Penguin Education

Modern Marketing Management

Edited by Raymond J. Lawrence
and Michael J. Thomas

Penguin Modern Management Readings

General Editor
D. S. Pugh

Modern Marketing Management

Selected Readings

Edited by Raymond J. Lawrence
and Michael J. Thomas

Penguin Education

Penguin Education
A Division of Penguin Books Ltd,
Harmondsworth, Middlesex, England
Penguin Books Inc., 7110 Ambassador Road,
Baltimore, Md 21207, USA
Penguin Books Australia Ltd,
Ringwood, Victoria, Australia

First published 1971
Reprinted 1973
This selection copyright © Raymond J. Lawrence and
Michael J. Thomas, 1971
Introduction and notes copyright © Raymond J. Lawrence and
Michael J. Thomas, 1971

Made and printed in Great Britain by
Cox & Wyman Ltd, London, Reading and Fakenham
Set in Intertype Times

Contents

Introduction

This book contains twenty-one articles addressed to some aspect of modern marketing management. Through them, the subject offers itself for inspection. The reader can decide whether the articles represent a unique standpoint in the field of management, despite the varied backgrounds and interests of the contributors. What is more important, he can find out whether marketing thought attracts and stimulates him into a new perspective on his own business activities.

The word marketing is often used loosely and vaguely. This is not surprising, because even after careful thought it remains a loose and vague word. Scores of formal definitions exist, ranging from the high-flown – 'the delivery of a standard of living' – to the pedestrian American Marketing Association version, 'the performance of business activities that direct the flow of goods and services from producer to consumer or user'. No single definition is adequate, except for limited purposes. In the following sections, we pursue the meaning of this elusive word. The purpose is partly to illustrate and clarify what marketing is about; partly to provide an overview of the subject, which may be helpful in going through the Readings; and partly to act as a guide to the principles on which the material in the book is based.

The marketing concept

The idea of starting with the customer, and working back from that point to the organization of a business, is by now well known. It contrasts with the production orientation, where the emphasis is on making things. Selling them is a subsidiary function to be taken care of later. Lee Adler describes this approach contemptuously as 'navel-gazing in the factory'. (The quotations and authors mentioned here, incidentally, all appear later in the Readings.)

The proposition that a company or individual should consider whether there is a potential buyer for the goods he makes before he makes them, sounds banal. It is such obvious common sense that the main principle of the marketing concept is recognized in all but the most sluggish organizations. What is much harder to do is to realize the implications of the marketing approach, viewed as an attitude and philosophy of management, right through the business. Wroe Alderson provides some good examples from his consultancy experience. Decisions about standards of quality control, about the type of stock records to keep, about plant investment and layout, prove to depend substantially on marketing considerations. The managers involved in such decisions often fail to appreciate this dependency. The problem is to diffuse an awareness of the outside world, and the customer as an all-important part of it, right through the staff of an organization.

The marketing outlook is deep-grained in men whose working experience has been with large, consumer goods companies. Because of competition, the heavy level of investment in brands and goodwill, and the ease with which housewives can and do switch between alternative products, such firms have necessarily sophisticated their marketing operations. They appoint and listen to marketing directors, who in turn run departments where a strong feeling of enthusiasm for marketing develops. Certain firms have been called the Marketing Universities, because they provide the living experience of the marketing concept at work and in control.

Men with a background of this type can be recruited to introduce marketing into a company where previously it has been weak or non-existent. It may even be essential to introduce new blood, since existing managers are perhaps too dominated by their lifetime experience as accountants, engineers, salesmen and so on. But there are disadvantages in the lack of training in other subject areas which marketing men often display. Their financial judgement may be limited, for example. To look at it from another point of view, a marketing department might claim responsibility for sales forecasting on the grounds that it knew about demand, competition, and buyer preferences. However, the marketing people could well make a hash of the job. Their actual method of forecasting might boil down to 'what we sold last time, plus a bit of upward trend to improve the look of the figures and five per cent on top to give the salesmen something to go for'. The man who actually has to schedule next month's production might find in practice that his own seat-of-the-pants estimates were more reliable.

The fact is that although marketing men may ask the right questions, they do not always come up with the right answers. The right questions are about the outside world, the trading environment, changes in distribution channels, competition, developments in customer requirements. The right answers require both information from the outside world and the ability to process it. The processing is no routine procedure. It calls for depth of understanding of marketing phenomena and customer psychology, experience, an eye for recurring relationships which can be modelled, and highly disciplined thinking. Our aim in this book has been to provide material which can contribute to the development of such skills. We believe that marketing can make an impact on management thought only by demonstrating an expertise, leading to sound decisions and recommendations which would not be reached otherwise. Waving the marketing flag is not enough; the subject only justifies itself if such expertise exists. If not, it must be accepted that marketing really came in with the Phoenicians, who were rather good at it, and that nothing has been added since, except a fancy word.

The systems approach

Many of the Readings talk of systems, a word much in vogue currently. It is perhaps no more than a convenient way of saying that things are interrelated, and cannot be adequately understood in isolation. An organ such as the liver, for example, only makes sense because it has a particular set of functions to perform in the context of the body as a total system. It would sound old-fashioned simply to say that the whole is greater than the sum of its parts. The systems approach has a fresh ring to it, and the phrase has helped to focus attention on part–whole relationships in a number of fields, including management science.

The saying 'Life is just one damned thing after another' has its parallel in business, where the in-tray and the telephone can produce a succession of unrelated events to which the manager merely reacts. The idea of a system can be useful in understanding what is going on. In particular, the concept draws attention to the relationships both within a given system and between systems. Links, interdependencies and conflict thereby come to light.

Wroe Alderson takes the widest approach. He considers modern industrial society as a single system. Its standards, growth, and capacity for innovation affect and are affected by manufacturers, channels of distribution, and households considered as separate subsystems with their own goals and means of realizing them. Marketing can be studied at the level of the social system, but to do so goes beyond the bounds of marketing management, which is a subsystem of the company or organization. Many of the Readings are basically concerned with the relationship between marketing and the company system, which has independent properties of its own. For example, the company system seeks a continued existence, or long term viability. It also sets objectives. Baumol discusses alternative goals, such as profit or sales revenue maximization, in the framework of economic analysis. McIver links new product development to the growth objectives supported by senior management. Gabor refers to some classic company ambitions – safety, independence and a quiet life. Marketing activities are clearly much affected by the company system of which they form a part. In the opposite direction, marketing feeds into the company system, particularly through its contribution to corporate strategy planning, which depends heavily on the developing pattern of events in the outside world.

Again, other departments in the firm are systems with their own purposes and methods of achieving them, which interact with the marketing system. (The terminology of system or subsystem is arbitrary, since to define a closed system is simply a means of saying that a particular entity is to be studied, and that influences on it from outside are to be ignored.) Forrester says that 'Marketing is a function which cannot exist by itself. It is intimately coupled to production, capital investment policies, product design, and the company's educational programs.'

Alderson suggests that the within-company systems can be studied in terms of group behaviour. The points of convergence and divergence between the several systems clearly bear on the major problem of company organization and structure.

Another development is to propose that subsidiary sets of tasks within the marketing function should be considered as systems in their own right. Adler makes the case for setting up marketing intelligence as a system, 'leading to a systematic *body of knowledge* about company markets rather than to isolated scraps of information'. It certainly makes sense to think about the collating, digesting and distributing of information as potentially a single, managed entity with a defined purpose. Ackoff makes a strong case that managers are swamped with more information than they can handle. Physical distribution is also worth consideration as a single system, although in their article Le Kashman and Stolle do not disguise the difficulties of a transformation in the distribution system.

As a final example of systems thinking, Adler applies the concept to the design and sale of products and services. He points out that buyers do not enjoy shopping for individual items in order to cover a single need: 'Customers don't want a grinding wheel, they want metal removed.' It is the responsibility of the seller to plan the system which the buyer really wants, whether the package covers metal removal, a holiday, a factory building, office records, or whatever it may be. One of the hardest marketing jobs is to deduce a latent demand – the system which the customer would in fact appreciate, perhaps after a period of education and persuasion, although he cannot now precisely define his need.

The marketing system

We have taken the view that marketing is the system within the firm responsible for the interface between the organization and the outside world, considered as customers or potential customers (thus excluding purchasing, which deals with the interface with suppliers). Interface is not an ideal word, but no other conveys quite the same sense. Two principal types of event occur at this interface: information exchanges and transactions. Transactions are sales, licensing agreements, credit extensions, franchising arrangements and so on. Although they are partly the objectives of marketing activities, they normally follow as the end point of an information exchange process which is a necessary condition for the transaction to occur.

Part Two of the Readings groups together articles dealing with information as an input to the marketing system. Market research is an important contributor, but Doina Thomas points out some of the disappointments which can arise from the misuse of research. Many of these can be thought of as failures in the marketing system. If no one knows what to do with information when it becomes available, for instance, that information has never been requisitioned as part of a continuing, organized approach to market intelligence. Failure to filter and condense information shows up the same deficiency, as described in Ackoff's pungent article. Perhaps the most frequently neglected input is cost data about the firm's own activities. Sevin says flatly that manufacturers typically do not know what profit contribution they obtain from their various products, customers and territories. Yet such figures are the logical basis for any rational product and development policy.

Part Three covers aspects of the information processing and decision making which lie at the heart of the marketing system. The emphasis is on the product mix, and the considerations which affect plans to extend, develop or cut back the product range. Gabor covers pricing – a particularly complex form of information processing since it involves internal inputs (costings, with varying criteria for the allocation of expense), external inputs (market reactions, the competitive situation), and an informational output (since price is commonly accepted as a signal about the quality of the goods). Evans writes about the job of the product manager, often the key figure of the whole processing system. He is the man most completely dependent on and responsible for the gathering and passing of information, since he seldom has authority to take important line decisions himself.

Part Four is concerned with management of the outward flow from the company to its environment, and particularly to its customers. The communications mix is perhaps the most important element, because successful trading depends ultimately on an intangible – a tiny share of the mind of present or potential customers. The housewife is aware of brands which she is prepared to buy. The industrial purchasing officer has in mind the names and reputations of certain companies, and his buying decision is dependent on such knowledge. Intangibles do not appear in balance sheets, but their management merits great care.

A company communicates in many ways. Simply being in business means communication. Customers and suppliers gain impressions of the firm as helpful, slow, rigid, easy to deal with and so on. A company image cannot be dispensed with. It exists, and changes as a result of every act identified with the company. An important task of communications management is to ensure that a customer's personal experience with the firm coincides with the company's intentions. If the firm – its whole manner and tone of dealing with the outside world – is not right, attempts to improve its image are not likely to be successful. The marketing department here interacts with other parts of the company system, since accountants, technical representatives and personnel managers, among others, are also dealing with the outside world and conveying what sort of company it is.

The management of communications requires an awareness of what the various paid-for media can achieve, when used to reach a particular target audience. The feedback loop is completed when general observations of audience psychology and specific reactions to a particular campaign serve as informational inputs for the marketing system, to be recycled through the internal data handling and decision-taking process, leading to adjusted information outputs from the firm.

Conclusion

The frustration of dealing with marketing is that so much must remain unsaid. We have not been able to deal with aids to the marketing system, particularly the use of models and quantitative techniques. However, these aids do not conform to the framework we have chosen. If it has been possible to sketch out a few columns of the marketing matrix, techniques and methods can be compared with the rows which run across every column. Linear programming, games theory, and simulation techniques, for example, can apply equally to the input, processing, and output variables. They cut across the information management system at many points.

Among the major omissions are sales forecasting and sales force operation and control. Both subjects are of great importance but could not be covered adequately in a limited space. Marketing management is a house of many mansions. We have only been able to show the way into a few of the larger rooms.

Some words from Levitt's article can serve as a final apologium. 'As with so many things in business, and perhaps uniquely in marketing, it is impossible to make universally useful suggestions regarding how to manage one's affairs.' It would be pleasant to offer a neat set of universally useful precepts, framed ready for hanging in the office. We do not pretend to do so. The hard work of finding out how a line of thought can be translated into a set of practical operating procedures suitable for a particular business must rest with the manager himself.

Part One
Dimensions of the Marketing Concept

The introductory essay to this volume has attempted to explain what we understand by the term 'the marketing concept'. It is not an easy concept to understand, much less to apply to the management of the marketing function. In the first section we have selected Readings that look at the concept in more than one dimension.

The extract (Reading 1) from Alderson's seminal work *Marketing Behavior and Executive Action* looks at the meaning for the firm, particularly the functional divisions of the firm, of applying the marketing concept. The book itself is a work of great originality, and is strongly recommended.

The application of the marketing concept should lead the firm away from a narrow emphasis on selling and maximizing sales revenue (the old marketing concept) to an emphasis on marketing and profit maximization. Many managers have difficulty understanding why sales (revenue) maximization may not maximize profit, a problem that Baumol (Reading 2) looks at in detail, discussing as well the relationship between expenditure components of the marketing mix, such as advertising, and the goals of the firm. The contribution of economic theory to this discussion will be clear, though too often the gap between economics and marketing seems to be very wide indeed. Alderson (Reading 3) analyses the marketing process using a framework familiar to economists, and in so doing provides some invaluable insights into what marketing does as an economic activity. Sorting theory is helpful in both understanding the behaviour of consumers and in defining marketing management tasks. A somewhat different dimension of the marketing concept is introduced by Adler (Reading 4), who applies the systems concept to marketing, exploring both the philosophical and managerial implications of treating marketing as a system, by the use of case studies.

Forrester (Reading 5) extends the systemic view from the company outwards to its markets and the market place, and suggests the value of modelling these relationships. The article makes very clear that information is the source of knowledge of the entire marketing system. Thus the management of marketing information is a critical element in the managerial task of the marketing manager, and Part Two looks at this area in further detail.

1 W. Alderson

A Marketing View of Business Policy

Excerpt from W. Alderson, *Marketing Behavior and Executive Action*, Irwin, 1957, pp. 444–63.

Some applications of the marketing viewpoint

Business policy may be defined as a set of working rules governing the use of the resources of the firm in gaining the firm's objectives. Policy rests on key decisions concerning the general course to be followed and guides executives in the day-to-day decisions involved in carrying out a detailed program. A business firm or any other operating organization can be analysed in terms of inputs and outputs. The primary output of the typical business firm is a flow of salable products. It is this output which justifies the existence of the enterprise and from which are derived such secondary but highly essential outputs as profits, wages and payments to suppliers. The inputs to be acquired and utilized in the business include labor, raw materials, plant equipment, working capital and executive talent. Issues arise in business as to the character of outputs and the direction in which inputs are to be expended, not merely their allocation within a fixed frame of reference. The function of policy is to deal with these issues.

Marketing considerations are the necessary foundation of policy in dealing with a complex pattern of relationships between inputs and outputs. This statement would be self-evident to any group of business executives were it not for the fact that so many have grown up in aspects of management which on the surface appear more stable and precise than marketing. Often, an executive who has spent all his working years in production, engineering, or finance takes over as the head of a company. It can well be a chilling thought that his most important decisions thereafter will be concerned with the uncertainties of the market place. There is no intention to deny that many successful executives have risen by these diverse routes. But they succeeded precisely because of their creative capacity to cope with uncertainty. Whether they recognize it or not, they are marketing men first of all from the time they accept top responsibility for the determination of company policy.

The pertinence of marketing considerations to every aspect of management will first be illustrated by a series of cases from the records of a consulting firm. These cases show how every major decision turns out to be a marketing decision or to be heavily involved with marketing decisions. Later sections will consider the formulation of policy within the marketing department, the relation of the marketing department to other departments, and the approach to company goals and their attainment in marketing terms. The intention is to picture the way in which an executive would operate if he adopted the perspective provided by marketing theory.

Marketing decisions and production methods

While marketing is the essential background for business policy, not all of the decisions governed by policy are marketing decisions. In fact, policy would not be very effective if it did not enable department heads and their subordinates to make decisions within a much narrower frame of reference than that required of the chief executive. Many decisions about the management of company resources can be defined as problems of plant layout, materials handling, inventory control, quality control, labor relations, or administrative organization. Some examples from the notebook of a management consultant will serve to illustrate the range of problems and policy issues arising in business firms, large and small. Ten examples will be presented, in five related pairs. Marketing considerations relevant to each case will be mentioned briefly. The succeeding sections will present in more general terms a conception of the place of marketing in policy formulation.

A moderate-sized plastics fabricator entered the postwar period with a reputation for quality work but with a prospective loss in volume through the completion of government contracts. The principals were men of some ingenuity in product engineering and design, but they lacked management experience. The inefficiency of production methods was obvious on the most casual inspection. Bench workers processing plastic components had to stoop down to get each blank from a box placed on the floor and stoop over again to place the finished piece in another box. Little thought appeared to have been given to the placement of machines in relation to the normal sequence of steps in the process.

A much larger plant was turning out vinyl film and plastic-coated textiles for upholstery and other purposes. While the machinery was largely automatic, the plant employed a surprising amount of unskilled labor. Materials used by each machine were brought in as needed on hand trucks or by small tractors from a warehouse a block away. Similarly, the finished product from each machine had to be carted some distance for storage. The business was growing, and the available floor space was crowded with equipment. It would have taken a major reorganization to bring stocks of raw materials up to the production line at one end and provide for more efficient movement of the product into storage at the other.

These cases would appear to call for the services of experts in plant layout and materials handling. Such specialists would necessarily have been involved in any program to make either plant fully efficient. Yet, marketing decisions had to be made before the production engineers could go to work. The plastic-fabricating plant had survived despite its inefficiency because of the high operating margin it enjoyed. The crucial issue was whether it could maintain an adequate volume in that class of work or whether it would have to be converted to the mass production of more competitive products. The process of tuning up the plant for efficient production would be quite different according to the outcome of that marketing decision. In the larger plant, nothing less than a major investment and construction program would have sufficed. Rapid shifts were going on in the demand for the various types of products the company manufactured. Plant reorganization could not be undertaken without key decisions concerning an investment program. The first requirement was for long-range forecasts based on thorough-going market studies.

Marketing approach to quality control

The next pair of cases is concerned with quality control. One company was a leader in its field, with procedures for quality control surpassing those of any of its competitors. One of its products had originated as a high-quality specialty and was manufactured to strict standards, including sanitary requirements. Later a volume market developed for a very similar product in a much less exacting field of use. Yet the control laboratory continued to employ the same strict standards, regardless of end use. With a quality level that was excessive in relation to actual use requirements, the volume product found it increasingly difficult to meet price competition.

The other case represented an extreme in the opposite direction. Because of numerous customer complaints, this firm introduced quality control, but with little conception of its significance. The method employed was 100 per cent inspection, but with no objective standards. In fact, the supervisor of the inspection crew was instructed to reject 3 per cent of the units produced each week, neither more nor less. This method was costly and ineffective and could scarcely be expected to lead to either a genuine improvement in the product or greater efficiency in production.

Both cases illustrate the need to begin with the market in designing appropriate quality control procedures. A study of each product in use would have disclosed the realistic requirements. An orderly method of recording, analysing and servicing complaints would provide a place to start. Rather than standardizing the percentage of rejects, it would be more to the point to standardize the number of complaints relative to volume of sales by adjusting the quality level upward or downward. The second company needed to apply objective procedures which would reduce the number of complaints to tolerable limits. The first company should actually have been concerned about the lack of complaints, which meant that it was producing a product which was both too perfect and too expensive for the particular need.

Marketing and control procedures

The third pair of cases is concerned with internal records and controls. A large retail jeweler was burdened with paperwork which had little real bearing on operating problems. Procedures have a way of accumulating in old and well-established companies and persisting after the operating heads have forgotten that they exist. In the jewelry trade a most laborious type of inventory records developed, based on the identification and registry of individual pieces. This method, appropriate to gems of great value, was gradually extended to each new line that was added, including some costume jewelry, plated silver and handbags. Despite this elaborate set of records, there was little current information for the guidance of buyers in the store under study. New business forms had been adopted to cover each aspect of purchase and sales transactions until more than twenty were in use.

The other extreme in record keeping was represented by a manufacturer of specialty leathers. There was nothing resembling a perpetual inventory control and the occasional physical inventories were scarcely more than a collection of estimates. Inventory continued to accumulate on some items which were being manufactured to stock, even though demand had been declining for several years. There were great variations in seasonal demand, item by item, and it seemed necessary to build up stocks months in advance of each peak. Capital was tied up in finished goods inventory, some of it of doubtful salability. Funds were lacking for effective purchasing of hides to take advantage of changes in the market. The management had attempted to improve its situation by instituting controls designed to reduce labor costs.

Solutions to both problems were attained without the use of extensive market surveys, although both were approached from a marketing viewpoint. The valuation of outputs, essential to the proper control of inputs, can sometimes be achieved by relatively simple means. One of the principal tools employed in these instances was sales analysis. The jewelry retailer agreed that there was little point in maintaining registry of pieces retailing for less than $30. Much to his surprise, an analysis of sales by size showed that 95 per cent of customer sales slips were for less than that amount, so that the items still requiring registry accounted for only 5 per cent of the sales transactions. Similarly, an analysis of the basic elements of both purchase and sales transactions showed that it was easily possible to standardize business forms, using only two as compared to more than ten times that number.

A somewhat more elaborate analytical procedure was followed in coping with the inventory problem of the leather manufacturer. An inventory control system was developed which would operate on the basis of advance orders, established seasonal patterns for each class of product and daily records of production and shipment. The entire business of the previous year was then put through this system as a dry run. The result of this test was to confirm the judgement that the inventory actually required to run the business and give satisfactory service to customers was only one third as great as the existing inventory. This finding not only made possible a great improvement in the financial position of the firm but also laid the basis for new policies in purchasing, sales and production.

Marketing analysis and organization problems

The fourth pair of cases has to do with organization difficulties and the delegation of executive responsibility. One very large company sold its entire line of products through territorial salesmen, with a single important exception. Included in its line was a class of products formerly manufactured by an independent company which had been acquired twenty years before. Actually, this firm had never been fully absorbed but continued to operate like a company within a company. Its products were originally consumed by a single industry and it was argued that only men specializing in this industry could supply it successfully. Territorial salesmen were not allowed to call on plants of this type and the particular product division continued to maintain its own national sales force.

The second case, out of many involving organization difficulties, is selected because of an interesting parallel to the first case. It was another instance of an enclave or a semi-autonomous unit persisting within a larger organization. A manufacturer had disposed of his entire output for many years through a single manufacturer's agent. Upon the death of the founder of the sales company it was acquired by the manufacturer. The intention was to have it become the sales department of the producing company. Assimilation was not easy because some of the sales executives continued to maintain the viewpoint appropriate to a separate company. They saw their primary function as that of keeping their traditional customers happy while drawing on a single source of supply for this purpose. It was especially difficult for sales and production to see eye to eye on new product possibilities, particularly when their proper development might involve new channels of trade.

Both of these organization problems were resolved by extensive market surveys. In the first case, involving industrial selling entirely, interviews were made with buyers representing all classes of customer firms. The purpose was to find out what kind of service these buyers expected from suppliers and to decide on the type of sales organization best equipped to give it to them. The conclusion was in favor of an intensification of territorial selling, with product specialists on call when the salesmen needed help. As to the semi-autonomous product division, the survey disclosed three trends which enabled management to see it in a new perspective. All of the companies in the industry served by the division were prospects for other products made by the company. Some of the leaders of this industry had expanded into new fields, so that it was no longer correct to regard them as belonging to a single industrial classification. Finally, some of the products originally sold to this group of firms only were now in demand in other industries.

In the case of the company absorbing the independent sales agency, it was found that the established methods and channels were still serving some segments of the market quite well, but missing the mark in others. While the company continued to enjoy a moderate growth in total sales, it was being outdistanced by competitors in some major new fields of use. The traditional distributors which the sales company had relied upon were not equipped to develop or serve these new markets. Appropriate changes were recommended in the sales program and sales organization. The real point of this story is that making policy from a marketing viewpoint does not necessarily mean relying on the judgement of the sales department. In the instance cited, the pressure for exploring broader marketing possibilities came from company executives whose background was in engineering and finance.

Marketing and investment planning

The final pair of cases deals with investment problems. They were chosen because of the contrasting attitudes of company executives. In one case it was recognized that investment decisions must rest eventually on marketing considerations, while in the other case it was not. The first company was one of the largest in the United States, long accustomed to gearing its tremendous operations to the market. It had developed a specialty product during the war which met certain needs of the military services. The demand was so great that a plant normally making other products was devoted exclusively to its production. After the war, this plant went back to its normal operations, and the question arose as to whether to invest millions of dollars in a plant to manufacture the new product. The problem was promptly defined as one of estimating the civilian demand for the product over the period required for the plant to pay for itself. An extensive market survey was undertaken, covering all the major fields of possible use. The survey results included a maximum and minimum estimate of the volume attainable within three years. These forecasts were considered under various assumptions as to the price of the product and the intensity of promotion. The minimum was only 40 per cent of the maximum. Even the minimum estimate, based on the most conservative assumptions, was so large that the proposed plant investment was amply justified.

The other case was that of a branch department store operating in a thriving suburban shopping center, but with indifferent success. A market survey, conducted at the instance of the landlord, indicated that the store was not living up to the potentialities of its location. Residents of the community appreciated the convenience of a neighborhood store but demanded goods of higher quality than this store provided. The survey results were shown to the department store manager.

The landlord agreed to enlarge the store, maintaining the same percentage lease basis, if the manager would undertake the relatively minor investment of improving and expanding the assortment of goods the store offered. The manager was skeptical about the survey findings concerning the market area and said that they did not check with his knowledge of his own customers. When pressed, he fell back on the argument that his downtown buyers were not experienced in higher-priced merchandise lines and he could not afford to have two sets of buyers. The landlord and the manager could not get together, and the lease was canceled shortly thereafter when it came up for renewal. Another organization occupied the store and accepted the survey findings as the basis of their merchandising program. During their first year they did four times as much business as the previous tenant had done the year before. Floor space has been increased three times to accommodate the steadily expanding business.

After this discussion of concrete instances, it remains to offer some general comments on the relation between marketing and management policy. Marketing is concerned with the primary output of a firm, which determines the outlook for its survival and growth. Marketing perspective is essential to the formulation of policy concerning production, finance and engineering. Finally, the marketing viewpoint should enter into policy making with respect to some problems precipitated by indefinite growth and expansion. These are problems for the whole community as well as for business, involving nothing less than the destiny of our free market economy and our society.

Marketing and production

The mass-production industries of today have arisen out of economies of scale. It is possible to perform many operations at a much lower cost per unit if the operation is to be performed a thousand or a million times rather than ten or twenty. Economies of scale have been in the forefront of both economic theory and business thinking in recent decades. This principle is a convenient place to begin in considering the relations between marketing policy and production policy.

Scale of production

There has been a tendency to regard economies of scale as a benefit accruing automatically as the size of business operations increases. Actually, the existence of a large volume of business under a single control does not in itself result in economies; it merely provides the opportunity to achieve them. Judgements as to the impact of economies of scale upon the individual firm or upon society as a whole have been both too optimistic and too pessimistic. Businessmen have too often assumed that if they could break into a specified volume range, costs would decline and profits increase. They often remark that there is nothing wrong with their company which cannot be fixed by an increase in volume. This cheerful outlook overlooks the fact that the achievement of economies of scale in certain phases of an operation may be accompanied by increases of cost in other phases. The most important example for our present purpose is the fact that the attainment of the volume which will result in the economies of large-scale production is often accompanied by large marketing expenditures to attain the necessary volume. It is true that the increase in marketing costs may often be less than the reduction in total cost. Nevertheless, there is little ground for the pessimistic view of economies of scale which has been expressed by some economic theorists. This is to the effect that the large firm, by achieving a much lower cost per unit, would soon be able to put all its small competitors out of business. The simple historic fact is that this gloomy prophecy has not been fulfilled, even though it has been made repeatedly for more than one hundred years.

There is an obvious and significant distinction between having plant capacity for a large volume of business and actually attaining that volume in any given year. Management must provide large capacity on the chance of achieving economies of scale; but capacity in itself merely represents large overhead costs, with constant uncertainty as to whether the volume will accrue to absorb these costs. The plant must operate close to capacity if the firm is to achieve the low production costs which it counted on in building the plant. Far from being able to rest securely in a monopolistic position, the management of such a firm is faced with a constant drive for volume to absorb its overhead.

This drive for volume tends to hold prices down to a competitive level established by other large firms with a similar need for volume. At the same time, it may push marketing costs up until the firm is obtaining only moderate profits and, frequently, a lower rate of profits than it earned when its volume of business was smaller. Marketing decisions must be made concerning the extent to which the economies achieved through mass production can be utilized in reducing prices and the extent to which these funds must be used in advertising and selling as alternative methods of increasing volume. The decision will turn on the extent of substitutability of the products of the firm for the products of competitors. If there were perfect substitutability among all products used for the same general purpose, then the large firm would doubtless utilize the low cost of the product for drastic price decreases, which might then put all small competitors out of business.

For most of the products of mass production, substitutability is very imperfect indeed. To enlarge its market share, a firm must persuade more and more consumers who lie on the fringe of its market position to buy. They must be convinced that they obtain a better value in buying the standardized product, even though it does not fit their needs or preferences quite so well as some competitive products. It takes large sums of money to carry out such a program of mass persuasion. The more that has to be spent for the purpose, the less remains of the margin of price advantage, which may be one of the claims made for the product. Marketing judgements must balance these two considerations and try to find the most favorable combination of an actually greater value and mass persuasion to convince consumers that a greater value is being offered.

Market segmentation

Another basic issue in the relations between marketing and production has to do with market segmentation and the degree to which the product will be differentiated to match differences in need and preferences from one segment to another. Assuming that there is a continuous range of variation as to the needs of consumers, the market for a given type of product might be divided into two, five, ten, or even more numerous segments. If only two product variations are offered, then it is obvious that differences in demand cannot be matched as precisely as if ten product variations were offered. Frequently, however, there is an inherent conflict in the requirements of marketing and production. The greater the range of product differentiation to meet consumer requirements, the less the opportunity to achieve economies of scale in production. Even assuming that all ten products can be made on the same machinery, there is a loss of efficiency in reducing the lot size and being obliged to make frequent changeovers in the plant from one product to another.

Sometimes, industries which grew up on the foundation of mass-production economies are obliged to dissipate these economies almost completely to meet variations in demand. Running a small lot through a plant built for continuous mass production is not the most efficient way of using plant equipment. It is the lesser of two evils, however, since the plant might be standing idle a large part of the time if it refused to make the various products demanded. The textile mills making upholstery fabrics provide an outstanding example of the dissipation of mass-production economies. At one time, looms could be set up to run for months at a time, with no variation in the pattern or color of the product. Today a plant that once made half a dozen patterns is making hundreds of variations in color and fabric. Each changeover from one lot to another is very expensive. Even though the loom is a prime example of mass-production equipment once it is set to run, a skilled worker has to tie some three thousand knots by hand in setting up the loom to run each new lot.

There are other mass-production industries which are somewhat more fortunate in their ability to adapt themselves to product variations. The first big automobile plants were operated on the assumption that any variations in the product would destroy the advantages of mass production. Today, improvement in production scheduling and in the control of both component parts and assembly make it possible for cars with many variations to roll in a steady stream from the same production line. The Ford Motor Company was known in the beginning for its rigid standardization on a single model. Today, it is said that Ford could produce a million and a half automobiles, no two of them exactly alike, without ever slowing up the production line. Somewhat similar achievements in production engineering have occurred in the great steel rolling mills. Several hundred variations in product can come off the rollers in the same day, without any interruption in the process. This result is achieved by a system of coordinated adjustments at various stages along the line as the new order reaches that stage in the process.

These partial reconciliations of marketing and production requirements are of great economic value and can doubtless be extended to many product fields. There are obvious limitations, depending on the character of product variations. Thus, while Ford might handle a million and a half variations in automobiles on the same assembly line, it obviously could not switch to refrigerators and then to watches and then back to cars again. The difficulty with the production of upholstery fabrics is that the switch from one lot to another in the character of the fabric is more like the change from automobiles to refrigerators than it is like a shift from blue to gray in the color of the automobile. For all mass-production industries, a cardinal issue of policy will continue to be that of market segmentation on the one hand versus economies of scale on the other.

The segmentation of a market can be made by geographic areas rather than by models of the product. The problem of whether to manufacture in a single large plant or in a number of smaller and scattered plants is largely a question of balancing transportation costs against the economies of mass production. Some economists have assumed that if production is to occur in decentralized plants, there is no economic justification for them to be under the control of a single firm. The weakness of this view is that it overlooks economies in marketing that can be achieved in a nation-wide operation. A unified sales organization supported by advertising through national media can sell a standardized product turned out by these localized plants more effectively than could be done by separate sales organizations and purely local advertising. Sometimes, however, decentralization of production is designed to meet marketing requirements as well as production requirements. The local plant may be able to give prompter and more individualized service to its major customers. In some cases, both production and marketing are rather fully decentralized, so that the economic advantage of the large concern lies in financial considerations and centralized staff services for research and planning.

Importance of production

A basic aim of management in most firms is the stabilization of production. Marketing programs are generally designed with this objective in mind. Production usually involves a larger number of workers as well as a much greater amount of fixed investment. It is better for the fluctuations and uncertainties of the market place to register their impact on marketing costs rather than on production costs. Stability of production in the short range requires production scheduling. Stability in the long range requires investment planning. The attempt to achieve these requisites of stable production may result in large expenditures on the marketing side, either on a regular or on an emergency basis.

Another reason for giving priority to the operating problems of production is the conservation of materials. Marketing contributes to this end by foreseeing demand and cutting down on the production of unwanted items. It also helps to keep finished goods inventory at reasonable levels, thus reducing inventory losses and the cost of carrying inventory. Keeping inventory within the limitations required by service to customers helps to remove a speculative element from business inherent in the possibility of major changes in demand or supply.

Importance of marketing

While there are all these reasons for giving priority to stability in production, management should not lose sight of the fact that the values achieved in production rest to a large extent on marketing decisions and marketing effort. Neither should the opportunity to reduce marketing costs be overlooked. The definition of the marketing task must take account of the fixed requirements of production. Once the marketing task is specified, functional analysis can be utilized, in order that the task may be performed as economically as possible.

There are some areas in which marketing economies should be given prior consideration. This would apply to products for which production costs are relatively small, such as packaged products in the drug and cosmetic fields. The largest possible savings in production might not be a critical factor in deciding the price at which such a product should be sold or the way it should be presented to consumers. Firms in this field must have a sound marketing program, first of all, in order to survive. Actually, many well-known companies in the drug and cosmetic industry are strictly marketing organizations, which have their products manufactured for them by someone else. It is true that they forego a manufacturing profit under this arrangement, but that is a minor loss compared to freeing themselves from manufacturing problems and financial hazards in order to concentrate on marketing. There are a number of other fields in which a company which plans to erect its own production facilities eventually may depend on outside production at the time a new product is launched. This policy is indicated when the market hazards are so great that a major plant investment might not pay off.

In summary, it might be said that marketing necessarily takes the lead in solving the issues that arise between marketing and production. In some cases the first concern of policy is stability and economy in production through appropriate marketing decisions. In other industries, where the cost structure is very different, it is appropriate for marketing to solve its own problems first because of the much greater magnitude of marketing costs and risks.

Marketing and finance

The subject of finance is concerned with the value of assets as compared to the preoccupation of marketing with the value of products. The first principle to be recognized in relating marketing and finance is that these two sets of values are not independent. The value of assets rests on the actual or potential output of products which can be achieved through their use. The term 'product' is used here to embrace all of the aspects of utility which an article has when it reaches the hands of the ultimate consumer. The assets involved in producing this utility consist of the capacity to market goods as well as the capacity to produce them. Assets employed in manufacturing are easier to evaluate, since they consist in large part of physical plant and equipment. The asset value of a well-integrated sales organization, with good morale based on an experience of success, has no value as collateral in floating a loan and, until quite recently, has had little recognition in financial analysis. The new emphasis on evaluating the market position of a firm and its ability to generate future sales may be regarded as a postwar phenomenon. This type of analysis is now frequently undertaken in considering mergers or acquisitions. The fact that statistical studies show that a high percentage of mergers have failed to live up to advance expectations is doubtless due in part to the very casual attention to marketing which was once prevalent in financial evaluation.

Both finance and marketing are concerned with the growth aspects of firms, the one from the standpoint of an expanding market position and the other from that of the accumulation of assets needed in transacting a larger volume of business. In financial terms, a firm can grow in two principal ways. One is to finance its growth by retaining some of the earnings generated by the company's operations. The other is to acquire either new capital or new assets from the outside. This growth from external sources may be effected by issues of stocks and bonds, followed by the purchase of the necessary equipment; or it can be effected by merger and the exchange of stock between two companies.

Growth through retained earnings

Growth through retained earnings has been criticized by economists as tending to remove from the market place some of the crucial decisions about the allocation of resources. Theoretically, if a company had to finance all expansion through the capital market, a sounder allocation would be made to precisely those users who were able to outbid all others in their demand for capital. First of all, it is obvious that small enterprise could seldom obtain its initial capital in this way. The owner or manager, by putting up his own funds, has a commitment to make the business succeed which is essential to its survival during the period of establishment. Even though a business may be well along its way toward gaining a solid foothold, it does not always have access to the public market for capital. The uncertainties may be too great and the integrity and drive of the management too dominant a consideration for capital to be obtained from outside sources. The chief way in which any small business can grow at all, therefore, is by financing growth through retained earnings. There are something like eleven hundred stocks listed on the New York Stock Exchange, or only a tiny fraction of all the companies which are interested in continued growth. Even among these listed stocks, most of the activity pertains to those of a few giant corporations.

These very large companies also depend to a considerable extent on retained earnings in financing expansion, but for a somewhat different set of reasons. The tax laws are of paramount importance in inducing corporate management to retain earnings rather than paying out the entire net earnings in dividends and then seeking capital funds for expansion. Retained surplus, within the legal limits, is subject to corporate taxes only, whereas dividends paid out and then reinvested are subject to both corporate taxes and personal taxes. The large company does not necessarily reinvest retained surplus in its own operations. Many companies have large portfolios of other stocks. Thus the criterion of a free market choice is at least partially observed, since a company treasurer and its board of directors will tend to invest surplus funds as profitably as possible, whether the assets they represent are used in the same company or in other companies. A large corporation is to some degree eliminating the middleman in its financial operations. That is to say that it generates large amounts of capital which it allocates to the most profitable uses available, without pouring it into the capital market and then calling it back to meet future uses.

This tendency in corporate policy is supported and reinforced by the prevailing attitudes of individual investors. Perhaps the majority are less interested in dividends than in increased values which can provide capital gains. The tax laws are again responsible for the predominant interest in capital gains. Since the owners of stocks want to see a company increase the value of its assets through growth, there is a constant pressure on management to move into new markets and to pioneer technical developments. The result is a highly competitive economy with moderate dividend rates, a constant drive for expansion, and a large part of total income being reinvested to support expansion. The specialist in finance who long ignored the marketing side of the business now indirectly helps to generate the pressure which makes marketing the crucial aspect of business today. The tax and fiscal policies of the government also support this trend, although they were not designed for this purpose.

Growth through new capital

The same forces are at work in a somewhat different way when a company requires outside capital for expansion. Many companies have growth goals which cannot be financed entirely from the inside because they call for a rate of growth which could not be sustained with retained earnings alone. For these companies, marketing considerations can play an important part in the effort to obtain new capital. To get money from outside investors a firm must be well known to the public. Some companies have been able to establish a public prestige which is out of proportion either to their size or to a cold-blooded evaluation of their relative prospects. Among the instruments which have been used in achieving standing with the public are public relations, institutional advertising and product promotion. A management with a good public relations sense uses every favorable development to build up a public image of itself which leads to confidence. Some companies succeed in getting capital funds relatively cheaply year after year. That is to say that they attract the money they need without paying out large dividends, although dividend payments are a factor of some importance in creating public interest in a company. Some of these companies early saw the value of institutional advertising and have spent large appropriations which were ostensibly aimed at customers for products but ultimately were directed at the purchasers of stock.

A refinement of this procedure is to advertise products but to make each product advertisements serve as institutional purpose. The product is presented as an example of the scientific ingenuity and management skill which the company exhibits in its operations generally. It may be described as one of a family of products, each offering exceptional values to the industrial or household consumer. This use of product promotion as an aspect of a financial program, in turn determines in some degree the company's marketing and product development program. Consumer products are more potent than industrial products in making a company known to the public. A company which derives its income largely from industrial markets may produce or sell one or more consumer products as a means of attaining public recognition. There is also a tendency for its financial policies to push a company in the direction of novel and newsworthy products. A new product may do more to gain prestige and, eventually, financial support than a much larger volume of sales in ordinary products.

Growth through acquisition of assets

Another way in which a large company continues to expand is by acquiring the assets of small companies. If the small company fits neatly into the established growth program of a larger company, its acquisition may represent a great saving in time as compared with the same expansion achieved from the inside. Acquisitions are frequently advantageous to both sides from a financial viewpoint. The larger firm, in effect, pays for the acquisition out of income generated by the new assets. The owners of the small firm may obtain a substantial amount of money which is subject to the capital gains tax only and which it would take many years to accumulate out of current income.

The tendency of firms of moderate size to sell out to larger companies is having an important effect on the size distribution of firms in the United States. Much of the uneasiness about the concentration of economic power and apparent trend toward monopoly is the result of this phenomenon. In many cases the initiative is on the side of the large firm looking to acquisitions in the effort to meet the pressure for steadily expanding sales. In other cases the initiative is exercised by the management of a smaller firm which has built up substantial productive assets but may no longer be interested in the day-to-day operation of the firm. This state of mind may result from the fact that the head of the firm is nearing retirement age. In other cases the deliberate aim is to build up an operation which some larger firm would be willing to buy. In getting ready to offer a company for sale, managements have been known to make drastic changes in policy, such as reducing prices and taking on new marketing channels in order to build up volume as quickly as possible while looking for a buyer.

Reference was made in an earlier chapter to the presumption of immortality implicit in the corporate form of organization. It may be that the true immortals consist of the limited number of large firms which are nationally known and whose shares are regularly traded on the stock exchange. Smaller companies, even though they adopt the corporate form of organization, may turn out to be mortal after all. In our present fiscal climate, there are thousands of small and moderate-sized firms in existence at any one time, because new ones are constantly being created. Only a very few of these will ever grow large enough to join the select circle of the great corporations. Of those which show enough vitality to survive the difficult periods of establishment and expansion, the great majority may disappear as independent entities by the route of acquisition. If this be true, it need not mean that the economy as a whole is any less effective or competitive. Earlier versions of the theory of the firm made the company the reflection of a single individual known as the 'entrepreneur'. A firm which survives only during the active career of an individual or a small group of principals is quite consistent with this earlier conception of business enterprise. Thus the dynamics of economic development involves continued interaction between the financial status of individuals and the marketing operations of firms. The resulting economic system is a mixed system in the sense that it consists of a limited number of large organizations, which may be expected to survive for the indefinite future, and many thousands of smaller organizations, which serve important marketing and financial objectives both while they are operating and as they cease to operate.

Marketing and engineering

Of the many staff activities which are a part of modern business, engineering is the oldest and possibly the most universal today. Marketing covers both staff and line activities, on the staff side being concerned with market research and market planning. These relatively new staff activities have had to make a place for themselves in a business environment in which the engineering staff was already well established. As in nearly all other phases of organization activities, the engineering staff and the marketing staff are partly competitive and partly complementary. The engineers in a company, aside from their functions of plant maintenance or product design, have usually been recognized as the group specifically trained for systematic planning. As the marketing staff has progressed from fact finding to planning and problem solving, it has brought a new point of view and a competitive claim for the confidence of management. The potential conflict between two staff groups which are not competing for line authority should not be difficult to resolve. Each is bringing its own technical perspective to problems of planning and policy making. Their joint aim is to illuminate these problems, which they should be able to do without wasteful duplication of effort and with a useful difference in emphasis.

The need for coordination

If the marketing staff and the engineering staff can work as a unified team, they can be the spearhead for company growth and expansion. As a member of this team, it is appropriate for the marketing man to assume that his fundamental job is to find adequate outlets for the engineering and production skills of his company. These skills are usually embodied in products as a means of harnessing them to demand, but the product is the vehicle for technology. Its command of technical know-how is what the company really has to sell.

W. Alderson 37

A corresponding attitude on the part of the research engineer would be that of being engaged in helping consumers and industrial users solve their problems. While there is a place for some research of a basic or general character in a large company, engineering research is concerned with application. Usually, there are many more problems of a technical nature than could be scheduled for effective work by the engineering staff. The assignment of priorities to problems regarded as of a higher degree of urgency is paramount in the management of engineering research. The marketing staff provides the channel through which the engineer can make contact with the needs and preferences of consumers. Just as the manufacturer needs retail stores as outlets for his product, so the engineering staff must rely on the marketing staff as an outlet for the technical possibilities at its command. As a team, engineering and marketing are concerned with expanding technology and changing markets and the best possible adjustment of one to the other.

Some leading companies have become increasingly concerned about the coordination of technical and marketing research. It is no longer regarded as efficient to complete a program of technical research resulting in a new product design and then to start a program of market research to find out how and where to sell the new product. The two types of research must work together from the inception of the product idea until its successful introduction on the market. A series of five steps has been suggested by B. F. Bowman as a convenient way of laying out such a coordinated program. These stages move from preliminary explorations through test marketing to the final launching of a full-scale marketing and production program. At each stage, there are essential activities on both the technical and the marketing side.

Aspects of coordination

While seeking coordination of marketing and technical research, there must be room for each to develop according to its own best possibilities. Neither one should be put in a strait jacket by being made too closely dependent on the other. At least three approaches can be observed in the engineering research of large companies, each having its most appropriate field of use. At the extremes are the basic research approach and the customer service approach. Some companies have emphasized basic research, assuming that the best results would be obtained by recruiting the finest talent available and giving it broad freedom for investigation in a general area. The expectation here is that discoveries and designs of novelty and value will emerge from time to time and that only the ideas of obvious merit will be considered for market introduction.

The customer service approach starts with the problems or complaints of individual customers and tries to develop new products or product improvements to meet customers' requirements. While this approach would appear on the surface to be one of matching technical skill directly against customer needs, it has serious disadvantages in many situations. The design which satisfied an individual customer may be so specialized that it cannot be sold to many other customers. The cost of developing the design may be so great that neither the supplier nor the customer is willing to absorb it. The customer is not always competent to define his own needs, and a better solution might be discovered by approaching the problem in a more general way.

The intermediate approach is probably the one which is more suitable in the majority of situations. It might be designated as the 'selected problem approach'. That is to say that out of a screening of ideas from customers and the technical staff, but with over-all guidance from marketing research, certain problems are given priority as the ones which will meet the needs of the greatest number of customers or which offer the greatest potential volume for business. Engineering research is assigned these selected problems, which are broader than problems of particular customers but more specific than those which might be identified from the viewpoint of basic research. A continuous process of screening to identify these selected problems may often result in the definition of whole families of related problems. Where this is true, research of a more basic nature may be undertaken in the underlying field to facilitate the solution of individual problems.

2 W. J. Baumol

The Firm and its Objectives

Excerpt from W. J. Baumol, *Economic Theory and Operations Analysis*, Prentice-Hall, 1965, pp. 295–310.

Alternative objectives of the firm

There is no simple method for determining the goals of the firm (or of its executives). One thing, however, is clear. Very often the last person to ask about any individual's motivation is the person himself (as the psycho-analysts have so clearly shown). In fact, it is common experience when interviewing executives to find that they will agree to every plausible goal about which they are asked. They say they want to maximize sales and also to maximize profits; that they wish, in the bargain, to minimize costs; and so on. Unfortunately, it is normally impossible to serve all of such a multiplicity of goals at once.

For example, suppose an advertising outlay of half a million dollars minimizes unit costs, an outlay of 1·2 million maximizes total profits, whereas an outlay of 1·8 million maximizes the firm's sales volume. We cannot have all three decisions at once. The firm must settle on one of the three objectives or some compromise among them.

Of course, the businessman is not the only one who suffers from the desire to pursue a number of incompatible objectives. It is all too easy to try to embrace at one time all of the attractive-sounding goals one can muster and difficult to reject any one of them. Even the most learned have suffered from this difficulty. It is precisely on these grounds that one great economist was led to remark that the much-discussed objective of the greatest good for the greatest number contains one 'greatest' too many.

It is most frequently assumed in economic analysis that the firm is trying to maximize its total profits. However, there is no reason to believe that all businessmen pursue the same objectives. For example, a small firm which is run by its owner may seek to maximize the proprietor's free time subject to the constraint that his earnings exceed some minimum level, and, indeed, there have been cases of overworked businessmen who, on medical advice, have turned down profitable business opportunities.

It has also been suggested, on the basis of some observation, that firms often seek to maximize the money value of their sales (their total revenue) subject to a constraint that their profits do not fall short of some minimum level which is just on the borderline of acceptability. That is, so long as profits are at a satisfactory level, management will devote the bulk of its energy and resources to the expansion of sales. Such a goal may, perhaps, be explained by the businessman's desire to maintain his competitive position, which is partly dependent on the sheer size of his enterprise, or it may be a matter of the interests of management (as distinguished from shareholders), since management's salaries may be related more closely to the size of the firm's operations than to its profits, or it may simply be a matter of prestige.

In any event, though they may help him to formulate his own aims and sometimes are able to show him that more ambitious goals are possible and relevant, it is not the job of the operations researcher or the economist to tell the businessman what his goals should be. Management's aims must be taken to be whatever they are, and the job of the analyst is to find the conclusions which follow from these objectives – that is, to describe what businessmen do to achieve these goals, and perhaps to prescribe methods for pursuing them more efficiently.

The major point, both in economic analysis and in operations-research investigation of business problems, is that the nature of the firm's objectives cannot be assumed in advance. It is important to determine the nature of the firm's objectives before proceeding to the formal model-building and the computations based on it. As is obviously to be expected, many of the conclusions of the analysis will vary with the choice of objective function. However, as some of the later discussion in this chapter will show, a change in objectives can, sometimes surprisingly, leave some significant relationships invariant. Where this is true, it is very convenient to find it out in advance before embarking on the investigation of a specific problem. For if there are some problems for which the optimum decision will be the same, no matter which of a number of objectives the firm happens to adopt, it is legitimate to avoid altogether the difficult job of determining company goals before undertaking an analysis.

The profit-maximizing firm

Let us first examine some of the conventional theory of the profit-maximizing firm. In the chapter on the differential calculus [not included here], the basic marginal condition for profit maximization was derived as an illustration. Let us now rederive this marginal-cost-equals-marginal-revenue condition with the aid of a verbal and a geometric argument.

The proposition is that no firm can be earning maximum profits unless its marginal cost and its marginal revenue are (at least approximately) equal, i.e. unless an additional unit of output will bring in as much money as it costs to produce, so that its marginal profitability is zero.[1]

It is easy to show why this must be so. Suppose a firm is producing 200,000 units of some item, x, and that at that output level, the marginal revenue from x production is $1·10 whereas its marginal cost is only 96 cents. Additional units of x will, therefore, each bring the firm some 14 cents = $1·10 − 0·96 more than they cost, and so the firm cannot be maximizing its profits by sticking to its 200,000 production level. Similarly, if the marginal cost of x exceeds its marginal revenue, the firm cannot be maximizing its profits, for it is neglecting to take advantage of its opportunity to save money – by reducing its output it would reduce its income, but it would reduce its costs by an even greater amount.

1. The word 'approximately' is inserted because, in practice, a precise adjustment may be impossible to achieve. A 230,773rd car may bring in $2 more than it costs to produce but the production of a 230,774th auto may cost somewhat more than the revenue it yields, so that perhaps only at something like an (impossible) 230,773¾ automobile output level would marginal cost and revenue be equal.

We can also derive the marginal-cost-equals-marginal-revenue proposition with the aid of Figure 1. At any output, OQ, total revenue is represented by the area $OQPR$ under the marginal revenue curve. Similarly, total cost is represented by the area $OQKC$ immediately below the marginal cost curve. Total profit, which is the difference between total revenue and total cost is, therefore, represented by the difference between the two areas – that is, total profits are given by the lightly shaded area TKP minus the small, heavily shaded area, RTC. Now, it is clear that from point Q a move to the right will increase the size of the profit area TKP. In fact, only at output OQ_m will this area have reached its maximum size – profits will encompass the entire area $TKMP$. But at output OQ_m marginal cost equals marginal revenue – indeed, it is the crossing of the marginal cost and marginal revenue curves at that point which prevents further moves to the right (further output increases) from

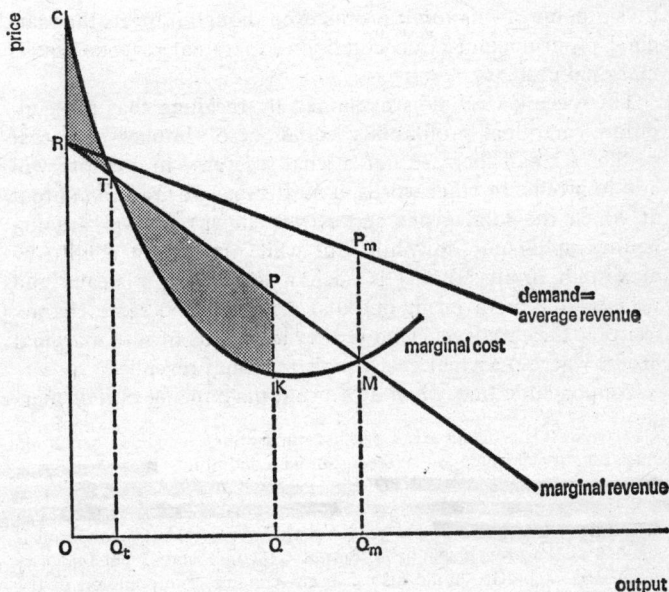

Figure 1

adding still more to the total profit area. Thus, we have once again established that at the point of maximum profits, marginal costs and marginal revenues must be equal.

Before leaving the discussion of this proposition, it is well to distinguish explicitly between it and its invalid converse. It is *not* generally true that any output level at which marginal cost and marginal revenue happen to be equal (i.e. where marginal profit is zero) will be a profit-maximizing level. There may be several levels of production at which marginal cost and marginal revenue are equal, and some of these output quantities may be far from advantageous for the firm. In Figure 1 this condition is satisfied at output OQ_t as well as at OQ_m. But at OQ_t the firm obtains only the net loss (negative profit) represented by heavily shaded area RTC. A move in either direction from point Q_t will help the firm either by reducing its costs more than it cuts its revenues (a move to the left) or by adding to its revenues more than to its costs. Output OQ_t is thus a point of *minimum* profits even though it meets the marginal profit-maximization condition, 'marginal revenue equals marginal cost'.

This peculiar result is explained by recalling that the condition, 'marginal profitability equals zero', implies only that neither a small increase nor a small decrease in quantity will add to profits. In other words, it means that we are at an output at which the total profit curve (not shown) is level – going neither uphill nor downhill. But while the top of a hill (the maximum profit output) is such a level spot, plateaus and valleys (minimum profit outputs) also have the same characteristic – they are level. That is, they are points of zero marginal profit, where marginal cost equals marginal revenue.[2]

We conclude that while at a profit-maximizing output mar-

2. Again, this problem arises because our marginal maximum condition must be supplemented by a second-order condition – that the second derivative of profits be negative, which means, in the present context, that the marginal revenue curve must cut the marginal cost curve from above (going from left to right). The reader should verify that this condition is satisfied at the profit-maximizing output OQ_m in Figure 1 but that it is violated at OQ_t. He should also give an economic interpretation of the condition.

ginal cost must equal marginal revenue, the converse is not correct – it is not true that at an output at which marginal cost equals marginal revenue the firm can be sure of maximizing its profits.

Application: pricing and cost changes

The preceding theorem permits us to make a number of predictions about the behavior of the profit-maximizing firm and to set up some normative 'operations research' rules for its operation. We can determine not only the optimal output, but also the profit-maximizing price with the aid of the demand curve for the product of the firm. For, given the optimal output, we can find out from the demand curve what price will permit the company to sell this quantity, and that is necessarily the optimal price. In Figure 1, where the optimal output is OQ_m we see that the corresponding price is Q_mP_m where point P_m is the point on the demand curve above Q_m (note that P_m is not the point of intersection of the marginal cost and the marginal revenue curves).

We have seen how our theorem can also enable us to predict the effect of a change in tax rates or some other change in cost on the firm's output and pricing. We need merely determine how this change shifts the marginal cost curve to find the new profit-maximizing price-output combination by finding the new point of intersection of the marginal cost and marginal revenue curves. Let us recall one particular result for use later in this chapter – the theorem about the effects of a change in fixed costs. It will be remembered that a change in fixed costs never has any effect on the firm's marginal cost curve because marginal fixed cost is always zero (by definition, an additional unit of output adds nothing to *fixed* costs). Hence, if the profit-maximizing firm's rents, its total assessed taxes, or some other fixed cost increases, there will be no change in the output-price level at which its marginal cost equals its marginal revenue. In other words, the profit-maximizing firm will make no price or output changes in response to any increase or decrease in its fixed costs! This rather unexpected result is certainly not in accord with common business practice and requires some further comment which will be supplied presently.

Extension: multiple products and inputs

The firm's output decisions are normally more complicated, even in principle, than the preceding decisions suggest. Almost all companies produce a variety of products, and these various commodities typically compete for the firm's investment funds and its productive capacity. At any given time there are limits to what the company can produce, and often, if it decides to increase its production of product x, this must be done at the expense of product y. In other words, such a company cannot simply expand the output of x to its optimum level without taking into account the effects of this decision on the output of y.

For a profit-maximizing decision which takes both commodities into account we have a marginal rule which is a special case of Rule 2 of Chapter 3 [not included here]:
Any limited input (including investment funds) should be allocated between the two outputs x and y in such a way that the marginal profit yield of the input, i, in the production of x equals the marginal profit yield of the input in the production of y.

The reasoning behind this result is straightforward. If the condition is violated the firm cannot be maximizing its profits, because the firm can add to its earnings simply by shifting some of i out of the product where it obtains the lower return and into the manufacture of the other.

Stated another way, this last theorem asserts that if the firm is maximizing its profits, a reduction in its output of x by an amount which is worth, say, \$5, should release just exactly enough productive capacity, C, to permit the output of y to be increased \$5 worth. For this means that the marginal return of the released capacity is exactly the same in the production of either x or y, which is what the previous version of this rule asserted.[3]

3. The earlier rule states that the marginal *profitability* must be the same in both uses, whereas now we have the marginal *revenue* of the input the same in the production of either x or y. But if a unit of resources costs D dollars, the marginal profit of i in the production of x (MP_{ix}) equals its marginal revenue minus its cost, so that if marginal profitability is the same in both uses we have

$$MP_{ix} = MR_{ix} - D = MR_{iy} - D = MP_{iy}$$

so that we must also have $MR_{ix} = MR_{iy}$, and conversely.

Still another version of this result is worth describing: suppose the price of each product is fixed and independent of output levels. Then we require that the marginal cost of each output be proportionate to its price, i.e. that $MC_x/P_x = MC_y/P_y$, where P_x and MC_x are, respectively, the price and the marginal cost of x, etc.[4]

In this discussion we have considered only the output decisions of a profit-maximizing firm. Of course, the firm has other decisions to make. In particular, it must decide on the amounts of its inputs including its marketing inputs (advertising, sales force, etc.) The main result here is that profit maximization requires for any inputs i and j

$$MP_i/P_i = MP_j/P_j$$

where MP_i represents the marginal profit contribution of input i and P_i is its price, etc.

Having discussed the consequences of profit maximization, let us see now what difference it makes if the firm adopts an alternative objective, one to which we have already alluded – the maximization of the value of its sales (total revenue) under the requirement that the firm's profits do not fall short of some given minimum level.

Price-output determination: sales maximization

Sales maximization under a profit constraint does not mean an attempt to obtain the largest possible physical volume (which is hardly easy to define in the modern multi-product firm). Rather, it refers to maximization of total revenue (dollar sales) which, to the businessman, is the obvious measure of the amount he has sold. Maximum sales in this sense need not require very large physical outputs. To take an extreme case, at a zero price physical volume may be high but dollar sales volume

4. To see how this follows from the preceding version of our rule, suppose that $1 in inputs produces K dollars worth of x and K dollars worth of y. Then if one unit of x requires, say $5 in inputs (marginal cost $5), one unit of x must be worth (approximately) $5K$ dollars. Similarly, if it costs $9 to produce a unit of y, that unit must be worth $9K$ dollars. Hence we must have

$$MC_x/P_x = 5/5K = 9/9K = MC_y/P_y.$$

All of these rules can also be derived with the aid of a Lagrange multiplier analysis. The reader can supply the proofs as an exercise.

will be zero. There will normally be a well-determined output level which maximizes dollar sales. This level can ordinarily be fixed with the aid of the well-known rule that maximum revenue will be obtained only at an output at which the elasticity of demand is unity, i.e. at which *marginal revenue is zero*. This is the condition which replaces the 'marginal cost equals marginal revenue' *profit*-maximizing rule.

But this rule does not take into account the profit constraint. That is, if at the revenue-maximizing output the firm does, in fact, earn enough or more than enough profits to keep its stockholders satisfied then it will want to produce the sales-maximizing quantity. But if at this output profits are too low, the firm's output must be changed to a level which though it fails to maximize sales, does meet the profit requirement.

We see, then, that two types of equilibrium appear to be possible: one in which the profit constraint does not provide an effective barrier to sales maximization, and one in which it does. This is illustrated in Figure 2, which shows the firm's total revenue, cost, and profit curves as indicated.

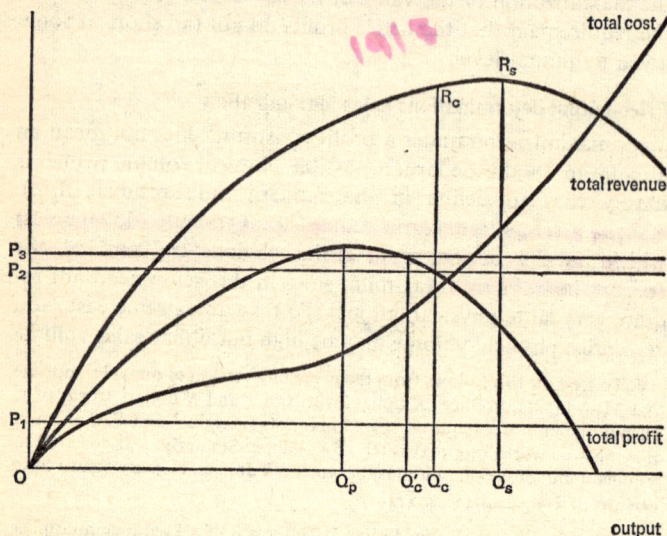

Figure 2

48 Dimensions of the Marketing Concept

The profit- and sales-maximizing outputs are, respectively, OQ_p and OQ_s. Now if, for example, the minimum required profit level is OP_1, then the sales-maximizing output OQ_s will provide plenty of profit, and that is the amount it will pay the sales maximizer to produce. His selling price will then be set at $Q_s R_s / OQ_s$. But if the producer's required profit level is OP_2, output OQ_s, which yields insufficient profit, clearly will not do. Instead, his output will be reduced to level OQ_c, which is just compatible with his profit constraint.

It will be argued presently that in fact only equilibrium points in which the constraint is effective (OQ_c rather than OQ_s) can normally be expected to occur when other decisions of the firm are taken into account.

The profit-maximizing output, OQ_p, will usually be smaller than the one which yields either type of sales maximum, OQ_s or OQ_c. This can be proved with the aid of the standard rule that at the point of maximum profit marginal cost must equal marginal revenue. For marginal cost is normally a positive number (we can't usually produce more of a good for nothing). Hence *marginal revenue will also be positive when profits are at a maximum*, i.e., a further increase in output will increase total sales (revenue). Therefore, if at the point of maximum profit the firm earns more profit than the required minimum,[5] it will pay the sales maximizer to lower his price and increase his physical output.

Advertising

The decision as to how far to carry advertising expenditure can also be influenced profoundly by the firm's choice of objectives – whether it chooses to maximize sales or profits. The relevant diagram for the advertising decisions is completely elementary. The horizontal axis in Figure 3 represents the magnitude of advertising expenditure, and the vertical axis represents total sales (revenue) and total profit. The drawing of the total revenue curve assumes, as most businessmen seem to do, that increased advertising expenditure can always increase physical volume, though after a point sharply diminishing returns may

5. If it earns less than the required minimum at this output, there is obviously no output which will satisfy the profit constraint.

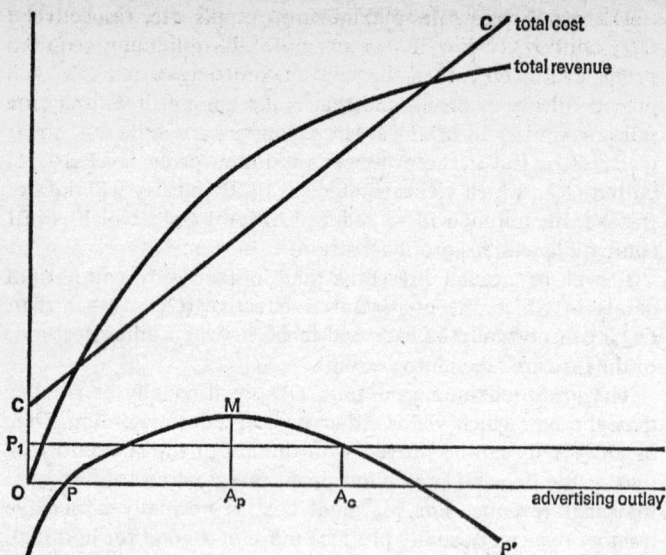

Figure 3

be expected to set in.[6] This means that total revenue must vary
with advertising expenditure in precisely the same manner. For,
unlike a price reduction, a *ceteris paribus* rise in advertising
expediture involves no change in the market value of the items
sold. Hence, whereas an increase in physical volume produced
by a price reduction may or may not increase dollar sales, depending on whether demand is elastic or inelastic, an increase in
volume brought about by added advertising outlay must always
be accompanied by a proportionate increase in total revenue.

If all other costs are added to advertising cost, we get the line
which depicts the firm's total (production, distribution, and selling) costs as a function of advertising outlay. Subtracting these

6. Of course, this is not necessarily true – potential customers may
perhaps be repelled by excessive advertising.
Incidentally, it should be noted that a more comprehensive analysis
would take into account the interdependence between pricing and advertising decisions. This could be done with the aid of a three-dimensional
diagram, with the axes representing price, advertising outlay, and revenue
(and costs).

50 Dimensions of the Marketing Concept

total costs from the level of dollar sales at each level of advertising outlay, we obtain a total profits curve, PP'.

We see that the profit-maximizing expenditure is OA_p, at which PP' attains its maximum, M. If, on the other hand, the sales maximizer's minimum acceptable profit level is OP_1, the constrained sales-maximizing advertising budget level is OA_c. It is to be noted that there is no possibility of an unconstrained sales maximum which is analogous to output OQ_8 in Figure 2. For, by assumption, unlike a price reduction, increased advertising always increases total revenue. As a result, it will always pay the sales maximizer to increase his advertising outlay until he is stopped by the profit constraint – until profits have been reduced to the minimum acceptable level. This means that sales maximizers will normally advertise no less than, and usually more than, do profit maximizers. For unless the maximum profit level A_pM is no greater than the required minimum OP_1, it will be possible to increase advertising somewhat beyond the profit-maximizing level OA_p without violating the profit constraint. Moreover, this increase will be desired since, by assumption, it will increase physical sales, and with them, dollar sales will rise proportionately.

The interrelationship between output and advertising decisions now permits us to see the reason for the earlier assertion that an unconstrained sales-maximizing output OQ_8 (Figure 2) will ordinarily not occur. For if price is set at a level which yields such an output, profits will be above their minimum level and it will pay to increase sales by raising expenditure on advertising, service, or product specifications. This is an immediate implication of the theorem that there will ordinarily be no unconstrained sales-maximizing advertising level. Since its marginal revenue is always positive, advertising can always be used to increase sales up to a point where profits are driven to their minimum level.

Choice of input and output combinations

The typical firm is a multi-product enterprise (frequently the number of distinct items runs easily into the hundreds or even thousands) and, of course, it employs a large variety of inputs. This section examines briefly the effect of sales (rather than profit) maximization on the amounts and allocation of the firm's various inputs and outputs.

We obtain the following result which may at first appear rather surprising: given the level of expenditure, the sales-maximizing firm will produce the same quantity of each output, and market it in the same ways as does the profit maximizer. Similarly, given the level of their total revenues, the two types of firm will optimally use the same inputs in identical quantities and will allocate them in exactly the same way. This result may be somewhat implausible because one is tempted to think of some products or some markets as higher-profit, lower-revenue producers than others and one would expect the profit-maximizing firm to concentrate more on the one variety and the sales-maximizing firm to specialize more in the other. But we shall see in a moment why this is not so.

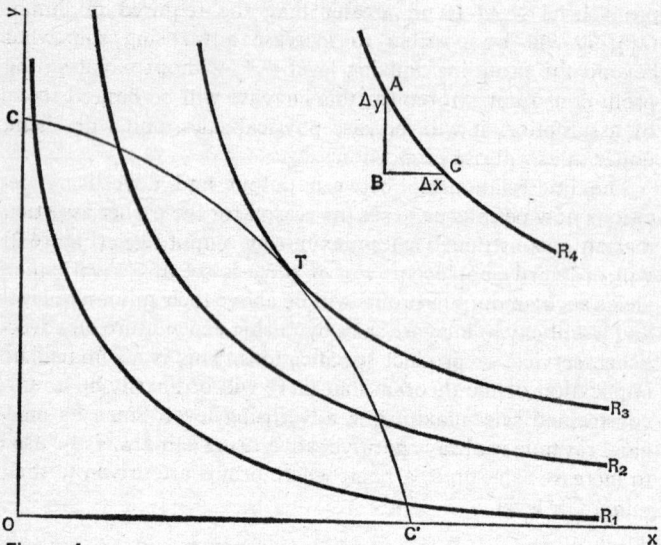

Figure 4

It is easy to illustrate our result geometrically. In Figure 4 let x and y represent the quantities sold of two different products (or sales of one product in two different markets) or the quantities bought of two different inputs. The curves labeled R_1, R_2, etc. are iso revenue curves, i.e., any such curve is the locus of all combinations of x and y yielding some fixed amount of revenue. Similarly, CC' represents all combinations of x and y which can be produced with a fixed outlay (total cost). The standard analysis tells us that the point of tangency, T, between CC' and one of the R curves, is the point of profit maximization. But it is also the point of revenue maximization because it lies on the highest revenue curve attainable with this outlay. This demonstrates our result.

A little reflection should now render the result quite plausible. The point is simply that, *given the level of costs,* since profit equals revenue minus costs, whatever maximizes profits must maximize revenues. Hence, differences between the profit and the sales maximizer's output composition or resource allocation must be attributed not to a reallocation of a given level of costs (or revenues) but to the larger outputs (and hence total costs and revenues) which, we have seen, are to be expected to accompany sales maximization.[7]

Explained in this way, our theorem is completely trivial. But when the sales maximizer's profit constraint is taken into account a more interesting but closely related conclusion can be drawn.

We may view the difference between maximum attainable profits and the minimum profit level expected by the sales maximizer as a fund of sacrificeable profits which is to be devoted to increasing revenues as much as possible. Since each output is produced beyond the point of maximum profits, *its marginal profit yield will be negative.* In other words, each time it increases the output of some product in order to increase its total revenue the firm must use up more of its fund of sacrificeable

7. We conclude that when the operations researcher encounters the problem of allocating optimally some *fixed* quantity of a firm's resources, the values of all other decision variables being given, his answer will be exactly the same whether he is dealing with a sales- or a profit-maximizing firm. Such analytically derived equivalences can clearly permit significant economies in research. In this case, for example, it means that the operations researcher may be able, when dealing with allocation problems, to avoid wasting effort in determining the order in which the company ranks sales and profit objectives.

profits. This fund of sacrificeable profits must be allocated among the different outputs, markets, inputs, etc., in a way which maximizes total dollar sales. The usual reasoning indicates that this requires the marginal revenue yield of a dollar of profit sacrificed, e.g. by product x to be the same as that obtained from a dollar of profit lost to any other product, y; i.e., we must have

$$\frac{\text{marginal revenue product of } x}{\text{marginal profit yield of } x} = \frac{\text{marginal revenue product of } y}{\text{marginal profit yield of } y}$$

This relationship indicates that, even in the sales-maximizing firm, relatively unprofitable inputs and outputs are to be avoided, whatever the level of outlay and total revenue.

Pricing and changes in fixed costs and taxes

Students consistently find one of the most surprising conclusions of the theory of the firm to be the assertion that fixed costs do not matter to pricing and output decisions.[8] This piece of received doctrine is certainly at variance with business practice, where an increase in fixed costs is usually the occasion for serious consideration of a price increase. It is easy to show, however, that this is precisely the sort of response one would expect of the firm which seeks to maximize sales and treats its profits as a constraint rather than as an ultimate objective. For if, in equilibrium, the firm always earns only enough to satisfy its profit constraint, then a rise in overhead cost must mean that earnings fall below the acceptable minimum. Outputs and/or advertising expenditures must then be reduced in order to make up the required profits. The purpose of any such decrease in production is, of course, to permit an increase in selling price.

This is very easily restated in terms of Figure 5. An increase in overhead costs means, geometrically, a uniform downward shift in the total profit curve by the amount of the overhead expenses. Hence, if overheads rise by amount CD, output will fall from OQ_c to OQ'_c, for at OQ_c profits will now be Q_cR,

8. However, it was shown earlier that the fixed charges can determine how many and which of the firm's *plants* or other facilities to use in a given operation.

which is less than the minimum acceptable level OP_m. By contrast, the change in overhead costs will leave the profit-maximizing output unchanged at OQ'_p. For the added costs reduce the height of the 'profit hill' uniformly, but they do not change the location of its peak. This result also has implications for tax policy. It has sometimes been held that there is nothing a company can do to shift any part of the corporation income tax on to the consumer or its employees. The profit-maximizing firm can gain nothing by raising its prices or changing its outputs in response to a change in corporation tax rates, provided that these rates are so structured that the higher the firm's earnings are before taxes the more it gets to keep after taxes. The argument is almost exactly the same as the fixed cost analysis. The corporation tax reduces the height of the total profit curve, but it moves the peak of the curve neither to the right nor to the left.

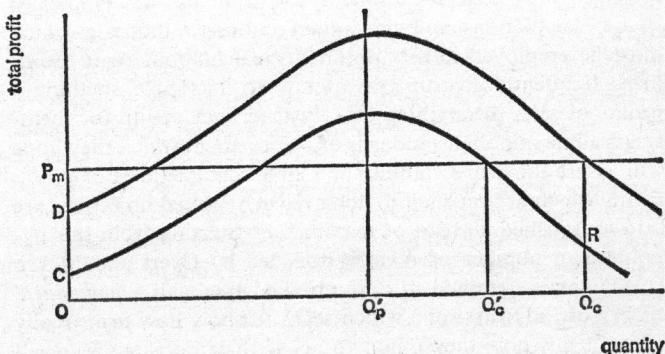

Figure 5

But, once again, if the firm wishes to maximize sales subject to a profit requirement, rather than maximizing profits, this conclusion loses its validity. When taxes are raised, the firm will be motivated to increase its price (and, therefore, to reduce its output) in order to make up its lost profits. The explanation of the shiftability of this apparently unshiftable tax is simple – the sales-maximizing firm will, in effect, have a reserve of profits which it has not claimed (it has not maximized profit) but which it can fall back on when driven to do so by a rise in tax costs, though it can get back to its old profits only by some sacrifice in its sales.

This concludes the discussion of the implications of a sales-maximization objective. In the present context the analysis is important primarily as an illustration of the effects of alternative objectives on the optimal decisions of the firm. It is designed to indicate the seriousness of the errors which can arise unless care is exercised in investigating the goals of a company before undertaking an analysis of its behavior and its policies.

Satisficing and behavior analysis

Professor Simon has offered yet another persuasive hypothesis about the objectives of firms. He has argued that in many cases management recognizes implicitly or explicitly the complexity of the calculations and the imperfections of the data which must be employed in any optimality calculation. As a result, firms frequently give up the attempt to maximize anything – profits or sales or anything else. Instead, they set up for themselves some minimal standards of achievement which they hope will assure the firm's viability and an acceptable level of profit. Firms which are satisfied to achieve such limited objectives are said to 'satisfice' instead of maximizing. Starting from this hypothesis, a number of investigators led by Cyert and March (1963) have attempted to develop what they call a *behavioral* theory of the firm – one which seeks to show how firms really act, not just how they ought to act if their decisions were all optimal. Using computers to simulate observed decision processes of a number of companies, they have achieved remarkable success in employing some of these programs to predict company decisions. Though one may question whether they have provided a theory or an empirical approach and evidence for the construction of a theory, the significance of the entire analysis is undeniable. Certainly we can no longer operate comfortably on the assumption that profit maximization adequately explains all of the observed business behavior.

References

BAUMOL, W. J. (1959), *Business Behavior, Value and Growth*, Macmillan Co., chs. 6–8.

CYERT, R. M., and MARCH, J. G. (1963), *A Behavioral Theory of the Firm*, Prentice-Hall.

HALL, R. L., and HITCH, C. J. (1939), 'Price theory and business behavior', *Oxford econ. Papers*, no. 2.

LESTER, R. A. (1946), 'Shortcomings of marginal analysis for wage-employment problems', *Amer. econ. Rev.*, vol. 36, no. 1.

MACHLUP, F. (1946), 'Marginal analysis and empirical research', *Amer. econ. Rev.*, vol. 36, no. 4. Reprinted in R. V. Clemence (ed.), *Readings in Economic Analysis*, vol. 2, Addison-Wesley, 1950.

SCITOVSKY, T. (1943), 'A note on profit maximization and its implications', *Rev. econ. Stud.*, vol. 11, pp. 57-60. Reprinted in G. J. Stigler and K. E. Boulding (eds.), *Readings in Price Theory*, Irwin, 1952.

SIMON, H. A. (1959), 'Theories of decision making in economics', *Amer. econ. Rev.*, vol. 49, no. 3.

SIMON, H. A. (1957), *Models of Man*, Wiley, ch. 14.

3 W. Alderson

The Analytical Framework for Marketing

W. Alderson, 'The analytic framework for marketing', in
D. J. Duncan (ed.), *Proceedings: Conference of Marketing Teachers from Far Western States*, University of California, 1958, pp. 15–28.

My assignment is to discuss the analytical framework for marketing. Since our general purpose here is to consider the improvement of the marketing curriculum, I assume that the paper I have been asked to present might serve two functions. The first is to present a perspective of marketing which might be the basis of a marketing course at either elementary or advanced levels. The other is to provide some clue as to the foundations in the social sciences upon which an analytical framework for marketing may be built.

Economics has some legitimate claim to being the original science of markets. Received economic theory provides a framework for the analysis of marketing functions which certainly merits the attention of marketing teachers and practitioners. It is of little importance whether the point of view I am about to present is a version of economics, a hybrid of economics and sociology, or the application of a new emergent general science of human behavior to marketing problems. The analytical framework which I find congenial at least reflects some general knowledge of the social sciences as well as long experience in marketing analysis. In the time available I can do no more than present this view in outline or skeleton form and leave you to determine how to classify it or whether you can use it.

An advantageous place to start for the analytical treatment of marketing is with the radical heterogeneity of markets. Heterogeneity is inherent on both the demand and the supply sides. The homogeneity which the economist assumes for certain purposes is not an antecedent condition for marketing. Insofar as it is ever realized, it emerges out of the marketing process itself.

The materials which are useful to man occur in nature in heterogeneous mixtures which might be called conglomerations since the mixtures have only a random relationship to human needs and activities. The collection of goods in the possession of a household or an individual also constitutes a heterogeneous supply, but it might be called an assortment since it is related to anticipated patterns of future behavior. The whole economic process may be described as a series of transformations from meaningless to meaningful heterogeneity. Marketing produces as much homogeneity as may be needed to facilitate some of the intermediate economic processes but homogeneity has limited significance or utility for consumer behavior or expectations.

The marketing process matches materials found in nature or goods fabricated from these materials against the needs of households or individuals. Since the consuming unit has a complex pattern of needs, the matching of these needs creates an assortment of goods in the hands of the ultimate consumer. Actually the marketing process builds up assortments at many stages along the way, each appropriate to the activities taking place at that point. Materials or goods are associated in one way for manufacturing, in another way for wholesale distribution, and in still another for retail display and selling. In between the various types of heterogeneous collections relatively homogeneous supplies are accumulated through the processes of grading, refining, chemical reduction and fabrication.

Marketing brings about the necessary transformations in heterogeneous supplies through a multiphase process of sorting. Matching of every individual need would be impossible if the consumer had to search out each item required or the producer had to find the users of a product one by one. It is only the ingenious use of intermediate sorts which make it possible for a vast array of diversified products to enter into the ultimate consumer assortments as needed. Marketing makes mass production possible first by providing the assortment of supplies needed in manufacturing and then taking over the successive transformations which ultimately produce the assortments in the hands of consuming units.

To some who have heard this doctrine expounded, the concept of sorting seems empty, lacking in specific behavioral content, and hence unsatisfactory as a root idea for marketing. One answer is that sorting is a more general and embracing concept than allocation which many economists regard as the root idea of their science. Allocation is only one of the four basic types of sorting, all of which are involved in marketing. Among these four, allocation is certainly no more significant than assorting, one being the breaking down of a homogeneous supply and the other the building up of a heterogeneous supply. Assorting, in fact, gives more direct expression to the final aim of marketing but allocation performs a major function along the way.

There are several basic advantages in taking sorting as a central concept. It leads directly to a fundamental explanation of the contribution of marketing to the overall economy of human effort in producing and distributing goods. It provides a key to the unending search for efficiency in the marketing function itself. Finally, sorting as the root idea of marketing is consistent with the assumption that heterogeneity is radically and inherently present on both sides of the market and that the aim of marketing is to cope with the heterogeneity of both needs and resources.

At this stage of the discussion it is the relative emphasis on assorting as contrasted with allocation which distinguishes marketing theory from at least some versions of economic theory. This emphasis arises naturally from the preoccupation of the market analyst with consumer behavior. One of the most fruitful approaches to understanding what the consumer is doing is the idea that she is engaged in building an assortment, in replenishing or extending an inventory of goods for use by herself and her family. As evidence that this paper is not an attempt to set up a theory in opposition to economics it is acknowledged that the germ of this conception of consumer behavior was first presented some eighty years ago by the Austrian economist Boehm-Bawerk.

The present view is distinguished from that of Boehm-Bawerk in its greater emphasis on the probabilistic approach to the study of market behavior. In considering items for inclusion in her assortment the consumer must make judgements concerning the relative probabilities of future occasions for use. A product in the assortment is intended to provide for some aspect of future behavior. Each such occasion for use carries a rating which is a product of two factors, one a judgement as to the probability of its incidence and the other a measure of the urgency of the need in case it should arise. Consumer goods vary with respect to both measures. One extreme might be illustrated by cigarettes with a probability of use approaching certainty but with relatively small urgency or penalty for deprivation on the particular occasion for use. At the other end of the scale would be a home fire extinguisher with low probability but high urgency attaching to the expected occasion of use.

All of this means that the consumer buyer enters the market as a problem-solver. Solving a problem, either on behalf of a household or on behalf of a marketing organization means reaching a decision in the face of uncertainty. The consumer buyer and the marketing executive are opposite numbers in the double search which pervades marketing; one looking for the goods required to complete an assortment, the other looking for the buyers who are uniquely qualified to use his goods. This is not to say that the behavior of either consumers or executives can be completely characterized as rational problem-solvers. The intention rather is to assert that problem-solving on either side of the market involves a probabilistic approach to heterogeneity on the other side. In order to solve his own problems arising from heterogeneous demand, the marketing executive should understand the processes of consumer decisions in coping with heterogeneous supplies.

The viewpoint adopted here with respect to the competition among sellers is essentially that which is associated in economics with such names as Schumpeter, Chamberlin and J. M. Clark and with the emphasis on innovative competition, product differentiation and differential advantage. The basic assumption is that every firm occupies a position which is in some respects unique, being differentiated from all others by characteristics of its products, its services, its geographic location or its specific combination of these features. The survival of a firm requires that for some group of buyers it should enjoy a differential advantage over all other suppliers. The sales of any active marketing organization come from a core market made up of buyers with a preference for this source and a fringe market which finds the source acceptable, at least for occasional purchases.

In the case of the supplier of relatively undifferentiated products or services such as the wheat farmer, differential advantage may pertain more to the producing region than to the individual producer. This more diffuse type of differential advantage often becomes effective in the market through such agencies as the marketing cooperative. Even the individual producer of raw materials, however, occupies a position in the sense that one market or buyer provides the customary outlet for his product rather than another. The essential point for the present argument is that buyer and seller are not paired at random even in the marketing of relatively homogeneous products but are related to some scale of preference or priority.

Competition for differential advantage implied goals of survival and growth for the marketing organization. The firm is perennially seeking a favorable place to stand and not merely immediate profits from its operations. Differential advantage is subject to change and neutralization by competitors. In dynamic markets differential advantage can only be preserved through continuous innovation. Thus competition presents an analogy to a succession of military campaigns rather than to the pressures and attrition of a single battle. A competitor may gain ground through a successful campaign based on new product features or merchandizing ideas. It may lose ground or be forced to fall back on its core position because of the successful campaigns of others. The existence of the core position helps to explain the paradox of survival in the face of the destructive onslaughts of innovative competition.

Buyers and sellers meet in market transactions each side having tentatively identified the other as an answer to its problem. The market transaction consumes much of the time and effort of all buyers and sellers. The market which operates through a network of costless transactions is only a convenient fiction which economists adopt for certain analytical purposes. Potentially the cost of transactions is so high that controlling or reducing this cost is a major objective in market analysis and executive action. Among economists John R. Commons has given the greatest attention to the transaction as the unit of collective action. He drew a basic distinction between strategic and routine transactions which for present purposes may best be paraphrased as fully negotiated and routine transactions.

The fully negotiated transaction is the prototype of all exchange transactions. It represents a matching of supply and demand after canvassing all of the factors which might affect the decision on either side. The routine transaction proceeds under a set of rules and assumptions established by previous negotiation or as the result of techniques of pre-selling which take the place of negotiation. Transactions on commodity and stock exchanges are carried out at high speed and low cost but only because of carefully established rules governing all aspects of trading. The economical routines of self-service in a supermarket are possible because the individual items on display have been pre-sold. The routine transaction is the end-result of previous marketing effort and ingenious organization of institutions and processes. Negotiation is implicit in all routine transactions. Good routines induce both parties to save time and cost by foregoing explicit negotiation.

The negotiated transaction is the indicated point of departure for the study of exchange values in heterogeneous markets. Many considerations enter into the decision to trade or not to trade on either side of the market. Price is the final balancing or integrating factor which permits the deal to be made. The seller may accept a lower price if relieved from onerous requirements. The buyer may pay a higher price if provided with specified services. The integrating price is one that assures an orderly flow of goods so long as the balance of other considerations remain essentially unchanged. Some economists are uneasy about the role of the negotiated transaction in value determination since bargaining power may be controlling within wide bargaining limits. These limits as analysed by Commons are set by reference to the best alternatives available to either partner rather than by the automatic control of atomistic competition. This analysis overlooks a major constraint on bargaining in modern markets. Each side has a major stake in a deal that the other side can live with. Only in this way can a stable supply relationship be established so as to achieve the economics of transactional routines. Negotiation is not a zero sum game since the effort to get the best of the other party transaction by transaction may result in a loss to both sides in terms of mounting transactional cost.

In heterogeneous markets price plays an important role in matching a segment of supply with the appropriate segment of demand. The seller frequently has the option of producing a streamlined product at a low price, a deluxe product at a high price, or selecting a price-quality combination somewhere in between. There are considerations which exert a strong influence on the seller toward choosing the price line or lines which will yield the greatest dollar volume of sales. Assuming that various classes of consumers have conflicting claims on the productive capacity of the supplier, it might be argued that the price-quality combination which maximized gross revenue represented the most constructive compromise among these claims. There are parallel considerations with respect to the claims of various participants in the firm's activities on its operating revenue. These claimants include labor, management, suppliers of raw materials and stockholders. Assuming a perfectly fluid situation with respect to bargaining among these claimants, the best chance for a satisfactory solution is at the level of maximum gross revenue. The argument becomes more complicated when the claims of stockholders are given priority, but the goal would still be maximum gross revenue as suggested in a recent paper by William J. Baumol. My own intuition and experience lead me to believe that the maximization of gross revenue is a valid goal of marketing management in heterogeneous markets and adherence to this norm appears to be widely prevalent in actual practice.

What has been said so far is doubtless within the scope of economics or perhaps constitutes a sketch of how some aspects of economic theory might be reconstructed on the assumption of heterogeneity rather than homogeneity as the normal and prevailing condition of the market. But there are issues raised by such notions as enterprise survival, expectations and consumer behavior, which in my opinion cannot be resolved within the present boundaries of economic science. Here marketing must not hesitate to draw upon the concepts and techniques of the social sciences for the enrichment of its perspective and for the advancement of marketing as an empirical science.

The general economist has his own justifications for regarding the exchange process as a smoothly functioning mechanism which operates in actual markets or which should be taken as the norm and standard to be enforced by government regulation. For the marketing man, whether teacher or practitioner, this Olympian view is untenable. Marketing is concerned with those who are obliged to enter the market to solve their problems imperfect as the market may be. The persistent and rational action of these participants is the main hope for eliminating or moderating some of these imperfections so that the operation of the market mechanism may approximate that of the theoretical model.

To understand market behavior the marketing man takes a closer look at the nature of the participants. Thus he is obliged, in my opinion, to come to grips with the organized behavior system. Market behavior is primarily group behavior. Individual action in the market is most characteristically action on behalf of some group in which the individual holds membership. The organized behavior system is related to the going concern of John R. Commons but with a deeper interest in what keeps it going. The organized behavior system is also a much broader concept including the more tightly organized groups acting in the market such as business firms and households and loosely connected systems such as the trade center and the marketing channel.

The marketing man needs some rationale for group behavior, some general explanation for the formation and persistence of organized behavior systems. He finds this explanation in the concept of expectations. Insofar as conscious choice is involved, individuals operate in groups because of their expectations of incremental satisfactions as compared to what they could obtain operating alone. The expected satisfactions are of many kinds, direct and indirect. In a group that is productive activity is held together because of an expected surplus over individual output. Other groups such as households and purely social organizations expect direct satisfactions from group association and activities. They also expect satisfactions from future activities facilitated by the assortment of goods held in common. Whatever the character of the system, its vitality arises from the expectations of the individual members and the vigor of their efforts to achieve them through group action. While the existence of the group is entirely derivative, it is capable of operating as if it had a life of its own and was pursuing goals of survival and growth.

Every organized behavior system exhibits a structure related to the functions it performs. Even in the simplest behavior system there must be some mechanism for decision and coordination of effort if the system is to provide incremental satisfaction. Leadership emerges at an early stage to perform such functions as directing the defense of the group. Also quite early is the recognition of the rationing function by which the leader allocates the available goods or satisfactions among the members of the group.

As groups grow in size and their functions become more complex, functional specialization increases. The collection of individuals forming a group with their diversified skills and capabilities is a meaningful heterogeneous ensemble vaguely analogous to the assortment of goods which facilitates the activities of the group. The group, however, is held together directly by the generalized expectations of its members. The assortment is held together by a relatively weak or derivative bond. An item 'belongs' to the assortment only so long as it has some probability of satisfying the expectations of those who possess it.

This outline began with an attempt to live within the framework of economics or at least within an economic framework amplified to give fuller recognition to heterogeneity on both sides of the market. We have now plunged into sociology in order to deal more effectively with the organized behavior system. Meanwhile we attempt to preserve the line of communication to our origins by basing the explanations of group behavior on the quasi-economic concept of expectations.

The initial plunge into sociology is only the beginning since the marketing man must go considerably further in examining the functions and structures of organized behavior systems. An operating group has a power structure, a communication structure and an operating structure. At each stage an effort should be made to employ the intellectual strategy which has already been suggested, that is, to relate sociological notions to the groundwork of marketing economics through the medium of such concepts as expectations and the processes of matching and sorting.

All members of an organized behavior system occupy some position or status within its power structure. There is a valid analogy between the status of an individual or operating unit within the system and the market position of the firm as an entity. The individual struggles for status within the system having first attained the goal of membership. For most individuals in an industrial society, status in some operating system is a prerequisite for satisfying his expectations. Given the minimal share in the power of the organization inherent in membership, vigorous individuals may aspire to the more ample share of power enjoyed by leadership. Power in the generalized sense referred to here is an underlying objective on which the attainment of all other objectives depends. This aspect of organized behavior has been formulated as the power principle, namely, 'The rational individual will act in such a way to promote the power to act'. The word 'promote' deliberately glosses over an ambivalent attitude toward power, some individuals striving for enhancement and others being content to preserve the power they have.

Any discussion which embraces power as a fundamental concept creates uneasiness for some students on both analytical and ethical grounds. My own answer to the analytical problem is to define it as control over expectations. In these terms it is theoretically possible to measure and evaluate power, perhaps even to set a price on it. Certainly it enters into the network of imputations in a business enterprise. Management allocates or rations status and recognition as well as or in lieu of material rewards. As for the ethical problem, it does not arise unless the power principle is substituted for ethics as with Macchiavelli. Admitting that the power principle is the essence of expediency, the ethical choice of values and objectives is a different issue. Whatever his specific objectives, the rational individual will wish to serve them expediently.

If any of this discussion of power seems remote from marketing let it be remembered that major preoccupation of the marketing executive, as pointed out by Oswald Knauth, is with the creation or the activation of organized behavior systems such as marketing channels and sales organizations. No one can be effective in building or using such systems if he ignores the fundamental nature of the power structure.

The communication structure serves the group in various ways. It promotes the survival of the system by reinforcing the individual's sense of belonging. It transmits instructions and operating commands or signals to facilitate coordinated effort. It is related to expectations through the communication of explicit or implied commitments. Negotiations between suppliers and customers and much that goes on in the internal management of a marketing organization can best be understood as a two-way exchange of commitments. A division sales manager, for example, may commit himself to produce a specified volume of sales. His superior in turn may commit certain company resources to support his efforts and make further commitments as to added rewards as an incentive to outstanding performance.

For some purposes it is useful to regard marketing processes as a flow of goods and a parallel flow of informative and persuasive messages. In these terms the design of communication facilities and channels becomes a major aspect of the creation of marketing systems. Marketing has yet to digest and apply the insights of the rapidly developing field of communication theory which in turn has drawn freely from both engineering and biological and social sciences. One stimulating idea expounded by Norbert Wiener and others is that of the feedback of information in a control system. Marketing and advertising research are only well started on the task of installing adequate feedback circuits for controlling the deployment of marketing effort.

Social psychology is concerned with some problems of communication which are often encountered in marketing systems. For example, there are the characteristic difficulties of vertical communication which might be compared to the transmission of telephone messages along a power line. Subordinates often hesitate to report bad news to their superiors fearing to take the brunt of emotional reactions. Superiors learn to be cautious in any discussion of the subordinate's status for fear that a casual comment will be interpreted as a commitment. There is often a question as to when a subordinate should act and report and when he should refer a matter for decision upstream. Progress in efficiency, which is a major goal in marketing, depends in substantial part on technological improvement in communication facilities and organizational skill in using them.

The third aspect of structure involved in the study of marketing systems is operating structure. Effective specialization within an organization requires that activities which are functionally similar be placed together but properly coordinated with other activities. Billing by wholesaler grocers, for example, has long been routinized in a separate billing department. In more recent years the advances in mechanical equipment have made it possible to coordinate inventory control with billing, using the same set of punch cards for both functions. Designing an operating structure is a special application of sorting. As in the sorting of goods to facilitate handling, there are generally several alternative schemes for classifying activities presenting problems of choice to the market planner.

Functional specialization and the design of appropriate operating structures is a constant problem in the effective use of marketing channels. Some functions can be performed at either of two or more stages. One stage may be the best choice in terms of economy or effectiveness. Decision on the placement of a function may have to be reviewed periodically since channels do not remain static. Similar considerations arise in the choice of channels. Some types of distributors or dealers may be equipped to perform a desired service while others may not. Often two or more channels with somewhat specialized roles are required to move a product to the consumer. The product's sponsor can maintain perspective in balancing out these various facilities by thinking in terms of a total operating system including his own sales organization and the marketing channels employed.

The dynamics of market organization pose basic problems for the marketing student and the marketing executive in a free enterprise economy. Reference has already been made to the competitive pursuits of differential advantage. One way in which a firm can gain differential advantage is by organizing the market in a way that is favorable to its own operations. This is something else than the attainment of a monopolistic position in relation to current or potential competitors. It means creating a pattern for dealing with customers or suppliers which persists because there are advantages on both sides. Offering guarantees against price declines on floor stocks is one example of market organization by the seller. Attempts to systematize the flow of orders may range from various services offered to customers or suppliers all the way to complete vertical integration. Another dynamic factor affecting the structure of markets may be generalized under the term 'closure'. It frequently happens that some marketing system is incomplete or out of balance in some direction. The act of supplying the missing element constitutes closure, enabling the system to handle a greater output or to operate at a new level of efficiency. The incomplete system in effect cries out for closure. To observe this need is to recognize a form of market opportunity. This is one of the primary ways in which new enterprises develop, since there may be good reasons why the missing service cannot be performed by the existing organizations which need the service. A food broker, for example, can cover a market for several accounts of moderate size in a way that the individual manufacturer would not be able to cover it for himself.

There is a certain compensating effect between closure as performed by new or supplementary marketing enterprises and changes in market organization brought about by the initiative of existing firms in the pursuit of differential advantage. The pursuit of a given form of advantage, in fact, may carry the total marketing economy out of balance in a given direction creating the need and opportunity for closure. Such an economy could never be expected to reach a state of equilibrium, although the tendency toward structural balance is one of the factors in its dynamics. Trade regulation may be embraced within this dynamic pattern as an attempt of certain groups to organize the market to their own advantage through political means. Entering into this political struggle to determine the structure of markets are some political leaders and some administrative officials who regard themselves as representing the consumer's interests. It seems reasonable to believe that the increasing sophistication and buying skill of consumers is one of the primary forces offsetting the tendency of the free market economy to turn into something else through the working out of its inherent dynamic forces. This was the destiny foreseen for the capitalistic system by Schumpeter, even though he was one of its staunchest advocates.

The household as an organized behavior system must be given special attention in creating an analytical framework for marketing. The household is an operating entity with an assortment of goods and assets and with economic functions to perform. Once a primary production unit, the household has lost a large part of these activities to manufacturing and service enterprises. Today its economic operations are chiefly expressed through earning and spending. In the typical household there is some specialization between the husband as primary earner and the wife as chief purchasing agent for the household. It may be assumed that she becomes increasingly competent in buying as she surrenders her production activities such as canning, baking and dressmaking, and devotes more of her time and attention to shopping. She is a rational problem solver as she samples what the market has to offer in her effort to maintain a balanced inventory or assortment of goods to meet expected occasions of use. This is not an attempt to substitute Economic Woman for the discredited fiction of Economic Man. It is only intended to assert that the decision structure of consumer buying is similar to that for industrial buying. Both business executive and housewife enter the market as rational problem solvers, even though there are other aspects of personality in either case.

An adequate perspective on the household for marketing purposes must recognize several facets of its activities. It is an organized behavior system with its aspects of power, communication and operating structure. It is the locus of forms of behavior other than instrumental or goal-seeking activities. A convenient three-way division, derived from the social sciences, recognizes instrumental, congenial and symptomatic behavior. Congenial behavior is that kind of activity engaged in for its own sake and presumably yielding direct satisfactions. It is exemplified by the act of consumption as compared to all of the instrumental activities which prepare the way for consumption. Symptomatic behavior reflects maladjustment and is neither pleasure-giving in itself nor an efficient pursuit of goals. Symptomatic behavior is functional only to the extent that it serves as a signal to others that the individual needs help.

Some studies of consumer motivation have given increasing attention to symptomatic behavior or to the projection of symptoms of personality adjustment which might affect consumer buying. The present view is that the effort to classify individuals by personality types is less urgent for marketing than the classification of families. Four family types with characteristically different buying behavior have been suggested growing out of the distinction between the instrumental and congenial aspects of normal behavior. Even individuals who are fairly well adjusted in themselves will form a less than perfect family if not fully adapted to each other.

On the instrumental side of household behavior it would seem to be desirable that the members be well coordinated as in any other operating system. If not, they will not deliver the maximum impact in pursuit of family goals. On the congenial side it would appear desirable for the members of a household to be compatible. That means enjoying the same things, cherishing the same goals, preferring joint activities to solitary pursuits or the company of others. These two distinctions yield an obvious four-way classification. The ideal is the family that is coordinated in its instrumental activities and compatible in its congenial activities. A rather joyless household which might nevertheless be well managed and prosperous in material terms is the coordinated but incompatible household. The compatible but uncoordinated family would tend to be happy-go-lucky and irresponsible with obvious consequences for buying behavior. The household which was both uncoordinated and incompatible would usually be tottering on the brink of dissolution. It might be held together formally by scruples against divorce, by concern for children, or by the dominant power of one member over the others. This symptomology of families does not exclude an interest in the readjustment of individuals exhibiting symptomatic behavior. Such remedial action lies in the sphere of the psychiatrist and the social worker, whereas the marketer is chiefly engaged in supplying goods to families which are still functioning as operating units.

All of the discussion of consumers so far limits itself to the activities of the household purchasing agent. Actually the term consumption as it appears in marketing and economic literature nearly always means consumer buying. Some day marketing may need to look beyond the act of purchasing to a study of consumption proper. The occasion for such studies will arise out of the problems of inducing consumers to accept innovations or the further proliferation of products to be included in the household assortment. Marketing studies at this depth will not only borrow from the social sciences but move into the realm of esthetic and ethical values. What is the use of a plethora of goods unless the buyer derives genuine satisfaction from them? What is the justification of surfeit if the acquisition of goods serves as a distraction from activities which are essential to the preservation of our culture and of the integrity of our personalities?

It has been suggested that a study of consumption might begin with the problem of choice in the presence of abundance. The scarce element then is the time or capacity for enjoyment. The bookworm confronted with the thousands of volumes available in a great library must choose in the face of this type of limitation.

The name hedonomics would appear to be appropriate for this field of study suggesting the management of the capacity to enjoy. Among the problems for hedonomics is the pleasure derived from the repetition of a familiar experience as compared with the enjoyment of a novel experience or an old experience with some novel element. Another is the problem of direct experience versus symbolic experience, with the advantages of intensity on the one hand and on the other the possibility of embracing a greater range of possible ideas and sensations by relying on symbolic representations. Extensive basic research will probably be necessary before hedonomics can be put to work in marketing or for the enrichment of human life through other channels.

This paper barely suffices to sketch the analytical framework for marketing. It leaves out much of the area of executive decision-making in marketing on such matters as the weighing of uncertainties and the acceptance of risk in the commitment of resources. It leaves out market planning which is rapidly becoming a systematic discipline centering in the possibilities for economizing time and space as well as resources. It leaves out all but the most casual references to advertising and demand formation. Advertising is certainly one of the most difficult of marketing functions to embrace within a single analytical framework. It largely ignores the developing technology of physical distribution. Hopefully what it does accomplish is to show how the essentially economic problems of marketing may yield to a more comprehensive approach drawing on the basic social sciences for techniques and enriched perspective.

4 L. Adler

Systems Approach to Marketing

L. Adler, 'Systems approach to marketing', *Harvard Business Review*, vol. 45, no. 3, 1967, pp. 105–18.

More and more businessmen today recognize that corporate success is, in most cases, synonymous with marketing success and with the coming of age of a new breed of professional managers. They find it increasingly important not only to pay lip service to the marketing concept but to do something about it in terms of (a) customer orientation, rather than navel-gazing in the factory, (b) organizational revisions to implement the marketing concept, and (c) a more orderly approach to problem solving.

In an increasing number of companies we see more conscious and formal efforts to apply rational, fact-based methods for solving marketing problems, and greater recognition of the benefits these methods offer. While these benefits may be newly realized, there is nothing new about the underlying philosophy; in the parlance of military men and engineers, it is the systems approach. For, whether we like it or not, marketing is, by definition, a system, if we accept Webster's definition of systems as 'an assemblage of objects united by some form of regular interaction or interdependence'. Certainly, the interaction of such 'objects' as product, pricing, promotion, sales calls, distribution and so on fits the definition.

There is an expanding list of sophisticated applications of systems theory – and not in one but in many sectors of the marketing front. The construction of mathematical and/or logical models to describe, quantify and evaluate alternate marketing strategies and mixes is an obvious case in point. So, too, is the formulation of management information systems (see Cox and Good, 1967) and of marketing plans with built-in performance measurements of predetermined goals. But no less vital is the role of the systems approach in the design and sale of products and services. When J. P. Stevens Company color-harmonizes lines and bedspreads and towels and bath mats, it is creating a product system. And when Avoco Corporation sells systems management to the space exploration field, involving the marriage of many scientific disciplines as well as adherence to budgetary constraints, on-time performance and quality control, it is creating a *service* system.

In this article I shall discuss the utilization of the systems concept in marketing in both quantitative and qualitative ways with case histories drawn from various industries. In doing so, my focus will be more managerial and philosophical than technical, and I will seek to dissipate some of the hocus-pocus, glamor, mystery and fear which pervade the field. The systems concept is not esoteric or 'science fiction' in nature (although it sometimes *sounds* that way in promotional descriptions). Its advantages are not subtle or indirect; as we shall see, they are as real and immediate as decision-making itself. The limitations are also real, and these, too, will be discussed.

Promising applications

Now let us look at some examples of corporate application of the systems approach. Here we will deal with specific parts or 'sub-systems' of the total marketing system. Figure 1 is a schematic portrayal of these relationships.

Products and services

The objective of the systems approach in product management is to provide a complete 'offering' to the market rather than merely a product. If the purpose of business is to create a customer at a profit, then the needs of the customer must be carefully attended to; we must, in short, study what the customer is buying or wants to buy rather than what we are trying to sell.

In the consumer products field we have forged ahead in understanding that the customer buys nutrition (not bread), beauty (not cosmetics), warmth (not fuel oil). But in industrial products this concept has been slower in gaining a foothold. Where it has gained a foothold, it expresses itself in two ways: the creation of a complete product system sold as a unit, or as a

component or components which are part of a larger consumption system.

Perhaps the most eloquent testimony to the workability and

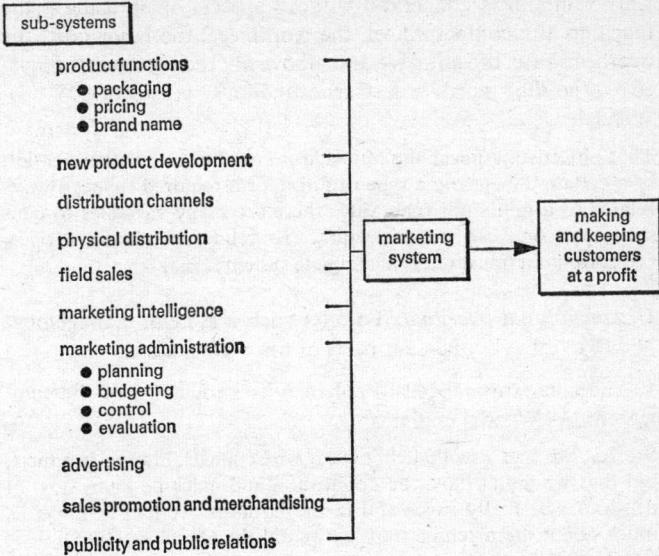

Figure 1 Marketing sub-systems and the total system

value of the systems approach comes from companies that have
actually used it. For a good example let us turn to the case of
The Carborundum Company. This experience is especially
noteworthy because it comes from industrial marketing, where,
as just indicated, progress with the systems concept has generally been slow.

Birth of the concept. Founded in 1894, the company was content
for many years to sell abrasives. It offered an extremely broad
line of grinding wheels, coated abrasives and abrasive grain,
with a reputed capacity for 200,000 different products of varying type, grade and formulation. But the focus was on the
product.

L. Adler 77

In the mid-1950s, Carborundum perceived that the market for abrasives could be broadened considerably if – looking at abrasives through customers' eyes – it would see the product as fitting into *metal polishing, cleaning,* or *removal systems.* Now Carborundum is concerned with all aspects of abrasing – the machine, the contact wheel, the workpiece, the labor cost, the overhead rate, the abrasive and, above all, the customer's objective. In the words of Carborundum's president, W. H. Wendel:

That objective is never the abrasive *per se,* but rather the creation of a certain dimension, a type of finish, or a required shape, always related to a minimum cost. Since there are many variables to consider, just one can be misleading. To render maximum service, Carborundum (must offer) a complete system (1965).

Organizational overhaul. To offer such a system, management had to overhaul important parts of the organization:

1. The company needed to enhance its knowledge of the total system. As Wendel explains:

We felt we had excellent knowledge of coated abrasive products, but that we didn't have the application and machine know-how in depth. To be really successful in the business, we had to know as much about the machine tools as we did the abrasives (1965).

To fill this need, Carborundum made three acquisitions – The Tysaman Machine Company, which builds heavy-duty snagging, billet grinding, and abrasive cut-off machines; Curtis Machine Company, a maker of belt sanders; and Pangborn Corporation, which supplied systems capability in abrasive blast cleaning and finishing.

2. The company's abrasive divisions were reorganized, and the management of them was realigned to accommodate the new philosophy and its application. The company found that *centering responsibility for the full system in one profit center* proved to be the most effective method of coordinating approaches in application engineering, choice of distribution channels, brand identification, field sales operations and so forth. This method was particularly valuable for integrating the acquisitions into the new program.

3. An Abrasives Systems Center was established to handle development work and to solve customer problems.

4. Technical conferences and seminars were held to educate customers on the new developments.

5. Salesmen were trained in machine and application knowledge.

Planning. A key tool in the systems approach is planning – in particular, the use of what I like to call 'total business plans'. (This term emphasizes the contrast with company plans that cover only limited functions.) At Carborundum, total business plans are developed with extreme care by the operating companies and divisions. Very specific objectives are established, and then detailed action programs are outlined to achieve these objectives. The action programs extend throughout the organization, including the manufacturing and development branches of the operating unit. Management sets specific dates for the completion of action steps and defines who is responsible for them. Also, it carefully measures results against established objectives. This is done both in the financial reporting system and in various marketing committees.

Quantitative methods. Carborundum has utilized various operations research techniques, like decision tree analysis and PERT, to aid in molding plans and strategies. For example, one analysis, which concerned itself with determining the necessity for plant expansion, was based on different possible levels of success for the marketing plan. In addition, the computer has been used for inventory management, evaluation of alternate pricing strategies for systems selling, and the measurement of marketing achievements against goals.

It should be noted, though, that these quantitative techniques are management tools only and that much of the application of systems thinking to the redeployment of Carborundum's business is qualitative in nature.

Gains achieved. As a consequence of these developments, the company has opened up vast new markets. To quote Carborundum's president again:

Customers don't want a grinding wheel, they want metal removed.
... The U.S. and Canadian market for abrasives amounts to $700
million a year. But what companies spend on stock removal – to
bore, grind, cut, shape and finish metal – amounts to $30 billion
a year (1966).

Illustrating this market expansion in the steel industry is Carborundum's commercial success with three new developments –
hot grinding, an arborless wheel to speed metal removal and cut
grinding costs, and high-speed conditioning of carbon steel
billets. All represent conversions from non-abrasive methods.
Carborundum now also finds that the close relationship with
customers gives it a competitive edge, opens top customer management doors, gains entrée for salesmen with prospects they
had never been able to 'crack' before. Perhaps the ultimate
accolade is the company's report that customers even come to
the organization itself, regarding it as a consultant as well as a
supplier.

Profitable innovation

The intense pressure to originate successful new products
cannot be met without methodologies calculated to enhance the
probabilities of profitable innovation. The systems approach
has a bearing here, too. Figure 2 (pp. 82–3) shows a model for
'tracking' products through the many stages of ideation, development, and testing to ultimate full-scale commercialization.
This diagram is in effect a larger version of the 'New Product
Development' box in Figure 1.

Observe that this is a logical (specifically, sequential), rather
than numerical, model. While some elements of the total system
(e.g. alternate distribution channels and various media mixes)
can be analysed by means of operations research techniques,
the model has not been cast in mathematical terms. Rather, the
flow diagram as a whole is used as a checklist to make sure 'all
bases are covered' and to help organize the chronological sequence of steps in new product development. It also serves as a
conceptual foundation for formal PERT application, should
management desire such a step, and for the gradual development of a series of equations linking together elements in the

diagrams, should it seem useful to experiment with mathematical models.

Marketing intelligence

The traditional notion of marketing research is fast becoming antiquated. For it leads to dreary chronicles of the past rather than focusing on the present and shedding light on the future. It is particularistic, tending to concentrate on the study of tiny fractions of a marketing problem rather than on the problem as a whole. It lends itself to assuaging the curiosity of the moment, to fire-fighting, to resolving internecine disputes. It is a slave to technique. I shall not, therefore, relate the term *marketing research* to the systems approach – although I recognize, of course, that some leading businessmen and writers are breathing new life and scope into the ideas referred to by that term.

The role of the systems approach is to help evolve a *marketing intelligence* system tailored to the needs of each marketer. Such a system would serve as the ever-alert nerve center of the marketing operation. It would have these major characteristics:

Continuous surveillance of the market.

A team of research techniques used in tandem.

A network of data sources.

Integrated analysis of data from the various sources.

Effective utilization of automatic data-processing equipment to distill mountains of raw information speedily.

Strong concentration not just on report findings but also on practical action-oriented recommendations.

Concept in use. A practical instance of the use of such an intelligence system is supplied by Mead Johnson Nutritionals (division of Mead Johnson & Company), manufacturers of Metrecal, Pablum, Bib, Nutrament, and other nutritional specialities. As Figure 3 shows, the company's Marketing Intelligence Department has provided information from these sources:

A continuing large-scale consumer market study covering attitudinal and behavioral data dealing with weight control.

Nielson store audit data, on a bi-monthly basis.

L. Adler 81

Market-trend anticipation

Market segmentation

Consumers

Trade and Industrial customers

Shareowners

Financial community

Market stretching

Creative marketing

Multibrand product

Multiproduct brand

Management determination of product fields and markets of primary interest

● Establish company mission (vision and definition of the business)

● Identify growth opportunities

● Evaluate company resources

● Analyse major problems

Market assessment of present size, growth potential, stability, etc.

Compatibility with company mission, policy and capabilities

Compatibility with law and public opinion

Identify idea sources — internal and external

Magnitude of investments

Analysis of market and product characteristics

Prospects for a competitive edge

Concept testing

Communicability of appeals

Market education required

Sales organization requirements

New product improvements

New products and services

New 'look at old products

Exploration

Assign responsibility for planned idea exploration

Screening

Set criteria; utilize existing data and informed opinion

Evaluation

Appoint product team to evaluate each selected idea

Employees

Plant communities

Suppliers

Government

Other interest groups and public policy

Distribution innovations

Merger and acquisition

Overseas expansion

Investment thinking

Unorthodox solutions

Revitalize marketing effort

Milking the product

Idea generation

Idea collection

Estimated layout

Degree of risk

Competition — present and potential

Patent and proprietary considerations

Period review of shelved ideas

Distribution requirements

Possible effects on other product lines

Producibility

Tentative specifications

Cost profit projections

Visual model of the product business

Product plan for management approval

Product Idea stage

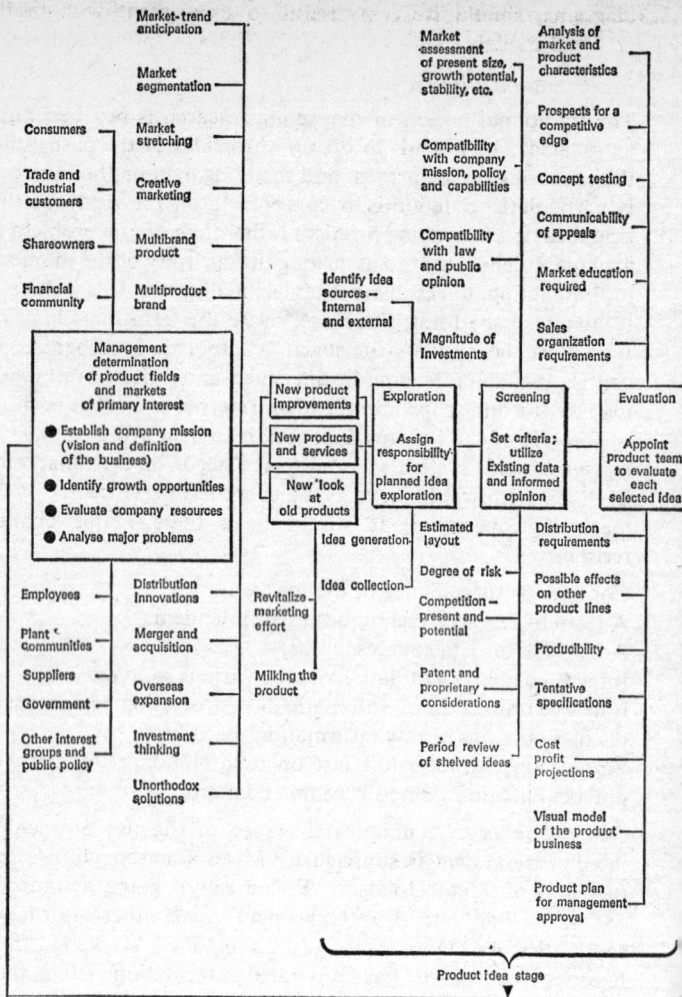

Figure 2 Work flow and systems chart for management of new products (developed by Paul E. Fank, President, and the staff of McCann/ITSM Inc.)

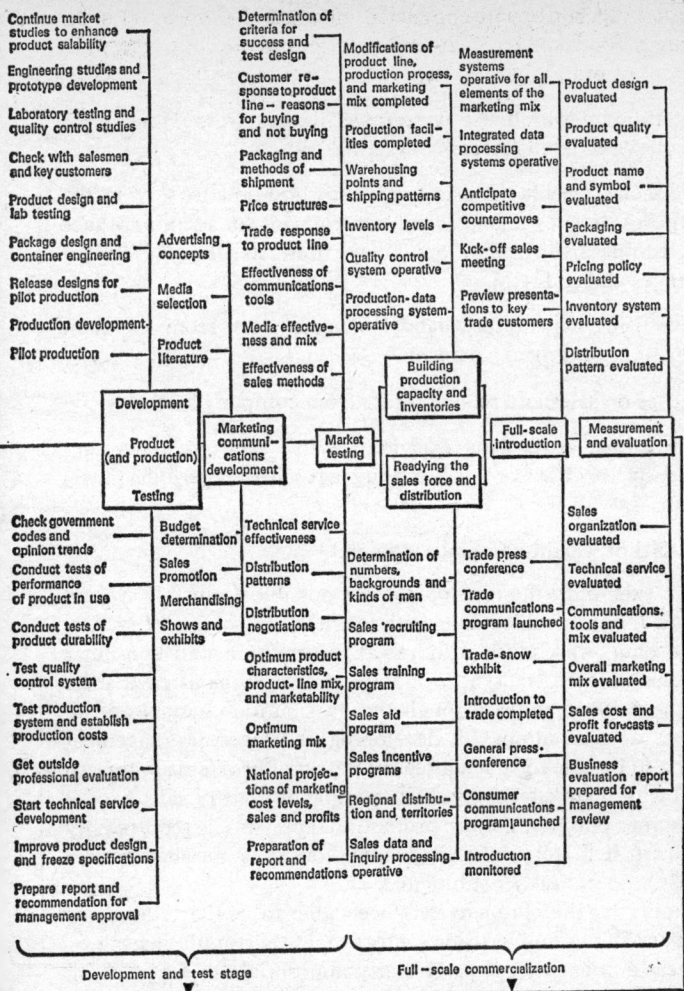

Continue market studies to enhance product salability

Engineering studies and prototype development

Laboratory testing and quality control studies

Check with salesmen and key customers

Product design and lab testing

Package design and container engineering

Release designs for pilot production

Production development

Pilot production

Determination of criteria for success and test design

Customer response to product line — reasons for buying and not buying

Packaging and methods of shipment

Price structures

Trade response to product line

Effectiveness of communications tools

Media effectiveness and mix

Effectiveness of sales methods

Modifications of product line, production process, and marketing mix completed

Production facilities completed

Warehousing points and shipping patterns

Inventory levels

Quality control system operative

Production-data processing system operative

Measurement systems operative for all elements of the marketing mix

Integrated data processing systems operative

Anticipate competitive countermoves

Kick-off sales meeting

Preview presentations to key trade customers

Product design evaluated

Product quality evaluated

Product name and symbol evaluated

Packaging evaluated

Pricing policy evaluated

Inventory system evaluated

Distribution pattern evaluated

Advertising concepts

Media selection

Product literature

Building production capacity and inventories

Development

Product (and production)

Testing

Marketing communications development

Market testing

Readying the sales force and distribution

Full-scale introduction

Measurement and evaluation

Check government codes and opinion trends

Conduct tests of performance of product in use

Conduct tests of product durability

Test quality control system

Test production system and establish production costs

Get outside professional evaluation

Start technical service development

Improve product design and freeze specifications

Prepare report and recommendation for management approval

Budget determination

Sales promotion

Merchandising

Shows and exhibits

Technical service effectiveness

Distribution patterns

Distribution negotiations

Optimum product characteristics, product-line mix, and marketability

Optimum marketing mix

National projections of marketing cost levels, sales and profits

Preparation of report and recommendations

Determination of numbers, backgrounds and kinds of men

Sales recruiting program

Sales training program

Sales aid program

Sales incentive programs

Regional distribution and territories

Sales data and inquiry processing operative

Trade press conference

Trade communications program launched

Trade-show exhibit

Introduction to trade completed

General press conference

Consumer communications program launched

Introduction monitored

Sales organization evaluated

Technical service evaluated

Communications, tools and mix evaluated

Overall marketing mix evaluated

Sales cost and profit forecasts evaluated

Business evaluation report prepared for management review

Development and test stage

Full-scale commercialization

A monthly sales audit conducted among a panel of 100 high-volume food stores in 20 markets to provide advance indications of brand share shifts.

Supermarket warehouse withdrawal figures from Time, Inc.'s new service, Selling Areas-Marketing, Inc.

Salesmen's weekly reports (which, in addition to serving the purposes of sales management control, call for reconnaissance on competitive promotions, new products launches, price changes and so forth).

Advertising expenditure data, by media class, from the company's accounting department.

Figures on sales and related topics from company factories.

Competitive advertising expenditure and exposure data, supplied by the division's advertising agencies at periodic intervals.

A panel of weight-conscious women.

To exemplify the type of outputs possible from this system, Mead Johnson will be able, with the help of analyses of factory sales data, warehouse withdrawal information and consumer purchases from Nielsen, to monitor transactions at each stage of the flow of goods through the distribution channel and to detect accumulations or developing shortages. Management will also be able to spot sources of potential problems in time to deal with them effectively. For example, if factory sales exceed consumer purchases, more promotional pressure is required. By contrast, if factory sales lag behind consumer purchases, sales effort must be further stimulated.

Similarly, the company has been able to devise a practical measurement of advertising's effectiveness in stimulating sales – a measurement that is particularly appropriate to fast-moving packaged goods. By relating advertising outlays and exposure data to the number of prospects trying out a product during a campaign (the number is obtained from the continuing consumer survey), it is possible to calculate the advertising cost of recruiting such a prospect. By persisting in such analyses during several campaigns, the relative value of alternative advertising approaches can be weighed. Since measurement of the sales – as opposed to the communications – effects of promotion is a horrendously difficult, costly and chancy process, the full significance of this achievement is difficult to exaggerate.

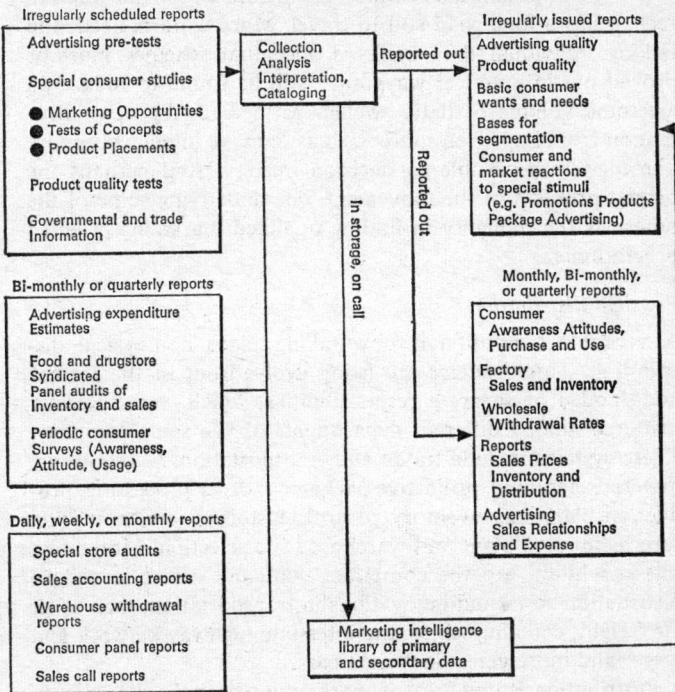

Irregularly scheduled reports

Advertising pre-tests
Special consumer studies
● Marketing Opportunities ● Tests of Concepts ● Product Placements
Product quality tests
Governmental and trade Information

Collection Analysis Interpretation, Cataloging

Reported out

Irregularly issued reports

Advertising quality
Product quality
Basic consumer wants and needs
Bases for segmentation
Consumer and market reactions to special stimuli (e.g. Promotions Products Package Advertising)

Reported out

In storage, on call

Bi-monthly or quarterly reports

Advertising expenditure Estimates
Food and drugstore Syndicated Panel audits of Inventory and sales
Periodic consumer Surveys (Awareness, Attitude, Usage)

Monthly, Bi-monthly, or quarterly reports

Consumer Awareness Attitudes, Purchase and Use
Factory Sales and Inventory
Wholesale Withdrawal Rates
Reports Sales Prices Inventory and Distribution
Advertising Sales Relationships and Expense

Daily, weekly, or monthly reports

Special store audits
Sales accounting reports
Warehouse withdrawal reports
Consumer panel reports
Sales call reports

Marketing Intelligence library of primary and secondary data

Figure 3 Mead Johnson's marketing intelligence system

Benefits realized. Mead Johnson's marketing intelligence system has been helpful to management in a number of ways. In addition to giving executive early warning of new trends and problems and valuable insights into future conditions, it is leading to a systematic *body* of knowledge about company markets rather than to isolated scraps of information. This knowledge in turn should lead ultimately to a theory of marketing in each field that will explain the mysteries that baffle marketers today. What is more, the company expects that the system will help to free its marketing intelligence people from fire-fighting projects so that they can concentrate on long-term factors and eventually be more consistently creative.

Despite these gains, it is important to note that Mead Johnson feels it has a long road still to travel. More work is needed in linking individual data banks. Conceptual schemes must be proved out in practice; ways must still be found to reduce an awesome volume of data, swelled periodically by new information from improved sources, so as to make intelligence more immediately accessible to decision makers. And perhaps the biggest problem of the movement, one underlying some of the others, is the difficulty in finding qualified marketing-oriented programmers.

Physical distribution

A veritable revolution is now taking place in physical distribution. Total systems are being evolved out of the former hodgepodge of separate responsibilities, which were typically scattered among different departments of the same company. These systems include traffic and transportation, warehousing, materials handling, protective packaging, order processing, production planning, inventory control, customer service, market forecasting and plant and warehouse site selection. Motivating this revolution are the computer, company drives to reduce distribution costs, and innovations in transportation, such as jet air freight, container ships, the interstate highway network and larger and more versatile freight cars.

Distribution is one area of marketing where the 'bread-and-butter' uses of the computer are relatively easily deployed for such functions as order processing, real-time inventory level reports and tracking the movements of goods. Further into the future lie mathematical models which will include every factor bearing on distribution. Not only will packaging, materials handling, transportation and warehouse, order processing and related costs be considered in such models; also included will be sales forecasts by product, production rates by factory, warehouse locations and capacities, speeds of different carriers, etc.

In short, a complete picture will be developed for management.

Program in action. The experiences of the Norge Division of Borg-Warner Corporation point up the values of the systems approach in physical distribution. The firm was confronted externally with complaints from its dealers and distributors, who were trying to cope with swollen inventories and the pressures of 'loading deals'. Internally, because coordination of effort between the six departments involved in distribution was at a minimum, distribution costs and accounts receivable were mounting persistently.

To grapple with this situation, Norge undertook a comprehensive analysis of its distribution system. Out of this grew a new philosophy. A company executive has described the philosophy to me as follows:

An effective system of physical distribution cannot begin at the end of the production line. It must also apply at the very beginning of the production process – at the planning, scheduling, and forecasting stages. Logistics, in short, is part of a larger marketing system, not just an evaluation of freight rates. We must worry not only about finished refrigerators, but also about the motors coming from another manufacturer, and even about where the copper that goes into those motors will come from. We must be concerned with *total flow*.

To implement this philosophy, the appliance manufacturer took the following steps:

1. It reorganized the forecasting, production scheduling, warehousing, order processing, and shipping functions into *one* department headed by a director of physical distribution.

2. The management information system was improved with the help of EDP equipment tied into the communications network. This step made it possible to process and report data more speedily on orders received, inventory levels and the actual movement of goods.

3. Management used a combination of computer and manual techniques to weigh trade-offs among increased costs of mul-

tiple warehousing, reduced long-haul freight and local drayage costs, reduced inventory pipe-line, and the sales value of an improved 'total' product offering. Also assessed were trade-offs between shorter production runs and higher inventory levels, thereby challenging the traditional 'wisdom' of production-oriented managers that the longer the run, the better.

4. The company is setting up new regional warehouses.

As a result of these moves, Norge has been able to lower inventories throughout its sales channels and to reduce accounts receivable. These gains have led, in turn, to a reduction of the company's overall investment and a concomitant increase in profitability.

It is essential to note that even though Norge has used operations research as part of its systems approach, many aspects of the program are qualitative. Thus far, the company has found that the development of an all-encompassing model is not warranted because of (a) the time and cost involved, (b) the probability that the situation will change before the model is completed, (c) a concern that such a model would be so complex as to be unworkable, and (d) the difficulty of testing many of the assumptions used. In addition, management has not tried to quantify the impact of its actions on distributor and retailer attitudes and behavior, possible competitive countermoves and numerous other factors contributing to results.

Toward total integration

The integration of systems developed for product management, product innovation, marketing intelligence, physical distribution and the other functions or 'sub-systems' embraced by the term *marketing* creates a total marketing system. Thus, marketing plans composed according to a step-by-step outline, ranging from enunciation of objectives and implementational steps to audit and adjustment to environmental changes, constitute a complete application of systems theory. Further, as the various sub-systems of the overall system are linked quantitatively, so that the effect of modifications in one element can be detected in other elements, and as the influences of competitive moves on each element are analysed numerically, then the total scheme becomes truly sophisticated.

Pluses and minuses

Two elements underlie the use and benefits of systems theory – order and knowledge. The first is a homely virtue, the second a lofty goal. Marketing is obviously not alone among all human pursuits in needing them; but, compared with its business neighbors, production and finance, marketing's need is acute indeed. The application of the systems concept can bring considerable advantages. It offers:

A methodical problem-solving orientation – with a broader frame of reference so that all aspects of a problem are examined.

Coordinated deployment of all appropriate tools of marketing.

Greater efficiency and economy of marketing operations.

Quicker recognition of impending problems, made possible by better understanding of the complex interplay of many trends and forces.

A stimulus to innovation.

A means of quantitatively verifying results.

These functional benefits in turn yield rich rewards in the marketplace. The most important gains are:

A deeper penetration of existing markets. As an illustration, the Advanced Data Division of Litton Industries has become a leader in the automatic revenue control business by designing systems meshing together 'hardware' and 'software'.

A broadening of markets. For example, the tourist industry has attracted millions of additional travelers by creating packaged tours that are really product-service systems. These systems are far more convenient and economical than anything the consumer could assemble himself.

An extension of product lines. Systems management makes it more feasible to seek out compatibilities among independently developed systems. Evidence of this idea is the work of automatic control system specialists since the early 1950s (Tustin, 1952). Now similar signs are apparent in marketing. For example, Acme Visible Records is currently dove-tailing the design and sale of its record-keeping systems with data-processing machines and forms.

A lessening of competition or a strengthened capacity to cope with competition. The systems approach tends to make a company's product line more unique and attractive. Carborundum's innovation in metal-removal systems is a perfect illustration of this.

Problems in practice

Having just enumerated in glowing terms the benefits of the systems approach, realism demands that I give 'equal time' to the awesome difficulties its utilization presents. There is no better evidence of this than the gulf between the elegant and sophisticated models with which recent marketing literature abounds and the actual number of situations in which those models really work. For the truth of the matter is that we are still in the foothills of this development, despite the advances of a few leaders. Let us consider some of the obstacles.

Time and manpower costs. First of all, the systems approach requires considerable time to implement; it took one company over a year to portray its physical distribution system in a mathematical model before it could even begin to solve its problems. RCA's Electronic Data Processing Division reports models taking three to five years to build, after which holes in the data network have to be filled and the model tested against history. Add to this the need for manpower of exceptional intellectual ability, conceptual skills and specialized education – manpower that is in exceedingly short supply. Because the problems are complex and involve all elements of the business, one man alone cannot solve them. He lacks the knowledge, tools and controls. And so many people must be involved. It follows that the activation of systems theory can be very costly.

Absence of 'canned' solutions. Unlike other business functions where standardized approaches to problem solving are available, systems must be tailored to the individual situation of each firm. Even the same problem in different companies in the same industry will frequently lead to different solutions because of the impact of other inputs, unique perceptions of the environment and varying corporate missions. These factors, too, compound time and expense demands.

'*Net uncertainties*'. Even after exhaustive analysis, full optimization of a total problem cannot be obtained. Some uncertainty will always remain and must be dealt with on the basis of judgement and experience.

Lack of hard data. In the world of engineering, the systems evolved to date have consisted all or mostly of machines. Systems engineers have been wise enough to avoid the irrationalities of man until they master control of machines. Marketing model-builders, however, have not been able to choose, for the distributor, salesman, customer and competitor are central to marketing. We must, therefore, incorporate not only quantitative measures of the dimensions of things and processes (e.g. market potential, media outlays and shipping rates), but also psychological measures of comprehension, attitudes, motivations, intentions, needs – yes, even psychological measures of physical behavior. What is needed is a marriage of the physical and behavioral sciences – and we are about as advanced in this blending of disciplines as astronomy was in the Middle Ages.

Consider the advertising media fields as an instance of the problem.

A number of advertising agencies have evolved linear programming or simulation techniques to assess alternate media schedules. One of the key sets of data used covers the probabilities of exposure to all or part of the audience of a TV program, magazine, or radio station. But what is exposure, and how do you measure it? What is optimum frequency of exposure, and how do you measure it? How does advertising prevail on the predispositions and perceptions of a potential customer? Is it better to judge advertising effects on the basis of exposure opportunity, 'impact' (whatever that is), messages retained, message comprehension, or attitude shifts or uptrends in purchase intentions? We do not have these answers yet.

Even assuming precise knowledge of market dimensions, product performance, competitive standing, weights of marketing pressure exerted by direct selling, advertising and promotion, and so on, most marketers do not yet know, except in isolated cases, how one force will affect another. For instance, how does a company 'image' affect the setting in which its salesmen work? How does a company's reputation for service affect customer buying behavior?

Nature of marketing men. Man is an actor on this stage in another role. A good many marketing executives, in the deepest recesses of their psyches, are artists, not analysts. For them, marketing is an art form, and, in my opinion, they really do not want it to be any other way. Their temperament is antipathetic to system, order, knowledge. They enjoy flying by the seat of their pants – though you will never get them to admit it. They revel in chaos, abhor facts and fear research. They hate to be trammeled by written plans. And they love to spend, but are loath to assess the results of their spending.

Obviously, such men cannot be sold readily on the value and practicality of the systems approach! It takes time, experience and many facts to influence their thinking.

Surmounting the barriers

All is not gloom, however. The barriers described are being overcome in various ways. While operations research techniques have not yet made much headway in evolving total marketing systems and in areas where man is emotionally engaged, their accomplishments in solving inventory control problems, in sales analysis, in site selection and in other areas have made many businessmen more sympathetic and open-minded to them.

Also, mathematical models – even the ones that do not work well yet – serve to bolster comprehension of the need for system as well as to clarify the intricacies among sub-systems. Many models are in this sense learning models; they teach us how to ask more insightful questions. Moreover, they pinpoint data gaps and invite a more systematized method for reaching judgements where complete information does not exist. Because the computer abhors vague generalities, it forces managers to analyse their roles, objectives and criteria more concretely. Paradoxically, it demands more, not less, of its human masters.

Of course, resistance to mathematical models by no means makes resistance to the systems approach necessary. There are many cases where no need may ever arise to use mathematics or computers. For the essence of the systems approach is not its techniques, but the enumeration of options and their implications. A simple checklist may be the only tool needed. I would even argue that some hard thinking in a quiet room may be enough. This being the case, the whole trend to more analysis and logic in management thinking, as reflected in business periodicals, business schools and the practices of many companies, will work in favor of the development of the systems approach.

It is important to note at this juncture that not all marketers need the systems approach in its formal, elaborate sense. The success of some companies is rooted in other than marketing talents; their expertise may lie in finance, technology, administration, or even in personnel – as in the case of holding companies having an almost uncanny ability to hire brilliant operating managers and the self-control to leave them alone. In addition, a very simple marketing operation – for example, a company marketing one product through one distribution channel – may have no use for the systems concept.

Applying the approach

Not illogically, there is a system for applying the systems approach. It may be outlined as a sequence of steps:

1. *Define the problem and clarify objectives.* Care must be exercised not to accept the view of the propounder of the problem lest the analyst be defeated at the outset.

2. *Test the definition of the problem.* Expand its parameters to the limit. For example, to solve physical distribution problems it is necessary to study the marketplace (customer preferences, usage rates, market size, and so forth) , as well as the production

process (which plants produce which items most efficiently, what the interplant movements of raw materials are, and so forth). Delineate the extremes of these factors, their changeability and the limitations on management's ability to work with them.

3. *Build a model*. Portray all factors graphically, indicating logical and chronological sequences – the dynamic flow of information, decisions and events. 'Closed circuits' should be used where there is information feedback or go, no-go and recycle signals (see Figure 2).

4. *Set concrete objectives*. For example, if a firm wants to make daily deliveries to every customer, prohibitive as the cost may be, manipulation of the model will yield one set of answers. But if the desire is to optimize service at lowest cost, then another set of answers will be needed. The more crisply and precisely targets are stated, the more specific the results will be.

5. *Develop alternative solutions*. It is crucial to be as openminded as possible at this stage. The analyst must seek to expand the list of options rather than merely assess those given to him, then reduce the list to a smaller number of practical or relevant ones.

6. *Set up criteria or tests of relative value*.

7. *Quantify some or all of the factors or 'variables'*. The extent to which this is done depends, of course, on management's inclinations and the 'state of the art'.

8. *Manipulate the model*. That is, weigh the costs, effectiveness, profitability and risks of each alternative.

9. *Interpret the results, and choose one or more courses of action*.

10. *Verify the results*. Do they make sense when viewed against the world as executives know it? Can their validity be tested by experiments and investigations?

Forethought and perspective

Successful systems do not blossom overnight. From primitive beginnings, they evolve over a period of time as managers and systems specialists learn to understand each other better, and learn how to structure problems and how to push out the frontiers of the 'universe' with which they are dealing. Companies must be prepared to invest time, money and energy in making systems management feasible. This entails a solid foundation of historical data even before the conceptual framework for the system can be constructed. Accordingly, considerable time should be invested at the outset in *thinking* about the problem, its appropriate scope, options and criteria of choice before plunging into analysis.

Not only technicians, but most of us have a way of falling in love with techniques. We hail each one that comes along – *deus ex machina*. Historically, commercial research has wallowed in several such passions (e.g. probability sampling, motivation research and semantic scaling), and now operations research appears to be doing the same thing. Significantly, each technique has come, in the fullness of time, to take its place as one, but only one, instrument in the research tool chest. We must therefore have a broad and dispassionate perspective on the systems approach at this juncture. We must recognize that the computer does not possess greater magical properties than the abacus. It, too, is a tool, albeit a brilliant one.

Put another way, executives must continue to exercise their judgement and experience. Systems analysis is no substitute for common sense. The computer must adapt itself to their styles, personalities and modes of problem solving. It is an aid to management, not a surrogate. Businessmen may be slow, but the good ones are bright; the electronic monster, by contrast, is a speedy idiot. It demands great acuity of wit from its human managers lest they be deluged in an avalanche of useless paper. (The story is told of a sales manager who had just found out about the impressive capabilities of his company's computer and called for a detailed sales analysis of all products. The report was duly prepared and wheeled into his office on a dolly.)

Systems users must be prepared to revise continually. There are two reasons for this. First, the boundaries of systems keep changing; constraints are modified; competition makes fresh incursions; variables, being what they are, vary, and new ones crop up. Second, the analytical process is iterative. Usually, one

L. Adler 95

'pass' at problem formulation and searches for solutions will not suffice, and it will be necessary to 're-cycle' as early hypotheses are challenged and new, more fruitful insights are stimulated by the inquiry. Moreover, it is impossible to select objectives without knowledge of their effects and costs. That knowledge can come only from analysis, and it frequently requires review and revision.

Despite all the efforts at quantification, systems analysis is still largely an art. It relies frequently on inputs based on human judgement; even when the inputs are numerical they are determined, at least in part, by judgement. Similarly, the outputs must pass through the sieve of human interpretation. Hence, there is a positive correlation between the pay-off from a system and the managerial level involved in its design. The higher the level, the more rewarding the results.

Finally, let me observe that marketing people merit their own access to computers as well as programmers who understand marketing. Left in the hands of accountants, the timing, content and format of output are often out of phase with marketing needs.

Conclusion

In about 1170 Reginald, a monk of Durham, wrote the following about St Godric, a merchant later turned hermit:

He laboured not only as a merchant but also as a shipman . . . to Denmark, Flanders and Scotland; in which lands he found certain rare, and therefore more precious, wares, which he carried to other parts wherein he knew them to be least familiar, and coveted by the inhabitants beyond the price of gold itself, wherefore he exchanged these wares for others coveted by men of other lands. . . .

How St Godric 'knew' about his markets we are not told, marketing having been in a primitive state in 1170. How some of us marketers today 'know' is, in my opinion, sometimes no less mysterious than it was eight centuries ago. But we are trying to change that, and I will hazard the not very venturesome forecast that the era of 'by guess and by gosh' marketing is drawing to a close. One evidence of this trend is marketers' intensified search for knowledge that will improve their command over their destinies. This search is being spurred on by a number of powerful developments. To describe them briefly:

The growing complexity of technology and the accelerating pace of technological innovation.

The advent of the computer, inspiring and making possible analysis of the relationships between systems components.

The intensification of competition, lent impetus by the extraordinary velocity of new product development and the tendency of diversification to thrust everybody into everybody else's business.

The preference of buyers for purchasing from as few sources as possible, thereby avoiding the problems of assembling bits and pieces themselves and achieving greater reliability, economy and administrative convenience. (Mrs Jones would rather buy a complete vacuum cleaner from one source than the housing from one manufacturer, the hose from another and the attachments from still another. And industrial buyers are not much different from Mrs Jones. They would rather buy an automated machine tool from one manufacturer than design and assemble the components themselves. Not to be overlooked, in this connection, is the tremendous influence of the US government in buying systems for its military and aerospace programs.)

The further development and application of the systems approach to marketing represents, in my judgement, the leading edge in both marketing theory and practice. At the moment, we are still much closer to St Godric than to the millenium, and the road will be rocky and tortuous. But if we are ever to convert marketing into a scientific pursuit, this is the road we must travel. The systems concept can teach us how our businesses really behave in the marketing arena, thereby extending managerial leverage and control. It can help us to confront more intelligently the awesome complexity of marketing, to deal with the hazards and opportunities of technological change, and to cope with the intensification of competition. And in the process, the concept will help us to feed the hungry maws of our expensive computers with more satisfying fare.

L. Adler 97

References

Cox, D. F., and Good, R. E. (1967), 'How to build a marketing information system', *Harv. Bus. Rev.*, vol. 45, no. 3, pp. 145–54.

Tustin, A. (ed.) (1952), *Automatic and Manual Control; Papers Contributed to the Conference at Cranford, 1951*, Butterworths.

Wendel, W. H. (1965), 'Abrasive maker's systems approach opens new markets', *Steel*, 27 December, p. 38.

Wendel, W. H. (1966), 'Carborundum grinds at faster clip', *Bus. Week*, 23 July, pp. 58, 60.

5 J. W. Forrester[1]

Modelling of Market and Company Interactions

J. W. Forrester, 'Modeling of market and company interactions',
Proceedings of the Fall Conference of the American Marketing Association,
1965, pp. 353–64.

All of you in marketing recognize that many linkages connect a
company to its market. Some of these linkages are tangible, like
the flow of orders toward the company and the counterflow of
product to the customer. Other linkages are obvious, like the
sales effort and advertising expended to communicate with the
market. But many linkages are subtle and tenuous, like those
that carry customer attitudes and needs back to the decision-
making points in the company.

But recognizing these linkages between company and market
does not mean that one can see clearly the time-varying responses caused by interactions between them. It is in the interplay of
forces caused by these interacting linkages that we find the
causes of company and product growth and conversely find the
influences which can cause stagnation and decline.

These company–market linkages form networks of feedback
loops. In these loops an action by the company causes a response in the market which in turn produces the information on
which decisions are based to control future company actions.
The dynamic behavior of these feedback loops is poorly
understood and contains many surprises.

The complexity of these interactions is far too great for analytical solution using conventional mathematical approaches.
With trivial exceptions, mathematics deals only with linear
systems. Yet some of the most important behavior mechanisms
in marketing depend for their very existence on non-linear relationships. The only effective tool for understanding non-
linear, multiple-loop, feedback systems is the construction of a

1. Professor Forrester is the author of *Urban Dynamics*.

model that permits simulation of the behavior relationships which we perceive within the company and market.

The construction of models to represent market dynamics is now possible. The problem is not, as often supposed, the need for more empirical data. The pace of progress will be set entirely by the availability of investigators who understand the kinds of factors that are important in feedback system behavior and who can conceptually structure the presently available information and data.

Some of the linkages between a company and market appear in Figure 1. The company uses incoming information from the market as the basis for generating the outputs from company to market. These outputs generated by the company include price and the quality of products and services. Another output from the company is delivery delay which reflects the relationship between incoming order rate and production capability. Product suitability reflects the adequacy of new product development and the degree of perception by the company of market needs. Sales effort is a result of the company's resource allocation policies.

In the opposite direction from market to company, there is, of course, a flow of orders and payments. But there are also other important information streams. These might be defined in a variety of ways. One useful structuring of information from the market to the company is in terms of reflections of those linkages which the company projects to the market. The company should be interested in the market reactions toward price, quality, delivery delay and product suitability.

Starting from Figure 1, to construct a dynamic simulation model requires that we define the responses that we believe exist in the two separate sectors – the company and the market. In each sector the task is to take the incoming inputs as a basis for generating the outputs. Within the company the time delays and policy interactions must be represented which convert market information into the outputs of price, quality, delivery delay, product suitability, sales effort and product flow. Within the market the characteristics must be conceptualized and defined which we believe react to the inputs from the company and generate a stream of orders as well as the sources of information flowing to the company. This means that the model represents our operational knowledge about the management processes in the company and the customer processes in the market.

Figure 1 implies the futility of attempting to teach marketing as an isolated corporate function. In the corporation, marketing shares with the area of management information systems the characteristic that it depends on an unusually high number of linkages to other parts of the business system. It is not self-sufficient. By contrast, production is a more self-contained corporate function. I feel that this high degree of inter-connectedness in marketing explains many of the difficulties encountered in attempting to teach the subject. Marketing can not be successfully isolated from its dynamic interactions with other company functions.

In Figure 1 we see implied many of the simpler feedback loops in the system. Company activities to generate quality lead to an actual product quality that produces a market reaction to quality and an information return to the company about the reaction to quality, which is one of the inputs to the future management of quality. Likewise, a loop connects company price policy through prices to the market and back through the

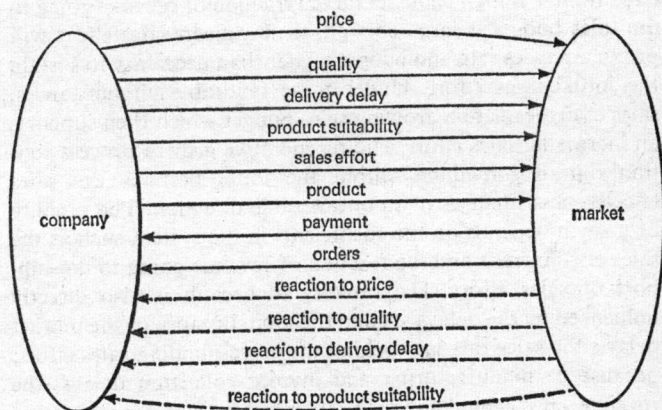

Figure 1 Company—market linkages

reaction of the market to price. But the system is not a collection of separate and isolated loops controlling the separate company outputs. There are many important cross couplings. For example, a policy which reduces price can reduce the payment stream and thereby company profits so that pressure is brought on the activities controlling quality, which then may lower the quality output from the company and in time cause a decrease in market orders. The feedback loops connecting company and market have many devious interconnections. The dynamic interactions within these loops can defeat our attempts at intuitive judgement about system behavior.

Some of the feedback loops between company and market are so-called 'negative feedback loops' which attempt to adjust system operation toward some reference goal. Other loops are 'positive feedback' in character and these latter account for the processes of growth and decline.

Figure 2 shows an example of a positive feedback loop involved in the growth of a new product. The sales effort operating at some sales effectiveness produces a sales rate. The sales effectiveness is a reflection of the desirability of the product and is a measure of the ease with which it can be sold. The sales rate generates revenue. A part of the revenue becomes available in the sales budget to support future sales effort. If the sales effectiveness is high enough and the fraction of revenue going to the sales budget is large enough, then a given sales effort will produce a sales rate and budget higher than necessary to sustain the initial sales effort. Under these favorable circumstances, sales effort leads to a growing sales budget which then supports an increasing sales effort. The regenerative growth process continues until something within the loop, perhaps the sales effectiveness, changes in an unfavorable direction. The rapidity of growth depends on the coefficients in the system such as the sales effectiveness and the fraction of revenue going to the support of sales effort. The rapidity of growth is also directly influenced by the delays around the loop. Because of the market delays, the sales rate lags behind the corresponding sales effort; because of manufacturing and invoice collection delays, the revenue lags behind the sales rate; because of the corporate budgeting procedures, the sales budget lags behind the in-

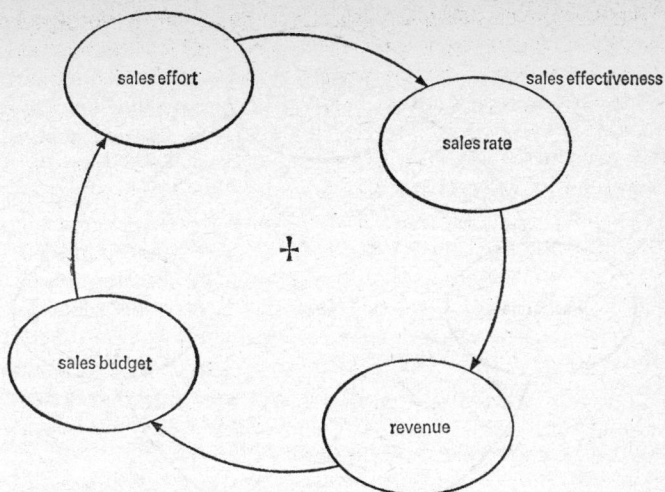

Figure 2 Positive feedback in sales growth

coming revenue; and because of the time to locate and train
salesmen, the sales effort lags behind the budget. Other conditions being equal, the rate of sales growth will be doubled if
the delays around this positive feedback loop can be reduced to
half.

Conversely, a positive feedback loop can show degenerative
decline. In the example of Figure 2, if the sales effectiveness is
low, the sales effort may not support its own sales budget leading to a future reduction in sales effort that further reduces
sales. Positive feedback loops can exhibit either growth or
decay. By contrast, negative feedback loops tend to adjust activity towards a reference goal, but in the attempt they often
produce fluctuation.

Figure 3 shows a negative feedback loop coupling sales rate,
order backlog, delivery delay and sales effectiveness. In this
diagram it is assumed that sales effort remains constant. The
relationship between order backlog and sales rate depends on
the production capacity characteristics of the company. For
illustration, assume that the production capacity is constant and
the sales effort is more than adequate to create the cor-

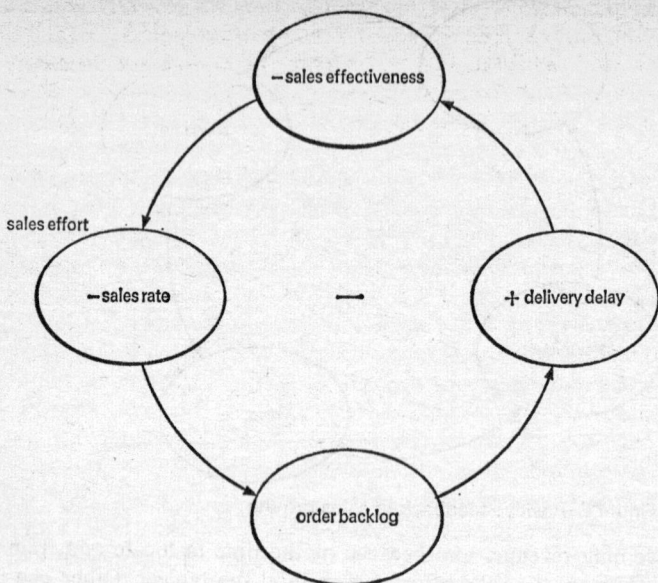

Figure 3 Negative feedback limiting sales

responding sales rate if delivery delay is short. Under these circumstances, sales rate will exceed production capacity and the order backlog will increase. The increase in the order backlog will continue until the resulting increase in delivery delay becomes sufficient that some customers become unwilling to wait for delivery. As the delivery delay becomes longer, the product becomes less attractive and the product becomes less easy to sell. This means that, as delivery delay increases, the sales effectiveness declines until sales rate falls to the production capability. This negative feedback loop is at work in any market situation where delivery delays are long enough to be of concern to the customer. A negative feedback loop as shown in Figure 3 can exhibit instability. There are delays at each point in the loop. The sales rate does not respond immediately to changes in delivery delay because many of the orders under negotiation are already committed and cannot be redirected. Order backlog is an accumulation over time of discrepancies between the sales rate and the production capacity and backlog lags behind a change in sales rate. Delivery delay here represents the delay recognized by the market, and this lags behind the true delay as indicated by the order backlog. These delays, coupled with the other characteristics of the loop, can lead to overcorrection. A sales rate which is too high goes unrecognized until the backlog builds up and until the delivery delay is recognized. By this time delivery delay is excessive and leads to a reduction in sales rate below the production capacity. Then, order backlog declines unduly before the low delivery delay is recognized and sales again rise.

An important part of the negative feedback loop of Figure 3 is the non-linear relationship between delivery delay and sales effectiveness as show in Figure 4. Sales effectiveness is a maximum when delivery is zero. For very small delivery delays (measured in seconds for a drugstore item and up to months for a digital computer) there is no reduction of sales as delivery delay increases. However, with longer delivery delays, a region of steep slope is encountered where the delay is sufficient to discourage a progressively larger fraction of customers. For still longer delays, the curve levels out as it approaches zero sales

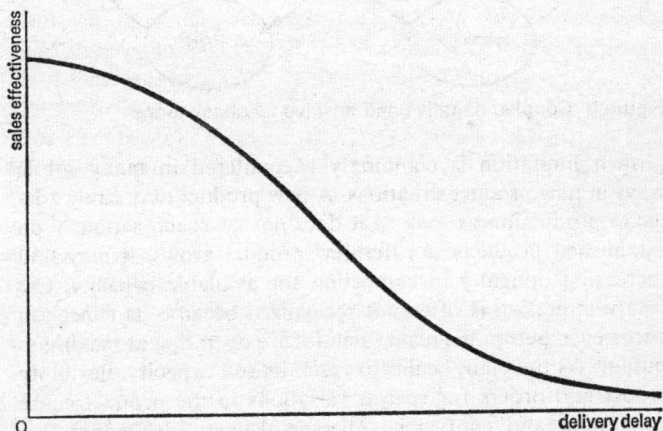

Figure 4 Non-linear relationship

effectiveness, representing the fact that a few customers find the product particularly suitable and are willing to plan ahead and wait unusually long.

Now what would happen in a coupled company and market system involving the two control loops of Figures 2 and 3? These are shown interconnected in Figure 5. Here, if we assume that only a limited production capacity is available, the positive feedback loop will regenerate a rising rate of sales until the production capacity limit is reached. When the production rate no longer increases with sales, the negative loop would show an increasing delivery delay, and this would produce a declining sales effectiveness to limit further growth. This process of

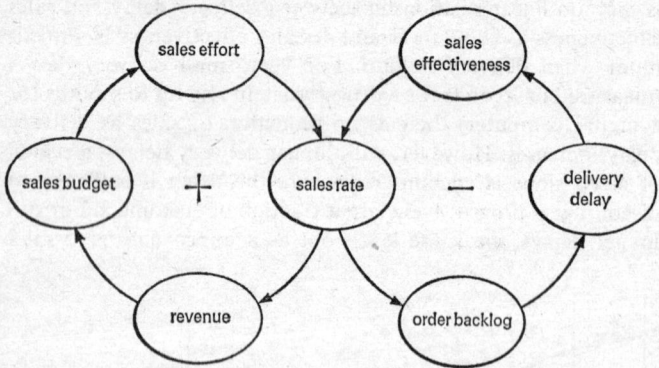

Figure 5 Coupled negative and positive feedback loops

growth limitation is commonly encountered in many subtle ways in new product situations. A new product may enjoy adequate production as long as it does not encroach seriously on established products. As the new product grows, it may find increasing difficulty in competing for available capacity. Capacity limitation is often not recognized because its effect can occur even before the plant facilities are operating at maximum output. As the plant begins to reach its full capacity, flexibility is lost and orders for special variations in the product cause congestion and confusion. Average delivery delay increases even though it appears that the manufacturing capacity is still

not fully occupied. Any situation where order backlogs are long
enough to be viewed unfavorably by customers implies that this
negative feedback loop is active in partially suppressing sales.
Figure 5 can be recognized as an extremely simplified subset of
the possible interactions contained in Figure 1. Even in this
severely simplified form of Figure 5, the implied system behavior cannot be intuitively estimated as one contemplates
changing the many factors within the two coupled loops.

The growth behavior of the double-loop system under one
set of system conditions is shown in Figure 6. The figure is
taken from a simulation run using 'industrial dynamics'
methods (Forrester, 1961) and the DYNAMO compiler (Pugh,
1963) for simulating the model. Growth in sales rate occurs
during the first 60 months. Thereafter sales tend to fluctuate
because the production capacity limit has been reached. During
the early period of growth, sales effectiveness remains constant
and high while at the same time the delivery delay remains
constant and low. As the sales rate begins to approach the production capacity, the delivery delay increases and the sales
effectiveness falls. After month 60, the system fluctuates be-

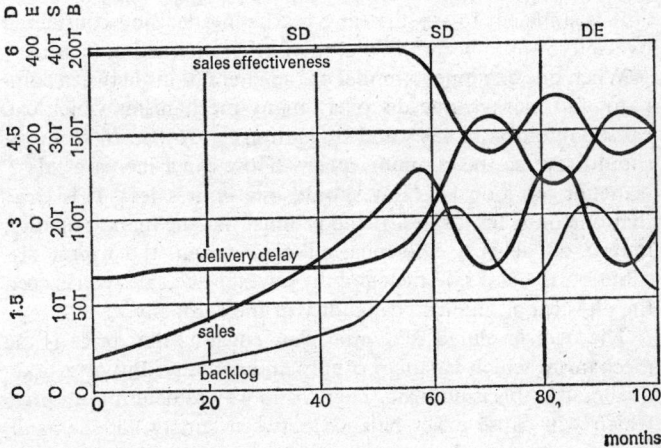

Figure 6 Growth and stagnation in sales

cause of the characteristics of the negative feedback loop in which readjustments within the loop are delayed and instability occurs on either side of the equilibrium position.

The major characteristics of Figure 6 – the rapidity of early growth and the fluctuation during the stagnation period – depend on the parameters and the time delays in the two loops. The positive feedback loop of Figure 2 is the primary determinant of the growth phase shown in Figure 6; and the negative feedback loop in Figure 3 is the primary determinant of the behavior after sales growth has been arrested by reaching the production capacity. In Figure 6 we see a transition from positive feedback loop behavior to negative loop behavior which is triggered by the non-linear characteristics represented in the production capacity and the sales effectiveness.

In Figures 5 and 6, the cessation of sales growth could not be forestalled by improved or expanded marketing activities. A larger fraction of revenue devoted to sales effort would only cause the delivery delay to increase further and drive down the sales effectiveness to still lower values. Similar interactions, within the multiple channels of the far greater complexity of real-life situations, can invalidate marketing decisions by the inner workings of the market–company system.

It is sufficient to say that any marketing decision considered by itself is apt to become a victim of other interacting factors.

When one examines a model of the interactions between company and market, one discovers many mechanisms which can cause limitation in sales and stagnation in growth. In fact, one should reverse the common query, 'How can I increase sales?' A better question is, 'How should one limit sales?' It is clear that one must limit sales. If the product has the highest quality, immediate delivery, the most suitable design, the widest distribution, the best salesmen and the lowest price, sales will exceed the physical or financial capability of the company.

The oversimplified economic view suggests that price is the mechanism which balances supply and demand. But as a practical matter this is not true. There is no way to determine a price which will cause exact balance between supply and demand. Price is established on the basis of manufacturing cost, past traditions, competitors' prices, or in response to financial pressures on the company. If the price is set lower than the economic equilibrium value, then other influences must share the burden of limiting orders. The first effect will usually be a rise in delivery delay to make the product less attractive. After a period of long deliveries, the company may grow careless and allow quality to decline so that the lower quality contributes to limiting sales. The company profitability is, however, very sensitive to the balance of factors at work in the limitation of sales. As more of the burden is shifted to long delivery delay, lower quality, obsolete design and unskilled salesmen, the price must be correspondingly lowered to maintain sales. Profit margins fall and create financial pressures which cause further deterioration in the product characteristics of interest to the customer. A degenerative spiral can then develop with lower quality forcing lower prices which exert financial pressure and further reduce quality.

Returning to Figure 1 we see a number of information channels flowing from market to company carrying information about market reactions to company performance. These information channels are of the utmost importance in determining the kinds of decisions made within the company. Yet these information channels are subject to many ills. The quality of an information channel can be measured in several ways – by its persuasiveness, delay, bias, distortion, error and cross-talk.

An information channel usually shows greater persuasiveness and influence on the decision-making processes as it deals with short-term factors and as it deals with information which is easily measured. Information is more persuasive when the method of measurement is well known and widely accepted. For example, inventory information is highly persuasive since it appears monthly on the balance sheet measured to five decimal places (even though it may not be truly meaningful even in the first decimal place). By contrast, information indicating what the customers think of the company's product quality lacks persuasiveness because it is difficult to measure and hard to define. Oftentimes the most important information is the least persuasive.

Delay represents the time it takes information to travel along a channel. Information delays can be very long. For example,

there can easily be a five-year delay between the quality actually produced in a product and the reputation for quality which
is prevalent in the market. The time taken to judge quality is
partly controlled by the natural life of the product. A meaningful measure of quality in an electric refrigerator can only be
made if one waits through the normal life of the refrigerator.
Even after quality is observed directly by a user, further delays
are encountered before this reputation is transmitted to potential customers who have not been users.

Bias is the offset in an information channel where the perceived information deviates consistently from the true
conditions. One often sees bias in a company's belief about the
degree to which customers are satisfied. The company wants to
believe it is doing well. Favorable reports bolster the self image
and are remembered and circulated. Unfavorable reports are
dismissed as exceptions or as unfortunate accidents.

Distortion is a deviation between the input and output of an
information channel, which is a function of the nature of the
information itself. Distortion is sometimes intentional as in an
averaging process. Averaging of sales data suppresses short-
term fluctuation while allowing longer term deviations to be
transmitted. The fidelity of the process therefore depends on the
periodicity of the information being transmitted.

Error refers to random deviations and mistakes in an information channel. More effort is expended in reducing error than
in reducing any of the other types of information deficiencies.
Yet of the six types of information degradation, error is probably least important in affecting the feedback systems that
couple a company to its market.

Cross-talk is a term borrowed from telephone usage and represents the tendency of information to be transposed from one
channel to another. Transposition of the meaning of information is conspicuously evident in the channels flowing from
market to company. There is a tendency for all customer dissatisfaction to take the form of indicating that the price is too high.
This can happen at many points in the information channels.
Price is too high for the low quality, or price is too high for the
poor delivery, or price is too high for the discourteous salesmen.
But the qualification is lost and only the reference to price is

transmitted. Suppose that the customer is dissatisfied with the performance of his last purchase. He has decided not to buy again. When the salesman appears, the socially acceptable and most expeditious reason for not buying is to say that the price is too high. That is a value judgement which the salesman cannot effectively counter. Were the customer to complain of quality, the salesman might offer to send a service engineer or he might explain how quality control at the factory has been improved. Or he might offer to take back the equipment for repair. But, if the customer wants none of these and wants not to be bothered, he says the price is too high. Suppose, however, that the customer does complain about the low quality and the obsolete design. Will the salesman risk the wrath of the development department and the factory by carrying these complaints back to the home plant? Probably not. He will simply report that the price is too high. But suppose that the salesman has courage to press complaints of an obsolete product. What will the management do to restore falling sales? It may well reduce price because it knows how to accomplish that, whereas a redesign is uncertain and far in the future.

From simulation of the information channels and decision-making policies that create the company–market system one can learn much about the behavior which in real life is so baffling. Interactions are complex. The human mind is not well adapted to intuitively estimating the behavior of complex feedback linkages. Marketing is a function which cannot exist by itself. It is intimately coupled to production, capital investment policies, product design and the company's educational programs. As one makes changes in a particular set of market linkages one may simply create greater difficulties in another area. It is only through knowledge of the entire system that successful coupling between company and market can be achieved.

References

FORRESTER, J. W. (1961), *Industrial Dynamics*, MIT Press.
PUGH, A. L. III (1963), *DYNAMO User's Manual*, MIT Press.

Part Two
Management of Marketing Information

Marketing managers have a responsibility for the management
of two types of flows – the flow of products (and/or services)
and the flows of information. Information flows are in two
directions. Advertising is obviously a flow from the firm to the
market. The salesman is a personal communicator between the
firm and its customers. There will of course be no disagreement
that these are marketing management responsibilities. In this
Part however, we deal with some rather less obvious and
perhaps rather more complex aspects of information
management, involving primarily flows of information from the
market into the firm.

Marketing managers and managers of market research do not
always work well together, a problem that is probably
commoner in the United Kingdom than in the United States.
The marketing manager must understand both the value of
good market research, and its limitations; the market research
manager must remember that he exists to facilitate problem-
solving and decision-making by marketing management.
Thomas (Reading 6) explores these problems, which are also
dealt with in a companion volume in this series (*Marketing
Research*, edited by J. Seibert and G. Wills). Making sure that
information is being used for its ultimate purpose, namely
decision-making, is a problem that managers may lose sight of
in our computer-aided management environment. Ackoff
(Reading 7) in a cautionary essay, offers some dramatic
examples of management misinformation systems and the
distress they cause marketing managers.

Information plays a critical role in the management of
marketing efficiency and productivity. The marketing manager

should for example, know how profitable every item in his product line is, how profitable his channels are, how relatively profitable each of his customers are, and how efficient and productive his salesmen and sales territories are. This requires the use of a wide variety of the information that is potentially at his disposal, in such a way as to reveal these facts. Sevin (Reading 8) describes a method of organizing information so that the profitability of products, accounts and sales territories is revealed. It breaks with traditional ways of classifying costs but is shown to be a powerful means of controlling the marketing function.

Reference

SEIBERT, J., and WILLS, G. (eds.) (1970), *Marketing Research*, Penguin.

6 D. Thomas

Riddles of Market Research

D. Thomas, 'Riddles of market research', *Management Today*, March 1968, pp. 101–6.

The boom in marketing, as the essence of business activity, has generated a boom in an even younger field of management – market research. Like advertising, research is heavily in the hands of outside agencies. Like advertising, research is subject to some suspicion from users who echo the old saw about half of all advertising being wasted. The classic problem with advertising is 'which half is wasted?' The answer with market research is presumably that part which contributes to the eight new products, out of every ten launched on to the market, that fail to survive infancy.

Nearly all companies, including the biggest and most efficient marketers in Britain and America, have had conspicuous and costly product failures, Ford Edsels of various shapes and sizes. American giants, supposedly more expert in all phases of marketing, have shown a remarkable ability to fail in Britain with American best-sellers like Betty Crocker cakes or Dial soap; while the cigarette firms, whose marketing is highly concentrated, have all had failures – such as Strand, whose copy line, 'You're never alone with a Strand', proved untrue.

What is impossible is to determine how far the failures are due to the use of market research or to its misuse. Research is the process that provides information about consumers in a market; it is not, as the name suggests, akin to conducting experiments in engineering or the sciences. There is some disagreement in the profession as to whether it is art or science; undoubtedly research does apply objective scientific methods to areas that shade from the apparently completely objective (how is the market for portable hair-dryers broken down?) into the wholly subjective areas of motivation and future intentions, where findings are often questionable and sometimes useless – such as the information that heavy smokers were bottle-fed babies, or the famous discovery that the convertible car symbolizes a mistress to the car-owning male.

Market research is about people: what they buy, why, where, and how often; how they use it; what they think of it. The technical instruments used to extract this information, mainly statistical, can be well or badly used. These tools of statistical science are subject to test in a way that sociology and psychology are not; yet the latter may have more bearing on the answers that the marketer wants to know, for one vital reason. All hard research information relates to actions of people in the immediate past, which is not always an infallible guide to their behaviour in the future. But only the future matters. Add to an imperfect science the opportunities for charlatanry that always surround crystal balls, and you have a perfect recipe for distrust.

In fact, the complaints about market researchers are numerous, but concern mostly minor, niggling irritants (which could still lead to major mistakes). Whatever the shortcomings, industry must be finding the information produced by research more than ever useful – to judge by its spending. Researchers are divided roughly into two camps as to the amount. One school guesstimates an annual turnover of between £10 million and £12 million: the other plumps for £15 million to £18 million. From this discrepancy alone, it is clear that the risk of errors in market research can be minimized. There are three distinct stages in the process – conception, execution and interpretation of the results – each of which has its own particular problems which affect the whole.

There are pitfalls all along the path. Even basic information may not be as solid as it seems – hence the well-known tendency for the market shares of all companies in a market, as provided by each of them, to add up to well over 100 per cent. Self-deception is a hazard at any stage. So is impatience and misinterpretation. An associate of British-American Tobacco wanted to launch a new menthol cigarette in Latin America. Every aspect of the product was research-tested – the blend, the size, the pack design, the image – over a period. Management decided to launch quickly. The product flopped. A post-mortem (often more instructive than the *post hoc* investigation of a success) showed why; the concept as a whole was unacceptable, even though the individual constituents had passed muster.

In another, happier case, a marketing man recalls two of his favourite launches. Both were hair-sprays, but produced by different companies. Intensive research into the acceptability of the first and comparison with existing brands showed that women in the test area considered the product the best on the market. The product promptly 'went national'. Later the marketing man moved on to new employers, where he tested another spray. The criteria were practically identical. That one also turned out to be considered the best on offer (the marketer has no complaints – both products were national successes).

The first decision that has to be faced is to go in for market research whole-heartedly. A certain amount of faith is needed, since all research tends to throw up more problems than it does clues to their solution. Once embarked on market research, it is very difficult to cry halt, or to see where one should stop. Market researchers, on the whole, think that there is too much discontinuity, that not enough continuous research is done. 'Managers realize the need to keep a check on stocks but they don't always see the need to watch markets in the same way', says Eric Shankleman of Marketing and Economic Research.

Subscription research, where facts on the market are available to any firm paying the fee, is the cheapest way of continuous watching. Stanley Orwell of Market Investigations believes this kind of research will increase, if only because researchers can make good profits from the sale of continuous information. The fortunes of the three largest agencies by turnover – Nielsen, Attwoods and Audits of Great Britain – are founded on precisely such surveys. Nielsen's has a retail audit, Attwoods a consumer panel; it also shared the British Television research contract with Nielsen, but this has just gone to AGB, which started off with its continuous housewife survey on consumer durable goods. Basically, this is a sample-polling business – Gallup, the famous political pollster, is also big in the commercial game through Social Surveys (UK).

D. Thomas 117

This kind of constant check on the market is indispensable to the big marketing firms. A large proportion of the research budgets of firms such as Beecham, Hoover, Rowntree and Ford is spent on continuous research, frequently designed to show up trends before they become problems. 'Very often when you want to know something it's too late to research', says Tom Moulson, manager of market research for Ford of Europe. At Ford research goes on constantly; since the researchers are on the staff, problems are researched as they come up, without prompting. 'As we're part of the firm, we know the kind of information it's necessary to present', adds Moulson. Another advocate of more continuous research is Andrew Ehrenberg of Aske Research, who believes it also offers the best field for another pet cause – more research into research results, in order to discover more about the science of marketing.

So far Ehrenberg has discovered five laws which he believes should be useful to marketing men, although the latter will have to be well versed in algebra. One law goes like this:

$$\left\{ 1 + a \sum_{i=1}^{t} T_i (1-u_i) \right\}^{-k}.$$

It describes a repeat buying theory. On the basis of continuous research, *ad hoc* projects can be formulated to explore specific problems. What is being explored, and why, is vital to success. Research is sometimes undertaken for reasons that could render the results useless. Although it should be gratuitous to say so, the objectives of any piece of research must be clearly defined and put into the context of general marketing policy before the research is discussed with outside researchers, and certainly before it is put into action. One research man recounts wrathfully how a potential client 'fancied having some research done' in a certain field. When asked what he would do with the results, he had no idea. 'The finest excuse for doing nothing is to do market research,' remarks Aubrey Wilson of Industrial Market Research (industrial research, the sibling of the consumer variety, accounts for a turnover of about £2 million a year).

When the research is presented, and the client still does not know what to do, he blames this on the research. Another popular and common misuse of market research is to commission it with the purpose, subconscious or otherwise, of confirming a certain decision. 'A lot of market research is bought because people want to back up a decision already taken,' points out Shankleman, 'and the report is judged accordingly.' Moreover, if the client does not state clearly what he wants, he may find that the research turns out to be broader and more expensive than he reckoned, since the researcher has had to cover for all eventualities. 'One cannot buy research as though it were a yard of cloth,' observes Eileen Cole of Unilever's Research Bureau.

Market researchers, once the problem is defined, occasionally despair of the way it is put to them. 'Marketing men should pose marketing problems to the researchers,' states Ehrenberg, 'but they have got to learn to translate the problem into terms answerable by research. Sometimes it seems as if the questions exist, and the answers exist, but never the twain shall meet.' There is a lack of common vocabulary between market researchers and marketing men, and between them and the rest of the world, because of the natural human tendency to use a verbal shorthand among members of the same profession. Jargon in young professions, often uncertain of their status, tends to be more obscure than normal – an explanation that embraces terms like 'thematic apperception tests', 'Guttman scaling' and 'Markov chain theory', helped along by equations only intelligible to an erudite statistician. The communication gap is not insuperable. There are people who speak both languages. 'We've had a market research manager for over twenty years,' says Peter Goode, associate director of marketing at Hoover. 'It would have been impossible to market without him.'

Agencies, like all outside consultancies, make a great plea for more information. Otherwise they are in great danger of re-inventing the wheel. Mary Griffin of Smith's Industries backs up this point. 'People get involved in spending far too much because they will not put down what they already know. It would be very extravagant not to do homework before commissioning research.' There is the story of the bearings firm that wanted to survey what it imagined to be a £500,000 market for possible gaps. Shortly after the research started, it was discovered that there were £5 million worth of imports, which changed the whole nature of the problem. However, getting information out of British industry has always been difficult – 'sometimes you don't even get to see the people who really matter,' according to one disgruntled researcher. This is quite obviously the worst way to get value for money.

The usual procedure, once the research objectives have been defined, is to discuss them with a short list of agencies who will then submit proposals and estimates. Short-listing agencies is undoubtedly difficult, and the 'biggest is best' rule does not always apply. Use of market research has grown so tremendously in the past ten years that some agencies and some individual researchers have grown up with their own specialities and have somewhat neglected all the other techniques. For example, there is one fairly small agency that is a specialist in the reactions of consumers to various colours and has concentrated solely on this.

Specialization is not the only possible stumbling-block. But thanks in part to professional bodies, such as the BIM, and the trade's own Market Research Society, which keep some check on agencies and their abilities, one market researcher is able to observe today that 'there are a lot less crooks about'. James Cameron, a refugee from market research who is now marketing services director for Beecham Products (UK), adds that 'you can't be sold a pup unless you're prepared to buy a pup'.

Agencies often insist that they are not very good at selling themselves (promptly contradicting this by saying that occasionally the temptation to blind with science is not resisted). But in their explanations of what market research can do, over-enthusiastic researchers can unintentionally lead the inexperienced client astray. As Cameron says, 'there are those who believe market research is going to solve all their problems. Really all market research can say is that the problem exists, and if you do this, that will probably result.' Tom Slack, marketing director of British-American Tobacco, remarks that 'market research is useful in our business from the point of view of reducing the risk. It warns you what not to do.' Another cigarette man, John Wilson, marketing director of W. D. & H. O. Wills, echoes this, but adds that market research only eliminates the negative factor. 'It doesn't eliminate the factor of judgement.'

Companies experienced in the use of market research by outside agencies choose the latter by three basic criteria – first, familiarity with the kind of research that is wanted in the particular field under study; second, general cooperativeness and enthusiasm; third, value for money. 'The question of economics comes in very strongly,' points out a product consultant. 'The question is really that, given a certain budget, would I spend it this way?' adds Cameron.

Rowntree, which employs outside agencies for the majority of its research (and whose After Eight mint chocolates are one of the more inspired product launches of recent years), comes down firmly in favour of the three criteria quoted. But Goode of Hoover points out that although 'the company has a definite market research budget, if additional research is needed that will take us over that budget, we will do it'. The first two points are obviously important because, if met, the clients can relax and trust the validity of the agency's work. It means less supervision, fewer progress meetings, and the agency will waste less time and money justifying its methods of operation. 'I try to chase progress as little as possible,' says Mary Griffin. 'This will ensure objectivity.'

It is not always understood that research can be carried out with varying degrees of precision according to the type of information wanted and the type of research done. 'There is often an over preoccupation with methodology relative to efficiency,' says Timothy Joyce of the British Market Research Bureau, a subsidiary of the J. Walter Thompson advertising agency. 'For example, in media research' (who reads or looks at what, etc.) 'methodology is very important. In cheaper research, such as group discussion, methodology (how to weigh participants, etc.) is not important.'

There are two common reasons given for over-concern with detail. The first puts the onus squarely on the client. British industry, according to a whole chorus of market researchers, is not as sophisticated as American about using research. 'The American marketing man, on the whole, can imagine the detail, and knows how much data he wants. In the UK there is a tendency to elaboration instead of decision – 'the British committee psychology at work,' remarks Shankleman. However, some blame is also borne by the market researchers. 'The tendency to be over-precise is partly the fault of market researchers who have not tried to sell the idea of varying degrees of precision,' says one researcher. 'Many people in market research came from academic backgrounds that stressed precision too much.'

Once the question of degree of precision is settled, the research is set up. 'Clients should take some interest in how the work is done and not take it for granted,' says Joyce. (Naturally, if the client understands what the researcher is talking about, life will be much easier.) 'We now know that many questionnaires have pitfalls,' he admits. 'We're well aware that many straightforward questions can be misconstrued.' For example, a simple question beginning 'why?' can give rise to useless, or misleading answers. People seldom admit why they do things. One has to get at it in a roundabout way. Asking a housewife to describe the typical user of the soap she buys, for example, is the best way to find the reasons for which she buys it. To a simple question like 'why do you buy brand X birdseed?', a most likely answer is 'because the budgie likes it'.

Dr Max Adler, who was in on the very beginnings of market research, has been known to say that there have been no important developments for twenty years. But Joyce points out that questionnaire and sample design have been tremendously improved. However, very elementary mistakes can still occur. Research men recount the story of a firm that wanted to enter the crisp market. It developed a crisp and tested it. The results were stupendously favourable. The firm's marketing men got excited and wanted to launch. But first they decided to have another look at the research. It was discovered that no distinction had been made between regular crisp eaters and non-crisp eaters. And it was the latter who liked the crisp. 'The people now handling market research are better equipped to handle research,' adds Eileen Cole. 'The actual execution is more efficient.'

Fieldwork, of course, offers great scope for mistakes, often amusing and always costly. Market researchers say soothingly that the days of kitchen table fieldwork (the part-time interviewer filling in the questionnaires at her kitchen table instead of tramping around door-to-door) are over. However, there is still plenty of room for less blatant ways of prejudicing the results – such as leading the interviewee to answer in a certain way by wrong delivery, intentional or otherwise, of the questions. The training of interviewers is very important. However accurate the sample, however clear and skilful the questionnaire, however clear the objectives, sloppy interviewing can ruin the lot. And it is on the information gathered in the field that trends are discovered, hypotheses built and advice based.

There are some agencies that are renowned for their accurate, well-supervised fieldwork. But training is so expensive that only the largest agencies can really afford to train sufficient interviewers to cope with large surveys. Bernard Audley, one of the founders of Audits of Great Britain, states that 'the essence of market research is grossing up from the relatively small. There is a tremendous danger of cutting corners.' In AGB's continuous field surveys, 'one has got to watch the interviewing side like a hawk. It's very remote from the office.' His firm has an associate director in charge and thirty-five national supervisors. 'The interviewers could be the weakest link in the chain,' observes Eileen Cole. 'The quality of interviewers is very important. We train and brief ours very carefully.' Inevitably, the majority of interviewers are part-time, and therefore in need of periodic retraining, since the work is sporadic and the most intelligent people are apt to get bored with it.

Some agencies will do fieldwork only, giving the mass of relatively unprocessed information back to the client to process. Cameron of Beechams sees this as a future trend of market research, with the larger marketing companies going to outside agencies only for those services they cannot find internally, perhaps large-scale processing of data as well as fieldwork. Ford of Europe puts out only the fieldwork of its surveys. Tom Moulson says that 'we brief the agencies in great detail, and specify how the computer output is to be arranged'. He regards the automotive industry as more difficult for outside market researchers to understand and adds that 'it is impossible for an agency to understand or solve our problems, because we cannot give them all the facts. For instance, we won't tell them our profits or corporate policy'.

There is some division of opinion as to whether agencies should be asked to interpret the research and give their opinions or whether they should just present it and leave the client to make his own deductions (which he should do anyway). Interpretation of research is a very subjective process; but sometimes, as in motivational research (investigation of why people do things, instead of what they have done), only the researcher can really interpret the results. An outside view will be more objective. But its very objectivity is a danger. The opinion of an outside agency will be influenced by what it knows of the company's policy and market, which may be little more than it has discovered during the process of the research. It may therefore make a recommendation that is quite out of keeping with the company's policy, capabilities or even product range.

There are many classics of successful motivation research, such as the cake-mix whose sales only soared when housewives were told to add an egg; before, when there was nothing for them to do, they felt guilty. Similarly, instant coffee only really took off when marketers learnt to stress the flavour, not the convenience. However, motivation research is perhaps peculiarly apt to come up with ideas that are brilliant, but only in their own context – that is, unworkable or impracticable in factory or marketplace. 'Sometimes research can come up with answers that are not feasible in engineering terms,' points out Hoover's Goode. Some allowance must, however, be made for vested interests at the client's end. 'No matter what recommendations are made, a research report that suggests change is bound to upset someone,' ruefully remarks one researcher – often because it faces people with the need to make a decision based on clear facts calmly, rather than being pushed into action by events.

Researchers and marketing men agree that, in the words of Cameron, 'research often goes wrong in the communication of results'. There are two main reasons for this. The first goes back to the initial reasons for the research. One sour market researcher observed that no man who is prepared to spend hundreds of thousands tooling up on the strength of a hunch is going to be persuaded by a £5,000 report that his hunch is wrong. 'We don't know what happens to half the reports we do for first-timers,' says Wilson. 'Lots of them probably never see daylight' (but 'half our business is repeat work'). Research that is commissioned merely to put off decision-making often ends up as no more than an impressive volume gracing a manager's desk. However, even wanted research reports can be very off-putting, and the difficulty of reading them can often obscure useful information.

'The mechanism whereby the information is presented is often wrong,' points out Shankleman. 'The firms have to be made to recognize that they are involved.' The second reason for the difficulty in putting over the results lies in the nature of market researchers. As research has only really expanded over the last decade, those at the top are young relative to the positions they hold. They have had to grow with the rapid expansion of research itself, which has often left them little time to develop anything but their immediate interests. 'Market research grew up with sociologists who were without terribly much knowledge of business fields,' observes Orwell of Market Investigations. 'Sometimes they tend to underestimate the intelligence of general management,' adds one company market researcher. Market research attracts a great many graduates who see it as a stepping stone to higher things, and the manpower turnover rate is fairly high (another factor which keeps the average age down). It is often difficult for managers to accept facts about their industry presented to them by very recent graduates. The fact that many of these are going to be women only makes it worse. One market research agency, taking a leaf out of its own book, always sends a man with its women researchers to presentations, because it increases the acceptability.

Market research attracts the kind of people who like to analyse problems and have a highly developed critical faculty. According to clients, this is not often balanced with an adequate ability to be constructive, which reinforces the accusation that market researchers, because of their academic origins, are introverted (there are a few whizzing extroverts around, but they tend to whizz wholly within the market research world) and also appear to lack sympathy for the client's problems, except as an interesting intellectual exercise. As with most specialists, researchers have a tendency to be somewhat arrogant when discussing their own subject. The unwary client who queries any part of a research may find himself dragged through a maze of interrelating, polysyllabic techniques that leave him little wiser. But if he has commissioned carefully, none of this should be necessary.

The real problem with market research is that it is a very sensitive process, although based on scientific techniques. 'At best it's an art,' says Aubrey Wilson, 'at worst a trade.' It is merely a marketing tool, not a magic wand, and human fallibility has all too many opportunities to invalidate the process. Moreover, no amount of market research is going to come up with a formula that will permit management to market without using judgement, exercising flair and deploying sheer business competence. Too many managers probably secretly hope that it will, which is where the trouble starts.

7 R. L. Ackoff

Management Misinformation Systems

R. L. Ackoff, 'Management misinformation systems',
Management Science, vol. 14, no. 4, 1967, pp. 147–56.

The growing preoccupation of operations researchers and management scientists with Management Information Systems (MISs) is apparent. In fact, for some the design of such systems has almost become synonymous with operations research or management science. Enthusiasm for such systems is understandable: it involves the researcher in a romantic relationship with the most glamorous instrument of our time, the computer. Such enthusiasm is understandable but, nevertheless, some of the excesses to which it has led are not excusable.

Contrary to the impression produced by the growing literature, few computerized management information systems have been put into operation. Of those I have seen that have been implemented, most have not matched expectations and some have been outright failures. I believe that these near- and far-misses could have been avoided if certain false (and usually implicit) assumptions on which many such systems have been erected had not been made. There seem to be five common and erroneous assumptions underlying the design of most MISs.

Give them more

Most MISs are designed on the assumption that the critical deficiency under which most managers operate is *lack of relevant information*. I do not deny that most managers lack a good deal of information that they should have, but I do deny that this is the most important informational deficiency from which they suffer. It seems to me that they suffer more from an *overabundance of irrelevant information*.

This is not a play on words. The consequences of changing

the emphasis of an MIS from supplying relevant information to eliminating irrelevant information is considerable. If one is-preoccupied with supplying relevant information, attention is almost exclusively given to generating, storing and retrieving information; hence emphasis is placed on constructing data banks, coding, indexing, updating files, access languages and so on. The ideal which has emerged from this orientation is an infinite pool of data into which a manager can reach to pull out any information he wants. If, on the other hand, one sees the manager's information problem primarily, but not exclusively, as one that arises out of an overabundance of irrelevant information, most of which was not asked for, then the two most important functions of an information system become *filtration* (or evaluation) and *condensation*. The literature on MISs seldom refers to these functions let alone considers how to carry them out.

My experience indicates that most managers receive much more data (if not information) than they can possibly absorb even if they spend all their time trying to do so. Hence they already suffer from an information overload. They must spend a great deal of time separating the relevant from the irrelevant and searching for the kernels in the relevant documents. For example, I have found that I receive an average of forty-three hours of unsolicited reading material each week. The solicited material is usually half again this amount.

I have seen a daily stock status report that consists of approximately six hundred pages of computer print-out. The report is circulated daily across managers' desks. I have also seen requests for major capital expenditures that come in book size, several of which are distributed to managers each week. It is not uncommon for many managers to receive an average of one journal a day or more. One could go on and on.

Unless the information overload to which managers are subjected is reduced, any additional information which an MIS makes available cannot be expected to be used effectively.

Even relevant documents have too much redundancy. Most documents can be considerably condensed without loss of content. My point here is best made, perhaps, by describing briefly an experiment that a few of my colleagues and I conducted on the OR literature several years ago. By using a panel of well-known experts we identified four OR articles that all members of the panel considered to be 'above average', and four articles that were considered to be 'below average'. We asked the authors of the eight articles to prepare 'objective' examinations (duration thirty minutes) plus answers for graduate students who were to be assigned the articles for reading. (The authors were not informed about the experiment.) Then we asked several experienced writers to reduce each article to two-thirds and one-third of its original length only by eliminating words. They also prepared a brief abstract of each article. Those who did the condensing did not see the examinations to be given to the students.

We then selected a group of graduate students who had not previously read the articles and gave each one four articles randomly selected, each of which was in one of its four versions: 100 per cent, 67 per cent, 33 per cent, or abstract. Each version of each article was read by two students. We gave all the students the same examinations, compared their average scores on the examinations.

For the above-average articles there was no significant difference between average test scores for the 100 per cent, 67 per cent, and 33 per cent versions, but there was a significant decrease in average test scores for those who had read only the abstract. For the below-average articles there was no difference in average test scores among those who had read the 100 per cent, 67 per cent, and 33 per cent versions, but there was a significant *increase* in average test scores of those who had read only the abstract.

The sample used was obviously too small for general conclusions but the results strongly indicate the extent to which even good writing can be condensed without loss of information. I refrain from drawing the obvious conclusion about bad writing!

It seems clear that condensation as well as filtration, performed mechanically or otherwise, should form an essential part of an MIS, and that such a system should be capable of handling much, if not all, of the unsolicited as well as solicited information that a manager receives.

Does the manager need the information that he wants?

Most MIS designers 'determine' what information is needed by asking managers what information they would like to have. This is based on the assumption that managers know what information they need and want it.

For a manager to know what information he needs he must be aware of each type of decision he should make (as well as does) and he must have an adequate model of each. These conditions are seldom satisfied. Most managers have some conception of at least some of the types of decisions they must make. However, their conceptions are likely to be deficient in a very critical way, a way that follows from an important principle of scientific economy: the less we understand a phenomenon, the more variables we require to explain it. Hence, the manager who does not understand the phenomenon he controls, plays it 'safe' and, with respect to information, wants 'everything'. The MIS designer, who has even less understanding of the relevant phenomenon than the manager, tries to provide even more than everything. He thereby increases what is already an overload of irrelevant information.

For example, market researchers in a major oil company once asked their marketing managers what variables they thought were relevant in estimating the sales volume of future service stations. Almost seventy variables were identified. The market researchers then added about half again and performed a large multiple linear regression analysis of sales of existing stations against these variables and found about thirty-five of them to be statistically significant. A forecasting equation was based on this analysis. An OR team subsequently constructed a model based on only one of these variables, traffic flow, which predicted sales better than the thirty-five variable regression equation. The team went on to *explain* sales at service stations in terms of the customers' perception of the amount of time lost by stopping for service. The relevance of all but a few of the variables used by the market researchers could be explained by their effect on such perception.

The moral is simple: one cannot specify what information is required for decision-making until an explanatory model of the decision process and the system involved has been constructed and tested. Information systems are sub-systems of control systems. They cannot be designed adequately without taking control in account. Furthermore, whatever else regression analyses can yield, they cannot yield understanding and explanation of phenomena. They describe and, at best, predict.

Improving a manager's decision-making

It is frequently assumed that if a manager is provided with the information he needs, he will then have no problem in using it effectively. The history of OR stands to the contrary. For example, give most managers an initial tableau of a typical 'real' mathematical programming, sequencing, or network problem and see how close they come to an optimal solution. If their experience and judgement have any value they may not do badly, but they will seldom do very well. In most management problems there are too many possibilities to expect experience, judgement, or intuition to provide good guesses, even with perfect information.

Furthermore, when several probabilities are involved in a problem the unguided mind of even a manager has difficulty in aggregating them in a valid way. We all know many simple problems in probability in which untutored intuition usually does very badly (e.g. What are the correct odds that two of twenty-five people selected at random will have their birthdays on the same day of the year?). For example, very few of the results obtained by queuing theory, when arrivals and service are probabilistic, are obvious to managers; nor are the results of risk analysis where the managers use their own subjective estimates of probabilities.

The moral: it is necessary to determine how well managers can use needed information. When, because of the complexity of the decision process, they cannot use it well, they should be provided with either decision rules or performance feedback, so that they can identify and learn from their mistakes.

More communication means better performance

One characteristic of most MISs which I have seen is that they provide managers with better current information about what other managers and their departments and divisions are doing.

Underlying this provision is the belief that better inter-departmental communication enables managers to coordinate their decisions more effectively and hence improves the organization's overall performance. Not only is this not necessarily so, but it seldom is so. One would hardly expect two competing companies to become more cooperative because the information each acquires about the other is improved. This analogy is not as far fetched as one might first suppose. For example, consider the following very much simplified version of a situation I once ran into. The simplification of the case does not affect any of its essential characteristics.

A department store has two 'line' operations: buying and selling. Each function is performed by a separate department. The purchasing department primarily controls one variable: how much of each item is bought. The merchandising department controls the price at which it is sold. Typically, the measure of performance applied to the purchasing department was the turnover rate of inventory. The measure applied to the merchandising department was gross sales; this department sought to maximize the number of items sold times their price.

Now by examining a single item let us consider what happens in this system. The merchandising manager, using his knowledge of competition and consumption, set a price which he judged would maximize gross sales. In doing so he utilized price–demand curves for each type of item. For each price the curves show the expected sales and values on an upper and lower confidence band as well (see Figure 1). When instructing the purchasing department how many items to make available, the merchandising manager quite naturally used the value on the upper confidence curve. This minimized the chances of his running short which, if it occurred, would hurt his performance. It also maximized the chances of being over-stocked, but this was not his concern, only the purchasing manager's. Say, therefore, that the merchandising manager initially selected price P_1 and requested that amount Q_1 be made available by the purchasing department.

In this company the purchasing manager also had access to the price–demand curves. He knew the merchandising manager

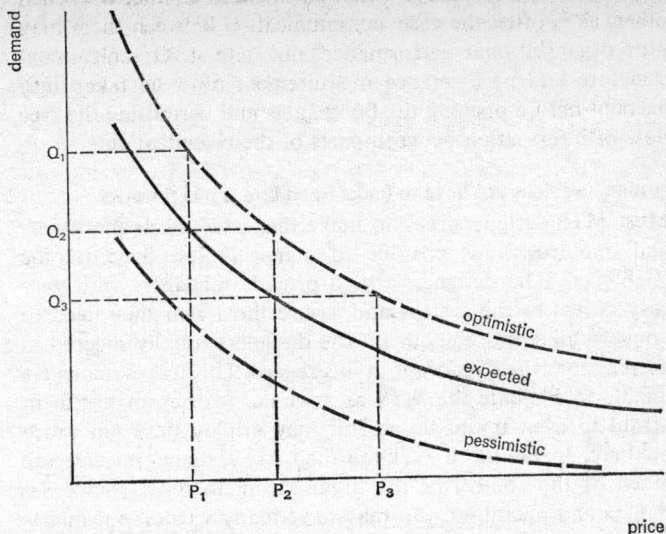

Figure 1 Price–demand curve

always ordered optimistically. Therefore, using the same curve
he read over from Q_1 to the upper limit and down to the
expected value from which he obtained Q_2, the quantity he
actually intended to make available. He did not intend to pay
for the merchandising manager's optimism. If merchandising
ran out of stock, it was not his worry. Now the merchandising
manager was informed about what the purchasing manager had
done so he adjusted his price to P_2. The purchasing manager in
turn was told that the merchandising manager had made this
readjustment so he planned to make only Q_3 available. If this
process – made possible only by perfect communication between departments – had been allowed to continue, nothing
would have been bought and nothing would have been sold.
This outcome was avoided by prohibiting communication between the two departments and forcing each to guess what the
other was doing.

Obviously I have caricatured the situation in order to make
the point clear: when organizational units have inappropriate

R. L. Ackoff 133

measures of performance which put them in conflict with each other, as is often the case, communication between them may hurt organizational performance, not help it. Organizational structure and performance measurement must be taken into account before opening the flood gates and permitting the free flow of information between parts of the organization.[1]

A manager does not have to understand how a MIS works

Most MIS designers seek to make their systems as innocuous and unobtrusive as possible to managers lest they become frightened. The designers try to provide managers with very easy access to the system and assure them that they need to know nothing more about it. The designers usually succeed in keeping managers ignorant in this regard. This leaves managers unable to evaluate the MIS as a whole. It often makes them afraid to even try to do so lest they display their ignorance publicly. In failing to evaluate their MIS, managers delegate much of the control of the organization to the system's designers and operators who may have many virtues, but managerial competence is seldom among them.

Let me cite a case in point. A chairman of a board of a medium-size company asked for help on the following problem. One of his larger, decentralized divisions had installed a computerized production-inventory control and manufacturing-manager information system about a year earlier. It had acquired about $2 million worth of equipment to do so. The board chairman had just received a request from the division for permission to replace the original equipment with newly announced equipment, which would cost several times the original amount. An extensive *justification* for so doing was provided with the request. The chairman wanted to know whether the request was really justified. He admitted to complete incompetence in this connection.

A meeting was arranged at the division at which I was subjected to an extended and detailed briefing. The system was large but relatively simple. At the heart of it was a re-order point for each item and a maximum allowable stock level. Re-

---

1. Sengupta and Ackoff (1965) provide a more rigorous discussion of organizational structure and the relationship of communications.

order quantities took lead-time as well as the allowable maximum into account. The computer kept track of stock, ordered items when required and generated numerous reports on both the state of the system it controlled and its own 'actions'.

When the briefing was over I was asked if I had any questions. I did. First I asked if, when the system had been installed, there had been many parts whose stock level exceeded the maximum amount possible under the new system. I was told there were many. I asked for a list of about thirty and for some graph paper. Both were provided. With the help of the system designer and volumes of old daily reports I began to plot the stock level of the first listed item over time. When this item reached the maximum 'allowable' stock level it had been re-ordered. The system designer was surprised and said that by sheer 'luck' I had found one of the few errors made by the system. Continued plotting showed that because of repeated premature re-ordering the item had never gone much below the maximum stock level. Clearly the programme was confusing the maximum allowable stock level and the re-order point. This turned out to be the case in more than half of the items on the list.

Next I asked if they had many paired parts, ones that were only used with each other; for example, matched nuts and bolts. They had many. A list was produced and we began checking the previous day's withdrawals. For more than half of the pairs the differences in the numbers recorded as withdrawn were very large. No explanation was provided.

Before the day was out it was possible to show by some quick and dirty calculations that the new computerized system was costing the company almost $150,000 per month more than the hand system which it had replaced, most of this in excess inventories.

The recommendation was that the system be redesigned as quickly as possible and that the new equipment not be authorized for the time being.

The questions asked of the system had been obvious and simple ones. Managers should have been able to ask them but – and this is the point – they felt themselves incompetent to do so. They would not have allowed a hand-operated system to get so far out of their control.

No MIS should ever be installed unless the managers for whom it is intended are trained to evaluate and hence control it rather than be controlled by it.

Designing an MIS

The erroneous assumptions I have tried to reveal can, I believe, be avoided by an appropriate design procedure, one of which I shall now outline.

Analysing the decision system

Each (or at least each important) type of managerial decision required by the organization under study should be identified and the relationships between them should be determined and flow-charted. Note that this is *not* necessarily the same thing as determining what decisions *are* made. For example, in one company I found that make-or-buy decisions concerning parts were made only at the time when a part was introduced into stock and was never subsequently reviewed. For some items this decision had gone unreviewed for as many as twenty years. Obviously, such decisions should be made more often; in some cases, every time an order is placed in order to take account of such factors as current shop loading, under-used shifts and delivery times from suppliers.

Decision-flow analyses are usually self-justifying. They often reveal important decisions that are being made by default (e.g. the make-buy decisions referred to above), and they disclose interdependent decisions that are being made independently. Decision-flow charts frequently suggest changes in managerial responsibility, organizational structure, and measure of performance which can correct the types of deficiencies cited.

Decision analyses can be conducted with varying degrees of detail, that is, they may be anywhere from coarse- to fine-grained. How much detail one should become involved with depends on the amount of time and resources that are available for the analysis. Although practical considerations frequently restrict initial analyses to a particular organizational function, it is preferable to perform a coarse analysis of all of an organization's managerial functions rather than a fine analysis of one or a sub-set of functions. It is easier to introduce finer information into an integrated information system than it is to combine fine sub-systems into one integrated system.

Analysing information requirements

Managerial decisions can be classified into three types:

1. Decisions for which adequate models are available or can be constructed and from which optimal (or near optimal) solutions can be derived. In such cases the decision process itself should be incorporated into the information system, thereby converting it (at least partially) to a control system. A decision model identifies what information is required and hence what information is relevant.

2. Decisions for which adequate models can be constructed, but from which optimal solutions cannot be extracted. Here some kind of heuristic or search procedure should be provided even if it consists of no more than computerized trial and error. A simulation of the model will, as a minimum, permit comparison of proposed alternative solutions. Here, too, the model specifies what information is required.

3. Decisions for which adequate models cannot be constructed. Research is required here to determine what information is relevant. If decision-making cannot be delayed for the completion of such research or the decision's effect is not large enough to justify the cost of research, then judgement must be used to guess what information is relevant. It may be possible to make explicit the implicit model used by the decision-maker and treat it as the second type of model.

In each of these three types of situation it is necessary to provide feedback by comparing actual decision outcomes with those predicted by the model- or decision-maker. Each decision that is made, along with its predicted outcome, should be an essential input to a management control system, a point which I shall return to later.

Aggregating decisions

Decisions with the same or largely overlapping informational requirements should be grouped together as a single manager's task. This will reduce the information a manager requires to do his job and is likely to increase his understanding of it. This may require a reorganization of the system. Even if such a reorganization cannot be implemented completely, what can be done is likely to improve performance significantly and reduce the information loaded on managers.

Designing information processing

Now the procedure for collecting, storing, retrieving and treating information can be designed. Since there is a voluminous literature on this subject I shall leave it at this except for one point. Such a system must not only be able to answer questions addressed to it; it should also be able to answer questions that have not been asked by reporting any deviations from expectations. An extensive exception-reporting system is required.

Designing control of the control system

It must be assumed that the system that is being designed will be deficient in many and significant ways. Therefore, it is necessary to identify the ways in which it may be deficient, to design procedures for detecting its deficiencies and for correcting the system so as to remove or reduce them. Hence the system should be designed to be flexible and adaptive. This is little more than a platitude, but it has a not-so-obvious implication. No completely computerized system can be as flexible and adaptive as can a man-machine system. This is illustrated by a system that is being developed and is partially in operation (see Figure 2).

The company involved has its market divided into approximately two hundred marketing areas. A model for each has been constructed as is 'in' the computer. On the basis of competitive intelligence supplied to the senior marketing manager by marketing researchers and information specialists, he and his staff make policy decisions for each area each month. Their tentative decisions are fed into the computer, which yields a forecast of expected performance. Changes are made until the expectations match what is desired. In this way they arrive at *final* decisions. At the end of the month the computer compares the actual performance of each area with what was predicted. If a deviation exceeds what could be expected by chance, the

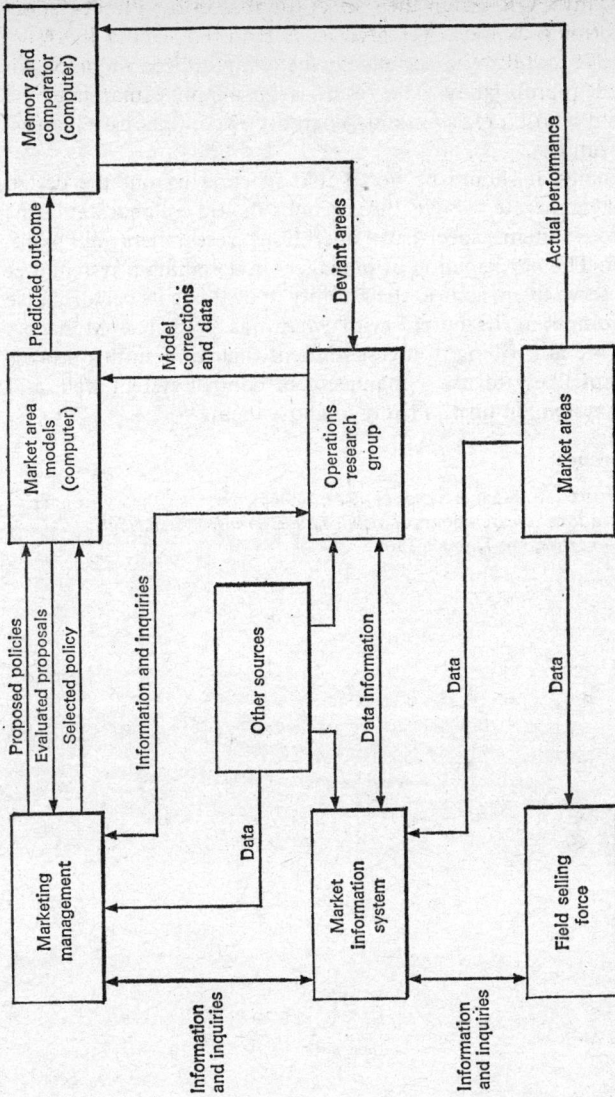

Figure 2 Simplified diagram of market-area control system

company's OR group then seeks the reason for the deviation, performing as much research as is required to find it. If the cause is found to be permanent the computerized model is adjusted appropriately. The result is an adaptive man-machine system whose precision and generality is continuously increasing with use.

Finally, it should be noted that in carrying out the design steps enumerated above, three groups should collaborate: information systems specialists, operations researchers *and managers*. The participation of managers in designing a system that is to serve them, assures their ability to evaluate its performance by comparing its output with what was predicted. Managers who are not willing to invest some of their time in this process are not likely to use a management control system well, and their system, in turn, is likely to abuse them.

Reference

SENGUPTA, S. S., and ACKOFF, R. L. (1965), 'Systems theory from an operations research point of view', *IEEE Trans. Systems Sci. Cybernetics*, no. 1, pp. 9–13.

8 C. H. Sevin

Marketing – Cost and Profitability Information: Manufacturing and Wholesaling

Excerpt from C. H. Sevin, *Marketing Productivity Analysis*, McGraw-Hill, 1965, pp. 11–32.

Judgement methods of estimating segmental marketing costs

Manufacturers and wholesalers generally do not know reasonably accurately the dollar marketing costs and the dollar profit (or loss) contribution of each of their products, customers, sales territories and other segments of their business.

In the case of wholesalers, the attempt is generally not even made to obtain this information. It is useful to recall that wholesalers generally stock and sell several thousand different products to a large number of customers. Probably most wholesalers arrive at judgements as to the relative profitability of the various items in their inventory on the basis principally of the product's gross margin percentage.

These judgements are tempered by taking into consideration such factors as the product's sales volume, turnover rate and estimates of its handling-expense rate. Where actual marketing-cost and profitability analyses have been made in wholesaling establishments, it has been demonstrated that:[1]

1. There are extremely wide variations in the marketing costs and profits (or losses) by segments within a wholesaling firm.

2. Judgement methods of estimating relative profitability by segments are grossly unreliable.

Naturally enough, there is great diversity in the methods by which manufacturers attempt to get marketing costs and profits for segments of their businesses, as for individual products. It appears reasonable, however, to generalize that the following

1. See Alderson and Haag (1931); Alderson and Miller (1930); Carroll (1934); Meserole and Sevin (1941); Millard (1928).

errors in the methods used by manufacturers are widespread. First, marketing costs are generally allocated to individual products, customers, territories, etc. on the basis of their dollar sales volumes. (By contrast with the methods described in the remainder of this reading, it will be shown that this method is completely erroneous.) Second, general and administrative costs are arbitrarily and erroneously allocated to segments, also on the basis of dollar sales volume. Third, many marketing costs are not allocated at all to segments, not being identified as marketing costs but, rather, being classified otherwise, i.e. as manufacturing or as general and administrative costs.

Marketing-profitability-analysis methods

Manufacturers and wholesalers can reasonably accurately determine their marketing costs and profits for segments – such as individual products, customer types, customer size classes and sales territories – according to the methods outlined in the remainder of this reading (Sevin, 1946). These methods are comprised of two principal elements that can be summarized as follows:

1. The marketing expenditures of a particular business, which are usually accounted for on a 'natural' expense basis, are reclassified into 'functional-cost' groups. These functional-cost groups bring together all the costs associated with each marketing activity, i.e. marketing function, performed by that company.

2. The functional-cost groups are 'allocated' to products, customers, territories and other segments of sales on the basis of measurable factors. These measurable factors or bases of allocation are product, customer and territory characteristics which bear a 'causative' relationship to the total amounts of the functional-cost groups.

Examples of functional-cost groups and bases of allocation are shown in Table 1. The methods of marketing-profitability analyses are also described in general detail in the following two sections of this chapter.

Functional classifications

The functional classification of marketing costs which would be used by any given firm is based on a study of the marketing activities performed by that firm. Most companies, especially those serving wide markets and producing and selling a number of products, have complex marketing organizations and engage in a wide range of marketing activities. Consequently, each company would need to construct its own functional classification to reflect its own marketing activities.

Direct marketing costs

The separable or direct marketing expenses associated with a specific segment of sales may, in some firms, constitute a significant proportion of the total marketing costs. This may be especially true of an organization engaging in extensive marketing activities, where separate departments are maintained for selling specific product groups and for soliciting specific customer classes. In such an instance, if the primary-expense accounts are kept in sufficient detail originally, or if provisions are made for subsequent divisions or sub-classifications of the primary-expense accounts, many marketing expenses may be assigned directly to either a product or a customer class or to a territory, instead of being allocated.

For example, when a single product group is sold through a single sales department to several classes of customers, the classification of the primary accounts by these departments will automatically assign the expense to the product. Likewise, when several product groups are sold through a single sales department to a single customer class, the classification of the primary-expense accounts by sales departments will automatically assign these selling expenses to customers.

Indirect marketing costs

Although the proportion of direct marketing costs may frequently be significant, the greater part of a firm's marketing costs are likely to be indirect. To facilitate their allocation to segments, as well as for purposes of expense control, these indirect marketing expenses are classified into functional groups. Usually, the activities performed in any one function will be of the same general kind. Such homogeneity facilitates the assignment of an entire functional-cost group by the use of a single basis of allocation, as will be described in the next section.

Table 1 Functional-cost groups and bases of allocation

| Functional-cost group (1) | Basis of allocation | | |
	To product groups (2)	To account-size classes (3)	To sales territories (4)
Selling – direct costs: Personal calls by salesmen and supervisors on accounts and prospects. Sales salaries, incentive compensation, travel, and other expense	Selling time devoted to each product, shown by special sales-call reports or other special studies	Number of sales calls times average time per call, as shown by special sales-call reports or other special studies	Direct
Selling – indirect costs: Field supervision, field sales-office expense, sales-administration expense, sales-personnel training, sales management. Market research, new-product development, sales statistics, tabulating services, sales accounting	In proportion to direct selling time, or time records by projects	In proportion to direct selling time, or time records by projects	Equal charge for each salesman
Advertising: Media costs such as TV, radio, billboards, newspaper, magazine, etc. Advertising production costs; advertising department salaries	Direct; or analysis of space and time by media; other costs in proportion to media costs	Equal charge to each account; or number of ultimate consumers and prospects in account's trading area	Direct; or analysis of media circulation records
Sales promotion: Consumer promotions such as coupons, patches, premiums, etc. Trade promotions such as price allowances, point-of-purchase displays, cooperative advertising, etc.	Direct; or analysis of source records	Direct; or analysis of source records	Direct; or analysis of source records

(1)	(2)	(3)	(4)
Transportation: Railroad, truck, barge, etc., payments to carriers for delivery of finished goods from plants to warehouses and from warehouses to customers. Traffic department costs	Applicable rates times tonnages	Analysis of sampling of bills of lading	Applicable rates times tonnages
Storage and shipping: Storage of finished goods inventories in warehouses. Rent (or equivalent costs), public-warehouse charges, fire insurance and taxes on finished goods inventories, etc. Physical handling, assembling, and loading out of rail cars, trucks, barges for shipping finished products from warehouses and mills to customers. Labor, equipment, space, and material costs	Warehouse space occupied by average inventory. Number of shipping units	Number of shipping units	Number of shipping units
Order processing: Checking and processing of orders from customers to mills for prices, weights and carload accumulation, shipping dates, coordination with production planning, transmittal to mills, etc. Pricing department. Preparation of customer invoices. Freight accounting. Credit and collection. Handling cash receipts. Provision for bad debts. Salary, supplies, space and equipment costs (teletypes, flexowriters, etc.)	Number of order lines	Number of order lines	Number of order lines

It is by no means as easy to classify marketing outlays in terms of functions as it is in terms of the so-called 'natural-expense' accounts. The difficulty lies in the fact that many natural-expense accounts relate to the performance of several functions, as, for example, when personnel perform more than one marketing function in the regular routine of their work.

But a natural-expense classification does not permit an allocation of the indirect marketing expenses to individual products, customers and other sales segments, nor does it provide an adequate basis for measuring efficiency and for controlling expenses. It is thus usually necessary to apportion many natural-expense items as they may appear in the ordinary accounting records among several functional-cost groups, since they relate to more than one functional activity. Where necessary, natural-expense items are divided among functional-cost groups by means of work-measurement study, space measurements, counts, managerial estimates and other methods.

Fixed versus variable costs

The functional-cost groups generally would include mixtures of fixed and variable costs. It is neither feasible nor useful to attempt to make an immutable or hard and fast distinction between fixed and variable marketing costs.

The distinction between fixed and variable marketing costs depends upon a number of factors, such as the size and nature of the particular segment of sales for which costs are being analysed, the permanency and range of a change in sales volume, the time interval, and the contractual arrangements of a particular business. Thus, in the short run, and with reference to small segments in sales volume, it may be generalized that most marketing expenses are in the nature of fixed costs.

Bases of allocation
Responsibility for marketing effort

After the indirect costs have been classified by functions, they are allocated to products, customers, territories and other segments of sales. The method followed is to charge the product or customer (or other segment of sales) with the cost of its or his share of the activity of each functional-cost group, that is, the cost of the portion of the marketing effort for which it or he is 'responsible'.

Another way of stating this allocation method is to say that the procedure is to determine, for each functional-cost group, the factor which 'controls' it, tending to increase or decrease it. As used here, the term control is meant to convey the concept that the total level of the functional cost is determined by the total level of the control factor. In other words, there is a 'cause-and-effect' relationship between the factor used as a basis of allocation and the dollar level of the corresponding functional-cost group (Sevin, 1952).

For example, a time series covering total number of salesmen's calls and total field selling expenses when plotted as a scatter diagram may exhibit a regular linear relationship (with the slope of the line of relationship at forty-five degrees). In such a case, the number of sales calls (rather than sales dollars) would be a reasonable basis for allocating field selling costs to individual customers. Functional-cost groups should not, in general, be allocated to products or customers or territories unless there are such clearly demonstrable and direct relationships between marketing costs and their bases of allocation.

Variable functional activity

The logical basis of allocation often becomes evident merely from analysis of the underlying data. Some functional activities vary largely according to certain characteristics of the product and are not greatly affected by customer characteristics. Others vary primarily according to certain customer characteristics regardless of what product is being purchased (Sevin, 1954).

For example, the costs involved in the storage of and investment in inventory depend almost solely on the bulk, weight, perishability and inventory value of the product stored and are affected but little by the customer who buys the product. Similarly, the credit function will usually vary according to the financial integrity and other credit characteristics of customers, with little regard to the nature of the product on which credit was extended.

The relationship among costs and product and customer characteristics is more complicated in the case of other functional-cost groups. There is every combination of customer, product and territory responsibility for the amounts of the different functional-cost groups.

Partial allocations

Accordingly, all functional costs are not allocated to products, customers, or territories. For example, storage and inventory investment costs usually would not be allocated to customers, because they would not be affected by short-run changes in the number of customers. Likewise, credit costs usually would not be allocated to products, since they would not be affected by the addition or elimination of products.

That is, those functional marketing costs which vary entirely with customer characteristics should not be allocated to products. Conversely, costs related solely to product characteristics should not be allocated to customers. However, some functional-cost groups would usually be allocated (as parallel operations) to customers and products and territories, as will be explained below.

There are usually several functional costs which are directly influenced by both products and customers. Product characteristics may influence some costs in one way, and customer characteristics may influence them in another. One technique for allocating such costs is to treat them as either product costs or customer costs. Another possible method is to treat these expenses as both product and customer costs. For example, certain functional costs may be allocated first to customers. Then, when product costs are being analysed, these same cost groups may be allocated on the basis of a controlling product characteristic. In this way, product and customer and territory marketing-cost-and-profit analyses are separate but parallel procedures (Sevin, 1950), as illustrated by the three 'bases-of-allocation' columns in Table 1.

Fixed- and variable-cost allocations

It is clear that both fixed and variable marketing costs would be allocated to products, customers and territories, since, as we have seen, the functional-cost groups comprise mixtures of these two types of costs. The question may arise as to the reasons for allocating so-called 'fixed' marketing costs to sales segments (in addition to the fact that there is not an immutable distinction between fixed and variable marketing costs).

It is useful to allocate portions of fixed marketing costs to specific segments of the business because there are nearly always alternative marketing uses for such 'pieces' of fixed costs. If it is discovered, for example, that a certain fixed marketing cost earns only x dollars in its present use, it may be possible to shift this marketing capacity to an alternative use that would bring in $2x$ dollars.

Allocation to products

Allocation bases are suggested below for assigning the more common functional-cost groups to products.

Investment

The product characteristic responsible for the expense of carrying an inventory of finished goods, such as taxes and insurance and interest, is generally its average inventory value. Consequently, this cost may be allocated to each product on the basis of the ratio of its average inventory value to the total average inventory value of all finished goods.

Storage

The product characteristic occasioning storage expenses is the space occupied by the finished goods inventory. Consequently, the measure of any product's portion of the storage expense is its share of the total storage space occupied.

Inventory control

The variable product activity giving rise to the expenses of this function is the number of postings made to the perpetual-inventory records, i.e. the number of invoice lines. Consequently, this cost is allocated to each product on the basis of its share of the total number of invoice lines.

Order assembly or handling

The expense of physically handling merchandise in the order-assembly process is mainly the cost of the time (man-hours) involved. Such factors as size, shape, weight, perishability, or nature of the package are only indirect handling-cost determinants. That is, they affect the time required to handle a single piece of merchandise. Thus, by work-measurement study, a 'standard handling unit' may be set up. If the standard handling unit is a case of goods, for example, then barrels, sacks, and other packages may be expressed as multiple or fractional handling units according to their time-of-handling relationship to that of the case of goods (the standard unit). Equipment and supply expenses, as well as wages, are included in the handling-cost group, but since wages are the largest and probably the governing factor of the entire group, the amount of these expenses is added to and distributed with wages.

Packing and shipping

Where possible, this functional-cost group should be assigned directly to each product group. Thus, the amount of shipping material used by each product group can often be determined by direct measurement. Shipping labor also can often be applied specifically to product groups and sub-groups, through labor-time tickets. And the overhead or indirect portion of this expense can be allocated on the direct labor-dollar basis. Where it is not feasible to assign these costs directly, periodic tests should be made of the labor-and-materials cost per ton necessary to ship each product sub-group. The expense of this function can then be prorated to products by multiplying the tonnage of shipments in each product classification by the shipping rate per pound determined through the test. Where weight is not available for any product group, a shipping unit (package, etc.) may be used as a basis for allocating these costs to products.

Transportation

Where common carriers are used, transportation charges should be analysed from a sampling of freight bills in all territories and an average rate per ton (or hundredweight) computed for each product sub-group. Transportation expense can then be assigned to each product by multiplying the tonnage of shipments by its average rate per ton.

Where the wholesaler or manufacturer makes deliveries by his own trucks, the following method can be used. The wage cost of loading and unloading the truck can be allocated to products on the basis of the number of standard handling units or the number of pieces of merchandise delivered. The actual cost of 'rolling the truck' – both truck and wage costs – can be allocated to commodities on the basis of bulk or weight.

Where there are important differences in the transportation costs of a given product to different sales territories, such differences should be reflected, rather than being averaged out.

Selling

Specific-product department selling costs are, of course, assigned directly. Much sales-promotion effort by 'full-line' salesmen (particularly in the case of wholesalers) is directed at customers rather than products. Such selling activities thus may vary more with customer characteristics and be only partly affected by product characteristics.

The relative time spent by salesmen in selling each product can be determined by a periodic work-measurement study of a sample of salesmen. Selling costs are then allocated on the basis of the relative amount of salesmen's time spent in promoting each product.

Advertising

Specific-product advertising should be assigned directly. Further allocation should be made directly to product sub-groups or lines or individual items advertised on the basis of the cost of space used for each. General institutional advertising that cannot be identified with any product (or customer) would not be allocated at all.

Other advertising and sales-promotion expenditures, such as advertising overhead and artwork, should also be assigned directly or distributed on a job-order basis, where possible. If direct assignment is not feasible, these expenses should be allocated to product (and customer) classes on the basis of relative appropriations or space and other direct advertising expenditures for each classification of sales. Otherwise, if no relationship can be traced, such items of expense should not be allocated.

Order routine and billing

These expense groups include the cost of the time spent by salesmen in routine order taking, as distinguished from promotion, as well as the cost of the time spent by office employees in the billing process. The total expense is mainly one of time (wages). The total order-routine time tends to be larger or smaller in accordance with the number of invoice lines processed. Consequently, a product's share of the total order-routine expense function depends on its share of the total number of invoice lines. The office-equipment and -supply expenses associated with the order routine may be added to and distributed with the wages.

Credit and accounts receivable

These functions are not directly affected by product characteristics. That is, as far as the individual item is concerned, new products could be added or old ones dropped without affecting the total amount of the credit activity or costs. The aggregate amount of this functional activity is determined entirely by customer characteristics. Consequently, this cost is not allocated to products.

Summary of product costing

There are thus certain data which must be known before marketing costs by products can be ascertained. In general, these data are of the following types:

1. The average inventory value of finished goods.

2. The amount of storage space occupied by these finished goods inventories.

3. The number of times the product is sold, i.e. the number of invoice lines.

4. The number of handling units of the product that are sold.

5. The weight or number of shipping units sold.

6. The proportion of sales time spent in promoting it.

7. The cost of the space or time in the various media that were used in advertising it.

Each of these factors must be determined separately for each product or product group to be costed. This means that a mass of data must be accumulated.

These product characteristics determine the shares of the corresponding functional-cost groups that are allocated to the product. The actual allocation of costs, in effect, is made by simple proportion. For example, if the average inventory value of product group X is 1/100 of the total average inventory value of all finished products, that group is charged 1/100 of the investment costs for the period. The sum of the shares of the various functional costs which are allocated plus any direct costs is subtracted from the dollar gross margin of the product (in costing products whose prices have previously been established). The dollar difference indicates the relative profit (or loss) contribution of the product.

The basic procedure is, of course, the same in costing major product groups, sub-groups, lines, and individual items or brands. The difference lies mainly in the detail with which product sales and gross margins are classified and the detail with which the functional costs are allocated.

Allocations to customers

The process of allocating marketing costs to customers is fundamentally the same as that of product marketing-cost analysis. As shown in Table 2, the functional-cost groups used in costing customers are basically the same as those used in costing products. Not all these cost groups are allocated to customers, however, and the bases of allocation differ somewhat. The bases for allocating the functional-cost groups to customers for a manufacturer or wholesaler are shown in Table 1 as well as in the right-hand column of Table 2. These bases of allocation are discussed below.

C. H. Sevin   153

Table 2 Functional-cost groups and bases of allocation

	Basis of allocation	
Functional-cost group	To products	To customers
Investment	Average inventory value	(Not allocated)
Storage	Floor space occupied	(Not allocated)
Inventory control	Number of invoice lines	(Not allocated)
Order assembly (handling)	Number of standard handling units	Number of invoice lines
Packing and shipping	Weight or number of shipping units	Weight or number of shipping units
Transportation	Weight or number of shipping units	Weight or number of shipping units
Selling	Work-measurement studies	Number of sales calls
Advertising	Cost of space, etc., of specific-product advertising	Cost of space, etc., specific-customer advertising
Order entry	Number of invoice lines	Number of orders
Billing	Number of invoice lines	Number of invoice lines
Credit extension	(Not allocated)	Average amount outstanding
Accounts receivable	(Not allocated)	Number of invoices posted

Investment and storage

These activities usually are only indirectly affected by customer characteristics. It is true, of course, that the costs are related to turnover rates, which depend partly on the rates at which customers purchase a specific product. But many other factors, such as the production policies of the manufacturer (and the purchasing policies of the wholesaler), determine merchandise turnover rates, and these are not related to customer characteristics.

Furthermore, these costs would not ordinarily be allocated to customers, for individual customers could be added or dropped – up to a certain point, of course – without affecting the aggregate amount of investment and storage costs.

Inventory control

Since the variable activity of inventory control is only remotely, if at all, affected by customer characteristics, in most cases this function would not be allocated to customers. In other words, customers could be added or eliminated – within broad limits, of course – without affecting the aggregate inventory-control expense.

Order assembly

This function is affected by both customer and product characteristics. Weight, bulk and perishability are product characteristics affecting the amount of order-assembly costs for which the customer is not responsible unless he purchases only certain particularly weighty, bulky, or perishable commodities. The frequency and size of his orders, however, are characteristics affecting the amount of order-assembly costs for which the customer is wholly responsible.

Thus, if there are no important variations in the kinds of products purchased by different classes of customers, i.e. where all customers purchase substantially the full product line, the number of his invoice lines over a period is the measure of each customer's responsibility for order-assembly cost.

Where some classes of customers purchase only certain products which are particularly weighty, bulky, or otherwise expensive to handle, the number of standard handling units or the number of invoice lines weighted for different classes of products would be a better basis of allocation. The customer who buys products less expensive to handle or who buys less frequently and in larger quantities thus is charged with less handling cost – as a percentage of sales – than the customer in the same class who over a period buys the same volume but more frequently and in smaller amounts. In other words, the latter is assessed a larger handling cost in proportion to the larger number of individual physical handlings of merchandise or more expensive merchandise handling for which he is responsible.

Packing and shipping

The shipping rates per pound of product multiplied by the corresponding tonnage of shipments in each product sub-group to each customer class can be used to allocate these costs to customers. Or if this is not feasible, an average shipping rate per

C. H. Sevin 155

pound of product or per unit for all products combined multiplied by the tonnage of shipments to customers would give the packing and shipping costs by customer classes.

Transportation

Where possible, transportation charges should be analysed from a sampling of freight bills by sales territories and assigned directly to customer classes or to individual customers. That is, the territorial rates per ton for major product groups multiplied by the corresponding tonnages delivered to each customer class – or an average territory rate per ton for all products combined multiplied by tonnages delivered to customer classes – can be used to allocate transportation costs to customers.

Where the manufacturer or wholesaler makes deliveries by his own trucks, the following method can be used. Truck-delivery activity and expense vary according to the customer characteristics of delivered-order weight or bulk and frequency of delivery. Where delivered-order weight or bulk and delivery-distance differences are not great, as between customers, the cost of delivery may be charged against individual customers on the basis of number of deliveries. Where only delivery-distance differences, as between customers, are great, the customers can be classified in zones, with costs per delivery weighted by distance. Where both weight or bulk and distance differences are significant, the ton-mile basis may be used. (It is not an easy task, however, to compute ton-miles by customers.)

Selling

Selling expense can be assigned to customers on the basis of the number of sales calls (whether orders are obtained or not). In assigning selling cost to customers on this basis, the view is taken that the time per sales call does not vary significantly as between customers. A more accurate basis would be to make a work-measurement study of a sample of sales calls or to have salesmen keep records of the time spent on each call and to allocate the cost of the actual total selling time to each customer.

Where travel distances, as between customers, are significant, the same classification of customers by zones which is used for weighting cost per delivery by distance probably can be used to establish a similar weighting of cost per salesman's call for salesmen's travel time and expense.

Advertising

Specific-customer-class advertising should be assigned directly to the particular customer classifications involved. General institutional advertising that cannot be identified with any customer class would not be allocated. Other advertising and sales-promotion expenditures, such as advertising overhead and artwork, should also be assigned directly or distributed on a job-order basis, where possible. If direct assignment is not feasible, these expenses should be allocated to customer classes on the basis of relative appropriations or space and other direct advertising expenditures for each classification of sales. Otherwise, if no relationship can be traced, such items of expense should not be allocated.

Order entry and billing

The order-routine expenses, like the physical-handling expense, depend on the number of orders and invoice lines, which, as an allocation basis, reflect the customer characteristics of frequency and amount of purchase.

Credit and accounts receivable

This expense is the cost of the clerical effort used in recording sales and collections and the financial cost of carrying accounts and making collections. The clerical portion of this expense is allocated on the basis of the number of payments made by customers, and the financial portion varies according to the average amount outstanding.

Summary of customer costing

The customer data needed for allocating the functional-cost groups to a customer class or customer are (see Table 2) as follows:

1. The number of invoice lines on all orders for the period.

2. The weight or number of shipping units of the merchandise bought by the customer.

C. H. Sevin 157

3. The number of sales calls made on the customer.

4. The cost of the space or time in the various media used to advertise to the customer class specifically.

5. The number of orders placed by the customer.

6. The average amount outstanding.

7. The number of invoices posted to accounts receivable.

Each of these factors would need to be measured for each customer group whose marketing costs and profits are to be determined. (As in the case of products, a mass of data is needed.)

These factors are used in allocating to the customer class a share of the functional-cost groups. The total of the shares of the allocated functional-cost groups plus any direct expenses gives the total customer cost. This cost deducted from the total dollar gross margin received from that customer class during the same period indicates the relative profitability of these customers.

It is possible and useful to management to make cost analyses for various groupings of customers. For example, the results for individual customers may be added together to show sales, gross margins, expenses and relative profits for channels of distribution and accounts classified by volume or purchases.

Allocation to units of sale and to territories

In general, a marketing-cost analyses by unit of sales is similar to product and customer costing, but it involves a different classification of sales, margins and costs. Instead of classifying sales by products or customers, the sales, margins and cost characteristics applying to unit-of-sale groups are determined. The unit of sale may refer to one of the following:

1. Number of units of product per invoice-line extension.
2. Dollar value per invoice-line extension.
3. Number of invoice lines per order.
4. Dollar value of the order.

The process of getting costs for the first two unit-of-sale groups, i.e. costs by invoice lines, is in general similar to the process of product costing and profitability analysis. Functional classifications of expenses and bases of allocation are much the same as those used for product costing. The allocation of costs to sales classified by order-size groups – whether order size is measured by dollar value or by number of invoice lines – is generally similar to the process of customer-costing and profitability analysis.

Marketing management is also interested in analysing marketing costs by territories. In many respects, costs by territories are the simplest ones to analyse. If the company's marketing activities are organized on a territorial basis, with the geographic limits of branches and districts clearly defined, a sufficiently detailed breakdown of the primary-expense accounts and their classification by branches and districts results in a direct assignment of a large proportion of marketing expenses to these territorial units. In some cases, however, it may be necessary to allocate to a territory certain branch and district expenses which are incurred jointly for several salesmen's territories. But even in such instances, there are some functional costs, difficult to allocate to products or customers or units of sale, which can be assigned directly to the sales territory.

Implementation of data requirements

Implementation of the marketing-cost and profitability-analysis procedures described in this Reading obviously entails a considerable burden of data collection and analysis. The considerable cost of this additional information is, of course, justified by the important benefits derived from the increased productivity of marketing effort. Further, the risk involved in undertaking a marketing-cost and profitability analysis before the benefits have been demonstrated can be at least reduced. This can be done by at first confining the analysis to a sampling of products, customers and territories and by making the analyses periodically rather than continuously. Finally, the use of computers frequently (but not always) reduces the data-gathering costs considerably.

References

ALDERSON, W., and HAAG, F., Jr (1931), *Problems of Wholesale Electrical Goods Distribution*, US Department of Commerce, Government Printing Office.

ALDERSON, W., and MILLER, N. (1930), *Problems of Wholesale Dry Goods Distribution*, US Department of Commerce, Government Printing Office.

CARROLL, E. G. (1934), *Wholesale Druggists' Operations*, US Department of Commerce, Government Printing Office.

MESEROLE, W. H., and SEVIN, C. H. (1941), *Effective Grocery Wholesaling*, US Department of Commerce, Government Printing Office.

MILLARD, J. W. (1928), *Analysing Wholesale Distribution Costs*, US Department of Commerce, Government Printing Office.

SEVIN, C. H. (1946), *Distribution Cost Analysis*, US Department of Commerce, Government Printing Office.

SEVIN, C. H. (1950), 'Controlling distribution costs', in L. Doris (ed.), *Corporate Treasurers' and Controllers' Handbook*, Prentice-Hall.

SEVIN, C. H. (1952), 'How to control your distribution costs', in J. K. Lasser (ed.), *Business Management Handbook*, McGraw-Hill, ch. 13.

SEVIN, C. H. (1954), 'Distribution and administrative cost analysis', in W. P. Fiske, and J. A. Beckett (eds.), *Industrial Accountant's Handbook*, Prentice-Hall, ch. 22.

Part Three
Management of the Product Mix

The discussion by Hood (Reading 9) reiterates in part the point we have touched on before (particularly in Reading 8), namely that the marketing manager must attempt to manage each product on the basis of its profitability. He must know, in a multi-product line of either industrial or consumer goods, which products are providing good profit, which are not, and trends. This level of knowledge is essential if other elements in the marketing mix are to be managed effectively. Products do not yield the same profit over time, and one factor determining profitability at a moment of time is the stage in its life cycle which the product has reached. Levitt (Reading 10) examines the product life-cycle concept and shows how the manager can use the concept to great advantage.

For a number of complex reasons, original product life-cycles, particularly in the United States, are tending to shorten. The effective marketing manager must therefore be an effective new product manager. The next two Readings deal with this subject. McIver (Reading 11) looks at the problem of new product introduction, suggesting that new product failure may in part be accounted for by poor management organization for it, not just to an unreceptive market, as many marketing managers would believe when they find they have an unsuccessful launch on their hands. Product mix management requires that managers make positive determination of the future of the unprofitable products in the line. Berenson (Reading 12) describes a simple five-variable model for evaluating products with a view to developing a cohesive product abandonment policy.

Product/price/quality relationships are obviously linked and a weak link may often be price. Pricing practices in both the United Kingdom and the United States tend to be somewhat primitive, particularly in the eyes of those trained in the theory of price. Gabor (Reading 13) explores the reasons for the gap between theory and practice and suggests how price management might become more consumer oriented.

Finally in this section we have included an article on product (brand) management (Reading 14). It is included because we believe that many firms that have begun to implement the marketing concept have failed to understand the organizational advantages of using a product manager system for managing a multi-product line.

9 P. Hood

How to Mix Products

P. Hood, 'How to mix products', *Management Today*, March 1970, pp. 57–64.

The ultimate objective of all companies should be to achieve a good return on their assets. Naturally, the objective varies in detail from one company to another in important respects such as the amount of the return and the time over which the return is sought. The profitable use of assets is a function of price, volume, cost and mix. Too many companies over-emphasize volume – as a means of encouragement and control of the sales force, as a justification for decisions and as an explanation for action. There is usually plenty of other information available. But interpretation and evaluation of, say, sales variance month by month, are complex, given that few companies have much control over their markets. What the marketing manager needs are simple indicators provided on a continuing basis. He wants to know what business the company would prefer to win and how to progress towards this ultimate objective.

Simplicity is the only advantage of depending on sales volume as an indicator. The difficulty is to persuade a marketing manager that this is so. If all his products can be sold at a profit, there is no denying that an increase in volume will raise profit absolutely. From an investment viewpoint, however, this increase may be bad, because the return on assets could – and often does – fall. This leads to two related weaknesses: complacency about the return, so long as volume rises, and failure to grasp opportunities to raise the return to a higher level. These opportunities relate to mix and to reinforcing what the company is good at; in a multi-product company this is the antithesis of the passive marketing attitude which maintains obstinately that 'all business is good business'. This criticism, however, only applies to the successful company. Subtlety often does not fit the needs of struggling or unprofitable businesses. For these, a brutish thrust for sales volume is often the first imperative.

Measures other than sales volume can be simple to calculate and understand. They are, of course, imprecise because an optimum plan is purely academic if markets are not controlled. They provide a continuing guide to the marketing manager, rather than an occasional *ad hoc* description of history, and this guide consists of a ranking of preferred business by product or market. Each of the three different measures given below suits a different case and is inferior in any other case. They are: 1. spare capacity and no constraining resources – *rank by profit contribution*, 2. a capacity limitation and a single dominant constraint – *rank by maximizing the earnings of the constraint*, 3. a capacity limitation and several constraining resources – *rank by the return on cost of value added*.

All these measures, however, go against the grain of normal practice. Volume of sales has traditionally been the way of measuring performance of salesmen. It is unusual to measure success in terms of contribution to profit. Commission systems, moreover, are usually based on volume. But the reasons given for rewarding volume rather than contribution given are often wholly unsound – for example, that the salesman is not bright enough to understand contribution, or that he cannot be trusted with data on profit margins. If either of these is true, how can he be trusted to act as the company's representative in any event?

Another common objection is that contribution differs from product to product and that one salesman may be fortunate in selling a high margin product while another does not. With the proviso that every salesman knows that chance plays its part, it should not be beyond the wit of his manager to devise a reward system which takes profitability into account. This does assume that the manager has agreed the potential of the salesman's territory beforehand – a requirement which applies regardless of the method of rewarding the salesman.

It is also argued that contribution is to a large extent outside the salesman's control. Most of the difficulty here can be avoided if the company uses standard costs. Contribution is calculated at standard, and variances which are no concern of the salesman are ignored. A selling price variance might be his responsibility or his manager's. True, sales volume is a good measure of performance if the salesman can only sell one product; or if there is no difference between the company's products in terms of value added, resources required to manufacture, or margin; or if the salesman has no discretion over price. But companies are rarely as uncomplicated as this.

The majority of marketing directors and managers have risen from the ranks of salesmen. Often they are outstanding personalities; individual rather than team or functional men; company men in the sense of dedication, but not in terms of seeing the business as a total integrated entity – in fact, the opposite is more usual. Their success in the field calls for identification with and understanding of the customer. This is in part fostered by the salesmen offering to win over 'them' in production, engineering or general management who are causing 'us' – the salesmen and customer – so much difficulty. Rarely have these managers risen from a marketing background with a training in business/profit/product planning. The inter-functional friction on which the salesman plays in the presence of his customer is retained in his later life as a manager. The parochial attitude 'all business is good business, and it's someone else's problem to design/manufacture/deliver on time' is all too common.

Two real life examples show the dangers. An electronics company discontinued a line of equipment previously sold to a foreign government and the tools were destroyed. Six years after the initial purchase, the marketing manager was again in negotiation with the same customer and won a very large order for the discontinued line. The quotation was made without regard for the cost and time required to retool or the displacement of more profitable work from overstretched resources. The manager frequently looked for credit for winning this high value order – but the profitable use of resources never entered his mind.

An engineering company wisely decided to broaden its range with a new product. The new product required a manufacturing technique in which the company was inferior to others. There were teething troubles, not in volume produced, but in large manufacturing cost variances. Prudence argued in favour of reducing sales activity on this line to give the production department time to master an unfamiliar method. Incidentally, the salesmen for the new product were also salesmen for the current range, for which demand still exceeded supply. The marketing manager refused to re-schedule the launch on the grounds that this would demoralize the salesmen and that initial losses on the product were due to production variances 'which are not my responsibility – it's my job to meet a forecast of £x,000 of orders'.

Convention expects the salesman to be 'thrusting, forceful, dynamic' in some loosely defined way. This dashing image of vigour is also expected in the salesman's manager. Plans clothed in terms of more sales are compatible with this. Plans based on more profit from less assets and possibly lower sales do not sound dynamic. Finally, measures other than sales volume are considered obscure and difficult to calculate. Certainly they involve additional calculation and presuppose a costing system. But they need not be at all complex.

No one should be deterred from using indicators because exact data are not available. This rarely matters for several reasons. First, the market cannot be controlled by the company, and so *exact* calculations are irrelevant. Second, alternative courses of action differ markedly in profitability. The second point follows from the first. These indicators do not give the optimum solution in a mathematical sense, if a company's products either share resources or there are several constraints. A mathematician can readily spell out an optimal solution, which may involve linear programming, but few companies bother with this because their information is imperfect; huge progress can be made without identifying the perfect course of action; perfection is unattainable; and the extra cost does not seem justified.

The aim is to make the most profitable use of resources. In the short term this means the resources currently available, because few of these can be changed. Profitable use is a function of utilization and margin. Therefore as a starting point we need

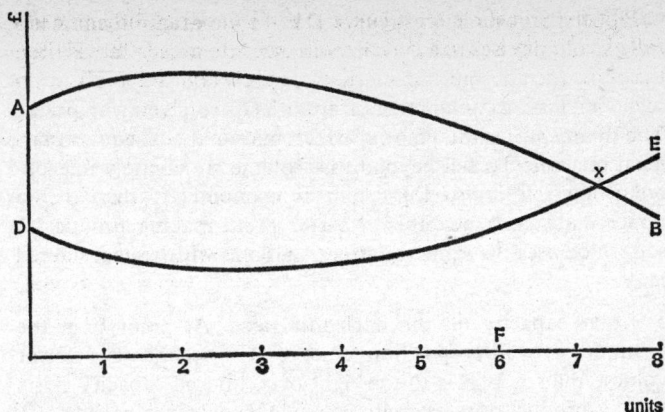

Figure 1

to know capacity, cost, forecast demand and selling price.

The principle is illustrated simply in the diagram. The manager is looking from a short term viewpoint: he has certain assets and resources to make product Z and these are fixed. (The majority of decisions taken by managers are made within this constraint.) Therefore the value of assets employed is ignored. The manager's objective is to maximize contribution. Here, in the first instance, one product is considered in isolation. By maximizing contribution the manager maximizes the return on resources required to make product Z. His method is to give preference to market segments with the highest profit contribution.

The right procedure is to take the following steps:

1. Let the vertical axis be money – cost per unit and selling price per unit.

2. Let the horizontal axis be number of units – demand and capacity (it is unlikely that these are the same).

3. Plot the demand for product Z – this is the line AB. It is implied in the example that prices will vary with volume. This arises because the market is segmented – home sales prices are higher than export, for example, or demand is price sensitive and bigger discounts give bigger sales.

P. Hood 167

4. Plot the unit direct cost curve DE. In the example unit costs fall as volume rises to a certain point, and then rise. Cases differ, the principle does not. Sooner or later AB and DE must intersect. For instance, market saturation leads to give-away prices. The intercept x is the point at which marginal cost equals marginal revenue. To sell beyond this volume is definitely uneconomic. To sell up to this point is economic if there is no opportunity cost: no other superior profit-making product to sell which uses the same resources – a point which is considered later.

5. Enter capacity on the horizontal axis. At point F in the example a healthy position emerges: F occurs at a lower volume than x. If F is to the right of x, unused capacity exists for this product or sales are to be made below marginal cost.

Finally, identify the customers, planned discount breaks or other factors, which give rise to orders beyond point F. Plan to avoid this business by a change in pricing, deployment of the sales force or some other means. This step may sound difficult. In fact it is straightforward if trivial price differences to markets and customers are ignored, and the order intake forecast for the product is built up with this end in view. This means grouping customers or markets in terms of price or discount and, of course, showing the expected volume of order intake for each.

There are two points to make about this example. First, companies stop selling a product before point x is reached, although they will have idle capacity as a result. This happens because fixed costs are looked upon as variable. This is not just a failure to classify sensibly. It arises because fixed costs are expressed as a percentage of variable costs, which can be convenient for play-safe book-keeping and budgeting, but can lead to wrong decisions in a competitive market. Second, sales manager A accepts orders up to point x for product Z, although sales manager B could sell product y which uses the same resources at greater profit. In other words, there is a 'sharing' problem to be considered.

The thinking here does not cope with the multi-product situation in which products share key resources. In other words, giving preference to products or markets on the basis of profit contribution is the wrong measure. The objective is to maximize the earning power of the prime resources of the business. The prime resources are often scarce resources. Maximizing the earning power of prime resources is not the same as giving preference to business or products which have the highest percentage contribution or the highest sales value.

Sales of a product or product group are often limited by the capacity of a single resource, although the products may pass through a number of cost centres in the course of manufacture. For instance, the limitation may be in design engineering, an extrusion press, or in manpower in fettling. Whatever the constraint is, if attention is concentrated on maximizing earning power through that constraint, then a very good plan for mix of business results. It is not claimed that the plan will always be the optimum. It will not be optimal if there is more than one constraint. However, since the optimum is seldom attainable because of market forces, an expensive search for perfection is downright irritating to a pragmatic manager.

The steps to go through are as follows:

1. Make an order intake forecast by product, segmenting the market by price as before.

2. Get the unit direct costs for each product in total.

3. Subtract 2. from 1. to give product profit contribution by unit.

4. Find out the time or cost – whichever is the key factor – for each product on the scarce resource. For example, Product A takes 0·10 press hours; Product B, 0·12 press hours; Product C, 0·20 press hours – or else Product A takes £0·5 fettling wages; Product B £0·75; Product C £0·2.

5. Now relate all the profit contribution to cost or time on this constraining resource, as below.

6. Find the capacity of the press in the forecast period. Say that the capacity is 2,000 hours. Take the product forecasts by market segment and multiply these by the press hours required. Now look at the products in the same sequence as above.

Table 1

Product	Market segment	Contribution	Press hours	Contribution per hour
A	1	£5	0·10	£50
A	2	£4·5	0·10	£45
B	1	£5	0·12	£42
A	3	£4·2	0·10	£42
B	2	£4·75	0·12	£40
C	1	£8·0	0·20	£40
C	2	£7·8	0·20	£39

Table 2

		Order (intake forecast)	Press time	Total PT by segment	Cumulative
A	1	2,000	0·10	200	200
	2	3,000	0·10	300	500
B	1	5,000	0·12	600	1100
A	3	1,000	0·10	100	1200
B	2	4,000	0·12	480	1680
C	1	2,000	0·20	400	2080

A segment may be a discount rate, territory or any other
logical division by price. The figures show that product C
business in market segment 2 and all segments below C2 are
not wanted. This illustrates the point that this calculation need
not be the same as giving preference to business with the highest
percentage contribution. Costs and selling price may well
appear thus:

Table 3

	Direct costs		Price	Contribution	
	Materials £	Labour £	£	£	%
A1	20	10	40	5	12½
B1	8	7	20	5	25
C1	12	12	32	8	25

The procedure described above is unsatisfactory if there are two or more limitations to output. The following variation is a simple method of finding the mix of business which maximizes the earning power of scarce resources – the mix which gives the best return on assets. For calculating capacity precisely linear programming is needed. But most situations are not complex.

Thus, there is a formula which gives a ranking of products. Subtract from forecast selling price those direct costs which do not add value; then divide by *direct costs which add value*. This gives the return on value added; however, the terms need explanation. In a manufacturing company the direct costs which do not add value contain such items as material, sales, distribution and administration expenses. Often these last three items are small in relation to total cost and do not vary much from product to product. In this case there is no point in including them; they will not affect the relative ranking of products which the formula produces. Direct costs which do add value contain adaptive or customer engineering; direct labour; other incremental costs of production. Applying this in the case above gives the following ranking according to return on value added:

Product A £$(40-20) \div 10 = 2$
Product B $(20-8) \div 7 = 1\cdot71$
Product C $(32-12) \div 12 = 1\cdot66$

There is no need to bring fixed costs or costs which depend on time into the calculation unless the decision which management is taking causes these to be changed. However, if the decision to sell some of product B forces management to invest in further capacity to make for product A, fixed costs must be added to the direct costs which add value – which may change the ranking.

By using these three methods, it is therefore simple to progress beyond volume of sales. To give preference to products with the highest percentage contribution is also unsound if there are capacity limitations – particularly if the proportion of value added varies from product to product. Ranking by return on expenditure on the key constraint or on the cost of value added clarifies the issue of mix, and changes in cost and selling price can be evaluated fast. Simplicity makes this a good indicator.

10 T. Levitt

Exploit the Product Life-Cycle

T. Levitt, 'Exploit the product life-cycle', *Harvard Business Review*, vol. 43, no. 6, 1965, pp. 81-94.

Most alert and thoughtful senior marketing executives are by now familiar with the concept of the product life-cycle. Even a handful of uniquely cosmopolitan and up-to-date corporate presidents have familiarized themselves with this tantalizing concept. Yet a recent survey I took of such executives found none who used the concept in any strategic way whatever and pitifully few who used it in any kind of tactical way. It has remained – as have so many fascinating theories in economics, physics and sex – a remarkably durable but almost totally unemployed and seemingly unemployable piece of professional baggage whose presence in the rhetoric of professional discussions adds a much coveted but apparently unattainable legitimacy to the idea that marketing management is somehow a profession. There is, furthermore, a persistent feeling that the life-cycle concept adds luster and believability to the insistent claim in certain circles that marketing is close to being some sort of science.[1]

The concept of the product life-cycle is today at about the stage that the Copernican view of the universe was 300 years ago; a lot of people knew about it but hardly anybody seemed to use it in any effective or productive way.

Now that so many people know and in some fashion understand the product life-cycle, it seems time to put it to work. The object of this article is to suggest some ways of using the concept effectively and of turning the knowledge of its existence into a managerial instrument of competitive power.

1. For discussions of the scientific claims or potentials of marketing, see Schwartz (1963) and Cox, Alderson and Shapiro (1964).

Since the concept has been presented somewhat differently by different authors and for different audiences, it is useful to review it briefly here so that every reader has the same background for the discussion which follows later in this article.

Historical pattern

The life story of most successful products is a history of their passing through certain recognizable stages. These are shown in Figure 1 and occur in the following order:

Stage 1: Market Development. This is when a new product is first brought to market, before there is a proved demand for it and often before it has been fully proved out technically in all respects. Sales are low and creep along slowly.

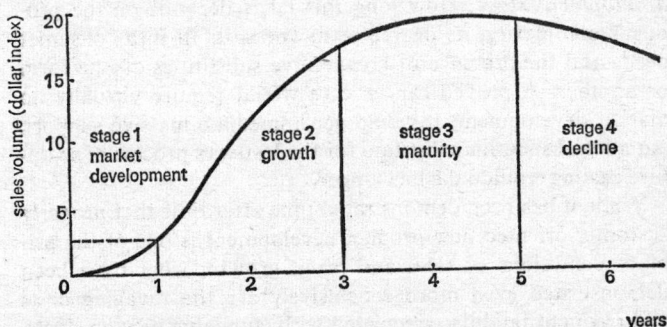

Figure 1 Product life-cycle – entire industry

Stage 2: Market Growth. Demand begins to accelerate and the size of the total market expands rapidly. It might also be called the 'Take-off Stage'.

Stage 3: Market Maturity. Demand levels off and grows, for the most part, only at the replacement and new family-formation rate.

Stage 4: Market Decline. The product begins to lose consumer appeal and sales drift downward, such as when buggy whips lost out with the advent of automobiles and when silk lost out to nylon.

Three operating questions will quickly occur to the alert executive:

Given a proposed new product or service, how and to what extent can the shape and duration of each stage be predicted?

Given an existing product, how can one determine what stage it is in?

Given all this knowledge, how can it be effectively used?

A brief further elaboration of each stage will be useful before dealing with these questions in detail.

Development stage

Bringing a new product to market is fraught with unknowns, uncertainties and frequently unknowable risks. Generally, demand has to be 'created' during the product's initial *market development stage*. How long this takes depends on the product's complexity, its degree of newness, its fit into consumer needs and the presence of competitive substitutes of one form or another. A proved cancer cure would require virtually no market development; it would get immediate massive support. An alleged superior substitute for the lost-wax process of sculpture casting would take lots longer.

While it has been demonstrated time after time that properly customer-oriented new product development is one of the primary conditions of sales and profit growth, what have been demonstrated even more conclusively are the ravaging costs and frequent fatalities associated with launching new products. Nothing seems to take more time, cost more money, involve more pitfalls, cause more anguish, or break more careers than do sincere and well-conceived new product programs. The fact is, most new products don't have any sort of classical life-cycle curve at all. They have instead from the very outset an infinitely descending curve. The product not only doesn't get off the ground; it goes quickly under ground – six feet under.

It is little wonder, therefore, that some disillusioned and badly burned companies have recently adopted a more conservative policy – what I call the 'used apple policy'. Instead of aspiring to be the first company to see and seize an opportunity, they systematically avoid being first. They let others take the first bite of the supposedly juicy apple that tantalizes them.

They let others do the pioneering. If the idea works, they quickly follow suit. They say, in effect, 'The trouble with being a pioneer is that the pioneers get killed by the Indians'. Hence, they say (thoroughly mixing their metaphors), 'We don't have to get the first bite of the apple. The second one is good enough'. They are willing to eat off a used apple but they try to be alert enough to make sure it is only slightly used – and they at least get the second big bite, not the tenth skimpy one.

Growth stage

The usual characteristic of a successful new product is a gradual rise in its sales curve during the market development stage. At some point in this rise a marked increase in consumer demand occurs and sales take off. The boom is on. This is the beginning of Stage 2 – the *market growth stage*. At this point potential competitors who have been watching developments during Stage 1 jump into the fray. The first ones to get in are generally those with an exceptionally effective 'used apple policy'. Some enter the market with carbon-copies of the originator's product. Others make functional and design improvements. And at this point product and brand differentiation begin to develop.

The ensuing fight for the consumer's patronage poses to the originating producer an entirely new set of problems. Instead of seeking ways of getting consumers to *try the product*, the originator now faces the more compelling problem of getting them to *prefer his brand*. This generally requires important changes in marketing strategies and methods. But the policies and tactics now adopted will be neither freely the sole choice of the originating producer, nor as experimental as they might have been during Stage 1. The presence of competitors both dictates and limits what can easily be tried – such as, for example, testing what is the best price level or the best channel of distribution.

As the rate of consumer acceptance accelerates, it generally becomes increasingly easy to open new distribution channels and retail outlets. The consequent filling of distribution pipelines generally causes the entire industry's factory sales to rise more rapidly than store sales. This creates an exaggerated impression of profit opportunity which, in turn, attracts more competitors. Some of these will begin to charge lower prices because of later advances in technology, production shortcuts, the need to take lower margins in order to get distribution and the like. All this in time inescapably moves the industry to the threshold of a new stage of competition.

Maturity stage

This new stage is the *market maturity stage*. The first sign of its advent is evidence of market saturation. This means that most consumer companies or households that are sales prospects will be owning or using the product. Sales now grow about on a par with population. No more distribution pipelines need be filled. Price competition now becomes intense. Competitive attempts to achieve and hold brand preference now involve making finer and finer differentiations in the product, in customer services, and in the promotional practices and claims made for the product.

Typically, the market maturity stage forces the producer to concentrate on holding his distribution outlets, retaining his shelf space and, in the end, trying to secure even more intensive distribution. Whereas during the market development stage the originator depended heavily on the positive efforts of his retailers and distributors to help sell his product, retailers and distributors will now frequently have been reduced largely to being merchandise-displayers and order-takers. In the case of branded products in particular, the originator must now, more than ever, communicate directly with the consumer.

The market maturity stage typically calls for a new kind of emphasis on competing more effectively. The originator is increasingly forced to appeal to the consumer on the basis of price, marginal product differences, or both. Depending on the product, services and deals offered in connection with it are often the clearest and most effective forms of differentiation. Beyond these, there will be attempts to create and promote fine product distinctions through packaging and advertising, and to appeal to special market segments. The market maturity stage can be passed through rapidly, as in the case of most women's fashion fads, or it can persist for generations with *per capita* consumption neither rising nor falling, as in the case of such staples as men's shoes and industrial fasteners. Or maturity can persist, but in a state of gradual but steady *per capita* decline, as in the case of beer and steel.

Decline stage

When market maturity tapers off and consequently comes to an end, the product enters Stage 4 – *market decline*. In all cases of maturity and decline the industry is transformed. Few companies are able to weather the competitive storm. As demand declines, the overcapacity that was already apparent during the period of maturity now becomes endemic. Some producers see the handwriting implacably on the wall but feel that with proper management and cunning they will be one of the survivors after the industry-wide deluge they so clearly foresee. To hasten their competitors' eclipse directly, or to frighten them into early voluntary withdrawal from the industry, they initiate a variety of aggressively depressive tactics, propose mergers or buy-outs, and generally engage in activities that make life thanklessly burdensome for all firms, and make death the inevitable consequence for most of them. A few companies do indeed weather the storm, sustaining life through the constant descent that now clearly characterizes the industry. Production gets concentrated into fewer hands. Prices and margins get depressed. Consumers get bored. The only cases where there is any relief from this boredom and gradual euthanasia are where styling and fashion play some constantly revivifying role.

Preplanning importance

Knowing that the lives of successful products and services are generally characterized by something like the pattern illustrated in Figure 1 can become the basis for important life-giving policies and practices. One of the greatest values of the life-cycle concept is for managers about to launch a new product. The first step for them is to try to foresee the profile of the proposed product's cycle.

As with so many things in business, and perhaps uniquely in marketing, it is almost impossible to make universally useful suggestions regarding how to manage one's affairs. It is certainly particularly difficult to provide widely useful advice on how to foresee or predict the slope and duration of a product's life. Indeed, it is precisely because so little specific day-to-day guidance is possible in anything, and because no checklist has ever by itself been very useful to anybody for very long, that business management will probably never be a science – always an art – and will pay exceptional rewards to managers with rare talent, enormous energy, iron nerve, great capacity for assuming responsibility and bearing accountability.

But this does not mean that useful efforts cannot or should not be made to try to foresee the slope and duration of a new product's life. Time spent in attempting this kind of foresight not only helps assure that a more rational approach is brought to product planning and merchandising; also, as will be shown later, it can help create valuable lead time for important strategic and tactical moves after the product is brought to market. Specifically, it can be a great help in developing an orderly series of competitive moves, in expanding or stretching out the life of a product, in maintaining a clean product line, and in purposely phasing out dying and costly old products (Kotler, 1965).

Failure possibilities . . .

As pointed out above, the length and slope of the market development stage depend on the product's complexity, its degree of newness, its fit into customer needs and the presence of competitive substitutes.

The more unique or distinctive the newness of the product, the longer it generally takes to get it successfully off the ground. The world does not automatically beat a path to the man with the better mousetrap.[2] The world has to be told, coddled, enticed, romanced and even bribed (as with, for example, coupons, samples, free application aids and the like). When the product's newness is distinctive and the job it is designed to do is unique, the public will generally be less quick to perceive it as something it clearly needs or wants.

2. For perhaps the ultimate example of how the world does *not* beat such a path, see the example of the man who actually, and to his painful regret, made a 'better' mousetrap, in Matthews, Buzzell, Levitt and Frank (1964, p. 4).

This makes life particularly difficult for the innovator. He will have more than the usual difficulties of identifying those characteristics of his product and those supporting communications themes or devices which imply value to the consumer. As a consequence, the more distinctive the newness, the greater the risk of failure resulting either from insufficient working capital to sustain a long and frustrating period of creating enough solvent customers to make the proposition pay, or from the inability to convince investors and bankers that they should put up more money.

In any particular situation the more people who will be involved in making a single purchasing decision for a new product, the more drawn out Stage 1 will be. Thus in the highly fragmented construction materials industry, for example, success takes an exceptionally long time to catch hold; and having once caught hold, it tends to hold tenaciously for a long time – often too long. On the other hand, fashion items clearly catch on fastest and last shortest. But because fashion is so powerful, recently some companies in what often seem the least fashion-influenced of industries (machine tools, for example) have shortened the market development stage by introducing elements of design and packaging fashion to their products.

What factors tend to prolong the market development stage and therefore raise the risk of failure? The more complex the product, the more distinctive its newness, the less influenced by fashion, the greater the number of persons influencing a single buying decision, the more costly, and the greater the required shift in the customer's usual way of doing things – these are the conditions most likely to slow things up and create problems.

... versus success chances

But problems also create opportunities to control the forces arrayed against new product success. For example, the newer the product, the more important it becomes for the customers to have a favorable first experience with it. Newness creates a certain special visibility for the product, with a certain number of people standing on the sidelines to see how the first customers get on with it. If their first experience is unfavorable in some crucial way, this may have repercussions far out of proportion to the actual extent of the underfulfillment of the customers' expectations. But a favorable first experience or application will, for the same reason, get a lot of disproportionately favorable publicity.

The possibility of exaggerated disillusionment with a poor first experience can raise vital questions regarding the appropriate channels of distribution for a new product. On the one hand, getting the product successfully launched may require having – as in the case of, say, the early days of home washing machines – many retailers who can give consumers considerable help in the product's correct utilization and thus help assure a favorable first experience for those buyers. On the other hand, channels that provide this kind of help (such as small neighborhood appliance stores in the case of washing machines) during the market development stage may not be the ones best able to merchandise the product most successfully later when help in creating and personally reassuring customers is less important than wide product distribution. To the extent that channel decisions during this first stage sacrifice some of the requirements of the market development stage to some of the requirements of later stages, the rate of the product's acceptance by consumers at the outset may be delayed.

In entering the market development stage, pricing decisions are often particularly hard for the producer to make. Should he set an initially high price to recoup his investment quickly – i.e. 'skim the cream' – or should he set a low price to discourage potential competition – i.e. 'exclusion'? The answer depends on the innovator's estimate of the probable length of the product's life-cycle, the degree of patent protection the product is likely to enjoy, the amount of capital needed to get the product off the ground, the elasticity of demand during the early life of the product and many other factors. The decision that is finally made may affect not just the rate at which the product catches on at the beginning, but even the duration of its total life. Thus some products that are priced too low at the outset (particularly fashion goods, such as the chemise, or sack, a few years ago) may catch on so quickly that they become short-lived fads. A slower rate of consumer acceptance might often extend their life-cycles and raise the total profits they yield.

The actual slope, or rate of the growth stage, depends on some of the same things as does success or failure in Stage 1. But the extent to which patent exclusiveness can play a critical role is sometimes inexplicably forgotten. More frequently than one might offhand expect, holders of strong patent positions fail to recognize either the market-development virtue of making their patents available to competitors or the market-destroying possibilities of failing to control more effectively their competitors' use of such products.

Generally speaking, the more producers there are of a new product, the more effort goes into developing a market for it. The net result is very likely to be more rapid and steeper growth of the total market. The originator's market share may fall but his total sales and profits may rise more rapidly. Certainly this has been the case in recent years of color television; RCA's eagerness to make its tubes available to competitors reflects its recognition of the power of numbers over the power of monopoly.

On the other hand, the failure to set and enforce appropriate quality standards in the early days of polystyrene and polyethylene drinking glasses and cups produced such sloppy, inferior goods that it took years to recover the consumer's confidence and revive the growth pattern.

But to try to see in advance what a product's growth pattern might be is not very useful if one fails to distinguish between the industry pattern and the pattern of the single firm – for its particular brand. The industry's cycle will almost certainly be different from the cycle of individual firms. Moreover, the life-cycle of a given product may be different for different companies in the same industry at the same point in time, and it certainly affects different companies in the same industry differently.

Originator's burdens

The company with most at stake is the original producer – the company that launches an entirely new product. This company generally bears most of the costs, the tribulations and certainly the risks of developing both the product and the market.

Competitive pressure

Once the innovator demonstrates during the market development stage that a solid demand exists, armies of imitators rush in to capitalize on and help create the boom that becomes the market growth, or take-off, stage. As a result, while exceedingly rapid growth will now characterize the product's total demand, for the originating company its growth stage paradoxically now becomes truncated. It has to share the boom with new competitors. Hence the potential rate of acceleration of its own take-off is diminished and, indeed, may actually fail to last as long as the industry's. This occurs not only because there are so many competitors, but, as we noted earlier, also because competitors often come in with product improvements and lower prices. While these developments generally help keep the market expanding, they greatly restrict the originating company's rate of growth and the length of its take-off stage.

All this can be illustrated by comparing the curve in Figure 2 with that in Figure 1 which shows the life cycle for a product. During Stage 1 in Figure 1 there is generally only one company – the originator – even though the whole exhibit represents the entire industry. In Stage 1 the originator is the entire industry. But by Stage 2 he shares the industry with many competitors. Hence, while Figure 1 is an industry curve, its Stage 1 represents only a single company's sales.

Figure 2 shows the life-cycle of the originator's brand – his

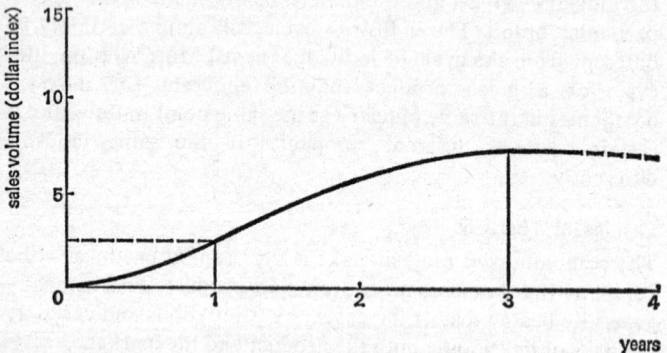

Figure 2 Product life-cycle – originating company

own sales curve, not that of the industry. It can be seen that between Year 1 and Year 2 his sales are rising about as rapidly as the industry's. But after Year 2, while industry sales in Figure 1 are still in vigorous expansion, the originator's sales curve in Figure 2 has begun to slow its ascent. He is now sharing the boom with a great many competitors, some of whom are much better positioned now than he is.

Profit squeeze

In the process the originator may begin to encounter a serious squeeze on his profit margins. Figure 3, which traces the profits per unit of the originator's sales, illustrates this point. During the market development stage his per-unit profits are negative. Sales volume is too low at existing prices. However, during the market growth stage unit profits boom as output rises and unit production costs fall. Total profits rise enormously. It is the presence of such lush profits that both attracts and ultimately destroys competitors.

Consequently, while industry sales may be rising nicely (as at the Year 3 point in Figure 1), and while the originating company's sales may at the same point of time have begun to slow down noticeably (as in Figure 2), and while at this point the originator's total profits may still be rising because his volume of sales is huge and on a slight upward trend, his profits per unit will often have taken a drastic downward course. Indeed, they will often have done so long before the sales curve flattened. They will have topped out and begun to decline perhaps around the Year 2 point (as in Figure 3). By the time the originator's sales begin to flatten out (as at the Year 3 point in Figure 2), unit profits may actually be approaching zero (as in Figure 3).

At this point more competitors are in the industry, the rate of industry demand growth has slowed somewhat, and competitors are cutting prices. Some of them do this in order to get business, and others do it because their costs are lower owing to the fact that their equipment is more modern and productive.

The industry's Stage 3 – maturity – generally lasts as long as there are no important competitive substitutes (such as, for example, aluminium for steel in 'tin' cans), no drastic shifts in

T. Levitt 183

influential value systems (such as the end of female modesty in the 1920s and the consequent destruction of the market for veils), no major changes in dominant fashions (such as the hourglass female form and the end of waist cinchers), no changes in

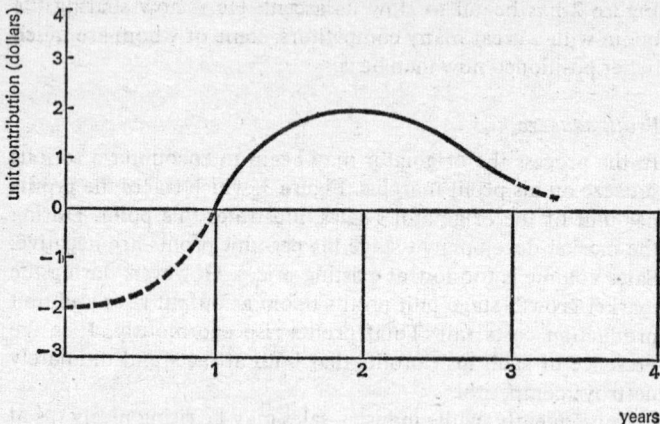

Figure 3 Unit profit contribution life-cycle – originating company

the demand for primary products which use the product in question (such as the effect of the decline of new railroad expansion on the demand for railroad ties), and no changes either in the rate of obsolescence of the product or in the character or introductory rate of product modifications.

Maturity can last for a long time, or it can actually never be attained. Fashion goods and fad items sometimes surge to sudden heights, hesitate momentarily at an uneasy peak and then quickly drop off into total obscurity.

Stage recognition

The various characteristics of the stages described above will help one to recognize the stage a particular product occupies at any given time. But hindsight will always be more accurate than current sight. Perhaps the best way of seeing one's current stage is to try to foresee the next stage and work backwards. This approach has several virtues:

It forces one to look ahead, constantly to try to reforesee one's future and competitive environment. This will have its own rewards. As Charles F. Kettering, perhaps the last of Detroit's primitive inventors and probably the greatest of all its inventors, was fond of saying, 'We should all be concerned about the future because that's where we'll have to spend the rest of our lives'. By looking at the future one can better assess the state of the present.

Looking ahead gives more perspective to the present than looking at the present alone. Most people know more about the present than is good for them. It is neither healthy nor helpful to know the present too well, for our perception of the present is too often too heavily distorted by the urgent pressures of day-to-day events. To know where the present is in the continuum of competitive time and events, it often makes more sense to try to know what the future will bring and when it will bring it, than to try to know what the present itself actually contains.

Finally, the value of knowing what stage a product occupies at any given time resides only in the way that fact is used. But its use is always in the future. Hence a prediction of the future environment in which the information will be used is often more functional for the effective capitalization on knowledge about the present than knowledge about the present itself.

Sequential actions

The life-cycle concept can be effectively employed in the strategy of both existing and new products. For purposes of continuity and clarity, the remainder of this article will describe some of the uses of the concept from the early stages of new product planning through the later stages of keeping the product profitably alive. The chief discussion will focus on what I call a policy of 'life extension' or 'market stretching'.[3]

To the extent that Figures 2 and 3 outline the classical patterns of successful new products, one of the constant aims of the originating producer should be to avoid the severe discipline imposed by an early profit squeeze in the market growth stage, and to avoid the wear and waste so typical of the market maturity stage. Hence the following proposition would seem

3. For related ideas on discerning opportunities for product revivification, see Adler (1964).

reasonable: when a company develops a new product or service, it should try to plan at the very outset a series of actions to be employed at various subsequent stages in the product's existence so that its sales and profit curves are constantly sustained rather than following their usual declining slope.

In other words, advance planning should be directed at extending, or stretching out, the life of the product. It is this idea of *planning in advance* of the actual launching of a new product to take specific actions later in its life cycle – actions designed to sustain its growth and profitability–which appears to have great potential as an instrument of long-term product strategy.

Nylon's life

How this might work for a product can be illustrated by looking at the history of nylon. The way in which nylon's booming sales life has been repeatedly and systematically extended and stretched can serve as a model for other products. What has happened in nylon may not have been purposely planned that way at the outset but the results are quite as if they had been planned.

The first nylon end-uses were primarily military – parachutes, thread, rope. This was followed by nylon's entry into the circular knit market and its consequent domination of the women's hosiery business. Here it developed the kind of steadily rising growth and profit curves that every executive dreams about. After some years these curves began to flatten out. But before they flattened very noticeably, Du Pont had already developed measures designed to revitalize sales and profits. It did several things, each of which is demonstrated graphically in Figure 4. This figure and the explanation which follows take some liberties with the actual facts of the nylon situation in order to highlight the points I wish to make. But they take no liberties with the essential requisites of product strategy.

Point A of Figure 4 shows the hypothetical point at which the nylon curve (dominated at this point by hosiery) flattened out. If nothing further had been done, the sales curve would have continued along the flattened pace indicated by the dotted line at Point A. This is also the hypothetical point at which the first systematic effort was made to extend the product's life. Du Pont, in effect, took certain 'actions' which pushed hosiery sales upward rather than continuing the path implied by the dotted line extension of the curve at Point A. At Point A action 1 pushed an otherwise flat curve upward.

At points B, C, and D still other new sales and profit expansion 'actions' (2, 3, 4, and so forth) were taken. What were these actions? Or, more usefully, what was their strategic content? What did they try to do? They involved strategies that tried to expand sales via four different routes:

1. Promoting more frequent usage of the product among current users.

2. Developing more varied usage of the product among current users.

3. Creating new users for the product by expanding the market.

4. Finding new uses for the basic material.

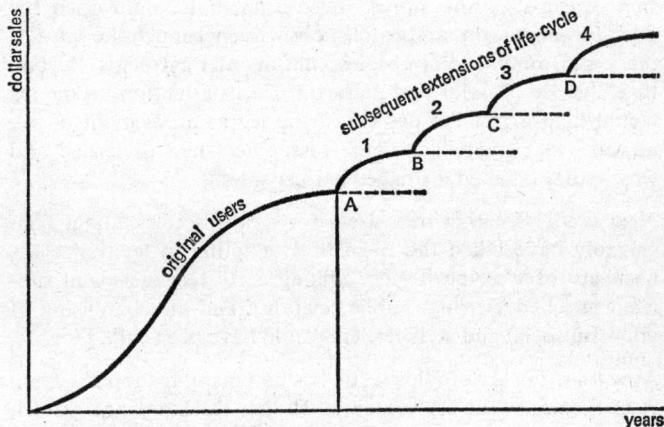

Figure 4 Hypothetical life-cycle – nylon

Frequent usage. Du Pont studies had shown an increasing trend toward 'bareleggedness' among women. This was coincident with the trend towards more casual living and a declining perception among teenagers of what might be called the 'social necessity' of wearing stockings. In the light of those findings, one approach to propping up the flattening sales curves might have been to reiterate the social necessity of wearing stockings at all times. That would have been a sales-building action, though obviously difficult and exceedingly costly. But it could clearly have fulfilled the strategy of promoting more frequent usage among current users as a means of extending the product's life.

Varied usage. For Du Pont, this stategy took the form of an attempt to promote the 'fashion smartness' of tinted hose and later of patterned and highly textured hosiery. The idea was to raise each woman's inventory of hosiery by obsolescing the perception of hosiery as a fashion staple that came only in a narrow range of browns and pinks. Hosiery was to be converted from a 'neutral' accessory to a central ingredient of fashion, with a 'suitable' tint and pattern for each outer garment in the lady's wardrobe.

This not only would raise sales by expanding women's hosiery wardrobes and stores' inventories, but would open the door for annual tint and pattern obsolescence much the same as there is an annual color obsolescence in outer garments. Beyond that, the use of color and pattern to focus attention on the leg would help arrest the decline of the leg as an element of sex appeal – a trend which some researchers had discerned and which, they claimed, damaged hosiery sales.

New users. Creating new users for nylon hosiery might conceivably have taken the form of attempting to legitimize the necessity of wearing hosiery among early teenagers and sub-teenagers. Advertising, public relations, and merchandising of youthful social and style leaders would have been called for.

New uses. For nylon, this tactic has had many triumphs – from varied types of hosiery, such as stretch stockings and stretch socks, to new uses, such as rugs, tires, bearings and so forth. Indeed, if there had been no further product innovations designed to create new uses for nylon after the original military, miscellaneous and circular knit uses, nylon consumption in 1962 would have reached a saturation level at approximately fifty million pounds annually.

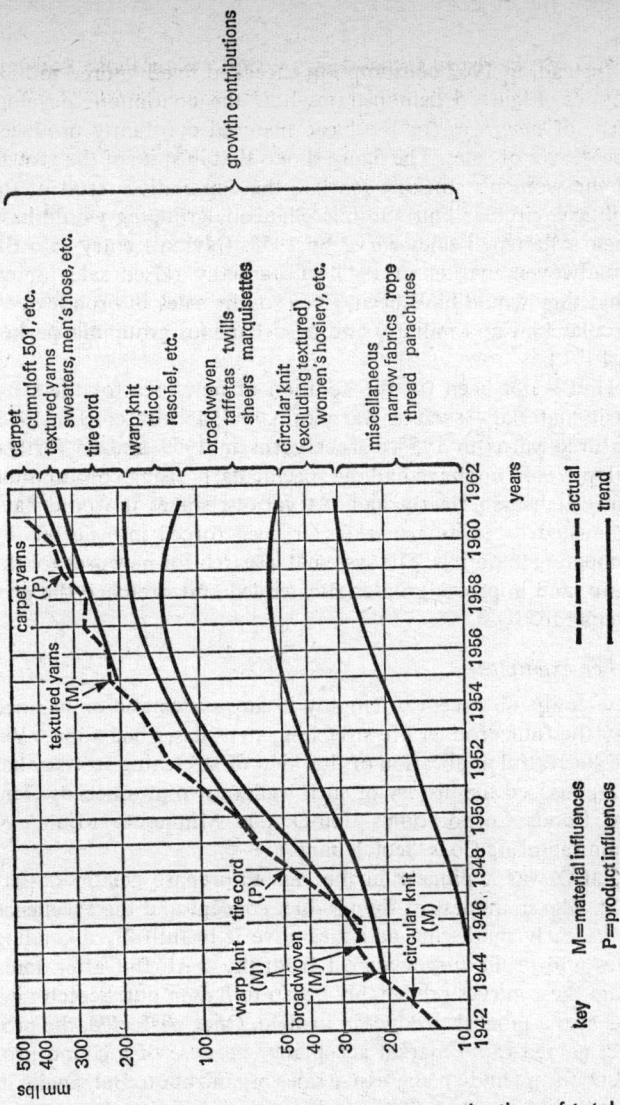

Figure 5 Innovation of new products postpones the time of total maturity – nylon industry (*Modern Textiles Magazine,* vol. 9. 1964, p. 33)

Instead, in 1962 consumption exceeded five hundred million pounds. Figure 5 demonstrates how the continuous development of new uses for the basic material constantly produced new waves of sales. The figure shows that in spite of the growth of the women's stocking market, the cumulative result of the military, circular knit and miscellaneous grouping would have been a flattened sales curve by 1958. (Nylon's entry into the broadwoven market in 1944 substantially raised sales above what they would have been. Even so, the sales of broadwoven, circular knit and military and miscellaneous groupings peaked in 1957.)

Had it not been for the addition of new uses for the same basic material – such as warp knits in 1945, tire cord in 1948, textured yarns in 1955, carpet yarns in 1959 and so forth – nylon would not have had the spectacularly rising consumption curve it has so clearly had. At various stages it would have exhausted its existing markets or been forced into decline by competing materials. The systematic search for new uses for the basic (and improved) material extended and stretched the product's life.

Other examples

Few companies seem to employ in any systematic or planned way the four product life-stretching steps described above. Yet the successful application of this kind of stretching strategy has characterized the history of such well-known products as General Foods Corporation's 'Jell-O' and Minnesota Mining & Manufacturing Co.'s 'Scotch' tape.[4]

Jell-O was a pioneer in the easy-to-prepare gelatin dessert field. The soundness of the product concept and the excellence of its early marketing activities gave it beautifully ascending sales and profit curves almost from the start. But after some years these curves predictably began to flatten out. Scotch tape was also a pioneer product in its field. Once perfected, the product gained rapid market acceptance because of a sound product concept and an aggressive sales organization. But, again, in time the sales and profit curves began to flatten out. Before they

4. I am indebted to my colleague, Dr Derek A. Newton, for these examples and other helpful suggestions.

flattened out very much, however, 3M, like General Foods, had already developed measures to sustain the early pace of sales and profits.

Both of these companies extended their products' lives by, in effect, doing all four of the things Du Pont did with nylon – creating more frequent usage among current users, more varied usage among current users, new users, and new uses for the basic 'materials':

1. The General Foods approach to increasing the frequency of serving Jell-O among current users was, essentially, to increase the number of flavors. From Don Wilson's famous 'six delicious flavors', Jell-O moved up to over a dozen. On the other hand, 3M helped raise sales among its current users by developing a variety of handy Scotch tape dispensers which made the product easier to use.

2. Creation of more varied usage of Jell-O among current dessert users involved its promotion as a base for salads and the facilitation of this usage by the development of a variety of vegetable flavored Jell-O's. Similarly, 3M developed a line of colored, patterned, waterproof, invisible and write-on Scotch tapes which have enjoyed considerable success as sealing and decorating items for holiday and gift wrapping.

3. Jell-O sought to create new users by pinpointing people who could not accept Jell-O as a popular dessert or salad product. Hence during the Metrecal boom Jell-O employed an advertising theme that successfully affixed to the product a fashion-oriented weight control appeal. Similarly, 3M introduced 'Rocket' tape, a product much like Scotch tape but lower in price, and also developed a line of commercial cellophane tapes of various widths, lengths and strengths. These actions broadened product use in commercial and industrial markets.

4. Both Jell-O and 3M have sought out new uses for the basic material. It is known, for example, that women consumers use powdered gelatin dissolved in liquids as a means of strengthening their fingernails. Both men and women use it in the same way as a bone-building agent. Hence Jell-O introduced a 'completely flavorless' Jell-O for just these purposes. 3M has also developed new uses for the basic material – from 'double-

coated' tape (adhesive on both sides) which competes with ordinary liquid adhesives, to the reflecting tape which festoons countless automobile bumpers, to marker strips which compete with paint.

Extension strategies

The existence of the kinds of product life-cycles illustrated in Figures 1 and 2 and the unit profit cycle in Figure 3 suggests that there may be considerable value for people involved in new product work to begin planning for the extension of the lives of their products even before these products are formally launched. To play for new life-extending infusions of effort (as in Figure 4) at this pre-introduction stage can be extremely useful in three profoundly important ways.

1. *It generates an active rather than a reactive product policy.*

It systematically structures a company's long-term marketing and product development efforts in advance, rather than each effort or activity being merely a stop-gap response to the urgent pressures of repeated competitive thrusts and declining profits. The life-extension view of product policy enforces thinking and planning ahead – thinking in some systematic way about the moves likely to be made by potential competitors, about possible changes in consumer reactions to the product and the required selling activities which best take advantage of these conditional events.

2. *It lays out a long-term plan designed to infuse new life into the product at the right time, with the right degree of care, and with the right amount of effort.*

Many activities designed to raise the sales and profits of existing products or materials are often undertaken without regard to their relationship to each other or to timing – the optimum point of consumer readiness for such activities or the point of optimum competitive effectiveness. Careful advance planning, long before the need for such activity arises, can help assure that the timing, the care and the efforts are appropriate to the situation.

For example, it appears extremely doubtful that the boom in women's hair coloring and hair tinting products would have been as spectacular if vigorous efforts to sell these products had preceded the boom in hair sprays and chemical hair fixers. The latter helped create a powerful consumer consciousness of hair fashions because they made it relatively easy to create and wear fashionable hair styles. Once it became easy for women to have fashionable hair styles, the resulting fashion consciousness helped open the door for hair colors and tints. It could not have happened the other way around, with colors and tints first creating fashion consciousness and thus raising the sales of sprays and fixers. Because understanding the reason for this precise order of event is essential for appreciating the importance of early pre-introduction life-extension planning, it is useful to go into a bit of detail. Consider:

For women, setting their hair has been a perennial problem for centuries. First, the length and treatment of their hair is one of the most obvious ways in which they distinguish themselves from men. Hence to be attractive in that distinction becomes crucial. Second, hair frames and highlights the face, much like an attractive wooden border frames and highlights a beautiful painting. Thus hair styling is an important element in accentuating the appearance of a woman's facial features. Third, since the hair is long and soft, it is hard to hold in an attractive arrangement. It gets mussed in sleep, wind, damp weather, sporting activities and so forth.

Therefore, the effective *arrangement* of a woman's hair is understandably her first priority in hair care. An unkempt brunette would gain nothing from making herself into a blond. Indeed, in a country where blonds are in the minority, the switch from being an unkempt brunette to being an unkempt blond would simply draw attention to her sloppiness. But once the problem of arrangement became easily 'solved' by sprays and fixers, colors and tints could become big business, especially among women whose hair was beginning to turn gray.

The same order of priorities applies in industrial products. For example, it seems quite inconceivable that many manufacturing plants would easily have accepted the replacement of the old single-spindle, constantly man-tended screw machine by a computerized tape-tended, multiple-spindle machine. The mechanical tending of the multiple-spindle machine was a necessary intermediate step, if for no other reason than that it required a lesser work-flow change and certainly a lesser conceptual leap for the companies and the machine-tending workers involved.

For Jell-O, it is unlikely that vegetable flavors would have been very successful before the idea of gelatin as a salad base had been pretty well accepted. Similarly, the promotion of colored and patterned Scotch tape as a gift and decorative seal might not have been as successful if department stores had not, as the result of their drive to compete more effectively with mass merchandisers by offering more customer services, previously demonstrated to the consumer what could be done to wrap and decorate gifts.

3. *Perhaps the most important benefit of engaging in advance, pre-introduction planning for sales-extending, market-stretching activities later in the product's life is that this practice forces a company to adopt a wider view of the nature of the product it is dealing with.*

Indeed, it may even force the adoption of a wider view of the company's business. Take the case of Jell-O. What is its product? Over the years Jell-O has become the brand umbrella for a wide range of dessert products, including cornstarch-base puddings, pie fillings, and the new 'Whip'n Chill', a light dessert product similar to a Bavarian Creme or French Mousse. On the basis of these products, it might be said that the Jell-O Division of General Foods is in the 'dessert technology' business.

In the case of tape, perhaps 3M has gone even further in this technological approach to its business. It has a particular expertise (technology) on which it has built a constantly expanding business. This expertise can be said to be that of bonding things (adhesives in the case of Scotch tape) to other things, particularly to thin materials. Hence we see 3M developing scores of profitable items, including electronic recording tape (bonding electron-sensitive materials to tape), and 'Thermo-Fax' duplicating equipment and supplies (bonding heat reactive materials to paper).

Conclusion

For companies interested in continued growth and profits, successful new product strategy should be viewed as a planned totality that looks ahead over some years. For its own good, new product strategy should try to predict in some measure the likelihood, character and timing of competitive and market events. While prediction is always hazardous and seldom very accurate, it is undoubtedly far better than not trying to predict at all. In fact, every product strategy and every business decision inescapably involves making a prediction about the future, about the market and about competitors. To be more systematically aware of the predictions one is making so that one acts on them in an offensive rather than a defensive or reactive fashion – this is the real virtue of preplanning for market stretching and product life extension. The result will be a product stategy that includes some sort of *plan for a timed sequence of conditional moves.*

Even before entering the market development stage, the originator should make a judgement regarding the probable length of the product's normal life, taking into account the possibilities of expanding its uses and users. This judgement will also help determine many things – for example, whether to price the product on a skimming or a penetration basis, or what kind of relationship the company should develop with its resellers.

These considerations are important because at each stage in a product's life-cycle each management decision must consider the competitive requirements of the next stage. Thus a decision to establish a strong branding policy during the market growth stage might help to insulate the brand against strong price competition later; a decision to establish a policy of 'protected' dealers in the market development stage might facilitate point-of-sale promotions during the market growth state and so on. In short, having a clear idea of future product development possibilities and market development opportunities should reduce the likelihood of becoming locked into forms of merchandising that might possibly prove undesirable.

This kind of advance thinking about new product strategy helps management avoid other pitfalls. For instance, advertising campaigns that look successful from a short-term view may hurt in the next stage of the life-cycle. Thus at the outset Metrecal advertising used a strong medical theme. Sales boomed until imitative competitors successfully emphasized fashionable slimness. Metrecal had projected itself as the dietary for the overweight consumer, an image that proved far less appealing than that of being the dietary for people who were fashion-smart. But Metrecal's original appeal had been so strong and so well made that it was a formidable task later on to change people's impressions about the product. Obviously, with more careful long-range planning at the outset, a product's image can be more carefully positioned and advertising can have more clearly defined objectives.

Recognizing the importance of an orderly series of steps in the introduction of sales-building 'actions' for new products should be a central ingredient of long-term product planning. A carefully pre-planned program for market expansion, even before a new product is introduced, can have powerful virtues. The establishment of a rational plan for the future can also help to guide the direction and pace of the on-going technical research in support of the product. Although departures from such a plan will surely have to be made to accommodate unexpected events and revised judgements, the plan puts the company in a better position to *make* things happen rather than constantly having to react to things that *are* happening.

It is important that the originator does *not* delay this long-term planning until after the product's introduction. How the product should be introduced and the many uses for which it might be promoted at the outset should be a function of a careful consideration of the optimum sequence of suggested product appeals and product uses. Consideration must focus not just on optimum things to do, but as importantly on their optimum *sequence* – for instance, what the order of use of various appeals should be and what the order of suggested product uses should be. If Jell-O's first suggested use had been as a diet food, its chances of later making a big and easy impact in the gelatin dessert market undoubtedly would have been greatly diminished. Similarly, if nylon hosiery had been promoted at the outset as a functional daytime-wear hosiery, its ability to replace silk as the acceptable high-fashion hosiery would have been greatly diminished.

To illustrate the virtue of pre-introduction planning for a

product's later life, suppose a company has developed a non-patentable new product – say, an ordinary kitchen salt shaker. Suppose that nobody now has any kind of shaker. One might say, before launching it, that (1) it has a potential market of x million household, institutional and commercial consumers, (2) in two years market maturity will set in, and (3) in one year profit margins will fall because of the entry of competition. Hence, once might lay out the following plan:

1. *End of first year: expand market among current users*
Ideas – new designs, such as sterling shaker for formal use, 'masculine' shaker for barbecue use, antique shaker for 'Early American' households, miniature shaker for each table place setting, moisture-proof design for beach picnics.

2. *End of second year: expand market to new users*
Ideas – designs for children, quaffer design for beer drinkers in bars, design for sadists to rub salt into open wounds.

3. *End of third year: find new uses*
Ideas – make identical product for use as a pepper shaker, as decorative garlic salt shaker, shaker for household scouring powder, shaker to sprinkle silicon dust on parts being machined in machine shops, and so forth.

This effort to prethink methods of reactivating a flattening sales curve far in advance of its becoming flat enables product planners to assign priorities to each task and to plan future production expansion and capital and marketing requirements in a systematic fashion. It prevents one's trying to do too many things at once, results in priorities being determined rationally instead of as accidental consequences of the timing of new ideas, and disciplines both the product development effort that is launched in support of a product's growth and the marketing effort that is required for its continued success.

References

ADLER, L. (1964), 'A new orientation for plotting a marketing strategy', *Bus. Horizons*, Winter, p. 37.

COX, R., ALDERSON, W., and SHAPIRO, S. J. (eds.) (1964), *Theory in Marketing*, Irwin.

KOTLER, P. (1965), 'Phasing out weak products', *Harv. Bus. Rev.*, vol. 43, no. 2, pp. 107–18.

MATTHEWS, J. B. Jr, BUZZELL, R. D., LEVITT, T., and FRANK, R. E. (1964), *Marketing: An Introductory Analysis*, McGraw-Hill.

SCHWARTZ, G. (1963), *Development of Marketing Theory*, South-Western.

11 C. McIver

Prosperity Comes from Products

C. McIver, 'Prosperity comes from products', *Management Today,
Annual Review of Management Techniques*, 1970, pp. 53–5.

It is said that Mrs Beeton's original recipe for jugged hare
(which does not appear in my new, improved edition) began
with the instruction 'first catch your hare'. A recipe for systematic new product development must begin at least as far
back – with snaring the basic idea that can be developed into a
successful new product. Any company which intends to launch a
succession of new products over the years (and a company without such intention has a limited life expectancy) should therefore start by agreeing, at top management level, a specific policy
for product development.

The new product policy statement – part of the corporate plan
if the company has become sufficiently formal – will provide
guidelines for the individual or group responsible for developing
and launching new products. It must not be so rigid as to exclude the off-beat bright ideas that can spring up anywhere,
given a favourable company climate, but it should be precise
enough to ensure that the programme of new products for development over, say, a ten-year period is reasonably coherent
and manageable. It should also save the marketing manager a
nightmare, when the board suddenly discovers that the only
thing that can save next year's turnover and profit is a successful
new product.

A new product policy statement should contain the following
elements:

1. The contribution to the company's turnover and profits expected of new products annually over the forward planning
period.

2. The acceptable minimum turnover and profit contribution for individual products.

3. The approximate amounts the company is prepared to invest in new product development.

4. A decision on whether acquisition, licensing, joint ventures, etc. are acceptable alternatives to internal development.

5. Identification of the market sectors in which the company intends to grow strong.

6. Recognition of the marketing, manufacturing and other skills which must be developed simultaneously.

7. A conscious appreciation of the type of business the company intends to be, in five or ten years' time, and the image it intends to project to the customer.

Usually, the answers to these questions are vaguely known to the management of a reasonably purposeful company. But anyone lumbered with responsibility for new product development would be well advised to get them specifically written down in his terms of reference – and to make sure there is provision for revising them as conditions change.

The appointment of a senior executive to spend much – if not all – of his time on devising, developing and agonizing over new products is the second step towards a successful product launch. Most companies have good intentions about new products but very few have good records. The reason, as often as not, is that nobody in the company – or at least nobody with sufficient status to make his voice heard – is totally committed to success in this area. It is simply not enough to write into the marketing manager's job specification that he 'will have a major responsibility for the development and introduction of new products'. He may well take this statement seriously, but when there is a crisis affecting one of the company's established lines (and when is there not some kind of crisis?) he cannot be expected to neglect the emergency to concentrate on a project that will, with luck, earn a profit the year after next. And time pressures apart, creating the company's future and administering its present call for separate qualities which may or may not be found in the same man.

A product development and diversification manager (a snappier title would be preferable) will not, if he is the right man for the job, demand a staff and start a period of Parkinsonian growth in personnel that a young company can ill afford. The product development manager's job is to find ideas, convert them into three-dimensional, marketable products and insinuate them as painlessly as possible into the company's day-to-day activities. He needs to work not alone but through other people. He needs to establish fruitful relationships with research and development, with production, sales and marketing, with the finance department and with general management that must provide the backing necessary to overcome organizational inertia.

The search for ideas will need to extend much further afield than the factory gates. The product development manager must study the market place, read not just the trade papers but a little sociology and perhaps even science fiction as well; he must visit trade fairs, get to know the industry and its research institutions, and talk with customers. He will certainly need access to design and R & D facilities, but he need not have them under his own control. Introducing products into the company's day-to-day operations is also better done through personal contacts with departmental managers, and *ad hoc* committees, than by building up a rival department. A one-man to three-man department, making use of outside as well as company facilities, is likely to be the most productive.

Management climate – a readiness by all concerned to say *oui* rather than *non* to new ideas – is, of course, at least as important as organization. Naturally, climate cannot be controlled to order but the chief executive's attitude will have a considerable bearing upon it, and his attitude toward innovation, in particular, could well be a critical factor. After living for a hundred years on the invention of a camera or a custard, it is unrealistic to assume that there will be no end to your prosperity, or that you can always invent another to carry the company through the next hundred years. Most new products are only modest improvements on existing products; most, if they are successful and are not invented more or less simultaneously by competing companies, will be imitated in very

C. McIver 201

short order. But most, in any case, betray the fond hopes of their progenitors by failing ever to earn an adequate profit. It is wise, therefore, where new products are concerned, not only to do the best possible job for each individual product but to seek safety in numbers.

Coming now to the actual steps towards a new product launch, the first stage might be labelled 'exploration' (or catching the hare). At this first stage an inescapable preliminary is a certain amount of *market research* – a detailed analysis of the market the company has decided to attack, and some form of motivational research to investigate consumer/trade needs and attitudes towards the product category. 'A certain amount' of research simply because at this early stage, as at every subsequent stage, the question of cost-input has to be considered in relation to potential profit-output. If the project is a major one, a five-figure research budget could be appropriate; if it is a minor one, unlikely to cost very much if it fails, or to earn very much if it succeeds, poor man's research may be all that can be afforded – desk research to quantify the market and small sample motivational studies among first-hand buyers (retailers or distributors) and consumers.

At the end of the research phase management should have a fairly clear idea of the size of the market and its overall growth rate, the sectors which are expanding and those which are in decline, the relative importance of different channels of distribution, the strengths and marketing methods of competitors, the extent to which distributors are happy about competitors' products and commercial methods, the basic physical requirements for a product to survive in the market, requirements for packaging and transportation, the pricing and terms structure that must be aimed at. On the basis of this information, the product development manager can then engage in some version of *gap analysis* – a procedure which has been elevated into a fairly elaborate technique but which boils down to the commonsense intellectual exercise of looking for a hole in the market (a neglected consumer group or section of the trade, a deficiency in existing products, a technical development capable of exploitation) which it is within the capacity of the company to fill.

Having picked its market, the company can choose between the high road of genuine originality and the low road of plagiarism (in a multiple new product development programme the two are not, of course, mutually exclusive). If it opts for the high road, it may well go on from gap analysis to the technique of *concept testing*. In its aboriginal form this consists, in effect, of asking a sample of consumers to choose between verbal descriptions of alternative versions of the company's gap-filling new product idea, and it suffers from the defect of all verbalizations, that words mean different things to different people. If the alternatives can be presented in mock-up form the response may be more significant, but consumers' assessments of products they cannot touch or taste or try out is still highly unreliable.

A more useful technique in the exploration stage is *brainstorming*, eliciting ideas from individuals of different disciplines – scientists, production men, researchers, designers, sales and marketing people brought together so that they interact with one another – on how to fill the identified market gap. The productiveness of brainstorming sessions depends very much on the atmosphere that the discussion leader creates; if he is successful in banishing embarrassment about putting forward half-witted ideas, yet prevents the meeting wandering from the point, the sessions can be very worthwhile. But whether concepts testing is used, or brainstorming, or simply a wet towel around the product development manager's head, the high road exploration process should lead to a number of alternative marketing briefs for research or development, detailing the physical specifications, performance characteristics and cost area to be aimed for. Little need be said about the low road of plagiarism except that it is as well not to be too contemptuous of it. Even large companies with powerful marketing departments and expensive research establishments will admit that some of their most cost-effective product development exercises have resulted from picking up a product already on the market (perhaps in another country) and either imitating it or buying up its manu-

facturer, or arranging to make it under license.

The exploration stage should end (only to begin again, of course, with exploration into the next group or generation of products) with a number of prototype products or ideas, the best of which can be selected to go forward to the second stage of 'development'. This stage should be much more controlled – by the two disciplines of time and money. The financial discipline will begin to be felt with a first attempt at a *product budget*, forecasting both development costs and the cash flow generated by the product over its expected lifetime – a forecast which must initially be highly speculative and will require periodic revision as the project becomes firmer. There are three good reasons for budgeting and rebudgeting through the development stage of a product development project. First, obviously, it helps management to keep the negative cash flow of the development period in some reasonable relationship to the eventual inflow that is hoped for; it avoids, in fact, spending more on developing its Concorde than can possibly be recovered in profit from forecast sales. Second, it forces management to consider the long-term financial implications of the project and make sure that the company has the resources to support it right through to the end. And third, each successive budgetary review offers an opportunity to liquidate the project if it becomes clear that the chances of success are minimal.

The discipline of time can be imposed in the form of a *critical path* network – one of the few business school techniques that has been widely accepted in everyday use. Timing can be vitally important in new product development. A product that misses this year's selling season may well be superseded or outmoded next year, yet attempts to short-circuit the development stage by neglecting checks on product performance, storage, transportation, consumer acceptance etc. frequently end in expensive disaster. Network analysis should make it possible to shorten the development period for the typical packaged consumer product by running development of (and tests on) the product itself in parallel with the development of packaging, advertising and promotional material. And time and cost can be kept under control by insisting that the critical decisions on ordering machinery, material and so on, are made by the cut-off dates.

If the product is a consumer product, the development stage should end, whenever possible, with a test in which the new product in its fully developed form is assessed, by a panel of consumers from the target market sector, against a standard – usually the current market leader. New products have successfully been introduced which failed to win a majority vote in this final test; sometimes popular taste is so conditioned to a dominant brand that even an objectively 'better' product will not at first be liked as well. But normally it is foolhardy to go ahead with a product launch without clear evidence that it is superior to established products – in the opinion of the customer as well as the manufacturer – at least in the characteristic on which it will be promoted.

By now the product should be as near right as successive modifications, plus laboratory and consumer testing, can make it. The marketing plan forecasts a break-even point after eighteen months and a healthy profit thereafter, provided that sales targets are met. There remains only the stage of 'implementation' – getting out and selling the thing.

The immediate question is – to test market or not to test market? Because the giant toiletry and food manufacturers (who have pioneered scientific marketing in this country) have made a practice of *test marketing* their new products, it has become almost an article of marketing dogma that every new consumer product should, before being launched nationally, first be sold in a limited area (almost invariably a TV region) with a scaled-down version of the national advertising and promotional plan. Of course this technique makes sense when the greater part of the new product's investment is not poured into plant and machinery (it may well be made on existing machinery) but consists of a million pounds of advertising and promotional money spent in the first year of national selling to buy a substantial share of the market. To spend say, 5 per cent or 10 per cent of this sum in a test area, getting the bugs out of the marketing plan and proving that the target market share is in fact attainable, has obvious attractions. But there is a price to be paid for test marketing, not least that it delays the national launch by a year or so – while results are evaluated and re-ordering patterns established – and thus gives competitors time to study the product and its marketing methods and prepare their counter measures. In many cases, particularly when there have been adequate small-scale tests of the individual factors that can go wrong, it may be more sensible to go straight into the national launch and accept the greater financial risk involved.

By the time of the national launch (or test market, if there is one) the product development manager will almost certainly have handed over the product and responsibility for it to the marketing manager. The product that has become a subject of major importance in his own life is now, in all probability, something of a nuisance to others. It may be a nuisance to the sales force who must take time out from selling the company's established lines; it may be a nuisance to distributors who must decide whether or not to find space for it (a large retail buyer will be offered a score or more of new products every month each of which seems much more indispensable to the salesman than to the buyer); it may be a nuisance even for the customer, for whom it was designed, if its purchase demands a change of habit or the direct mail used to promote it clutters his waste bin.

If nuisance is to be accepted, the launch must contain provisions for establishing temporary superiority over competition both outside and inside the company. For the salesmen, excitement must be created by the way the product and its role are presented, by the supporting promotional material and (if this is consistent with the company's incentives policy) by differential rewards for selling the new product on top of established lines. For retailers there must be some form of introductory offer, enabling them both to buy on special terms and to pass on some special inducement to the consumer to encourage an initial purchase; and, even more important, there must be reasonably convincing evidence – based on the initial market research, product and consumer tests – that the product meets a real need and a continuing demand is likely.

For consumers of the product it is essential to provide enough promotional support, both through media advertising and at the point of sale, to create at least an awareness of the product's existence amid a hubbub of competing promotions. All of this, of course, costs money, which is why the principle of a two or three-year pay-out for new products with a reasonably long life expectancy has been widely adopted for consumer products – accepting, for example, a substantial loss in the first year, a breakeven in the second year and recovery of the first year's losses in the third before the product starts becoming properly profit-earning. It is also why the principle of *segmentation*, according to which a company concentrates its promotional fire on a selected market sector instead of dissipating it over too wide a target, has become so important.

Obviously, success is not guaranteed by following the marketing rule book. The casualty rate in new product launches is extremely high. Yet the possible causes of disaster are so varied, and the imaginative and creative (as opposed to the purely rational) elements in a product launch are so significant, that innumerable cases can be quoted where no mistakes were made – at least that could be identified until after the event – and the whole operation was still a resounding flop. All that can reasonably be expected is that adopting an organized and rational procedure for product development, with special emphasis on the preliminary research and planning stages, will increase the success rate sufficiently to justify the extra cost in time, money and management effort. Perhaps that claim is enough.

12 C. Berenson

Pruning the Product Line

C. Berenson, 'Pruning the product line', *Business Horizons*,
Summer 1963, pp. 63–70.

In recent years, a great deal of attention has centered upon
problems associated with the introduction of new products.
While this emphasis has been productive and valuable, it has
tended to obscure another part of the product-line complex: the
concomitant problems of eliminating unprofitable items. Yet
the firm's profits and future health can suffer unless the product
line is effectively pruned; the retention of marginal products
constitutes a significant barrier to increased profits and lessens
the firm's ability to adapt to a changing environment.

The whole subject of product elimination has been neglected
by marketing managers and economists. The literature on product abandonment is extremely sparse and vaguely defined; no
body of knowledge exists that can be referred to for guidance in
this area. A comprehensive perspective cannot be obtained
through a synthesis of the small amounts of isolated data and
bits and pieces of information lodged in many places. The
formulation of a new concept would require a different evaluative approach toward product abandonment decisions and
would force the analyst to do primary research involving a
multitude of factors and a labyrinth of detail.

The purpose of this article is to present a conceptual framework for structuring into a uniform and cohesive entity the numerous factors that bear on product abandonment decisions.
The structure is built upon a thorough mining of the literature
of marketing, management, psychology, finance and politics, as
well as on extensive field work with many firms and executives.
Models developed from it have been tested and found to be
operationally useful. With this framework as a guide, it is possible to handle long and complicated chains of reasoning sys-

tematically and to weigh all variables in compatible terms. Within the framework, widely disparate viewpoints concerning criteria for product abandonment are reconciled. The result should be an effective tool for pruning the product line.

The traditional approaches

Before trying the new approach, it will be helpful to set the stage by reviewing some traditional lines of thought. Product abandonment has traditionally been dominated by four different viewpoints: the accountant's, the economist's, the sales manager's, and, perhaps to a lesser extent, the government policy maker's.

The accountant

The accountant's customary view of a product line deletion involves a comparison of the dollar costs of retention with the dollar costs of abandonment. In essence, his approach is concerned with the quantitative aspects of depreciation, current expenditures and revenues. It places great importance on the dollar and cent values of sunk costs. In other words, the accountant's primary emphasis is on quantifiable financial items.

The real virtue of the accounting viewpoint lies in its applicability as a yardstick combining several important criteria. Properly used, it provides a standard for identifying specific products or product groups that need to be closely examined.

But because its confines are narrow, the accounting viewpoint has dangerous limitations. It does not indicate the possible market effects of dropping a product. Nor does it measure profitability in relation to the life-cycle of a product, the stage of product development, or the product's potential. These shortcomings necessitate the adoption of a wider compass in our evaluative procedures.

The economist

The economist has also significantly influenced our mode of thought concerning product abandonment. In a succinct statement of the economist's thinking, product abandonment is a matter of emphasizing the future and leaving the past for the historical record. The prime considerations in this approach are alternative choices and marginal costs. It involves questions of incremental profits – for example, the possibility that the product may be in the black on an out-of-pocket cost basis and can therefore make some contribution to general overhead.

The chief element of strength in the economist's approach is its future orientation and its emphasis on costs and revenue *opportunities*. The economist tries to balance present costs against projections of future revenues and alternative opportunities. He strives to obtain the greatest long-run rate of return and is concerned about distinguishing between products that merely contribute to overhead on a short-term basis and products that show long-term returns on a fully allocated basis.

But we find serious flaws in this major avenue of traditional thought. The element of out-of-pocket cost can be stressed so heavily that it becomes exceedingly difficult to abandon anything; as long as a product returns one dollar above cash costs, it stays in the line. Most economists would claim, no doubt, that this is a badly truncated and distorted version of the proper analytic method. And indeed it is. But it is an all too common version. A spokesman for one of the top ten chemical firms, a mature and experienced executive with large responsibilities, told me recently, 'Perhaps only once or twice in my career have I seen a loser based on out-of-pocket costs.' A second and closely related problem frequently arises from overzealous attention to the out-of-pocket cost criterion, in that alternative opportunities are often slighted in favor of barely marginal products.

The sales manager

In the sales manager's thinking, we might expect to find a synthesis of the accounting and economic viewpoints. It would also seem reasonable to look for evaluative procedures that include consideration of the important intangibles in a marketing strategy. But, in fact, this expectation is usually unfulfilled. The sales manager's approach to pruning the product line has been largely intuitive. It stresses the factors that may make the line easier to sell but not necessarily more profitable – for example, it favors carrying a full line and seeking to build volume at the expense of overall, long-term profit.

The sales manager's opinions receive varying weight in different companies. In some sales-oriented companies, the sales manager's views are heavily discounted for emotional bias, but in other companies the sales manager's full-line argument is accepted without qualification despite its tendency to parochialism. In a recently completed survey of chemical companies, I found that a majority of the firms are strongly inclined to accept as final the judgements of their sales staffs. This attitude is reflected in the statement of a high executive of a major chemical firm: 'If the sales manager says we need it, that's it.' In one of the companies surveyed, I found a product manager making highly optimistic forecasts for his line when more objective study would have revealed a steady downtrend in sales and profits sufficient to warrant elimination of the line. In discussing the problem, one company executive said, 'There are not a host of openings for product managers in large and profitable lines so that here, as in other companies, the present product manager of a marginal line will hesitate before putting himself in the position of starting all over again.'

The extent to which the subjective opinions of the sales manager will influence product decisions depends in part upon the personalities of the individuals involved and their roles in the enterprise. A strong and stubborn individual may retain a product beyond the time when all objective criteria dictate its deletion. Another factor to be considered is that the sales manager frequently tends to emphasize volume rather than profit. Despite its deficiencies, however, the sales manager's outlook is important, for the company image, sales enthusiasm and similar considerations are important factors in an abandonment decision.

The government policy maker

The last of the four principal strands in our traditional thinking on product abandonment is that of government influence. The decision criteria in this case relate to the public interest. The government tends to consider continued satisfaction of the consumer as an overriding criterion. Hence, railroads regulated by the ICC cannot readily abandon trackage or other services when the line as a whole is making a profit. Even in deciding which

C. Berenson 211

plants to close during war emergencies, governments have set aside questions of operating efficiency and market dislocations in an effort to minimize labor dislocation – this policy was characteristic of both the Allies and the Axis powers during the Second World War.

Although the government's views are less relevant to non-regulated industries' policies in peacetime, they remain an important element in product abandonment considerations. Deletion actions taken by the firm today can be the forerunner of government scrutiny tomorrow. The firm's deletion policy, therefore, should recognize that government influence is involved and that, although it is at present relatively inactive, this force is potentially important.

A new conceptual approach

The approaches outlined above reflect the major approaches in traditional product elimination thinking. Unfortunately, individually taken, they raise many questions and answer few. What is the relative importance of these different concepts? How should the firm actually abandon a product? What other criteria should be used to help in determining when to abandon products? Can the study of the factors affecting deletion situations be systematized? These difficult issues are clouded by the fact that the accountant, the economist, the sales manager and the government all have different opinions; each party considers some factor to be of primary importance that another regards as trivial. It is obvious that aid is required to simplify the complex of inter-relationships bearing upon abandonment situations. Without such aid, it would be extremely difficult and risky to reduce these many factors and concepts to clearly stated alternative courses of action.

A framework for integrating the factors germane to product abandonment decisions is shown in analogue form in Figure 1. The presentation is intended to unite concisely and compatibly the significant variables in the product abandonment decision. The factors amenable to quantification and those ordinarily valued only in qualitative terms are combined to provide an orderly context in which deletion decisions can be consistently made.

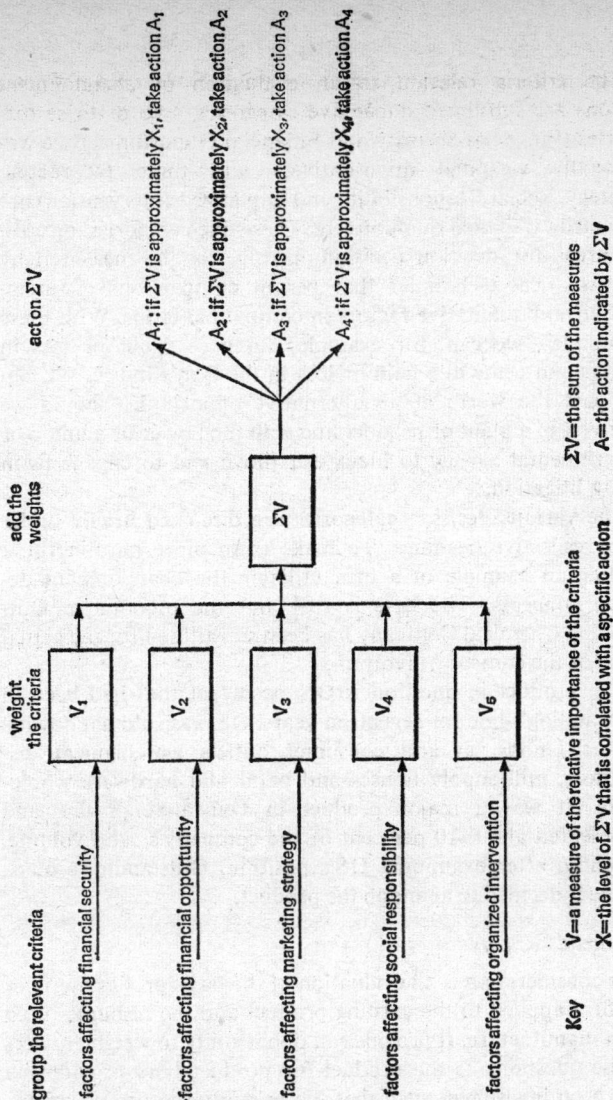

Figure 1 A schematic representation of the general model for product abandonment decisions

The criteria relevant to an evaluation of abandonment actions are subsumed under five categories; two of these categories (Financial Security and Financial Opportunity) are traditionally weighted quantitatively and three (Marketing Strategy, Social Responsibility and Organized Intervention) are ordinarily weighted qualitatively. These five categories, or critical areas for deletion decision-making, can be measured by mathematical techniques that permit comparisons of quantitative and qualitative factors in compatible terms. With these techniques, we can, for example, compare profit or loss in dollars and cents to a gain or loss in the firm's image. We can compare the worth of an alternative opportunity should we disinvest in a plant or product line with the power of a union or governmental agency to block our move and to engage us in costly litigation.

The various decision categories are discussed briefly under their respective headings. To make them more meaningful, I include an example of a firm utilizing the abandonment decision concepts. The case is real, but the pseudonym Outstanding Chemical Company has been substituted for the actual name of the company involved.

The product in question is OS, a solvent that had been in Outstanding's line for seventeen years. OS was sold nationwide to such industrial and consumer outlets as chemical distributors, mill supply houses and paint and hardware wholesalers. It was a major product in Outstanding's line and represented about 10 per cent of the company's sales volume. Recently, after examining OS's position, Outstanding's management decided to abandon the product.

Financial security

This consideration is an evaluation of the basic profit criteria of the firm applied to the existing product and the resources used in its manufacture. It provides an opportunity to weigh answers to the question, 'Is the product (or product line) providing a return on investment such that the *minimum* return on investment desired by management is being achieved?' Naturally, the level of return expected in different industries or segments of an industry will vary considerably. The different goals set for rate of return are merely a reflection of the different risks inherent in these specific fields.

For the past two years, OS had yielded a rate of return below the minimum desired by the company. This fact, taken with other considerations centering about the firm's goals for return on investment (OS's future prospects, for example), indicated an unattractive situation insofar as financial security was concerned. The evaluation of the financial security objective can be quantified by several operations research techniques; the quantification is represented by V_1 (see Figure 1). For illustrative purposes, we can establish a simple scale in which more desirable product prospects are allocated more points than less desirable prospects. In the case of OS, V_1 will receive relatively few points.

Financial opportunity

This consideration provides an opportunity to consider the profitability of the product (or plant, product line, or division) in terms of opportunity costs, phase of the product's life cycle and the amount of return in excess of the firm's minimum goal. The norm set by management merely represents the profit necessary if the firm is to remain in a healthy state; the standard of financial opportunity, however, is a consideration of the firm's opportunity to derive a profit *greater* than the goal set by management. The prime distinction, then, between financial security and financial opportunity is that the former weighs the degree to which the firm's basic profit needs are met, while the latter weighs the effect of alternative opportunities and superior returns.

OS was competing in a saturated market. Outstanding was engaged in battle for its market share with seven strong competitors, each of whom had been in the market for at least ten years. In the twenty years since the product's introduction, the price of OS had been reduced to the point where it had been at a relatively stable low level for five years prior to the date of the abandonment decision. Total industry sales had been constant in these five years while Outstanding's share of the market had declined slightly.

Outstanding's management found that the firm could produce alternative products utilizing the OS plant's equipment, men and resources. It was estimated that these products would provide a return on investment at least 100 per cent greater than that yielded by OS.

A quantitative valuation of these data, via reference to predetermined point schedules set by management, provides V_2. If we assume that V_2 reflects an unattractive financial opportunity, then V_2 will be given relatively few points.

Marketing strategy

Here we consider many factors that are not usually measured in quantifiable terms, or that cannot be so measured. Thus, marketing strategy includes the following: patent and trademark positions, market leadership, market share, marketing agreements, reliability of supply, users' buying habits, number and type of customers, distribution factors, sales force, selling problems, advertising, sales promotion, reciprocity, the company image, corporate objectives, service policies, rounding out the line, emotional involvement and other considerations.

When considering the deletion of a product, all of these factors must be weighed. Legitimate reasons may exist for selling a full line even though certain items will not be profitable. The loss items may contribute to the overall profit of the line, by, for example, giving the salesmen entrée to important accounts. But in many instances, retaining a full line is not worthwhile, and time and energy are wasted on poor performers. The extent to which these strategic factors operate upon any specific situation must, therefore, be weighed; some effort must be made to determine the relative importance of out-of-pocket cost, company image, reciprocity dealings and so on. Only by adopting a viewpoint toward product deletions that incorporates a quantified consideration of strategic elements can one be sure that important parts of the abandonment problem are being considered.

A consideration of the strategic factors surrounding OS indicates that the product's abandonment would not hurt Outstanding very much or for very long. Since Outstanding had been well known as a supplier of OS, the company image would suffer to some extent. Outstanding's management felt that the company's sales force would encounter some resistance in attempting to sell other products in the line to customers who had been purchasing OS. It was believed, however, that Outstanding's new products would soon erase the bad effects of the abandonment.

These strategic factors must be quantified to obtain V_3. Once again using a simple point scale, V_3 can be obtained. In this case, a modest number of points is accorded to V_3, reflecting the fact that while the firm will suffer some harmful effects, these effects are moderate and unlikely to persist for too long.

Social responsibility

The effects of abandonment actions are so widely dispersed that economic dimensions are no longer sufficient to provide a total view of a deletion decision. Starting from the economic and strategic criteria that may apply to contemplated abandonments, it is apparent that the decision areas have moved into the realms of politics and culture. Thus, another problem that must be considered in abandonment decisions is that of social responsibility, that is, the firm's responsibility to its employees, its customers, its suppliers and the communities in which it operates. Although the first responsibility of management is to the enterprise, it is well to note that the business environment has social as well as economic dimensions and that if the former are ignored, the long-term consequences to the firm may well be inimical. It must be borne in mind that in today's business world, the manager is often considered to be a trustee not only for the owners of his firm but for society as a whole.

Social considerations were not a factor in the abandonment of OS. The plant was to be kept open and its labor force employed on new products; some customers might be moderately inconvenienced for a short time, but with seven vigorous alternative suppliers fighting for Outstanding's market share, that possibility did not militate significantly against abandonment.

Once again, quantification of this category can be effected via a point allocation system. The system would give few points to situations in which there is a low degree of social responsibility and more points to cases in which there is a high degree of social responsibility. For OS, V_4 would be negligible.

Organized intervention

This decision category consists of the actual or potential actions of governments or labor unions regarding product abandonment. The government's view has been outlined above. Labor unions' organized intervention in management's product abandonment actions is growing rapidly. At the present, union intervention plays a minor role in the deletion decisions of the vast majority of firms. An executive of one leading chemical company stated, 'It has to be weighed. . . . We recognize it, but it is a minor part of the total picture.' A spokesman for another large chemical firm dismissed the subject as one that could not affect his company by saying, 'We would not sign a union contract that would limit our freedom of action.'

While the conditions that exist in most industries today do not appear to be restrictive in the area of organized intervention, this prospect will undoubtedly change in the future. The government is re-examining its relation to business and to the public, and it appears that a new attitude, one less benevolent toward the corporation, may be formulated. In addition, labor unions have begun to lobby for regulations to discourage plant abandonment. The AFL-CIO recently stated in its policy manual on economic problem areas that '. . . federal action is necessary . . .' and called for collective bargaining agreements that will ease the effects of plant movements.

Management's recognition of this network of restrictive regulations and contracts and its implications for free decision-making is essential. While most abandonments in the past have taken place within the frame of 'enlightened self-interest' on the part of the enterprise, this frame is now threatened. Since enforced recognition of the social obligations of the firm is thoroughly undesirable, management should structure its present and future abandonment policies to reduce the pressure for organized control over abandonments. This requirement may necessitate another look at the amount of enlightenment contained in the self-interest policies that are pursued at the present. Also, it may require that management mount a vigorous attack upon this strangling network of restraints. In any event, the potential for trouble is real – and all considerations of abandonment should encompass a view of this issue.

No threat of organized intervention is found in the case of OS. The labor force will remain employed and the market will continue to be satisfied in a convenient and economical manner. Quantification of this category via a point allocation scheme would result in V_5 receiving a rating of zero (no points).

Adding the weights

Now that all five factors have been quantified, they are added to obtain an overall rating for the product on trial. Referring once again to Figure 1, this overall ranking is termed ΣV. ΣV must now be measured on a yardstick that correlates values of ΣV with the firm's alternative actions.

Let us assume that ΣV in the OS situation was equal to X_1. From Figure 1, the action taken on X_1 is A_1, which (for illustrative purposes only) indicates that OS should be removed from the product line.

What has really been done in developing this new approach is to recognize that the traditional views of product abandonment all have some merit but that no one of them is satisfactory to use as a single criterion for pruning the line. An eclectic path has been taken in integrating the relevant viewpoints of these approaches into a new conceptual frame; this frame has been found to be useful in dealing with abandonments on a logical and consistent basis. With its help, a product that might have been dropped at Monday morning's executive committee meeting would also have been dropped at Thursday afternoon's meeting. Objectivity has been substituted for subjectivity and emotionalism. In addition, a full consideration of all significant factors affecting deletions has replaced a partial analysis of some factors.

The five critical areas are evaluated with a quantitative treatment that permits them to be compared in common terms. Of course, different industries and various companies within an industry will attach different values to the possible actions to be taken in a particular situation. But whatever these values may be, their evaluation within this framework should furnish the manager with the necessary tools for product-line decisions, and should provide the firm with a way to give its products a suitable burial to complement its procedures for a proper birth.

13 A. Gabor

Pricing in Theory and Practice

A. Gabor, 'Pricing in theory and practice', *Management Decision*,
Summer 1967, pp. 28–33.

If you ask a student of economics what price is, he will answer that it is the factor which equates supply with demand. He is likely to add that, in a competitive market, price will tend to settle at a level at which no excess profits are made by the producers and the distributors, while a monopoly will fix prices so that its profits should be at a maximum. It is generally agreed, I think, that whether or not these statements contain an element of truth, they are of no use whatever to the business-man.

If you then ask the man of business what price is, the odds are that he will say it is the cost of the article plus his margin of profit. While this is undoubtedly true, it is not very helpful to the economist and, since it is a mere description rather than a working definition, it gives no effective guidance to the price setter in business either. Clearly, it all turns on the evaluation of cost on the one hand and, on the other hand, on the actual size of the margin which is added to it.

The just price
Before we take up these points, let us briefly consider another aspect of price, the origins of which go back to antiquity, and which has once again become a very live issue. I am referring to the 'just price', that is to say, the price which could be called correct on the basis of social considerations.

In the distant past, the just price of bread and the just wage were annually decided by the justices of the peace; a practice which here and there survived in Britain until the end of the eighteenth century. Controlled prices, as used during both World Wars and for some time after, were not quite the same thing, and this applies also to the guaranteed farm prices decided annually by the Minister of Agriculture, simply because practically all the prices so manipulated were and still are subsidized. Hence there is not one price in each of these instances but two, and the price received by the farmer is often considerably above that paid by the consumer. The proper 'just price', the price which is morally right, is supposed to be one which is accepted as such both by the consumer and the producer, because it serves the community better than any other price possibly could.

In Britain, concern with this problem has received new impetus with the institution of the Prices and Incomes Board, the central task of which is to pronounce social judgements on proposed increases. There exists no set of rules which the members of the Board could use as a guide line, but one or two observers have given expression to the hope that some sort of principle will eventually arise out of their decisions. So far this has not been substantiated.[1]

Signs of a revival of the belief in the just price are also visible in the United States. While the typical American businessman is still likely to proclaim that any profit is *ipso facto* justified if you can get away with it, housewives have, on occasion, effectively forced supermarkets to reduce their prices to an earlier level or at least to abstain from increasing them further.

Both in Britain and in America the main concern seems to be the maintenance of the *status quo* and this helps to give us an idea of what the just price means to the man in the street or, perhaps more properly, to the housewife in the supermarket. It appears that it is simply the customary price, and since human life is short and human memory even shorter, it can often be identified as the ruling price during a recent period of relative stability.[2]

A fundamentally different approach to the problem can be discerned in the East. Until 1955, the official doctrine of the Soviet Union was that the prices arbitrarily determined by the planners were unquestionably correct, even though at the retail

1. See Wray (1966). For a collection of earlier views on the related issue of wages, see Healy (1966).
2. There are exceptions to this rule; see Gabor and Granger (1965).

level practically all of them either included a heavy tax or were artificially lowered below the cost of production by a subsidy. Then this doctrine was suddenly dropped and Soviet economists were encouraged to develop the principles on which a just structure of prices should be based. The public discussion which ensued has been going on for the last eleven years and has not so far been closed. It has produced a number of ingenious propositions, some of which are in fact being tried out in the USSR and certain other countries within the Soviet sphere. Their essence is the abandonment of the original idea of the just price because, in one form or another, they tend to reassert the law of the market.

Let us take another look at this issue. It is of course agreed that a price which does justice both to the producer and to the consumer must cover cost and also a reasonable reward to the producer and the distributors, and this leads us back to the point which we were to take up again. So the question is now how costs are to be defined for this purpose and how wide the 'just' profit margin should be. We shall deal with profits first and with the problems of cost determination afterwards.

Profitability and other business aims

There can be little doubt that the first aim of any business is survival. This is certainly true in the field of private enterprise, and even the nationalized corporations were enjoined in the nationalization acts to avoid losses at least in the long run, taking one year with another.

There are times when survival alone is justifiably looked upon as a creditable achievement. Such a time was the Great Depression of the 1930s and, in some respects, the present period of the squeeze also falls into this category. It is small wonder that the device known as the break-even chart was born in the depression period and hailed at the time as a useful guide to the businessman. Today it has once again become relevant.

In Figure 1, B is the break-even point which indicates the minimum volume of sales M required to keep the firm out of the red. In a way, this is useful knowledge but it should be noted that it is based on some pretty bold assumptions. Total sales returns are shown as strictly proportionate to the volume of sales, which means that prices are supposed to be invariant, and also that the product-mix remains the same whatever the total quantity sold. Furthermore, it assumes that costs can strictly be divided into two categories: overheads which do not vary with the output (F), and direct costs which vary proportionately with the output. This is not always unacceptable in the region of the break-even point, but if the chart is of any help at all, it is only in connection with the first aim of a business which is, as we said, survival.

True success, however, is more than just staying alive. It means also profitability and this is an issue which deserves closer consideration.

Striving for profits is described in economics as profit maxi-

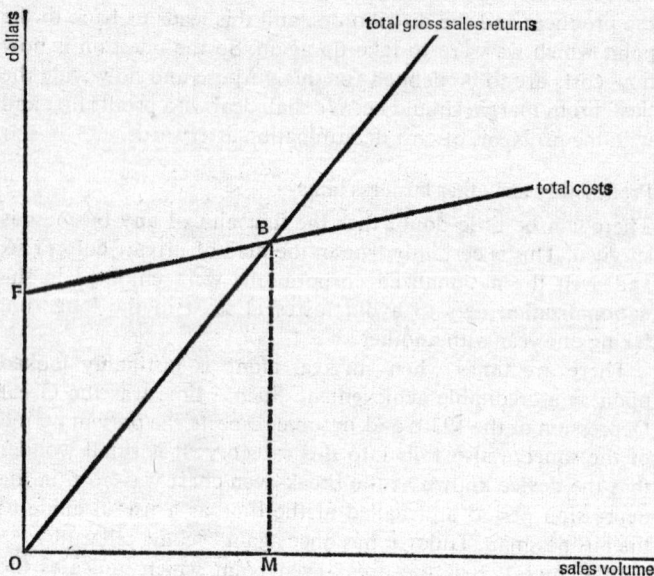

Figure 1 Break-even chart showing relationship between volume of sales and total sales returns. This assumes that overheads, prices and product-mix all remain constant, while direct costs alone vary proportionately with output

mization; a term which does not seem to appeal to businessmen. If asked, they will usually say that they are striving for a reasonable rate of profit, not maximum profits. However, if we press the issue further, and ask why they are not charging higher prices, the answer is likely to be that this would have a detrimental effect on sales. If now we ask why don't they reduce their prices, they will say that this would not help either. In some cases they will be afraid of starting a price war, in other cases the belief will be expressed that the customers would welcome the decrease in price but would not thereby be induced to buy more. Summing up, what the businessman has told us is that he can see no way in which he could increase his profits and this is, of course, exactly what the economist means by profit maximization.

It cannot be denied that there are exceptions to such behaviour. There exist businessmen, mostly in charge of relatively small firms, who deliberately restrict their activities, who feel sure that they could make higher profits if they were prepared to work harder and assume greater risks and responsibilities; there are others who refuse to avail themselves of an opportunity of increasing their profits because this would mean that they would not any longer be in sole charge of their enterprise. The aims of such people may not in every instance be in harmony with the national interest, but they are legitimate all the same. Safety, independence and the quiet life are sensible aims, though it should be noted that those who pursue them are often unaware that the head of a successful large firm is likely to be in a safer position, more independent and less hard worked than the owner of a small corner shop.

An optimal price policy is one which serves the central aims of the business best and, after due regard has been paid to the exceptions, it remains true that the road to most aims leads through profit maximization. But profit maximization itself can mean at least four different principles, each of which demands a separate policy. Let us consider them in turn.

1. *Maximization of total profits*. Though oft quoted, it is an acceptable aim only if we assume that the capital of the firm is unalterable. Otherwise it is palpably wrong. Because it cannot be a matter of indifference to the owners of capital how large

the resources tied down in the firm are. An example will make this clear: say that a shop in which £5,000 has been invested returns a profit of £1,000 per year. Should the owner, who can command further capital, invest another £5,000 to expand the shop? If the calculations show that this would raise total profits from £1,000 to about £1,100, he would be very unwise to do so, even though total profits would be increased, simply because the return on the additional capital would be a mere 2 per cent, which is hardly satisfactory.

2. *Maximization of the rate of return on capital* is the principle to which we have been led by this reasoning, but since 'capital' can mean two different things, there are again two principles under this heading:

(a) *total assets* is one definition, including both the capital of the owners of the firm and all loan capital, whether the loan is in the form of debentures, bank overdraft or trade credit, and

(b) *net worth* is the other definition, that is to say, the capital which would remain after all creditors have been paid off.

At the first blush net worth appears to be the appropriate concept of capital for the purpose of maximizing the rate of return. After all, loan capital has its price; if borrowed at 6 per cent, say, anything over this goes to swell the return on the net worth. However, this is misleading simply because the return on the net worth cannot be at a maximum unless the return on total assets has been maximized. To accept loan capital at 6 per cent and use it so that it earns 9 per cent, say, is not an optimal policy if there are other investment possibilities open, whether within the firm in question or outside it, where 15 per cent could have been earned. In other words, the true cost of capital is not what has to be paid for its use but the best return which could be obtained on it.

3. *Maximization of the rate of return on total sales,* also called maximization of the mark-up rate, is the last principle we shall discuss. Clearly, it is the proper one for a retail cooperative society only, which pays dividends on its sales and not on its capital, and even the cooperative movement realizes nowadays that it is at least partly this policy which is responsible for the fact that it is losing ground in its fight against the large mul-

tiples. The commercial supermarket can cut its mark-up rate and yet increase profits by enhanced turnover, while a cooperative society following the same policy would have to reduce its dividend and would in consequence lose trade rather than gain new customers.

It is remarkable that, according to the recent report of the Monopolies Commission, the large American firm Procter and Gamble judges its profits in relation to its total sales and never endeavours to work out what this means in terms of the capital tied down in the enterprise concerned. One wonders if there was not some misunderstanding between the members of the Monopolies Commission and the executives of Procter and Gamble. However, it is also possible that Procter and Gamble's method rests on the consideration that since prices are the result of competition and therefore not fully under their control, they must set their aims in terms of a high and increasing share of the market and keep costs at or below a certain proportion of wholesale prices.

The long-run aim of a firm may well be profit maximization, and it is my opinion that it should be so and that it is the rate of return on the total assets of the firm which should be the centre of attention, but in any particular venture the short-run aim may demand an entirely different policy. Perhaps one should also mention here the interesting proposition recently forwarded by a leading American economist, according to which business success is measured by growth rather than by profits and that, consciously or unconsciously, many firms follow a policy which aims at the highest rate of growth attainable without lowering the rate of return to the shareholders below a certain practical minimum (Baumol, 1964).

Formulating pricing policies

The next question is the translation of the aim set by the owners or chief executives of a firm into an effective pricing policy.

It is, of course, fully recognized that pricing is only one facet of product development and merchandising, and that it should be discussed in conjunction with a number of other aspects of the complete process. However, it is in many cases perfectly proper to start by determining the most appropriate price and then to shape the product accordingly. This method, sometimes referred to as backward costing, finds its most conspicuous use in the clothing trade where conventional prices rule absolutely in the lower price ranges. Marks and Spencer's is well known for its prices which invariably end in 11 pence, but the same policy is also widely used by manufacturers. For example, ladies' stockings selling below 10s. are traditionally priced at one shilling intervals from 1s. 11d. to 9s. 11d.

Even if the price is not the starting point, if the product was invented or developed without any immediate consideration of selling price, it is mostly possible to choose between various price ranges to which it could be adapted. This can be done fairly easily before the product is introduced; later on there is proper freedom of movement in the downward direction only, and even that is not without its dangers. But, whatever evils inflation may engender, it makes the correction of earlier pricing mistakes a relatively simple matter in either direction. Whether this will remain so in this new era of the Prices and Incomes Board remains to be seen.

What is then the price which should be selected for a new product? Joel Dean's distinction between the two main policies which can be pursued is often quoted (Dean, 1951). One of them is that of the *skimming price*, set at the level of at least three or four times the cost of the article at the factory door, which can be gradually lowered over the life of the product should it become necessary to fight competition, or when it appears desirable to bring the product within the reach of the lower income groups. The alternative to this policy is the selection of a *penetration price*, that is to say, a price at which the product is hoped to go over big. There are many instances where this is an absolute necessity because only the economies of mass production can bring the cost down to an acceptable level. This is the case where the unit cost would be so high at low levels of output that the corresponding skimming price would be prohibitive even to the upper income groups.

We have now arrived at the problem of determining the most appropriate penetration price for a new product, taking into account the central aim of the business. It seems that there are two main ways in which this problem can be approached, one of which is through unit costing and the other through market oriented pricing.

Pricing through unit costing

Once again, there are two methods which go under this heading. One of them is based on the direct cost of the product only, while the other takes the full cost into consideration, including an allowance for all overheads. The latter is sometimes referred to as absorption costing.[3]

Before we go any further, we should clearly distinguish between two fundamentally different situations. One of them is typically that of the branded consumer good, the price of which is declared and, if the product is successful, will soon become generally known to the public. This applies also in the absence of retail price maintenance: the price may vary somewhat from shop to shop and even from day to day but only within relatively narrow limits. In other words, the general level is still a matter which the producer can himself determine.

The other case is typically that of the product which has to be sold to industrial buyers, either for use within the business or for the purpose of incorporating it in another article. If a rigid price list with quantity rebates is issued and is being strictly adhered to, the case is very much the same as that of the branded consumer product, but if each order is negotiated on the basis of a special quotation, the pricing policy of the firm must be embodied in the method of price determination and not just in the price finally arrived at.

It should be noted that, contrary to popular belief, the industrial buyer is not altogether different from the layman in his attitude to price. To both of them, price has two aspects: one which provides a measure of the cost a purchase would involve, and the other is the role of price as an indicator of quality.

I have reported the findings of my research in this field elsewhere (Gabor and Granger, 1966) and I should like to emphasize it here that to use price as an indicator of quality does not in

3. Since I consider marginal costing not so much a method of pricing proper, rather a device which may be helpful in deciding whether certain orders should be accepted or not, I have made no mention of it in this Reading. For a very good summary of the issues invoked see Sizer (1966).

general imply that one is subject to a delusion. Sure enough, it would be rather foolish to enter an Eastern bazaar with the idea that the higher the price, the better the bargain, but it is perfectly rational to go, say, to almost any tailoring establishment in this country to select the grey suit which we want guided simply by the shade of the cloth and the price.

It is generally held that industrial buyers base their decisions essentially on specification and that they award the order in full knowledge of what the product should cost. But this can apply only if the specification is truly all-embracing and if, in addition, the buyer has himself experience in the manufacture of the item concerned. Otherwise, all he will know is the cheapest price in the market and not what it could be if the suppliers were more efficient or prepared to satisfy themselves with a narrower profit margin.

If the product is new or in some way unique, the industrial buyer will have neither the knowledge nor the power to prescribe what he would consider a just price; say one which would give the supplier of a component a profit margin similar to that associated with the finished product.

I will illustrate this by some actual examples, related to me by the people actually involved in the events concerned. A friend of mine, acting as an agent for a large London firm of oil producers, was selling oil to industrial users. Oil at this stage is sold by specification and sample rather than by brand name, the specification being the analyst's report on the composition of the product. Now the composition of oil varies both with the oil field from which the crude oil has been obtained and with the processing to which it has been subjected. My friend found that in the line which he carried there was one item which no buyer would touch even though it was an excellent oil and the price was relatively very low. The reason given for its rejection was in every case the unusual composition of the product.

Having unsuccessfully tried to sell this product to every one of his customers, he decided on a new tack. He let the matter rest for a year, then took out his sample again and went round to the customers. This time, however, he did not apologize for the product by saying that it was very cheap because it had an unusual composition. On the contrary, he proudly presented the analyst's report, saying to the buyer: 'Now I have brought you something you have never seen before. It is very expensive, but just look at this analysis.' To cut a long story short, he was so successful with the high price which he quoted that his principals soon asked him to reveal his secret to them because, in the hands of all the other agents, this oil was a non-starter.

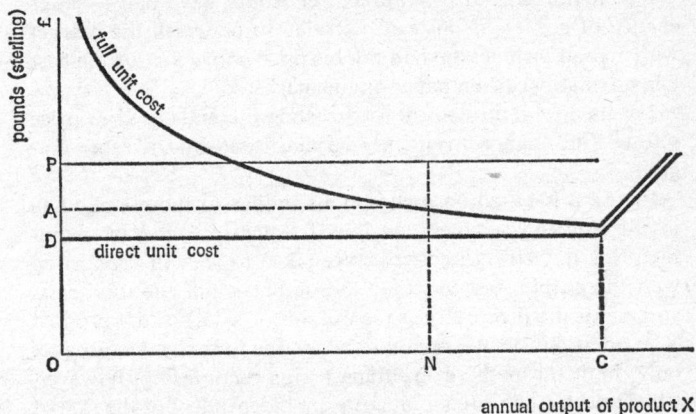

Figure 2 Full unit costs of a single product fall slowly until the capacity point C is reached. Beyond this point, overtime rates or shiftwork coupled with the problems of equipment being fully utilized lead to sharp increases in direct costs.

Another case known to me is that of a foreign manufacturer who tried to introduce his carbon paper in the London market. He had a very reputable agent who managed to sell several of the chemicals produced by his firm but never a single sheet of carbon paper. In the end, the manufacturer came himself to London to explore the situation. His agent said to him that instead of a long explanation, he would take him along to the buyer of one of the leading firms of chartered accountants in the City of London. The buyer readily admitted that the sample submitted was good and that the price was so competitive that the annual savings would be quite substantial if it were substituted for the very expensive carbon paper actually used by his firm. When asked why he still refused to give an order, the

A. Gabor 231

buyer said that the experiment with a cheap carbon paper could be so costly that he would not dare to recommend it to the partners. 'One illegible carbon copy sent to a client could cause us such trouble that even a saving of several thousand pounds would not be worth the risk of such an occurrence,' he declared.

I feel sure that this manufacturer would have had a better chance of success if, instead of trying to undersell the market with a good product, he had put his price *above* that of the best known quality carbon paper on the market.

Let us now return to the two costing methods used in price setting. Both can conveniently be illustrated by the same diagram.

Figure 2 is based on assumptions similar to those embodied in the break-even chart. As it is frequently found in manufacturing industry, direct costs are taken to vary in proportion with the output, but this time the output is not the total sales volume of the firm but just the output (or sales) of the product X in question. (In the rare case where the firm has one product only, both mean the same thing.) This relationship, however, which means that direct unit costs are independent of the rate of output, applies only until the capacity point C is reached. Beyond that overtime rates or shiftwork, coupled with the usual difficulties which arise when equipment is fully utilized, sharply increase the direct unit cost. Assuming that all the non-direct costs are fixed, the share to be carried by each unit of the product X will fall all the way through; it will be halved every time output is doubled. Hence the full unit cost will also fall until the capacity point is reached, and will begin to rise almost immediately beyond it.

A selling price, like the one indicated by P in the diagram, can be arrived at in two ways. If only direct costs are used in the estimation, a margin of DP is added to them, this margin being so set that it should cover the full cost and the profit margin which is itself a translation of the aim of the firm into a pricing rule. Clearly, the rule must also involve an estimate of the volume of sales, says N, which may represent normal utilization of capacity. By way of example, it is put at approximately two thirds of C in the diagram.

If the price is set on the basis of full absorption cost, the procedure is similar, except insofar as A will be taken as representing cost and the margin added to it will be AP only.

Now with price based on direct cost plus a margin DP, even though this margin will necessarily include some assumption about the rate of utilization of plant capacity, price will not be expected to vary if output varies between O and C. But if, as executives of firms often maintain, they add their profit margin to the full cost, every time with due regard to the fact that it varies with output, prices should increase every time output is reduced.

The only firms which can afford to behave in this way are monopolies, such as British Rail, and even it often finds that price increases in a shrinking market reduce rather than increase profits. And it considerably surprised me to see that when a few months ago one of the chief executives of the British Motor Corporation declared publicly that the reduction in home demand caused by the squeeze will mean higher prices of its products, the government did not respond by immediately referring the motor industry to the Monopolies Commission. That this was not due to oversight can be seen by the subsequent approval of the proposed increases by the Prices and Incomes Board. No firm in a competitive market would dare to increase its prices in the face of a shrinking demand.

I have, I hope, demonstrated the main reason why I hold that if unit costing is used as the basis of price determination, it should rest on direct cost rather than full absorption cost. But before I leave this issue, I should like to quote from a report on an earlier enquiry into pricing carried out by some of my colleagues at the University of Nottingham. They followed the only procedure which is correct for such studies; they analysed the firm's records before they approached the executives with their questions. This is what the report says:

Nothing could shake Mr W. (one of the executives of the firm investigated) from the contention that cost plus was a rigorous rule allowing only of rare exceptions. . . . The percentage mark-up was the 'customary' one. It was suggested to Mr W. that if this rule were in fact inflexibly applied, the fact ought to be reflected in the accounts of the company. He replied that the fluctuating margin was a feature of the accounts which he had previously noted and which had never ceased to puzzle him. He could offer no explanation (Pearce, 1956).

This firm produced only a small percentage for stock. In the main, every order was separately bespoken and, except in the case of repeats, an individual price was fixed for each. While all the executives maintained that the price was the full cost plus a fixed percentage for profits, the accounts showed considerable variation from year to year. And when the individual costing sheets were examined, it turned out that in the year when the average margin was about 14 per cent, individual orders carried margins which varied between *minus* 4 per cent and *plus* 44 per cent.

The just rate of profit

Let us stop here for a moment and consider if anything can be said about the rate of profit which a business should correctly charge. The opinion of the laymen (a group which also includes practically all politicians) is of little help here. I have not tested this, but I would expect that if we asked a representative group of consumers what they thought of a profit margin of 5 per cent, the great majority would call it modest, and that they would judge a rate of 10 per cent as reasonable. Anything above 10 per cent would probably be considered excessive.

The trouble is, of course, that the layman fails to distinguish between the mark-up rate and the rate of return on investment and he also tends to forget that, especially in retail establishments, the mark-up rate has to cover all the costs of the business not included in the wholesale price of the article.

We get somewhat more guidance from the business world. Investment projects are frequently judged by the pay-off period and it is customary to consider seven years as the maximum in the case of projects which carry relatively little risk of early obsolescence. Where this risk is considerable, the required pay-off period may be considerably shorter; four years or even less. Curiously enough, very much the same principle has been in use in the Soviet Union for some considerable time.

The rough equivalents in terms of the rate of return on the capital tied down by the project are 15 to 25 per cent *gross*, that is to say, before any allowance for depreciation on the equipment concerned.[4] The considerably more sophisticated Discounted Cash Flow Method, strongly promoted by its modern protagonists Merrett and Sykes, is an attempt to improve upon this simple device by taking the estimated life of the project, changes in the rate of the cash flow, taxation and the cost of capital into consideration (Merrett and Sykes, 1963). As a systematic approach to the problem of investment, the DCF method is commendable, though several aspects of it are open to criticism. Its use is spreading only slowly, even though the National Economic Development Council has also come out in its favour in a booklet on investment decisions (NEDC, 1965). Poor Neddy got itself rather confused on the crucial issue of the cut-off rate. It notes that 15 per cent tends to be looked upon as the minimum in the business world and while it is, of course, in the national interest to let capital flow where its productivity is greatest, it considers it still deplorable that projects promising less than 15 per cent tend to be rejected, even though they would add to the profits of the firm concerned and would also increase the national product. But even Neddy can't have it both ways; if it wants the best, it should not encourage firms to lower their sights.

It has been proposed by some economists and business experts both in this country and America that the rate of return firms require is simply what keeps the capital market sweet, so that it will serve them whenever the need for new capital arises. They suggest that since a return of about 6 per cent, consisting partly of dividends and partly of appreciation in the value of ordinary shares is about all the investor gets in the long run, any investment project promising a net return of not less than 6 per cent should be adopted. I myself think that this is a very naive view, because it pays no attention to the fact that many promising ventures fail and that hence the cut-off rate has to be set considerably above what is then generally achieved in the long run by the successful firms. I would say that the 15 to 25 per

4. The coy expression of the cost accountant for this return is not profit but cost saving. In the Soviet Union it is called the effectiveness of capital investment. Profit seems to have become a dirty word; people still make it but it is not done to refer to it by its proper name.

cent guide line, varied in individual cases in accordance with the estimated risk, provides quite a sound principle. But let me repeat that these are *gross* rates, before depreciation and taxation.

Towards a modern system of customer oriented pricing

I will finish by reiterating my main tenets and by examining how they can be utilized in developing a modern system of pricing.

First of all, there is no uniform formula by which a price could be judged. It will be a good price or a bad price according to how well it serves the aims of the firm rather than the personal aim of the salesman. Thus for example the cheapest item in a product line may be a loss-leader, the aim of which is to gain new customers for the firm in the hope that they will then gradually turn to the more expensive items. But the purpose of the cheapest item may be merely to demonstrate to the purchaser that the firm can compete with all comers and not to push the sales of that particular item. 'Yes, we can supply at the same price as Bloggs & Company, but this is not what you want. Nobody can produce a decent widgeon at that price, and I would not sell it to an old customer of the firm like you even if you asked for it,' is the sort of sales talk to go with it. It is therefore absolutely essential to take a clear-cut decision on the central aim or aims of the firm and on the application of the principle so arrived at to the case in hand.

Next, there is the point which I consider to be of paramount importance, which is that the price is not just the cost but an essential feature of the product itself. By that I do not mean that anything will sell if the price is high enough, though I could quote examples to show how often this principle does prevail. But if you have a good product, don't spoil it by trying to sell it too cheaply. In other words, give the consumer the price which he wants and remember that it is not necessarily the cheapest price which will give him the greatest satisfaction.

I have discussed elsewhere the methods by which the most promising price can be located for a product to be launched in the retail market (Gabor and Granger, 1965, 1966). Since this method is not applicable to the industrial market I will try to indicate what I consider the right approach in that market.

Full freedom in pricing is available only when the product is launched for the first time. Later on, downward adjustments are relatively easy but not upward adjustments. If the launching is not successful, it is best to withdraw the product and come forward with a different version of it at a more promising price.

But before the product is launched, there is an opportunity to examine the market. The method is no novelty, it has been used since times immemorial, but it tends to be avoided nowadays, especially by large firms. I will quote (and somewhat para-phrase) a version of it which I found many years ago in an otherwise not particularly outstanding textbook of economics written by a Belgian professor for his students (de Bodt, 1956, p. 58). He described how a cloth manufacturer whose mill has just produced a new type of cloth or, perhaps, just a new pattern, will find the right price for it. He will take a sample of it to one of the wholesalers, and ask him what he thinks of it. If the wholesaler likes the sample, the manufacturer will name the highest price within reason, adding at once that the article has not yet been properly costed and that the final price may come out above or below his preliminary estimate. If the wholesaler reacts unfavourable, and especially if he produces comparable samples from a competitor at a lower price, the manufacturer will approach the next wholesaler with a somewhat lower price estimate, and so on. Gradually, he will get the feel of the market, he will see how his buyers react to different prices and, with some skill, he will even find out what competition he is likely to meet if he puts that particular product on the market. A somewhat similar process was recently mentioned in an article by Michael White (1966).

Much has been written about the price strategy a firm may have to follow through the life of a product. This, I would say, is something about which no general rules can be laid down, since so much depends on the type of competition which is being encountered, to say nothing of possible changes in taste.

Competition has to be watched closely, but not at the expense of watching the consumer. In some interesting cases the firm concerned stepped out of the competitive field by bringing out a product with distinctive features at a price high above the prevailing level. Parker Pens are, of course, an outstanding example. In other cases firms in the industry were so afraid of starting a price war that they clung rigidly to their existing prices, until one of them or, in some cases, an outsider, boldly undercut the market which responded by expanding beyond expectation. This was, of course, what Henry Ford did with motor cars.

Some of my contentions might expose me to the charge of cynicism. I started by discussing the 'just price' and then suggested that the proper price may be what the market will bear. So before closing I should like to say two things. One of them is that I have some very definite ideas about consumer protection but this was not the topic I set out to discuss. The other is that though I maintain the general principle that price should cover cost, this does not mean that I approve of the present system of control of company accounts and taxation which sets no effective limits on the promotion costs and fails to give sufficient encouragement to innovation.

References

BAUMOL, W. J. (1964), 'Company goals, growth and the multi-product firm', in R. Cox, W. Alderson and S. J. Shapiro (eds.), *Theory in Marketing*, Irwin, pp. 322–32.

de BODT, J. P. (1956), *La Formation des Prix*, De Visscher.

DEAN, J. (1951), *Managerial Economics*, Prentice-Hall.

GABOR, A., and GRANGER, C. W. J. (1965), 'The pricing of new products', *Sci. Bus.*, vol. 3, no. 10, pp. 141–50.

GABOR, A., and GRANGER, C. W. J. (1966), 'Price as an indicator of quality', *Economica*, vol. 33, no. 2, pp. 43–70.

HEALY, S. J. (1966), *The Just Wage 1750–1890*, Nijhoff, The Hague.

MERRETT, A. J., and SYKES, A. (1963), *The Finance and Analysis of Capital Projects*, Longman.

NATIONAL ECONOMIC DEVELOPMENT COUNCIL (1965), *Investment Appraisal*, H.M.S.O.

PEARCE, I. F. (1956), 'A study in price policy', *Economica*, vol. 23, no. 90, pp. 114–27.

SIZER, J. (1966), 'The accountant's contribution to the pricing decision', *J. manag. Stud.*, vol. 33, no. 2, pp. 129–49.

WHITE, M. (1966), 'Pricing industrial products', *Bus.*, February, pp. 59–62.

WRAY, M. (1966), 'The new "just price"', *Westminster Bank Rev.*, August, pp. 15–26.

14 G. H. Evans

The Product Manager's Job

Excerpt from G. H. Evans, *The Product Manager's Job*,
American Management Association Research Study 69, 1964, pp. 49–62.

A product manager may be a brilliant marketing man, an out-standing salesman, an advertising genius, a peerless planner, an expert in each of the many functions affecting his product; but unless he can coordinate all of these activities, unless the pieces can be fitted together so that they spell 'profit', his special skills will have been wasted. More than any other factor, it is his skill in working harmoniously with key people in the various func-tional disciplines that will heavily influence the success of the product and, of course, his own future with the company.

In working to get the sales department to do the best possible job on his products, the product manager can take several different kinds of action. One of his first concerns is likely to be that of securing sufficient actual selling time to be devoted to his goods. In many forward-looking firms this is present by plan, at least in broad terms. Before taking part in planning meetings held for this purpose, the product manager can gather facts which, if valid, may win more field selling time than previously allocated to him. Of course, if all product managers are equally diligent, management may be forced to add salesmen in order to tap actual profit potential. One product manager in a large industrial goods firm successfully convinced his superiors that substantial profits were being lost at the field sales level due to inattention to his product; he asked for and got his own small sales force.

Although more and more medium-size and large firms now plan and measure profits at the district sales level, attaining maximum profit in a certain sales district does not auto-matically lead to maximum total profits for a specific product.

The product manager is acutely conscious of product profits, and a number of the product managers interviewed spoke of differences between their viewpoints and those of salesmen. For example, one said:

Sales people are rarely profit-minded. ... There is a real difference of viewpoints involved. One's attitude changes, coming from sales to product management – you get a broader picture. The sales group has a very serious blind spot in regard to profit. I'm interested in the profit as it appears on this year's income statement. But the sales people have become very lenient with the customer. They may say, 'Let's give this man credit,' or 'Let him return the goods if they're not entirely satisfactory.' Either one of these things could ruin today's profits, but they might very well improve future sales. The sales group must live with the customer next year and the year after that. He will remain friendly towards us if we offer him favors. Sales must emphasize customer service and customer accommodation. But too much can ruin the current profit picture, and that's what I'm responsible for. Of course, this difference in our perspectives is not all bad; both have to exist in a company. If you take a narrow profit viewpoint, you are apt to ruin the goodwill on which your success has been based. As a matter of practically managing these matters, I make it a rule that if the sales manager feels very strongly about a problem, much more strongly than I do, I'll go along with him. Unless you're willing to do this, even though you may think it's a downright mistake, you're liable to build up a suspicious and negative attitude in sales. It's very easy to get yourself in such a position.

These sentiments on the importance of the product manager's cooperative coexistence with sales are echoed in the following paragraph taken from a typical product manager's job description:

He [the product manager] must work cooperatively with the sales manager. He must seek the sales manager's counsel and advice, those all-important elements in the product program. Remember, the sales manager and his sales force are those who actually execute the product manager's plans. It thus behooves both the sales manager and the product manager to work in close harmony, and they must do so if maximum results are to be had. However, if opposite points of view are strongly held and a meeting of minds between the two men is impossible, the vice-president of marketing will decide between them.

To impress upon the sales department the fact of the product manager's responsibility for profits, many companies make a point of granting the product manager the right to examine sales costs and make suitable recommendations. Indeed, if he is to work effectively, his right to any relevant cost information – or any other information – must be clearly understood by all concerned, and complementing this right is his right to submit suggestions and give advice to both functional personnel and senior management. Product managers stress the crucial importance of both these rights. However, the manner in which the product manager exercises these rights is perhaps an even more critical matter. If he is too demanding, he may defeat his own purpose. He is far more likely to obtain the desired results by persuasion – by making the sales force as profit-conscious as he is. He strives to do this at every possible opportunity, particularly at the district-level meetings where he has a chance to personally hammer this message home.

However, maintaining a cordial working relationship with sales yields its greatest benefits during negotiations for selling time. In a typical multi-product company which has a shared sales force, the bidding among product managers for selling time is fiercely competitive. Indeed, the product manager's success in selling his product to salesmen and sales management is often a critical factor in his evaluation by higher management. One former product manager remarks: 'You must know how to get things done in sales. You may even have to be demanding. If you roll over and play dead, you won't get what you want.' Occasionally, the jockeying for selling time goes to extremes. A director of product management comments: 'From time to time, things get a little too rough. I have to get everybody together and give them a lecture on good corporate citizenship.'

The product manager, lacking any clear-cut authority, must rely heavily on personal tact, diplomacy and powers of persuasion in selling his product internally. He may frequently find that the dice have been loaded against him; for example, differential commission rates set by higher levels of management may favor other products. In such instances he will have to convince his superiors in the marketing department that *his* product should benefit from such incentives. Here again, his persuasive powers, backed with concrete information and realistic plans for promoting the product, will determine whether he receives this support. Indeed, the sales department looks to the product manager to provide a continuing flow of data about the product, such as periodic bulletins describing price and model changes, special promotions, advertising tie-ins, point-of-purchase displays – anything that will be useful in improving the competitive position of the product. They do not look for this kind of assistance but they expect it to materialize in the form of useful sales tools such as brochures or flyers depicting new product applications, catalogues and package-deal promotions rather than gratuitous advice, irksome reminders to watch costs, or unrealistic sales quotas. For this reason, many firms recruit product managers from the field sales force on the assumption that they have a first-hand knowledge of the product, its markets and customer expectations. These companies feel that the salesman, or sales-manager-turned-product-manager, can acquire the other pertinent skills through practical experience and on-the-job training. At least one major chemical company continues to follow this approach with salutary results. The only difficulty is that a field sales manager is sometimes reluctant to give up his field 'command' to become a product manager.

The product manager's face-to-face dealings with field sales people usually occur at planning meetings attended by top-level marketing managers, product managers, field sales managers and, of course, the salesmen. At these meetings, the group blocks out each salesman's time, and specific product campaigns are scheduled to avoid conflicts. Such meetings provide no guarantee that the following year will be – in the words of Robert Browning – 'roses, roses, all the way'; but Lever Brothers, for one, has found that special meetings of this kind have been particularly effective in identifying and resolving difficulties.

One of the most common criticisms of the product manager concept originates with salesmen in the field who feel that the product manager usurps many of their functions – that his 'interference' is more of a hindrance than a help. Those in favor of product managers often attempt to minimize such criticism by emphasizing the 'value added' potential of the product manager; they point out that he is ideally situated to reinforce their sales efforts by supplying data on special product applications, by expediting special orders, and by making personal sales presentations when necessary. This is especially true of the product manager in an industrial goods company, where his special knowledge of the product's performance characteristics and technological subtleties may provide the clincher in closing an important sale. More often, however, the product manager plays a passive role in relation to field sales. He acts chiefly as an observer. He listens carefully to salesmen, customers and district office personnel; notes their comments, suggestions, and complaints; and takes these back to the home office for consideration and action. In fact, as a matter of practice some companies go even further to emphasize the non-authoritarian nature of the product manager's relations with the salesmen. L & F Products Division of Lehn & Fink Products Corporation, for example, states in its comprehensive *Brand Manager's Manual:* 'No instructions are to be given to field personnel by brand management personnel unless a specific request to do so is made by the sales manager.'

The multiplicity of reports and forms that salesmen must complete is a common source of contention between the product manager and the field. He must constantly evaluate his need for a continual flow of sales data against the reluctance of the salesmen to take time away from their primary function of selling, to fill factual reports and memorandums. If he overpowers them with data-gathering tasks, he may find that the reports are carelessly prepared or even ignored.

His relationship to advertising

Although 'product manager' and 'brand manager' are synonymous terms in many large packaged goods firms, today's product manager is often thought to be a direct descendant of the brand manager; the advertising specialist of the consumer goods company of the late 1920s and early 1930s. While the product manager has acquired considerably broader duties and responsibilities over the years than were held by the original brand managers, he often retains this strong relationship to advertising and exercises a dominant influence in developing and implementing advertising campaigns for his product. He may be authorized to work directly with the advertising agency, plan the overall advertising strategy for his product line, deploy the tactical weapons which implement that strategy, and modify it as the competitive situation dictates or new markets appear. There are exceptions but in most consumer packaged goods companies the responsibility-without-authority problem does not arise where advertising is concerned. Advertising plans are often approved along conventional reporting lines — that is, by the product manager's own chief.

However, when the organizational set-up requires lateral communication, the product manager's goal is to persuade the art, copy and media experts of the advertising department to create advertising themes and campaigns that will vividly express the consumer's expectations of the product. If the product manager's concept of what the consumer looks for in the product is valid, then half the battle is won. If he miscalculates in choosing the appeals that he wants to build into the product and package design, if the copy does not carry through the basic theme, then no matter what pressure he applies to the sales force and no matter what media he uses to reach his market, his campaign will be seriously compromised and he will spend most of his time attempting to patch up a vessel that was waterlogged before it was launched. However, there are usually others involved in the final decision to proceed with the campaign and veto power must exist somewhere. Final approval of annual advertising plans may go as high as the president or even the board of directors; but once the budget has been approved, authorization of specific plans often rests with the product group manager or the director of marketing. As regards consumer packaged goods, it is not uncommon for the product manager to be able to say, 'no' to ad agency plans.

In contrast, an indication of advertising department power is found in the advertising policy bulletin of a manufacturer of printing equipment, which says, 'To insure a consistent external picture, significant changes in advertising styles or approaches are subject to clearance by the General Office Director of Advertising.' And the advertising department in one typical pharmaceutical concern is watchdog over ethical standards and may vote down a product manager's proposal for an advertising campaign which it considers marginal.

In many firms, written policies or other guides help to provide common standards for all those responsible for advertising. Salada Foods, Ltd, sets forth some rather firm rules:

Our advertising must project and reflect quality, and a continuing search for even greater quality, with respect to every product bearing a label of the company.

No claim should be made in any advertisement which the company would be unwilling to back with an unconditional money-back guarantee. The guarantee itself may or may not be included in any advertisement. Judgement and mechanical requirements will be the deciding factors.

It must be dynamic in reflecting an active and progressive determination to keep in step with changing consumer habits and tastes.

It should recognize news, either in the form of new products or new uses of old products, as one of its most vital ingredients.

It should employ a maximum degree of continuity, recognizing that attitudes are slow to change and that pleasant familiarity with a brand is a powerful selling force.

In execution, it should build solid confidence through adherence to the following rules:

(a) All claims used should be supportable.

(b) It must be in good taste by scrupulously avoiding anything that reflects on religious beliefs, or that could offend racial or political minorities. Naturally, also, it should never depend on a suggestive *double entendre* or sexy connotation for attention value or humorous effect.

(c) It must not unfairly attack the reputation or product claims of competitors.

The solving of some problems is usually a matter of bargaining and company politics; but in some cases it is reduced to a system. An ingenious system for controlling the allocation of advertising expense has been adopted in a ranking company in the proprietary drug field. The company explains it as follows:

We work on what we call an *advertising-to-sales* ratio. In short, it's called 'A to S'. Every brand has an A-to-S percentage established for it. This determines what per cent of sales may be spent on advertising. As you see, there is an automatic effect: if sales go down, the budget for that brand automatically goes down. If sales go up, advertising goes up. The thinking is that we should put our money behind our winners, and not behind our losers. The advertising department is constantly reviewing sales and adjusting budgets accordingly. ... It is their job to drop one budget down and pull another budget up. The result is that the product managers do not have to fight all along the line for their advertising share *most of the time*. This is decided for them. However, there is, of course, always the question of the starting base. The product group may make recommendations for a change in the A-to-S ratio. We may suggest to higher-ups that we spend a higher percentage of money on a given brand.

I don't want to give the impression, however, that we are entirely inflexible. The general thinking is that it is unwise to put money behind a poor seller. Other companies think otherwise. The instinctive reaction of management is to do just the wrong thing in a falling market. However, we are in an industry where sales are very sensitive to advertising. If we get a very hot product (and this may be the result of very good copy or other factors), we are not reluctant to put advertising funds behind it by altering the A-to-S ratio. The percentage is primarily a limit, a protection on the *down side*, but there is no arbitrary ceiling on the *top side*. We're willing to take flyers, and we have taken them. Sometimes we will spend 50 per cent more than we ordinarily would do on a very high selling brand. But when a brand is declining and we still have to make a profit on it, profit comes out of advertising savings.

Several degrees of control over the advertising function are possible. The most complete control exists when the company's advertising department, and hence the agencies used by it, report directly to the product manager or to the head of product management. The over-riding importance of advertising to consumer goods companies has led some companies to replace competent sales-oriented product managers with executives who have been extremely successful in advertising. In those instances where a manager is particularly adept in one area, he is frequently given a subordinate who is strong in another. In one such case, the product manager was an advertising specialist; he was supported by a field sales contact man whose skills and experience made him a natural complement to the product manager.

A slightly less stringent degree of control is found where the advertising personnel, although they do not report directly to the product manager, still must yield to his judgement on everything substantive about his product and his advertising campaign. Here the product manager can decide the content and wording of the copy, its art, the media in which it will be placed and when it will appear.

Yet, in some companies, the product manager may have even less authority than this. Such instances perhaps are found most often in companies that make technically complex products for industrial customers; here, the product manager may have the right only to reject – veto – advertising copy. He may ask the advertising and sales promotion staff to emphasize certain product advantages in copy and art, may recommend media and may propose direct mail approaches and lists; but he may not demand that his recommendations be followed. The reason this limited control appears more often in industrial goods firms is that the industrial product manager is rather technically oriented and has been chosen for his background in applications work or engineering rather than for the training and experience in advertising that characterize his counterpart in the consumer goods company. Under the circumstances, the head of marketing may feel that it is better to rely on the skills of an experienced advertising specialist within the company or in an outside agency.

Needless to say, product managers would like as much control as possible over other marketing staffs. More than one product manager mentioned in an interview that it would also be desirable to have market research for his product report to him, or that the market research function report to his director of product management. They feel that only in this way can market research be properly integrated with product management.

Some years ago, when National Biscuit Company first began to use product managers, the rumor spread that the company had a 'vice-president in charge of Fig Newtons'. While this title was invented in jest, it does convey the genuinely high regard that functional chiefs have for product managers. They realize that the product manager bears a considerable portion of the total responsibility for profitable volume for a given product or segment of the line and they treat him accordingly.

His relationship to finance

It is common practice for product managers to conduct campaigns to reduce the inequitable allocation of fixed costs to certain items, to study other cost factors, to analyse and evaluate the implications of price changes and to develop profit plans for a specific product or market. In a conventional marketing organization there may be no one specifically assigned to accomplish these tasks. Consequently a product may be overpriced or underpriced and languish far behind its true market potential, simply because no one has time to explore the revenue and profit possibilities in terms of cost structures and return on investment.

Today's product manager has a working knowledge of financial principles and can discuss them intelligently with cost estimators, accountants and financial experts in his continuing effort to increase his product's profits, as well as the overall profits of the firm. However, he is not an accountant; even in a small firm, the product manager will have to call on financial specialists to insure a profitable result. And in the large multi-product, multiplant company, the complexity of product and the frequency of cost, price, or design changes of the product itself will largely determine the number of people assigned to cost analysis and control.

In a conventional functional organization the finance department usually develops the profit plan, if there is to be one. However, many finance men lack the marketing knowledge, experience and insight of the product manager. The advisability of having a finance man at the product level is, again, a function of profitability. Perhaps the 'business teams' of Union Carbide's Chemical Division provide a workable compromise.

In many companies the profit responsibility for a given product rests with the group product manager, or marketing manager, rather than with the product manager himself. However, when profit responsibility is specifically assigned to him, the product manager works closely with accounting or finance people to develop a budget for his product. This budget is essentially a profit plan which will subsequently provide, to a great extent, the basis for evaluating his performance at the end of the year. He plays a major role in developing the estimates that make up the profit plan and, consequently, must bear the responsibility for explaining any undesirable variances that may occur. Over all, the product manager's day-to-day working relationship with finance – either directly or through the group product manager – consists chiefly of arranging for merchandising deals, price changes, premium offers and occasional unplanned activities arising from changing market conditions or the necessity to counter a competitor's tactical moves.

His relationship to manufacturing

The extent to which the product manager becomes involved in manufacturing depends mainly on the nature of the product. If the product is relatively easy to make and represents a minimal capital investment, his dealings with manufacturing will be occasional and informal. If, however, the product requires a sizable investment in raw stock, expensive machinery and technical manpower, then the product manager will devote a significant portion of his time to the analysis of costs, schedules, productive capacities (including make-or-buy decisions) and quality control.

Few product managers qualify as experts in developing shop costs, but those fortunate enough to have had some experience in production can at least recognize when manufacturing costs seem out of line. In one chemical manufacturing company, for example, a product manager objected to the manufacturing expenses charged to his product. He made a detailed analysis of these costs and was able to prove that the costs were overstated. Thus, because he knew something of the manufacturing process, the materials involved and the man-machine requirements, he was able to control an important component of his total cost picture and improve his profit potential accordingly. Such knowledge not only minimizes the possibility of manufacturing overcharges but can be instrumental in developing competitive price structures.

There are difficulties in estimating shop costs, of course. It is not simply a question of applying historical data and the cost of current facilities. A competitor may enter the field with new and more efficient equipment that will permit him to lower his costs and selling price – and perhaps run away with the market. One method of preventing just such occurrences is through the development of 'design-cost systems'. This approach provides estimates based on the use of the best possible equipment and facilities, rather than the existing plant capabilities. As one executive commented:

By using 'design costs' we can arrive at a hypothetical price based on the use of the most advanced and efficient processes, materials, handling techniques and the like. This is the lowest cost at which our product could be made.

By constantly referring to the difference between the ideal design cost and the actual shop costs, the product manager is in a position to exert pressure for low-cost production. He has a reliable yardstick for measuring cost improvements. Furthermore, he is able to anticipate the effect of competitive activities if it becomes apparent that the competition is installing the same type of machines upon which the ideal design costs were based.

The problems of scheduling, inventory control and production lot sizes are second in importance; only manufacturing costs deserve more attention. Again, these problems will be of more or less interest to the product manager, depending on the nature of his product. They are virtually non-existent in some companies. A producer of proprietary drugs comments:

Our product is physically very small and chemically very simple. We can keep a year's inventory in a medium-size room. Our manufacturing process is almost primitive and capital equipment is inexpensive. I have little to worry about in my relations with manufacturing.

When the product is bulky and costly to produce and distribute, however, the product manager may find it advisable to become more deeply involved in production problems. If the product requires long production runs and extensive warehousing facilities or has a markedly seasonal sales pattern, then the product manager probably should investigate the pros and cons of economic lot quantity planning (ELQ), which attempts to balance output costs against warehouse costs and deterioration losses. He might find that costs could be reduced significantly by the use of ELQ planning.

In many companies, the product manager is responsible for telling manufacturing how much of a given item will be needed per year, quarter, or month; in such a situation, his statement is often binding on manufacturing. The manufacturing manager may ask the product manager: 'How much of product X will you need during the next year, and how much should I make?' 'Will you verify that our inventory level is such and such?' The product manager often must answer these questions. From manufacturing's viewpoint, this is all to the good. As one executive puts it: 'Manufacturing now has someone to put its finger on, someone who will give a hard, quantitative answer.' It is not surprising that in many companies manufacturing is not at all unfriendly toward the product manager in this connection.

Another area of consideration for some product managers arises when they become involved in the formulation of plant expansion or contraction decisions. Since the product plan must include forecasts[1] of future demand, the question of capacity must arise. Often it is part of the product manager's job to act as a liaison with manufacturing on this question. Manufacturing is of course most interested in the product manager's predictions of future sales levels. He is the specialist on the market: and if his judgement is trusted, manufacturing will listen keenly to his views on how much more or less capacity will be needed next year, or five years from now. This is especially true with the introduction of new products. Production routine has not yet been set, and manufacturing must rely heavily on the product manager's ideas of sales level and production timing. Conversely, the product manager must be careful to see that he does not stimulate a premature demand which manufacturing is incapable of meeting. As one company puts it in its product manager job description: 'Specific planning must be done on end product requirements. They must be announced

1. For an example of the form the product manager's forecast may take see AMA Special Report (1955, pp. 142–5).

early enough for production to have merchandise ready in kind and quantity.'

Make-or-buy decisions constitute potentially one of the most difficult problems facing the product manager in his dealings with manufacturing. As guardian of a product's profitability, he may discover that it is easier and cheaper to buy his supply outside the company rather than to manufacture it in-house. At this point, a conflict with manufacturing is almost sure to arise. Alfred N. Watson, professor of business at the Graduate School of Business Administration of Columbia University and a former vice-president – marketing of U S Rubber, says:

This problem arises because in some industries as, say, the chemical industry, productive capacity is growing faster than consumption. Certain companies will have difficulty even keeping plants open and reaching their break-even points. Beyond this, they [the products] can sell at lower *incremental costs*. The product manager of a potential buyer will realize that his plant's production will be charged to him at *average* cost. If he buys astutely –and certainly this is one of the qualifications of a product manager – he will see chances to buy cheaper outside. The manufacturing function will, of course, fear being put out of business. So it must be equally astute in meeting competitive production prices.

The coordination of the interest of marketing and production with the overall interests of the company is often a major problem of senior management. An executive may wonder, for example, if he should place the company at the mercy of a competitor-supplier, even if a great temporary advantage might be secured by purchasing products from it.

Finally, the product manager must keep in touch with product quality. In many lines, quality is a significant factor in product sales. Traditionally, quality control has been the responsibility of manufacturing and in most companies this is still the rule.

But the product manager must be concerned with the customers' reaction to the overall quality level. He has a valid interest in complaints, especially where the alleged defect may be serious or frequent enough to undermine the product's reputation. He is often charged with making sure an investigation is made and corrective action is taken.

His relationship to research and development

As with manufacturing, the product manager's relationship to research and development will depend to a great extent on his product. If the product is subject to innovation, or requires frequent customer service of a highly technical nature, the product manager will work closely with the R & D people; if not, he will seldom have occasion to see them. In most organizations, the research and development group is a separate entity and has few day-to-day dealings with marketing and the product manager. Celanese Fibers Company, a division of Celanese Corporation of America, is an exception to this rule. Dr Robert D. Williams, who has charge of both product management and the division's research and development activities, cites some of the advantages of his dual responsibility:

The advantage of having R & D in the same house with product management is that we have available a large number of competent people who are able to think analytically. They are able to act as a kind of auxiliary marketing staff. This definitely improves the working relationship. Otherwise, our access to our R & D people would be slower and less close. In the same house we have a tremendous benefit in terms of quick responses to new product developments. All the complaints one hears about the marketing department being unable to get service from R & D may be true enough, but not in this division.

Perhaps it is in the area of new product development that the product manager finds his closest working relationship with research and development. His knowledge of customer expectations and market requirements is of particular significance in this phase of the product's life. If he can persuade the research and development scientists and engineers to build these expectations and requirements into the design and packaging components of the product, then he will have served his company well.

The product manager's authority

Typically, the product manager has the authority to make a wide range of analyses and marketing plans for the product line assigned to him, subject of course to budget and policy limits. He may have authority over promotional aids or advertising copy. Occasionally he has authority to set prices in his line. He has almost unlimited authority to communicate with persons in other departments which design, sell, schedule, make, inspect, or bill for his product line. But, as a rule, he may only request, or persuade, these people to act in the ways he believes will advance the sales and net income from the product line.

Responsibility for profits

Marketing executives consulted in the preparation of this AMA Study repeatedly spoke of the product manager as 'the watchdog for profits'. In what sense is this true? And to what extent is he accountable for the components of profits – sales and costs? The profit of the product line for which he is responsible is a very real concern of the product manager and is constantly in his mind. Yet, paradoxically, there is a very real question of how much direct authority he has over the conditions which create or destroy profit. J. M. Juran has sketched the situation in this way (1964, pp. 190–91):

This man is a planner and coordinator for a particular product or market. He has the main voice as to some matters – the content of the product line, through what channels it should be sold, how it should be promoted and priced. He is decisive [as] to the sales forecast and the profit budget. He has the right and duty to sound the alarm when an impasse looms ahead. However, he does not command the technical departments, the manufacturing departments, or the field sales forces. When we tell this man, 'You are responsible for profit', we are more wrong than right. He *is* responsible for the profit planning, for some of the ingredients of profit performance, for coordinating and for needling. Whether a profit results from all this depends on many things beyond him – so many, in fact, that to hold him 'responsible' is usually unrealistic and sometimes ludicrous. Paying him based on this profit is another matter. Even if he is not 'responsible', it may be a good thing to make his bonus (and, for that matter, the bonus of the others) depend on the profit.

A senior marketing executive interviewed for this study puts it this way:

You cannot really be responsible for anything unless you have it under your direct control. The product manager can't be responsible for manufacturing costs, because he doesn't run the factory. He can't be directly responsible for sales, because he doesn't have working control of the salesmen. You simply can't eliminate either, or both, of these aspects of profit and say that the product manager is responsible for the end result. I suppose in some companies you could make a case that since he is part of marketing, his influence with the sales people is greater. Perhaps in some places he is the dominant factor in field sales, or at least his superior is. But in very few companies is this true with manufacturing. If either one of the manufacturing or sales elements is taken away from a fellow, you can't say that he is running the whole product – he is only having something to do with running it.

The general manager of a product division has authority over more of the factors that govern profit. Thus he may reasonably be charged with a greater degree of profit responsibility than can be attached to the product manager. To quote J. M. Juran (1964, p. 190):

This man is put in charge of a profit centre or division of the company. He has broad responsibility over design, manufacture, and marketing of the product, including command of the respective departments. He also commands some but not all of the supporting services. He does not have the full latitude that is enjoyed by the head of an independent company, but he has a lot to say. When we tell the general manager, 'You are responsible for profit', we are more right than wrong. When we go a step further and tell him, 'We will make your bonus depend on this profit', we are on sound ground.

This element of authority is a key distinction between the product manager arrangement and the general manager arrangement. The typical product manager cannot be held fully accountable for profit in the same sense that the general manager can. Yet the product manager has a very real *influence* over profit and may be the key factor in making a profit exist for a specific product. His special knowledge, plans, stimulus and persuasion can clearly give the needed competitive edge to his product.

Can his authority be increased?

Basically, marketing executives point out that a good product manager has the possibility of spurring sales and profits in his field, yet can be blocked in his efforts by one or two intransigent executives in other functions – particularly sales, advertising, or production. In this respect he is in a position which is similar to that of the personnel manager or the director of industrial engineering. If the full potential of any of these positions is to be realized, the executive in charge must be able to communicate and persuade. It is impractical to give him formal authority to command everyone his job touches, so he must earn much of his authority with the quality of his ideas.

The product manager often wishes he had command authority over each of the various groups which play important parts in marketing or producing the products he is concerned with. There are only two ways this could be done. One is to give any such group as many bosses as there are product managers. The image of confusion, missed schedules, uncontrolled costs and frustrated group supervisors brought to mind by this idea normally causes it to be dismissed without further thought.

The second possibility is to subgroup the people engaged in a particular function according to product specialization and place the subgroup under the direction of the product manager responsible for the same product. This has been found to be somewhat more practicable. When carried to its extreme in most of the major functions, this arrangement becomes a general manager system as defined in this report.

However, many in-between applications of this concept also are found in practice; in a number of companies the product manager has direct authority over one or two functions vital to his success. The limiting factors are duplication of jobs and facilities and difficulties in coordinating the subgroups, training them and balancing their workloads. Where these factors are paramount – as in production – the product manager is rarely given line authority. Where they are less serious as liabilities, the product manager is sometimes given authority. Advertising is perhaps the best example. Some companies (for example, Vick Chemical Division of Richardson-Merrell) assign an advertising man to the product manager. Others (Colgate-Palmolive and Mennen, to name only two) have organized to give the product manager direct access to an advertising agency; in effect, he serves as advertising manager for his line of products. In such arrangements the product manager gains in control over results but in exchange for some disadvantage in other sectors. Obvious among these is greater difficulty in coordinating advertising programs on a companywide basis, since the authority gained by the product manager has been lost by the manager who had companywide authority over advertising. Now *his* mission must be carried out largely through persuasion.

In most of the major company functions, the problems that would be generated by giving the product manager direct authority seem too great to be tolerated. So, as noted earlier, he must generally keep work moving by explaining and persuading. This is not to say that the product manager's superiors cannot help to make his responsibility for product success tenable. Where it is impractical to give him formal authority, they can help the product manager to break down roadblocks by giving their support and by setting up procedural guidelines.

Resolving the problem of limited authority

In any organizational arrangement, a man consults his chief if he finds his work seriously or consistently hampered by someone whose cooperation he needs to reach his goal. The superior then negotiates for a better solution at a higher level. If he fails to get one, he can take the issue to a still higher level. The outcome of a number of such debates over a period of months or years does much to establish the informal authority – or lack of authority – of the product manager. A kind of case law develops. If a product manager differs with an advertising man on specifics of copy a number of times, for example, and the judgement of the superiors goes generally with the product manager, then usually the advertising man finds it prudent to allow fewer copy matters to reach the appeal stage. In this case the product manager gains informal authority. If, on the other hand, the advertising man's ideas are more often supported, then the product manager loses informal authority in this area. The aggregate of such decisions in many fields does much to establish the image of importance or unimportance of the job of product manager in the company as a whole, and so to influence the willingness of others to honor his requests.

G. H. Evans 257

In this and other ways the attitude of top management is revealed and comes to be reflected by people of the various departments who work with the product manager. The respect higher managers show for the job – in deeds even more than in words – is a vital factor. The caliber of person they choose for the post of product manager is one such signal to the organization. In one company he may be paid $24,000 a year; in another, $10,000. If the salary is low, it may be necessary to accept a candidate of limited qualifications. Because of his inexperience this man may make quite a few decisions which do not work out well; or he may make recommendations which are not accepted by the departments to which they are directed and, on appeal, the recommendations are found inadequate. The result is low informal authority. Where the top marketing executive wants to strengthen the hand of the product manager he must be prepared not only to act in a supportive way but also to select product managers of knowledge and experience so their day-to-day actions will be supportable.

Minimizing friction

To sum up: prudent management will go a long way to prevent problems in the relationships between product managers and functional units, through careful selection of people. But even in the best-managed firms there will be unavoidable friction, misunderstanding and disagreement. The means used to minimize the frequency of unpleasant incidents include:

Periodic planning meetings to allocate time and spell out special responsibilities for specific products.

'As needed' meetings between product management and functional units to discuss unforeseen problems.

Written procedures to clarify, where necessary, relationships between product managers and functional specialists. These descriptions also may spell out limits of activity with respect to advertising and other outside agencies.

Appointment of counterparts to each product manager, in manufacturing, finance and other functions, to complement his efforts and thus speed action on specific product needs.

Coordination of product managers' recommendations to functional groups, to minimize any tendency to favor one man's products at the expense of those of others.

A number of executives have pointed out the importance of establishing a favorable climate when the position of product manager is first set up. When the job is first created and the product manager (or his immediate superior, the group product manager) is made responsible for a profit center, these executives feel it is vital to communicate his role in creating revenue and profit to the managers of the departments he will be dealing with. Some suggest that it is valuable, especially in early stages, for higher-level marketing, production and other managers to aid in establishing direct lines of communication between the product manager and those at the same managerial level in sales, advertising, production control, quality control, accounting and other functional areas.

It is common for a higher-level marketing executive to arrange periodic meetings between product managers and the sales manager, the advertising manager and other functional managers concerned to allocate time and efforts. Since the several product managers are usually competing with each other for time of the same group of salesmen, for example, it is necessary to take some such approach to reconciling their pressures by agreeing on priorities or time allocations. There is apt to be a similar need to work out priorities for work in the factory, particularly where the products are made on a job-order basis.

Because the work of the product managers interacts with that of so many people in the company, managerial-level procedures may be written to facilitate crossing organizational lines where promotional arrangements, packaging modifications, price changes, complaint handling and other important actions are involved. Such memos or manuals clarify the part that is to be played by each department, the clearances that have to be secured on various kinds of proposals or plans, the lead time that is normally to be allowed and like matters.

Finally, of course, special conferences may be called, as needed, to smooth the way for specific programs or resolve conflicts between the product manager and representatives of other departments.

G. H. Evans 259

References

American Marketing Association (1955), *Successful Production Planning and Control*, Special Report No. 5.

JURAN, J. M. (1964), *Managerial Breakthrough*, McGraw-Hill.

Part Four **Management of Communications**

Wroe Alderson has said (Reading 3) 'For some purposes it is useful to regard marketing processes as a flow of goods and a parallel flow of informative and persuasive messages.' Part Four deals with these two types of outward flow from the organization to its environment.

The three main ingredients in communications management are objectives, people and money. Baumol (Reading 2) showed that the total company objective, either to maximize sales or profit, profoundly affected the level of advertising expenditure. The setting of specific communications targets is a recurring theme in the following Readings. Management by objectives is accepted in many other areas, but advertising decisions are still often based on habit, caution and rule-of-thumb.

The people in the communications process are the target audience, defined in terms of age, occupation and other socio-economic characteristics as a first step. The harder questions are: what interests people in this target group? Why do they buy one product rather than another? Which messages lead to purchasing and which ones make no impact? The choice of advertising theme depends on well-informed answers to these questions. Without understanding of audience psychology, advertising expenditure may be money wasted.

Kotler (Reading 15) discusses five models of what happens inside the 'black box', or the mind of the potential customer. He relates each model to the type of product for which it is likely to be most applicable and quotes references to the original studies on which his conclusions are based. These are well worth following up.

The article by Colley (Reading 16) is the classic statement of the 'communication task' approach to setting advertising objectives. However, his view of buyer psychology – that advertising's function is to move the consumer, step by step, closer to conviction and buying action – is sharply questioned by Palda (Reading 17). Palda reviews the evidence that attitude change precedes buying, which is the assumption on which many techniques for evaluating advertising effects rest. Regression analysis (a technique to establish whether market share is predictable from weighted combinations of other factors, such as brand awareness) indicates that high awareness coincides with a high rate of buying, but still does not prove that one causes the other. Palda quotes many of the important research studies into advertising effectiveness and his bibliography provides valuable further reading. He ends by doubting the usefulness of black box measurements, suggesting that it may be better to investigate directly the connection between advertising expenditure and the level of sales.

Watson (Reading 18) helps to broaden our understanding of advertising influence. Using Emery's model of the persuasion process, Watson gets away from the elemental effect of one advertisement on one individual at the moment of exposure. He suggests that we consider all the relationships which are implicit in the situation. The reader or viewer knows that the presenter of the message is speaking on behalf of an advertiser and that both stand in a special relationship toward the product advertised. The reader allows for these relationships in interpreting what is going on. For example, he may expect the advertiser to exaggerate his claims, and doubt whether the presenter is as sincere as he appears. Simultaneously, the reader may have other information about the advertiser ('a big company') and the presenter ('an actor I always like'). All these elements come into play in the advertising situation, in a complex interaction process.

Money comes into communications management when the executive has to fix his budget and decide where to spend it, guided by objectives and his understanding of how advertising can influence the target market. Majaro (Reading 19) shows how advertising budgets are decided in practice. It seems that setting objectives does pay off in increased sales – and that companies marketing industrial goods are least likely to set them. Majaro strikes a sensible balance between putting objectives in action (sales) or communications terms, discussing the circumstances in which each applies best. Lawrence (Reading 20) adopts a pragmatic approach. He suggests that most companies know a level of advertising which 'works' currently. The main problem is whether to move in the direction of spending more or less. The way to find out is through deliberately planned experimentation, in a constant effort to probe the reactions of the market.

The physical flow of goods is the subject of a final article by Le Kashman and Stolle (Reading 21). Distribution costs are hard to disentangle from company accounts and tend to lie in a managerial no-man's land, but potential savings are considerable. The multiple side-effects of changes in the distribution system call for very careful study, backed by top management support.

15 P. Kotler

Behavioural Models for Analysing Buyers

P. Kotler, 'Behavioral models for analysing buyers',
Journal of Marketing, vol. 29, no. 4, 1965, pp. 37–45.

In times past, management could arrive at a fair understanding
of its buyers through the daily experience of selling to them.
But the growth in the size of firms and markets has removed
many decision-makers from direct contact with buyers. Increasingly, decision-makers have had to turn to summary statistics
and to behavioral theory and are spending more money today
than ever before to try to understand their buyers.[1]

Who buys? How do they buy? And why? The first two questions relate to relatively overt aspects of buyer behavior and
can be learned about through direct observation and interviewing.

But uncovering *why* people buy is an extremely difficult task.
The answer will tend to vary with the investigator's behavioral
frame of reference.

The buyer is subject to many influences which trace a complex course through his psyche and lead eventually to overt
purchasing responses. This conception of the buying process is
illustrated in Figure 1. Various influences and their modes of
transmission are shown at the left. At the right are the buyer's
responses in choice of product, brand, dealer, quantities and
frequency. In the center stands the buyer and his mysterious
psychological processes. The buyer's psyche is a 'black box'
whose workings can be only partially deduced. The marketing
strategist's challenge to the behavioral scientist is to construct a
more specific model of the mechanism in the black box.

1. For a comprehensive collection of readings and articles on behavioral
models, see Day (1964). For a view that relates consumer decision strategies and risk reduction techniques to the concepts of brand loyalty,
personal influence, and prepurchase deliberation, see Bauer (1960).

Unfortunately no generally accepted model of the mechanism exists. The human mind, the only entity in nature with deep powers of understanding, still remains the least understood. Scientists can explain planetary motion, genetic determination and molecular behavior. Yet they have only partial, and often partisan, models of *human* behavior.

Nevertheless, the marketing strategist should recognize the potential interpretative contributions of different partial models for explaining buyer behavior. Depending upon the product, different variables and behavioral mechanisms may assume particular importance. A psychoanalytic behavioral model might throw much light on the factors operating in cigarette demand, while an economic behavioral model might be useful in explaining machine-tool purchasing. Sometimes alternative models may shed light on different demand aspects of the same product.

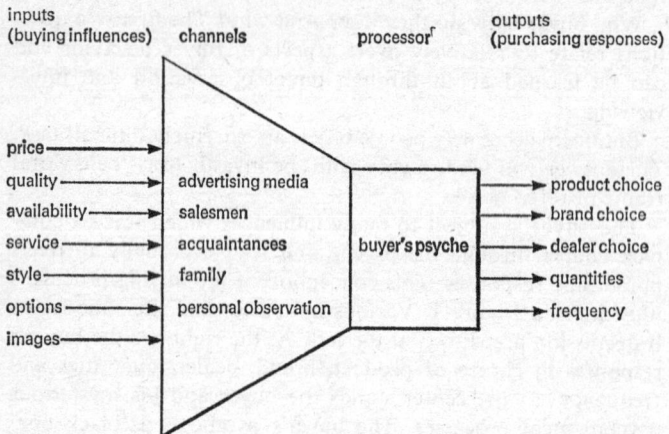

Figure 1 The buying process conceived as a system of inputs and outputs

What are the most useful behavioral models for interpreting the transformation of buying influences into purchasing responses? Five different models of the buyer's 'black box' are presented in the present article, along with their respective marketing applications: the Marshallian model, stressing economic motivations; the Pavlovian model, learning; the Freudian model, psychoanalytic motivations; the Veblenian model, social-psychological factors; and the Hobbesian model, organizational factors. These models represent radically different conceptions of the mainsprings of human behavior.

The Marshallian economic model

Economists were the first professional group to construct a specific theory of buyer behavior. The theory holds that purchasing decisions are the result of largely 'rational' and conscious economic calculations. The individual buyer seeks to spend his income on those goods that will deliver the most utility (satisfaction) according to his tastes and relative prices.

The antecedents for this view trace back to the writings of Adam Smith and Jeremy Bentham. Smith set the tone by developing a doctrine of economic growth based on the principle that man is motivated by self-interest in all his actions (Smith, 1937 edn). Bentham refined this view and saw man as finely calculating and weighing the expected pleasures and pains of every contemplated action (Bentham, 1907 edn).

Bentham's 'felicific calculus' was not applied to consumer behavior (as opposed to entrepreneurial behavior) until the late nineteenth century. Then, the 'marginal-utility' theory of value was formulated independently and almost simultaneously by Jevons (1871 edn) and Marshall (1927 edn) in England, Menger (1950 edn) in Austria and Walras (1954 edn) in Switzerland.

Alfred Marshall was the great consolidator of the classical and neoclassical tradition in economics; and his synthesis in the form of demand-supply analysis constitutes the main source of modern micro-economic thought in the English-speaking world. His theoretical work aimed at realism, but his method was to start with simplifying assumptions and to examine the effect of a change in a single variable (say, price) when all other variables were held constant.

He would 'reason out' the consequences of the provisional assumptions and in subsequent steps modify his assumptions in the direction of more realism. He employed the 'measuring rod of money' as an indicator of the intensity of human psychological desires. Over the years his methods and assumptions have been refined into what is now known as *modern utility theory*: economic man is bent on maximizing his utility, and does this by carefully calculating the 'felicific' consequences of any purchase. . . .

Marketing applications of Marshallian model

From one point of view the Marshallian model is tautological and therefore neither true nor false. The model holds that the buyer acts in the light of his best 'interest'. But this is not very informative.

A second view is that this is a *normative* rather than a *descriptive* model of behavior. The model provides logical norms for buyers who want to be 'rational'. Although the consumer is not likely to employ economic analysis to decide between a box of Kleenex and Scotties, he may apply economic analysis in deciding whether to buy a new car. Industrial buyers even more clearly would want an economic calculus for making good decisions.

A third view is that economic factors operate to a greater or lesser extent in all markets, and, therefore, must be included in any comprehensive description of buyer behavior.

Furthermore, the model suggests useful behavioral hypotheses such as: the lower the price of the product, the higher the sales; the lower the price of substitute products, the lower the sales of this product, and the lower the price of complementary products, the higher the sales of this product; the higher the real income, the higher the sales of this product, provided that it is not an 'inferior' good; the higher the promotional expenditures, the higher the sales.

The validity of these hypotheses does not rest on whether *all* individuals act as economic calculating machines in making their purchasing decisions. For example, some individuals may buy *less* of a product when its price is reduced. They may think that the quality has gone down, or that ownership has less status value. If a majority of buyers view price reductions negatively, then sales may fall, contrary to the first hypothesis.

But for most goods a price reduction increases the relative value of the goods in many buyers' minds and leads to increased sales. This and the other hypotheses are intended to describe average effects.

The impact of economic factors in actual buying situations is studied through experimental design or statistical analyses of past data. Demand equations have been fitted to a wide variety of products – including beer, refrigerators and chemical fertilizers (Nemmers, 1962). More recently, the impact of economic variables on the fortunes of different brands has been pursued with significant results, particularly in the case of coffee, frozen orange juice and margarine (Telser, 1962; Massy and Frank, 1965).

But economic factors alone cannot explain all the variations in sales. The Marshallian model ignores the fundamental question of how product and brand preferences are formed. It represents a useful frame of reference for analysing only one small corner of the 'black box'.

The Pavlovian learning model

The designation of a Pavlovian learning model has its origin in the experiments of the Russian psychologist Pavlov, who rang a bell each time before feeding a dog. Soon he was able to induce the dog to salivate by ringing the bell whether or not food was supplied. Pavlov concluded that learning was largely an associative process and that a large component of behavior was conditioned in this way. . . .

The model has been refined over the years and today is based on four central concepts – those of *drive, cue, response,* and *reinforcement* (Dollard and Miller, 1950).

Drive. Also called needs or motives, drive refers to strong stimuli internal to the individual which impels action. Psychologists draw a distinction between primary physiological drives – such as hunger, thirst, cold, pain and sex – and learned drives which are derived socially – such as cooperation, fear and acquisitiveness.

Cue. A drive is very general and impels a particular response only in relation to a particular configuration of cues. Cues are weaker stimuli in the environment and/or in the individual which determine when, where, and how the subject responds. . . .

Response. The response is the organism's reaction to the

configuration of cues. Yet the same configuration of cues will not necessarily produce the same response in the individual. This depends on the degree to which the experience was rewarding, that is, drive-reducing.

Reinforcement. If the experience is rewarding, a particular response is reinforced; that is, it is strengthened and there is a tendency for it to be repeated when the same configuration of cues appears again. . . .

Forgetting, in contrast to extinction, is the tendency for learned associations to weaken, not because of the lack of reinforcement but because of non-use.

Cue configurations are constantly changing. The housewife sees a new brand of coffee next to her habitual brand, or notes a special price deal on a rival brand. Experimental psychologists have found that the same learned response will be elicited by similar patterns of cues; that is, learned responses are *generalized*. . . .

A counter-tendency to generalization is *discrimination*. When a housewife tries two similar brands and finds one more rewarding, her ability to discriminate between similar cue configurations improves. Discrimination increases the specificity of the cue-response connection, while generalization decreases the specificity.

The modern version of the Pavlovian model makes no claim to provide a complete theory of behavior – indeed, such important phenomena as perception, the subsconscious and interpersonal influence are inadequately treated. Yet the model does offer a substantial number of insights about some aspects of behavior of considerable interest to marketers. . . .[2]

Light introductory advertising is a weak cue compared with distributing free samples. Strong cues, although costing more, may be necessary in markets characterized by strong brand loyalties. For example, Folger went into the coffee market by distributing over a million pounds of free coffee.

To build a brand habit, it helps to provide for an extended period of introductory dealing. Furthermore, sufficient quality must be built into the brand so that the experience is re-

2. The most consistent application of learning-theory concepts to marketing situations is found in Howard (1963).

inforcing. Since buyers are more likely to transfer allegiance to similar brands than dissimilar brands (generalization), the company should also investigate what cues in the leading brands have been most effective. Although outright imitation would not necessarily effect the most transference, the question of providing enough similarity should be considered.

The Pavlovian model also provides guide lines in the area of advertising strategy. The American behaviorist, John B. Watson, was a great exponent of repetitive stimuli; in his writings man is viewed as a creature who can be conditioned through repetition and reinforcement to respond in particular ways (Watson, 1925). The Pavlovian model emphasizes the desirability of repetition in advertising. A single exposure is likely to be a very weak cue, hardly able to penetrate the individual's consciousness sufficiently to excite his drives above the threshold level.

Repetition in advertising has two desirable effects. It 'fights' forgetting, the tendency for learned responses to weaken in the absence of practice. It provides reinforcement, because after the purchase the consumer becomes selectively exposed to advertisements of the product.

The model also provides guide lines for copy strategy. To be effective as a cue, an advertisement must arouse strong drives in the person. The strongest product-related drives must be identified. . . .

The Freudian psychoanalytic model

The Freudian model of man is well known, so profound has been its impact on twentieth-century thought. It is the latest of a series of philosophical 'blows' to which man has been exposed in the last 500 years. . . .

According to Freud, the child enters the world driven by instinctual needs which he cannot gratify by himself. Very quickly and painfully he realizes his separateness from the rest of the world and yet his dependence on it.

He tries to get others to gratify his needs through a variety of blatant means, including intimidation and supplication. Continual frustration leads him to perfect more subtle mechanisms for gratifying his instincts.

As he grows, his psyche becomes increasingly complex. A part of his psyche – the id – remains the reservoir of his strong drives and urges. Another part – the ego – becomes his conscious planning center for finding outlets for his drives. And a third part – his super-ego – channels his instinctive drives into socially approved outlets to avoid the pain of guilt or shame.

The guilt or shame which man feels toward some of his urges – especially his sexual urges – causes him to repress them from his consciousness. Through such defence mechanisms as rationalization and sublimation, these urges are denied or become transmuted into socially approved expressions. Yet these urges are never eliminated or under perfect control. . . .

The individual's behavior, therefore, is never simple. His motivational wellsprings are not obvious to a casual observer nor deeply understood by the individual himself. If he is asked why he purchased an expensive foreign sports-car, he may reply that he likes its maneuverability and its looks. At a deeper level he may have purchased the car to impress others, or to feel young again. At a still deeper level, he may be purchasing the sports-car to achieve substitute gratification for unsatisfied sexual strivings.

Many refinements and changes in emphasis have occurred in this model since the time of Freud. The instinct concept has been replaced by a more careful delineation of basic drives; the three parts of the psyche are regarded now as theoretical concepts rather than actual entities; and the behavioral perspective has been extended to include cultural as well as biological mechanisms. . . .

Marketing applications of Freudian model

Perhaps the most important marketing implication of this model is that buyers are motivated by *symbolic* as well as *economic-functional* product concerns. The change of a bar of soap from a square to a round shape may be more important in its sexual than its functional connotations. A cake mix that is advertised as involving practically no labor may alienate housewives because the easy life may evoke a sense of guilt.

Motivational research has produced some interesting and occasionally some bizarre hypotheses about what may be in the buyer's mind regarding certain purchases. Thus, it has been suggested at one time or another that:

Many a businessman doesn't fly because of a fear of post-humous guilt – if he crashed, his wife would think of him as stupid for not taking a train.

Men want their cigars to be odoriferous, in order to prove that they (the men) are masculine.

A woman is very serious when she bakes a cake because unconsciously she is going through the symbolic act of giving birth.

A man buys a convertible as a substitute 'mistress'.

Consumers prefer vegetable shortening because animal fats stimulate a sense of sin.

Men who wear suspenders are reacting to an unresolved castration complex.

There are admitted difficulties of proving these assertions. Two prominent motivational researchers, Ernest Dichter and James Vicary, were employed independently by two separate groups in the prune industry to determine why so many people dislike prunes. Dichter found, among other things, that the prune aroused feelings of old age and insecurity in people, whereas Vicary's main finding was that Americans had an emotional block about prunes' laxative qualities (Scriven, 1958). Which is the more valid interpretation? Or if they are both operative, which motive is found with greater statistical frequency in the population?

Unfortunately the usual survey techniques – direct observation and interviewing – can be used to establish the representativeness of more superficial characteristics – age and family size, for example – but are not feasible for establishing the frequency of mental states which are presumed to be deeply 'buried' within each individual.

Motivational researchers have to employ time-consuming projective techniques in the hope of throwing individual 'egos' off guard. When carefully administered and interpreted, techniques such as word association, sentence completion, picture interpretation and role-playing can provide some insights into the minds of the small group of examined individuals; but a 'leap of faith' is sometimes necessary to generalize these findings to the population.

Nevertheless, motivation research can lead to useful insights and provide inspiration to creative men in the advertising and packaging world. Appeals aimed at the buyer's private world of hopes, dreams and fears can often be as effective in stimulating purchase as more rationally-directed appeals.

The Veblenian social-psychological model

While most economists have been content to interpret buyer behavior in Marshallian terms, Thorstein Veblen struck out in different directions.

Veblen was trained as an orthodox economist, but evolved into a social thinker greatly influenced by the new science of social anthropology. He saw man as primarily a *social animal* – conforming to the general forms and norms of his larger culture and to the more specific standards of the subcultures and face-to-face groupings to which his life is bound. His wants and behavior are largely molded by his present group-memberships and his aspired group-memberships.

Veblen's best-known example of this is in his description of the leisure class (1899). His hypothesis is that much of economic consumption is motivated not by intrinsic needs or satisfaction so much as by prestige-seeking. He emphasized the strong emulative factors operating in the choice of conspicuous goods like clothes, cars and houses.

Some of his points, however, seem overstated by today's perspective. The leisure class does not serve as everyone's reference group; many persons aspire to the social patterns of the class immediately above it. And important segments of the affluent class practice conspicuous underconsumption rather than overconsumption. There are many people in all classes who are more anxious to 'fit in' than to 'stand out'. As an example, William H. Whyte found that many families avoided buying air conditioners and other appliances before their neighbors did (1954).

Marketing applications of Veblenian model

The various streams of thought crystallized into the modern

social sciences of sociology, cultural anthropology and social psychology. Basic to them is the view that man's attitudes and behavior are influenced by several levels of society – culture, subcultures, social classes, reference groups and face-to-face groups. The challenge to the marketer is to determine which of these social levels are the most important in influencing the demand for his product.

Culture. The most enduring influences are from culture. Man tends to assimilate his culture's mores and folkways and to believe in their absolute rightness until deviants appear within his culture or until he confronts members of another culture.

Subcultures. A culture tends to lose its homogeneity as its population increases. When people no longer are able to maintain face-to-face relationships with more than a small proportion of other members of a culture, smaller units or subcultures develop, which help to satisfy the individual's needs for more specific identity.

The subcultures are often regional entities, because the people of a region, as a result of more frequent interactions, tend to think and act alike. But subcultures also take the form of religions, nationalities, fraternal orders and other institutional complexes which provide a broad identification for people who may otherwise be strangers. The subcultures of a person play a large role in his attitude formation and become another important predictor of certain values he is likely to hold.

Social class. People become differentiated not only horizontally but also vertically through a division of labor. The society becomes stratified socially on the basis of wealth, skill and power. Sometimes castes develop in which the members are reared for certain roles, or social classes develop in which the members feel empathy with others sharing similar values and economic circumstances.

Because social class involves different attitudinal configurations, it becomes a useful independent variable for segmenting markets and predicting reactions. Significant differences have been found among different social classes with respect to magazine readership, leisure activities, food imagery, fashion interests and acceptance of innovations. . . .

Reference groups. There are groups in which the individual has no membership but with which he identifies and may aspire to – reference groups. Many young boys identify with big-league baseball players or astronauts, and many young girls identify with Hollywood stars. The activities of these popular heroes are carefully watched and frequently imitated. These reference figures become important transmitters of influence, although more along lines of taste and hobby than basic attitudes.

Face-to-face groups. Groups that have the most immediate influence on a person's tastes and opinions are face-to-face groups. This includes all the small 'societies' with which he comes into frequent contact: his family, close friends, neighbors, fellow workers, fraternal associates and so forth. His informal group memberships are influenced largely by his occupation, residence and stage in the life cycle.

The powerful influence of small groups on individual attitudes has been demonstrated in a number of social-psychological experiments (Asch, 1953; Lewin, 1952). There is also evidence that this influence may be growing. David Riesman and his co-authors have pointed to signs which indicate a growing amount of *other-direction*, that is, a tendency for individuals to be increasingly influenced by their peers in the definition of their values rather than by their parents and elders (1950).

For the marketer, this means that brand choice may increasingly be influenced by one's peers. For such products as cigarettes and automobiles, the influence of peers is unmistakable.

The role of face-to-face groups has been recognized in recent industry campaigns attempting to change basic product attitudes. For years the milk industry has been trying to overcome the image of milk as a 'sissified' drink by portraying its use in social and active situations. The men's-wear industry is trying to increase male interest in clothes by advertisements indicating that business associates judge a man by how well he dresses.

Of all face-to-face groups, the person's family undoubtedly plays the largest and most enduring role in basic attitude formation. From them he acquires a mental set not only toward religion and politics, but also toward thrift, chastity, food, human relations and so forth. Although he often rebels against parental values in his teens, he often accepts these values eventually. Their formative influence on his eventual attitudes is undeniably great.

Family members differ in the types of product messages they carry to other family members. Most of what parents know about cereals, candy and toys comes from their children. The wife stimulates family consideration of household appliances, furniture and vacations. The husband tends to stimulate the fewest purchase ideas, with the exception of the automobile and perhaps the home.

The marketer must be alert to what attitudinal configurations dominate in different types of families and also to how these change over time. For example, the parent's conception of the child's rights and privileges has undergone a radical shift in the last thirty years. The child has become the center of attention and orientation in a great number of households, leading some writers to label the modern family a 'filiarchy'. This has important implications not only for how to market to today's family, but also on how to market to tomorrow's family when the indulged child of today becomes the parent.

The person. Social influences determine much but not all of the behavioral variations in people. Two individuals subject to the same influences are not likely to have identical attitudes, although these attitudes will probably converge at more points than those of two strangers selected at random. Attitudes are really the product of social forces interacting with the individual's unique temperament and abilities.

Furthermore, attitudes do not automatically guarantee certain types of behavior. Attitudes are predispositions felt by buyers before they enter the buying process. The buying process itself is a learning experience and can lead to a change in attitudes.

P. Kotler 277

Alfred Politz noted at one time that women stated a clear preference for GE refrigerators over Frigidaire, but that Frigidaire continued to outsell GE (Politz, 1958). The answer to this paradox was that preference was only one factor entering into behavior. When the consumer preferring GE actually undertook to purchase a new refrigerator, her curiosity led her to examine the other brands. Her perception was sensitized to refrigerator advertisements, sales arguments and different product features. This led to learning and a change in attitudes.

The Hobbesian organizational-factors model

The foregoing models throw light mainly on the behavior of family buyers.

But what of the large number of people who are organizational buyers? They are engaged in the purchase of goods not for the sake of consumption, but for further production or distribution. Their common denominator is the fact that they are paid to make purchases for others, and operate within an organizational environment.

How do organizational buyers make their decisions? There seem to be two competing views. Many marketing writers have emphasized the predominance of rational motives in organizational buying (Copeland, 1924). Organizational buyers are represented as being most impressed by cost, quality, dependability and service factors. They are portrayed as dedicated servants of the organization, seeking to secure the best terms. This view has led to an emphasis on performance and use characteristics in much industrial advertising.

Other writers have emphasized personal motives in organizational buyer behavior. The purchasing agent's interest to do the best for his company is tempered by his interest to do the best for himself. He may be tempted to choose among salesmen according to the extent they entertain or offer gifts. He may choose a particular vendor because this will ingratiate him with certain company officers. He may shortcut his study of alternative suppliers to make his work day easier.

In truth, the buyer is guided by both personal and group goals; and this is the essential point. The political model of Thomas Hobbes comes closest of any model to suggesting the relationship between the two goals (1887 edn). Hobbes held that man is 'instinctively' oriented toward preserving and enhancing his own well-being. But this would produce a 'war of every man against every man'. This fear leads men to unite with others in a corporate body. The corporate man tries to steer a careful course between satisfying his own needs and those of the organization.

Marketing applications of Hobbesian model

The import of the Hobbesian model is that organizational buyers can be appealed to on both personal and organizational grounds. The buyer has his private aims, and yet he tries to do a satisfactory job for his corporation. He will respond to persuasive salesmen and he will respond to rational product arguments. However, the best 'mix' of the two is not a fixed quantity; it varies with the nature of the product, the type of organization, and the relative strength of the two drives in the particular buyer.

Where there is substantial similarity in what suppliers offer in the way of products, price and service, the purchasing agent has less basis for rational choice. Since he can satisfy his organizational obligations with any one of a number of suppliers, he can be swayed by personal motives. On the other hand, where there are pronounced differences among the competing vendors' products, the purchasing agent is held more accountable for his choice and probably pays more attention to rational factors. Short-run personal gain becomes less motivating than the long-run gain which comes from serving the organization with distinction.

The marketing strategist must appreciate these goal conflicts of the organizational buyer. Behind all the ferment of purchasing agents to develop standards and employ value analysis lies their desire to avoid being thought of as order-clerks, and to develop better skills in reconciling personal and organizational objectives (see Strauss, 1962, for an insightful account).

Summary

Think back over the five different behavioral models of how the buyer translates buying influences into purchasing responses.

Marshallian man is concerned chiefly with economic cues – prices and income – and makes a fresh utility calculation before each purchase.

Pavlovian man behaves in a largely habitual rather than thoughtful way; certain configurations of cues will set off the same behavior because of rewarded learning in the past.

Freudian man's choices are influenced strongly by motives and fantasies which take place deep within his private world.

Veblenian man acts in a way which is shaped largely by past and present social groups.

And finally, Hobbesian man seeks to reconcile individual gain with organizational gain.

Thus, it turns out that the 'black box' of the buyer is not so black after all. Light is thrown in various corners by these models. Yet no one has succeeded in putting all these pieces of truth together into one coherent instrument for behavioral analysis. This, of course, is the goal of behavioral science.

References

ASCH, S. E. (1953), 'Effects of group pressure upon the modification and distortion of judgments', in D. Cartwright and A. Zander (eds.), *Group Dynamics*, Row, Peterson, pp. 151–62.

BAUER, R. A. (1960), 'Consumer behavior as risk taking', *Proc. Summer Conference Amer. Marketing Assn*, pp. 389–98.

BENTHAM, J. (1907), *An Introduction to the Principles of Morals and Legislation*, Clarendon Press. First published 1780.

COPELAND, M. T. (1924), *Principles of Merchandising*, McGraw-Hill.

DAY, R. L. (ed.) (1964), *Marketing Models Quantitative and Behavioral*, International Textbook Co., pp. 3–268.

DOLLARD, J., and MILLER, N. E. (1950), *Personality and Psychotherapy*, McGraw-Hill, ch. 3.

HOBBES, T. (1887), *Leviathan*, Routledge & Kegan-Paul. First published 1651.

HOWARD, J. A. (1963), *Marketing Management: Analysis and Planning*, Irwin.

JEVONS, W. S. (1871), *The Theory of Political Economy*, Macmillan Co.

LEWIN, K. (1952), 'Group decision and social change', in T. M. Newcomb and E. L. Hartley (eds.), *Readings in Social Psychology*, Holt, Rinehart Winston.

MARSHALL, A. (1927), *Principles of Economics*, Macmillan. First published 1890.

MASSY, W. F., and FRANK, R. E. (1965), 'Short-term price and dealing effects in selected market segments', *J. Marketing Res.*, vol. 2, no. 2, pp. 171–85.

MENGER, K. (1950), *Principles of Economics*, Free Press. First published 1871.

NEMMERS, E. E. (1962), *Managerial Economics*, Wiley, pt 2.

POLITZ, A. (1958), 'Motivation research – opportunity or dilemma?', in R. Ferber and H. G. Wales (eds.), *Motivation and Marketing Behavior*, Irwin, pp. 57–8.

RIESMAN, D., DENNEY, R., and GLAZER, N. (1950), *The Lonely Crowd*, Yale University Press.

SCRIVEN, L. E. (1958), 'Rationality and irrationality in motivation research', in R. Ferber and H. G. Wales (eds.), *Motivation and Marketing Behavior*, Irwin, pp. 69–70.

SMITH, A. (1937), *An Inquiry into the Nature and Causes of the Wealth of Nations*, Modern Library. First published in 1776.

STRAUSS, G. (1962), 'Tactics of lateral relationship', *Admin. Sci. Q.*, vol. 7, September, pp. 161–86.

TELSER, L. G. (1962), 'The demand for branded goods as estimated from consumer panel data', *Rev. Econ. Stats.*, vol. 44, August, pp. 300–324.

VEBLEN, T. (1899), *The Theory of the Leisure Class*, Macmillan Co.

WALRAS, L. (1954), *Elements of Pure Economics*, Irwin. First published 1874.

WATSON, J. B. (1925), *Behaviorism*, The People's Institute Publishing Co.

WHYTE, W. H., Jr (1954), 'The web of word of mouth', *Fortune*, vol. 50, November, pp. 140 ff.

16 R. H. Colley

Defining Advertising Goals

Excerpt from R. H. Colley (ed.), *Defining Advertising Goals for Measured Advertising Results*, Association of National Advertisers of New York, 1961, pp. 49–60.

Understanding advertising's purpose

It is a fact of modern business life that many different people are involved in the creation and approval of advertising. . . . For a small advertiser, there may be a half-dozen different people concerned, while a larger advertiser may have dozens of people involved in the advertising of a single product, hundreds of people concerned with the entire product line.

Do all of these people have a common understanding of the purpose of advertising?

We have already indicated what would be the result if you were to conduct a little survey among these individuals asking: 'What are we trying to accomplish with this campaign or ad for this product at this time?' The same diversity of opinion would undoubtedly result if the survey asked the more general question: 'What is advertising's purpose in our company?'

The President may be strongly minded toward building a 'corporate image'. The Sales Manager may regard advertising as a means of getting larger orders from retailers. Financial people may regard advertising as an expense, chargeable to a given fiscal period. The Advertising Manager or the agency account executive may regard advertising as an investment, directed toward building a brand image and increasing share of market.

The job of gaining a common understanding of advertising's contribution is highly important. Few of those who influence and approve key advertising decisions have had any direct advertising experience. But the final decision-makers in American industry are reaching out for a better understanding of advertising and how it can be employed most profitably in the business.

Robert F. Elder, President of the Plax Corporation, expressed the feeling voiced by many other chief executives, in these words: 'Most management men want to understand advertising and are eager to listen attentively when you talk to them about it in simple, realistic, down-to-earth terms – and what it means to corporate sales and profits.'

Discussions of the advertising process, what it is, and how it operates may be helpful in gaining a general understanding of advertising's function and contribution in various kinds of business situations.

What is advertising?

Those who have spent their lives in advertising may, on first consideration, feel it is naïve to pose the question, 'What is advertising?' Such a question, they may say, is appropriate only for students and trainees, but not for experienced and sophisticated marketing and sales executives.

However, different meanings are frequently attached to the terms 'advertising', 'sales promotion',[1] 'publicity', 'selling', and

1. There is no universally accepted distinction between 'advertising' and 'sales promotion'. In some companies 'advertising' includes all forms of mass paid communication directed toward influencing the *end consumer*, whereas 'sales promotion' includes those forms of mass communication directed toward informing and influencing the *channels of distribution:* salesmen, distributors, dealers. In other companies, 'sales promotion' includes mass communication materials (literature, catalogs, displays, films) which are used *by* the channels of distribution (salesmen, retailers) as selling aids. Hence, a piece of product literature mailed directly to a customer is advertising; literature distributed by the salesman or dealer is sales promotion. Still another (and perhaps the most traditional) distinction between advertising and sales promotion is that advertising consists of time, space and preparatory costs in *commissionable media*. All other mass commercial communications are regarded as 'sales promotion'. In some industries and channels of distribution the term 'sales promotion' is used to refer to any and all activities used to promote sales including: premium offers and other special inducements to consumers, special price offers, sales drives and contests, as well as advertising. Under such usage the term 'sales promotion' becomes almost synonymous with 'merchandising' and even 'marketing'. The first important consideration is that some agreed-upon definition be arrived at, as a basis for common understanding within the company and between company and agency. Resolving industry-wide semantic differences is a longer-range effort.

R. H. Colley 283

'marketing'. Terminology differs from industry to industry and within an industry. Differences of opinion on 'what is advertising?' are clearly demonstrated when a budget is prepared. In some companies the advertising budget includes only paid space and time. In others it includes practically all forms of the printed word including sales literature, price sheets, publicity releases, house organs, employee communications, etc. (One advertising manager thought it was going a little too far to charge his budget for repair and maintenance of the clock over the branch office building.) It is important that those within a given company have a common understanding of terminology.

We start with the obvious fact that advertising is a form of communication. So is a letter or a personal call by a salesman on a customer. The difference is that advertising is *mass* communication. So is a story in a newspaper or magazine, or a play on television. So is a sermon or a political speech. As a matter of fact, all of the fine arts – music, poetry, painting, drama – are forms of communication. They convey a frame of mind. By whatever the means, somehow these forms of art make contact and thereby transmit a mood or 'message' from one human mind to another.

We begin to separate advertising from the many other forms of communication when we add the term 'commercial' or 'paid'. It is paid for by a sponsor who expects to induce some kind of action on the part of the reader or listener that will be beneficial to the advertiser. To sum up in a definition: advertising is mass, paid communication, the ultimate purpose of which is to impart information, develop attitude and induce action beneficial to the advertiser (generally the sale of a product or service).

Paid political announcements, recruitment ads, even the 'lost dog' ad in the classified columns of the newspaper are all advertising. They are mass communications, paid for by a sponsor who wishes to achieve some end: the election of a candidate, the hiring of personnel, or the recovery of the family pet. But the bulk of all advertising aims toward the ultimate sale of a product or service. It is this area of advertising as a marketing force with which we are primarily concerned.

How the advertising process works

The ultimate purpose of most advertising is to help bring about the sale of a product or service.

To come to grips with this question of the purpose of advertising we ask two very simple and obvious questions:

1. When? (Speed of reaction)

2. How much of the sales-making load is to be carried by advertising?

Answers to the question 'When is advertising expected to bring about a sale?' will run the complete gamut. A department store runs an ad in the evening paper announcing a sensational sale of an item. Next morning, people are lined up waiting for the doors to open. An hour later clerks are saying, 'Sorry, we're sold out.'

A corporation runs a 'corporate image' ad aimed at prospective employees at the student level. Ten years later a man who read the ad may apply for a job, or he may specify the company's products on a purchase order, or he may buy some of the company's stock.

Of course, the time objective of most advertising falls somewhere in between these two extremes. The advertiser of automobiles, insurance, farm equipment or machine tools does not expect people to rush out and buy his product. But he does expect to move the prospect a little closer to the purchase of his product. Advertising's job is to increase *propensity* to buy – to move the prospect, inch-by-inch, closer to a purchase. If one out of ten or even one out of a hundred of the people who are exposed to the ads take *near-term buying action* we may have a huge success on our hands.

Let's examine the second question: 'How much of the selling load is advertising expected to carry?'

At one extreme we have a mail-order advertiser who would say, '100 per cent', because advertising is the only commercial communication force. At the other extreme is the industrial company in which personal selling is the key sales-making force. Advertising assists by carrying part of the communicating work load. One corporation, having a line of both

R. H. Colley 285

consumer and industrial products, figured the advertising-to-sales ratio varied from a high of 25 per cent to a low of 0·25 per cent.

Between these extremes we have the wide range of products where advertising is blended with packaging, promotion, price and personal selling; all of these forces contributing to the consummation of a sale.

To repeat, we have two variables:

1. The speed of reaction to advertising.

2. The share of the communicating work load to be carried by advertising.

The communications spectrum

The concept of the 'Marketing Communications Spectrum' . . . offers a starting approach to the solution of our problem. This concept is applied common sense. It breaks the subject up into logical and comprehensible steps. It begins with the obvious assumption that advertising is a communication force. Advertising does not physically impel the consumer toward the purchase of goods; its purpose is to create a state of mind conducive to purchase. Advertising, therefore, is one of several communication forces which, acting singly or in combination, move the consumer through successive levels of what we have termed the communications spectrum. These levels as shown in Figure 1 are Unawareness, Awareness, Comprehension, Conviction and Action.

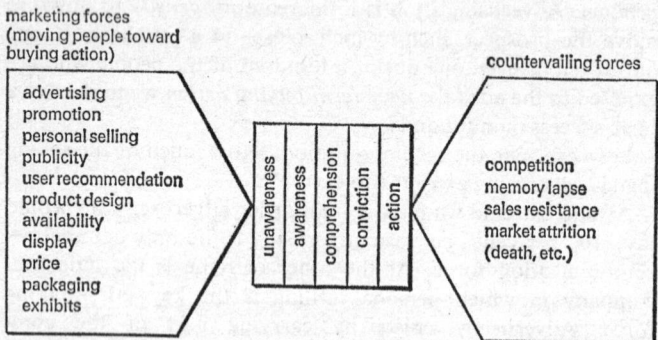

Figure 1 Marketing communications spectrum

The lowest level of this communications spectrum is Unawareness. At this level are the people who have never heard of our product or company. The messages about the product have not penetrated to the point where the consumer recognizes or recalls the brand or company name. Now it is conceivable that people buy products or vote for candidates whose names are unknown to them. The chances are, however, that such a product makes few sales and such a candidate gets few votes. As a bare minimum, we strive for achieving consumer Awareness.

The next level above Awareness in the communications spectrum is that of Comprehension. In this state the consumer not only is aware of the product or service, but knows the brand name and recognizes the package or trademark and, in addition, possesses some degree of comprehension of what the product is and does. He may say, 'Brand A is a headache remedy which the maker claims will give fast relief and will not upset the stomach,' or 'The B company is a manufacturer of earthmoving equipment that will scoop up twenty tons in one bite.'

The next level of the spectrum, Conviction, can be illustrated by a consumer who says, 'Brand B is a name for a polyester fiber made by the X Company. Garments made of this fiber dry faster, wear longer and hold their shape better. I intend to buy this product in the future.' It may also be illustrated by a woman who prefers a particular brand of lipstick or a man who prefers a particular brand of beer on an emotional rather than a strictly rational basis.

Finally, there is Action, in which the consumer has made some overt move toward the purchase of the product. He may have visited a dealer's showroom and asked for a demonstration. He may have asked for literature or for a salesman to call. He may have asked for or reached for the brand at the retail store. Consummation of the sale may have been beyond the power of advertising: the dealer did not have the brand in stock, the salesman failed to follow up the lead, the price was considered too high, or the product lacked appeal when physically examined. However, the advertising induced action.

Advertising performs its role when it contributes to moving the consumer through one or more levels in the spectrum: awareness of the existence of the product, comprehension of the

R. H. Colley 287

features and advantages, rational or emotional conviction of the benefits and, finally, action leading to a sale.

The marketing communications mix

Advertising is one of several forces contributing to awareness, comprehension, conviction and action. Other forces will vary, depending upon whether this is a 'consumer' or 'industrial' product or service. They may include: person-to-person selling, recommendation of user or retailer, publicity and various other forms of mass communication such as displays, exhibits, films, literature, etc.

Rarely does a single communication force move a prospect through the entire cycle. The exceptions prove the rule. Mail-order type advertising can move a reader through the entire spectrum from unawareness to cash-in-advance sale in a few hundred words. Door-to-door salesmen and street-corner demonstrators can sell kitchen utensils, cosmetics, brushes, etc. to consumers in a few minutes of persuasive selling.

But the use of advertising or personal selling to achieve the wrapped-up, one-shot sale is but a tiny fraction of total advertising and selling effort. All of the forces of marketing communication are brought together in a 'mix' or 'blend' to move the prospect step by step, even inch by inch, toward the ultimate goal of a satisfied customer.

The purpose of advertising is to perform certain parts of the communicating job with greater economy, speed and volume than can be accomplished through other means.

In some instances – notably consumer package goods – advertising may be called upon to carry the major part of the marketing communicating work load: from awareness, through comprehension, conviction and right through to action. Consider a product sold through self-service grocery and drug outlets. Advertising is the major communicative force between manufacturer and consumer. The function today of the package goods retailer is mainly to make the goods conveniently available at a price and to provide facilities for the physical exchange between goods and money.

In other product lines, notably industrial goods, advertising is a complementary communicative force. The typical company salesman calling on industrial accounts may make only three or four calls a day. If we subtract the time he spends behind a steering wheel, in reception rooms, in handling various service duties and in building friendly relations, the actual face-to-face time spent in *presenting the merits of his product* to the customer is small. The cost per sales call and per selling minute is high; the rate of penetration of sales messages to the many thousand of buying influences is slow. *Advertising's job is to increase the productivity of the salesman by relieving him of a substantial part of his communication work load.*

Falling somewhere in between these two extremes are consumer durables and semi-durables (autos, appliances, home furnishings, jewelry, clothing, etc.) Advertising's job is to deliver people who are informed and emotionally favorable to a brand, across the retailer's threshold (and, of course, advertising informs and influences the retailer, too). Consummation of a sale hinges upon product appearance, price, availability in desired size and color and a dozen other factors.

Advertising's job may vary with the season or the stage of a product's development. It may be to introduce a new product or a new use of an old product. It may be to hammer away at product benefits or to create a favorable emotional disposition toward a company or brand. In some cases the primary function of advertising is to remind people to buy or to stimulate impulse purchases.

In every case the function of advertising is to perform a commercial communication task more economically than by some alternate means.

Advertising is automated marketing communications

We tend to regard automation as a relatively recent development in American industry, and so it is when applied to the factory or office. We tend to overlook the fact that advertising is 'automated marketing communication'. Automation can be a powerful force for increased productivity *if* it is applied selectively. It would be foolish to propose that every operation in a factory or office should be automated. The process of boring cylinders in an engine block may lend itself to automation, whereas the assembly of carburetors may not. It may be economical to put factory payroll or finished goods inventory on an electronic computer in one company and not feasible in another company.

In a similar manner, we approach marketing communications on a 'task basis':
What are the communicating tasks to be done?
What parts of the total communicating job is advertising uniquely and economically qualified to perform?
What is the ideal 'mix' of these communication forces for *each* product at this particular stage in its marketing development?

Marketing mix in action

If we refer again to Figure 1, we see that advertising is one of several marketing forces acting upon potential customers and moving them toward buying action. Seldom does a single force, such as advertising or personal selling, perform the entire task alone. And rarely is a single force powerful enough to move a prospect through the entire spectrum, from unawareness to action, through a single message. Advertising's function is to move the consumer, step by step, closer to buying conviction and finally, to buying action.

In some situations, advertising may be designed to work at all levels at the same time. Let's assume that the market is equally divided into the five levels. (See Figure 2.)

action	20% are presented users of the product (action)
conviction	20% are convinced but haven't gotten around to buying
comprehension	20% comprehend the product but are not convinced
awareness	20% are aware of the product but don't know its advantages
unawareness	20% never heard of it

Figure 2

Let's assume that, as a result of an advertising campaign, half of those at each level move up one rung on the ladder. Then we would have Figure 3.

Advertising in this instance has worked 'across the board', moving some people from unawareness to awareness, others to comprehension, conviction and action.

Under certain market conditions (such as intense competition), advertising may perform a valuable economic function if it succeeds in *holding its present share of the consumer mind*. In addition to replacing customers lost to competition, the advertising has succeeded in counteracting such opposing forces as memory lapse and the losses that occur through death and through customers 'outgrowing' the need for the product (example: baby food).

Consider some entirely different situations. The force of advertising may be directed at one particular level in the spectrum, rather than 'across the board'. Some situations call for advertising that is entirely action-oriented. (See Figure 4.)

For example, consider a leading brand of razor blades. Everyone is acquainted with the product. And while not 100 per cent of the people are convinced, the brand's high share of industry indicates that this is not the key problem. What is advertising job? It may well be to *remind* people to buy: men

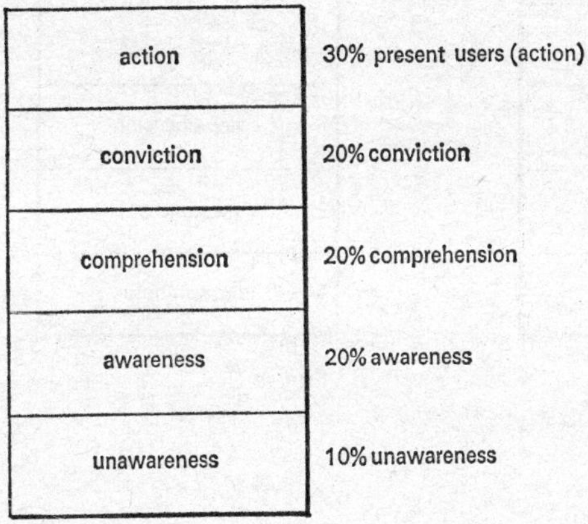

action	30% present users (action)
conviction	20% conviction
comprehension	20% comprehension
awareness	20% awareness
unawareness	10% unawareness

Figure 3

forget to buy blades, use old blades beyond their normal length of life. Similarly, advertising of such impulse items as soft drinks is strongly action-oriented.

A leading established brand in a highly competitive situation – let's say a headache remedy – may channel the bulk of its advertising efforts toward the *conviction* level of the spectrum. Advertising's job is to demonstrate product superiority and create a brand preference. Action occurs when a consumer with high-buying propensity is confronted with the need and is exposed to the product at the point of purchase. (See Figure 5.)

In a similar way we have situations in which the major advertising emphasis is placed at the comprehension or awareness level. Then there are other situations in which the emphasis changes from one season to another: announcement advertising to introduce a product or feature; demonstration advertising to build comprehension and conviction; image advertising to build emotional preference; and finally, 'buy now' advertising to get action.

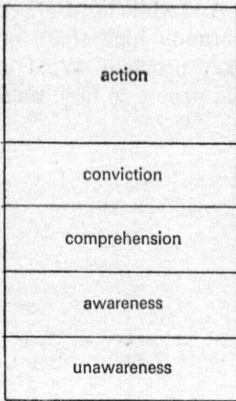

Figure 4

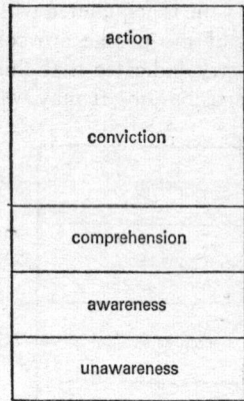

Figure 5

17 K. S. Palda

The Hypothesis of a Hierarchy of Effects: A Partial Evaluation

K. S. Palda, 'The hypothesis of a hierarchy of effects: a partial evaluation', *Journal of Marketing Research*, vol. 3, no. 1, 1966, pp. 13–24.

In 1961 Lavidge and Steiner presented a model for the predictive measurement of advertising effectiveness (Lavidge and Steiner, 1961). They postulated a hierarchical sequence of effects, resulting from the perception of an advertisement, which moves the consumer ever closer to purchase. In diagram form the model is as follows:

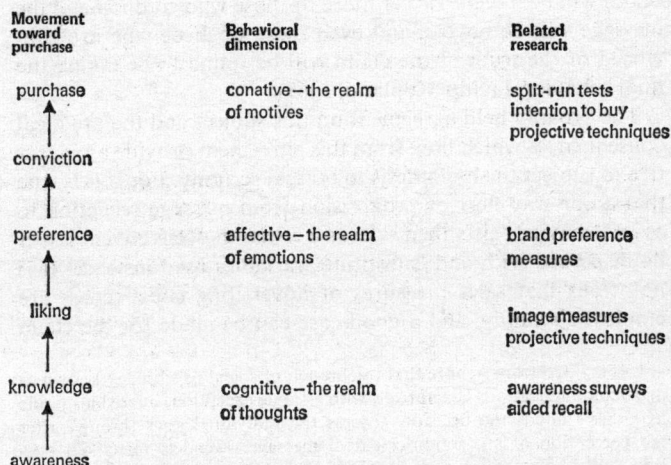

Movement toward purchase	Behavioral dimension	Related research
purchase	conative – the realm of motives	split-run tests intention to buy projective techniques
↑		
conviction		
↑		
preference	affective – the realm of emotions	brand preference measures
↑		
liking		image measures projective techniques
↑		
knowledge	cognitive – the realm of thoughts	awareness surveys aided recall
↑		
awareness		

Figure 1

Lavidge and Steiner claim that this sequence is based on what they term a classic psychological model, which divides behavior into cognitive, affective and conative (or motivational) states.[1]

The Lavidge-Steiner hypothesis of a hierarchy of effects offers in a concise and clear manner viewpoints widely held in advertising circles for many years. Attention, interest, desire and action (Sandage and Fryburger, 1963); awareness, acceptance, preference, intention to buy and provocation of sale (Wolfe, Brown, and Thompson, 1962); awareness, comprehension, conviction and action are but a few of similar but more sketchy views of the internal psychological process a typical consumer is supposed to experience from the perception of an ad to purchase (Colley, 1961).

Some recent refinements of the hypothesis are symptoms of its growing popularity. Copland, for instance, states that it cannot be expected that a purchase will take place only if the individual has passed through each of the stages of awareness, comprehension and conviction. Rather, it is to be expected that some people who are merely aware of the existence of the brand will be buyers, rather more of those who comprehend the message will be buyers, and even more of those who are convinced of the truth of the claim will be found to be taking the final behavioral jump (Copland, 1963).

The broadly held agreement on this subject and the practical consequences which flow from this agreement provide an incentive to subject the hypothesis to critical scrutiny. For if it is true that a one-way flow of progression from message reception to overt behavior exists, then sales as a criterion of effectiveness can be dispensed with and 'substitute' variables used instead.[2] It is notorious that sales measures of advertising effectiveness are employed scantily, and a good case can be made for the claim

1. It is interesting to note that the branch of social psychology known as mass communications has not yet, with a single exception, offered a specific hypothesis about the decision process the individual goes through after the perception of an 'action-oriented' message. Mendelsohn (1962) prosides both the exception and a critique of mass communications theory on this point.

2. I have dealt elsewhere with the assertion that a firm can find the optimum size of its advertising appropriation, even though avoiding the use of sales as the ultimate yardstick of effectiveness; it cannot (Palda, 1964b).

that the general acceptance of the idea of a hierarchy of advertising effects is to a large extent responsible for this.[3]

Voices of skepticism and dissent have not been entirely absent in advertising literature (Mindak, 1956). Criticism seems, however, to have been directed at each individual step in the hierarchy rather than at the hypothesis as a whole.[4] Furthermore, the criticism appears to have been predominantly concerned with the methodological soundness of the research methods employed to ascertain the effectiveness of an advertisement to bring about awareness, recall, attitude change, etc. It has not tended to the question, until very recently, of the plausibility of the assumption that each of these steps contributes to an increased probability of purchase.[5]

In the following sections, the assumption that movement up each step of the hierarchy increases the probability of *purchase* on the part of a consumer will be critically evaluated. (The methodological soundness of the various methods measuring the impact of advertising on the '*intermediate*' variables will only be touched upon.) First, a survey of some of the literature and empirical evidence concerning the various hierarchical steps will be made; second, an analysis of some data which have been gathered; third, and finally, objections in the form of a table will be presented, and questions on the economic soundness of not using sales as *the* criterion of advertising effectiveness will be posed.

Published sources that would be of relevance to the testing of the hypothesis of hierarchical effects with regard to the link between each step and *buying behavior* have been checked. Confidence in this bibliographical survey was strengthened when the bibliographical survey of the Advertising Research Foundation appeared and dovetailed with it (Krueger and Ramond, 1964).

3. A good example is the privately available *Program for Measuring the Effectiveness of General Motors' Advertising* drawn up in 1963.

4. In their recent book, Lucas and Britt present a systematic evaluation of the research methods dealing with each step in the hierarchy (1963).

5. The important recent exception is Haskins (1964).

Cognitive dimensions

Awareness

Studies of change of awareness accompanying changed amounts of advertising effort are so numerous that it is impossible to survey them. With one exception, there is no good evidence that such changes in awareness precede rather than follow purchase.[6] Several studies, in which the relationship between change in awareness and change in sales was investigated, in addition to other hierarchical effects, are reviewed below.

Knowledge, recall and recognition

The position of advertisers and their agencies with regard to measurement of awareness, recognition or recall was stated by Heller as follows (1956). Advertisers hypothesize that if advertising is to sell, it must communicate, and that the ad that communicates best is the one that will produce the greatest memory impression. The assumption is that the memory production of an advertisement is related to its sales effectiveness. Until data are obtained to the contrary, this is an assumption that advertising management and research personnel accept and work with, concludes Heller.

Such data to the contrary, in fairly persuasive form and quantity, have been assembled by Haskins (1964). He is interested in the relationship between factual learning and attitudes, or factual learning and sales. (This article centers on the latter relationship.)

Haskins first surveyed those few private advertising research studies which he could find. Two used sales as the criterion. In the first, awareness was, but gain in knowledge was not, related to increased sales. From the second, which was a massive experiment, it appeared that knowledge was not a prerequisite to sales, but attitude and belief changes preceded sales, and there was a relationship between the two measures.

Searching through *Psychological Abstracts* for 1954–63, he found seventeen studies dealing with the correlation of knowledge changes with attitude or behavioral changes. Two showed

6. The exception (NBC, 1953) is discussed later.

a positive relationship between changes in knowledge/recall and the criterion variable (mostly attitudes), two a negative relationship and the remaining thirteen little or no relationship.

Against this evidence might be set the ancient popularity of Starch's service and his series of articles about Netapps (1961). Starch asserts that when users are divided into those who recall and those who do not recall the advertisement, the difference between them can be attributed to advertising. And that, typically, those who recall buy more than those who do not.

Rotzoll, in a recent summary of the usual objections to Starch, points out why high purchase and high recall could both be present without one necessarily being the cause of the other:

1. Product interest could affect willingness to be exposed to advertising for a product;
2. Post-purchase doubts about the wisdom of choosing a product could lead to exposure to that product's advertising in order to allay such doubts;
3. 'Yea-saying' tendencies may inflate readership-purchase correlation;
4. Starch relies on the assumption, possibly unsound, that perceivers-buyers closely resemble nonperceivers-buyers in all significant aspects except for exposure to the advertising message and purchase of the brand (Rotzoll, 1964).

To those objections the following, from among many others, might be added:

5. The possibility that many factors, other than the printed ad in question, were not eliminated from the test situation: frequency of exposure to previous ads of the brand, similarity to previous or other ads, numbers of claims in ad, etc.
6. Purchasers of the brand may be better 'rememberers' because it may be easier to associate recent experience and recent perception.

The *methodological* pitfalls surrounding *recognition and recall* tests are discussed in Lucas and Britt (1963).[7]

7. Particularly pp. 60 and 101. Note also their conclusion that *portfolio* tests of advertisements are so insensitive to changes in variables of interest as to be of little practical value (pp. 77–8).

A search uncovered the following studies in which recall is measured against purchasing and which appear relevant to testing the hierarchical hypothesis.

A study undertaken at Scott Paper deserves brief mention because it claims to have used experimental methods to determine the relationship between changes in recall, attitudes and market shares (Roens, 1961). From the published report it is, however, impossible to determine with any degree of confidence what went on.[8]

NBC undertook an expensive study in the Davenport, Iowa, metropolitan area in 1952 to determine the effects of television viewing on purchases (NBC, 1953). A special effort was made to find out whether viewing leads to purchase, rather than purchase to the remembering of viewing.

Interviewed were 2,452 women, first in February and then in May, on a particular TV program viewed and the brand advertised. Table 1 was constructed, where the first algebraic sign (+ or —) refers to buying or viewing in February, and the second to buying or viewing in May.

Table 1 Respondents Viewing a Particular TV Program and/or Buying the Brand Advertised, in February and May

| Viewing | Buying | | | | |
	++	+—	—+	——	Total
++	460	173	191	351	1175
+—	76	59	44	113	292
—+	86	27	53	80	246
——	175	104	113	347	739
Total	797	363	401	891	2452

Source: National Broadcasting Company (1953), Table 5 in Appendix A.

A chi-square statistic of eighty-nine calculated from this table points to a strong relationship between viewing and buying.

If it were true that buyers are better rememberers of adver-

8. Thus, for instance, on p. 66 it is stated that there was no advertising or promotion in control markets (while test markets received special direct mail advertising). But a chart on p. 68 gives an index of changes in recall of such advertising in control markets as well. A section heading is General Industry Awareness and Attitude Study, but the word attitude cannot subsequently be found in the entire section.

tising exposure than non-buyers, then it would be reasonable to expect that: (*a*) relatively more buyers than non-buyers should claim they started viewing between surveys; (*b*) relatively more buyers should claim they continued to view the program. But the Davenport data did not bear this out. Though not conclusive, the evidence presented in this NBC study appears to indicate that recall precedes buying.

A similar study, gathering information on magazine readership as well as television viewing, was reported by the project director for the NBC Davenport study (Coffin, 1963). It appeared that TV viewing did, but magazine reading did not, contribute to an increase in sales. A subsequent critique by Semon (1964) of this article points to some of the weak spots in this and other NBC studies. In particular, it attempts to show that the 'start and stop' viewing or reading analysis is of dubious value in this context.

Bridging the cognitive and affective behavioral dimensions is survey evidence gathered by the NBC Hofstra television study (NBC, 1950). Matched panels of New York metropolitan area television owners and non-owners (3270) were interviewed about buying behavior on two occasions, in January and May, 1949. The surveys covered purchases of brands advertised on television and competing brands not on television, among such products as gasoline, cigarettes, coffee, soap, watches, refrigerators, etc.

Most striking are the results of the second survey, which asked about seventeen brands bought lately and about recent (last month) and remote (before last month) TV exposure. Table 2 summarizes the results. The base for the figures is the

Table 2 Relative Sales Increase at Various Levels of Exposure to TV Advertising (base = unexposed non-TV-owners)

Non-owner, seen TV	12·8%
Total owners	41·7
Seen program recently	54·9
Seen program regularly	59·6
Seen commercial recently	64·3
Liked commercial recently	70·2

Source: National Broadcasting Company (1950, p. 49)

K. S. Palda 299

percentage of non-owners unexposed to T V who have bought the brand in the past month: 23·5 per cent. There appears to be a steady progression in sales increases for ever higher levels of awareness, recall and liking of commercials.

Nevertheless, more detailed analysis shows that the memory (cognitive) effect may be more important than the liking (affective effect) of commercials: of the several thousands of 'likers' and 'dislikers' interviewed, 34·5 per cent who have seen the commercial *recently* and disliked it, purchased the brand; only 33·8 per cent of those who liked the commercial and saw it *'remotely'* did buy a brand (N B C, 1950, p. 42).

The key issue in this study is how well the set owners were matched with the non-owners. For every T V owner, a non-owner was obtained from the same block, resembling the T V owner as closely as possible in family composition and standard of living. Eleven variables were used in pairing respondents. However, the fundamental question was not resolved: was not remembrance of advertising increased as a result of buying rather than vice versa?

Affective dimensions

Without question the strongest conviction held by the advertising community with regard to the hierarchy relates to the link between attitude (or change in attitude) and sale of the advertised product (or change in sales).

What criterion, then, *can* be measured which provides a predictive copy test; what criterion is related to sales or brand usage? My answer is attitude *shift*. ... And why do I believe this? Because there is considerable and growing evidence that attitude shift is related to brand image; and because there is an abiding logic backing up this evidence (Achenbaum, 1964).

Is there such a logic; is there such evidence? There are really two aspects to the problem of a link between attitude (or attitudinal change) and behavior (or behavioral change): (1) Is attitude a mechanism which tends to direct behavior? (2) Must a change in attitude precede, rather than follow, a change in behavior?

Consider the first aspect. Many psychologists have for a long time been very careful about the definition of attitude. Helen Peak deserves to be quoted on this subject:

Attitude is (defined as) a hypothetical construct which involves organization around a conceptual or perceptual nucleus and which has affective properties. ... It is often said that an attitude is a 'readiness for action' which seems to imply that behavior is directly determined by attitudes. We regard this at best as a greatly over-simplified statement of the relationship between attitude and action ... an attitude should not be expected to serve as an adequate basis for predicting all behavior, since it is rarely more than one of several components of motive structure (Peak, 1955).

In any case, a very large number of attitude studies undertaken by social psychologists are *not* concerned with an eventual prediction of behavior on the basis of ascertained attitudes. Almost thirty years ago it was pointed out that while critics deem the 'merely verbal' aspect of attitude measurement to be its Achilles' heel, actions are no more 'valid' inherently than words. Actions are frequently designed to conceal or distort 'true' attitude quite as fully as verbal behavior (Murphy, Murphy, and Newcomb, 1937). This caution about the meaning and purpose of attitude measurement is not, however, observed universally either among psychologists or advertising men. As Festinger puts it:

What I want to stress is that we have been quietly and placidly ignoring a very vital problem. We have essentially persuaded ourselves that we can simply assume that there is, of course, a relationship between attitude change and subsequent behavior and, since this relationship is obvious, why should we labor to overcome the considerable technical difficulties of investigating it? But the few relevant studies certainly show that this 'obvious' relationship probably does not exist and that, indeed, some non-obvious relationships may exist (Festinger, 1964).

It is symptomatic that 'applied' social psychologists, working in fields in which it is important to predict behavior, have been aware for some time that it is not easy to infer behavior from attitudes and vice versa. The best summary of their thinking on this subject was recently presented by Vroom (1964). He points out that there appears to be no tendency for persons with preju-dicial attitudes toward Negroes and Jews to express their prejudices when their interaction is within the context of a formal role relationship demanding a lack of discrimination. He also stresses that in no sense should employee attitudes be regarded as causes of effective job performance. He argues that 'the conditions which produce positive attitudes on the part of employees toward their jobs are not necessarily those that motivate them to perform effectively on these jobs'. Substitute 'consumer, product, purchase' for 'employee, job, perform' and the similarity of this problem between industrial relations and advertising becomes apparent.

Consider now the second aspect. It is easy to imagine a purchasing situation in which advertising, effective as a reminder of a particular brand name, caused the consumer to select this rather than another brand. Satisfaction with the consequences of the purchase evoked a favorable attitude where none existed before, or strengthened a weak preference. That attitude change can follow behavioral change is now widely accepted – the literature stretches from racial prejudice research to empirical studies of cognitive dissonance (Deutsch and Collins, 1951; Straits, 1964). Yet, there seems to be only one published empirical study of advertising effectiveness in which attitudes are measured after exposure to advertising, but *before* any buying takes place, and matched against subsequent purchases (DuBois, 1960).

This should not imply that there are many published reports of studies delving into the *concurrent* relationship between attitude (change) and buying (change). Their relative scarcity is indicated by the fact that of the ninety-eight cases presented in the National Industrial Conference Board's monograph *Measuring Advertising Results* (1962), only one makes some attempt in the direction of attitude-sales measurement (Case 35, Tea Council of the USA).

DuBois (1960) reported on a study by Foote, Cone and Belding designed to find out whether attitudes influence sales. Data were obtained on use and attitude for 40 assorted grocery store brands by 228 respondents in a panel in one city. Most of the analysis was based on a composite of all 40 brands, which, when multiplied by 228 respondents, gave a total of 9120 cases for the composite brand (XL).

Among users who called the brand 'one of the best' at the outset, 68 per cent continued using the brand. Among those who were only mildly favorable, 50 per cent continued using it. Among the handful less than favorable, only 28 per cent continued use.

Among non-users who called the brand one of the best at the outset, 25 per cent became users in the next few months, in contrast to 17 per cent of those non-users who had called the brand 'good', and 9 per cent of those who rated it at anything less than good.

Both types of attitude effect, holding users and generating new users, were observed to continue for a considerable period of time, after two months, after six months, and even (in a separate study) after a full year.

In a different kind of analysis of the same data, the 40 individual brands were ranked according to the percentage of users who called them one of the best. It was found that the higher this proportion, the higher also the proportion of users who keep on using the brand. Similarly, the brands were re-ranked according to the percentage of non-users who called them one of the best. Again, the larger this percentage, the larger also was the percentage of non-users who became users within the next few months.

The study also provided evidence that changes in attitudes are conducive to changes in action. If the attitudes became more favorable, the users were more likely to stay with the brand than if attitudes remained mildly favorable. And, on the other hand, a deterioration of attitude among users seemed to lead to a falling off in the percentage of those remaining with the brand. Similar effects of attitude change were observed among non-users. An increase in favorability went with larger percentages of conversion. A decline in favorability of attitude led to lower percentages of conversion.

Here the evidence, as reported, appears to bear out the ideas that attitudes do *precede* and causally influence buying. Unfortunately, the paucity of technical information (how were the observations pooled, what composite measure constituted a 'favorable attitude', how was the pre-test effect coped with, etc.) given in this one-page paper published in the proceedings of a conference precludes the thorough critique such a study would merit.

A very interesting study of recall, association and, especially, attitude change (as measured by the semantic differential), offering a wealth of technical detail, was reported by Mindak (1956). It stopped short, however, of looking at purchasing behavior. Nevertheless, a brief passage from it merits quotation:

From a research point of view, a further-reaching consequence was the introduction of more evidence supporting the hypothesis that high levels of association or recall did not necessarily mean a favorable attitude or disposition to buy the product. In addition, it seemed that high levels of recall did not even necessarily mean that the consumers understood the core idea of intensive and expensive advertising campaigns (Mindak, 1956, p. 371).

Conative dimensions
Intention to buy
There appear to be no published studies of the predictive power (with regard to sales) of *advertising induced* intentions to buy.[9] The classic warnings about difficulties of using intentions to forecast sales, concisely uttered fifteen years ago by Lorie and Roberts, are still valid (1951). The problems faced in this area, but restricted to the relatively easier subject matter of consumer durables, are exhaustively discussed by Juster (1964).

More than one dimension
The following two studies which are briefly reviewed cover more than one behavioral dimension of the hierarchy.

At first sight, NBC's Fort Wayne study (NBC, 1955) looks like a massive test in which the hierarchy of effects is well documented. 'How television works to condition customers all along the road to purchase is a research area explored for the first time in this study. ... It advances viewers along every step in the creation of customers for a brand. It turns strangers into acquaintances ... acquaintances into friends ... friends into

9. Wells and Dames drew attention to the effect 'exaggerators' might have on survey results when both exposure to media and intentions to buy are measured (1962). But this problem has no relation with the hierarchy of effects.

customers' (NBC, 1955, p. 9). After wading through the quag-mire of results and technical appendices, it becomes apparent that no such thing was documented.

Over 5,000 housewives were interviewed in Fort Wayne in the Fall of 1953 before the first local television station went on the air. They were re-interviewed six months later. The emphasis was on respondents who acquired a TV set between the two surveys. Some or all of the TV buyers were measured on brand awareness, brand-product association, slogan identification, trademark recognition, brand reputation, or brand preference with regard to about thirty-five advertised brands and then compared to the 'unexposed' respondents. There is little question about the sturdy increase in the level of the 'communications' variables among the set buyers as opposed to those 'unexposed'. However, information about percentage changes in the various effects, *and* the percentage change in purchases, is given out on Scotties face tissues only; no mention is made of Halo in this context, although all of the measurements taken on Scotties were also taken on Halo; and the percentage change in purchases of other brands is presented in aggregate form only. Scotties registered a net absolute increase (difference between set buyers and the unexposed) in slogan identification of 46 per cent, in brand reputation of 6 per cent, in brand preference of 20 per cent. Characteristically, only the absolute increase (per cent of set buyers who bought Scotties during the last four weeks before the second interview *minus* the percentage of the same interviewees who bought Scotties in the last four weeks before the first interview) in Scotties' purchases is given – 20 percentage points. The increase in buying in the control (unexposed) group is not presented.

Anyone who is seriously interested in the technical quality of advertising effectiveness research is advised to go carefully over this study, which is ambitious, costly and typical.

A recent massive and analytically conscientious study, John B. Stewart's *Repetitive Advertising in Newspapers* (1964), turned some of its attention to the hierarchical steps. Chapters 5, 6 and 7 are devoted to consumer awareness of brands, Chapter 8 to product knowledge imparted by advertising, Chapter 9 to product images and 10 to purchase intent.

K. S. Palda 305

The book reports on a massive experiment in Fort Wayne, Indiana, with advertising campaigns for two products. As usual, a higher level of awareness and better product knowledge was exhibited by purchasers than non-buyers; as usual there is no information on precedence in time, except that 'those who planned to try' scored about one-third higher on product knowledge than those who did not. With regard to the attitude towards the advertised products, Stewart says 'Apparently product usage was a more powerful influence on the image than was exposure to advertising' (1964, p. 192).

Intent to purchase was not matched with actual purchase. Five respondents out of the 1,314 subjects who were not exposed to advertising declared that they intended to purchase either product: of the 1,903 subjects who were exposed, seventeen declared their readiness to buy one product, and twenty-seven declared intent to purchase the other product (p. 211). After the campaign ran for several weeks, however, the differences between the exposed and non-exposed groups tended to disappear.[10]

In his concluding chapter, Stewart writes:

What means can management use to evaluate a specific advertisement? Judging from this campaign, the only safe measure would appear to be trial purchase. As a more thorough understanding of persuasion through advertising is obtained, it may become possible to evaluate advertisements accurately before they are actually run. But it would not have been possible to do a good job in evaluation with the 'before purchase' measures used in this study (p. 300).

Two private studies of advertising effect which throw some light on the hierarchical hypothesis are now analysed; first, because they provide an opportunity of looking at some length at original data, and second, because they are typical of many other unpublished research studies. The first study attempts only to link awareness of product with purchasing, but it gives a substantial amount of data. The second deals with many of the hierarchical steps; the data, however, are not abundant.

The first study concerned a newly launched brand of a house-

10. The study did find that the advertising campaign for one product was successful and that it probably was not for the other; this, however, has no bearing on the subject of this paper.

hold utility product, not a regularly purchased item, priced between $6 and $8, which was to some extent functionally differentiated from other brands of the same product class. Three telephone surveys were undertaken in March, May and July of the same year. In March and July the same thirty-nine medium-to-small-sized cities from coast to coast were the locale of the survey; in May, however, only thirty of them. The universe from which the sample was taken were households listed in telephone directories; about 400 names were selected at random in each city's directory on each occasion. Thus, the sample had different subjects for each time.

First a question was asked designed to yield information about the respondent awareness of the brand. Then a question was asked whether the respondent purchased the product within the last three months and, if so, which brand. The two variables in the study are awareness and market share and are expressed in percentages of total respondents. Information was also gathered about level of advertising activity (Table 3).

Table 3 Market Shares, Awareness and Advertising Intensity in 39 Cities Disclosed during March, May and July Surveys

City	Y_1	Y_2	Y_3	X_1	X_2	X_3	D
1	6·3	11·8	3·9	14·4	13·8	9·4	1·5
2	1·4	—	4·1	5·6	—	13·1	0
3	11·8	—	5·3	11·3	—	8·1	1
4	2·7	—	6·1	8·3	—	11·7	1
5	1·9	—	6·2	7·4	—	9·1	1
6	2·2	—	6·3	11·4	—	12·8	0
7	15·1	—	6·7	10·8	—	12·3	1
8	12·0	10·4	6·9	11·0	13·4	14·7	1
9	6·6	13·7	7·1	12·8	22·2	14·8	1·5
10	6·2	—	7·4	12·4	—	13·0	1
11	1·5	6·6	7·5	9·8	9·1	13·3	1
12	9·4	2·1	7·8	16·3	14·6	18·4	1
13	4·8	9·0	8·4	5·4	9·9	13·8	1
14	9·9	5·9	8·4	13·3	10·6	19·6	2
15	7·5	—	9·9	14·3	—	18·8	1
16	2·8	7·3	10·1	10·9	12·4	10·6	1·5
17	11·5	8·7	10·4	18·0	14·7	18·9	2

Table 3 continued

City	Y_1	Y_2	Y_3	X_1	X_2	X_3	D
18	6·1	8·0	11·6	8·0	9·1	12·6	1
19	10·0	11·1	13·5	12·8	13·9	14·4	1·5
20	14·8	9·9	13·6	21·8	18·3	27·4	3
21	12·8	5·0	14·6	15·4	21·5	22·2	4
22	20·5	15·3	22·9	24·8	19·6	18·7	1
23	11·1	7·4	15·7	7·7	11·8	21·8	3
24	15·0	18·3	15·7	20·7	23·8	23·6	1·5
25	12·9	13·8	15·8	25·0	23·7	30·8	4
26	1·6	6·9	16·0	9·8	14·4	17·9	1
27	5·7	3·2	16·7	18·9	15·9	25·2	3
28	17·4	23·3	18·1	35·2	34·4	31·8	1·5
29	21·1	11·9	18·8	16·2	14·3	23·0	3
30	9·6	8·7	18·9	22·5	23·6	29·3	3
31	19·0	25·6	19·0	24·9	32·5	30·2	4
32	9·3	—	19·4	15·1	—	25·7	0
33	21·2	23·7	19·8	27·3	35·7	30·6	1
34	25·0	21·9	20·0	31·4	34·5	35·6	1
35	9·4	17·9	22·2	15·4	22·9	29·6	2
36	15·2	21·7	24·7	29·5	37·0	33·8	1
37	29·1	12·5	25·0	29·9	27·1	40·0	1
38	30·0	24·2	28·6	35·1	36·1	43·5	1
39	13·3	25·3	29·2	19·5	28·3	31·5	3

Note: The Y's represent market shares in the various cities in percentages. The X's are percentages of respondents in corresponding cities who are aware of the brand. The subscripts stand for the March (1), May (2) and July (3) surveys. D is a variable which represents six different levels of combined TV and newspaper activity supporting the brand in question in the various cities. The data are arranged in ascending order of magnitude of Y_3.

Table 4 cross-classifies period-to-period changes in awareness with changes in market share. Since a χ^2 based on the cross-classification of $\triangle X_3$ with $\triangle Y_3$ is equal to 5·9 ($\chi^2_{1,0\cdot50}=3\cdot8$), it appears that a relationship between the two variables exists which is not attributable to chance alone. Further estimation of this relationship led to regression analysis.

Table 4 Number of Changes in Market Shares and Awareness
from March–May to May–June

Change in market share	Change in awareness				
	$\triangle X_2$		$-\triangle X_2$		
	$\triangle X_3$	$-\triangle X_3$	$\triangle X_3$	$-\triangle X_3$	Total
$\triangle Y_3$	5	2	2	0	9
$\triangle Y_2$	1	4	0	2	7
$-\triangle Y_3$	—	—	—	—	—
Subtotal	12		4		16
$\triangle Y_3$	4	0	7	1	12
$-\triangle Y_2$	2	0	0	0	2
$-\triangle Y_3$	—	—	—	—	—
Subtotal	6		8		14
Total	18		12		30

Note: Where $\triangle X_i = X_i - X_{i-1}, \triangle Y_i = Y_i - Y_{i-1}$.

The following linear multiple regressions were run:

GROUP I

(a) $Y_t = f(X_t)$
$\quad Y_t = f(X_t, D_i)$

(b) $Y_t = f(\log X_t)$
$\quad Y_t = f(\log X_t, D_i)$

(c) $\log Y_t = f(\log X_t)$
$\quad \log Y_t = f(\log X_t, D_i)$,

where $t = 1$, or 2, or 3 representing, respectively, data from the
first, second, and third survey, and D_i's are dummies representing
four levels of combined TV and newspaper advertising activity:
$D_1 = 1$ when $D = 1$; otherwise its value is zero; and, similarly,
$D_2 = 1$ when $D = 1\cdot5$ or 2; $D_3 = 1$ when $D = 3$ or 4. The values
of these dummy variables do not change from period to period.

GROUP II

(a) $Y_{t+1} = f(X_t)$ $\qquad\qquad Y_{t+1} = f(X_t, D_i)$
$\quad Y_{t+1} = f(X_{t+1}, X_t)$ $\qquad\quad$ etc.
$\quad Y_{t+2} = f(X_t)$
$\quad Y_{t+2} = f(X_{t+1})$
$\quad Y_{t+2} = f(X_{t+2}, X_{t+1})$
$\quad Y_{t+2} = f(X_{t+2}, X_{t+1}, X_t)$

Subgroups (*b*) i.e. the semilogarithmic, and (*c*), i.e. the logarithmic versions were also run.

GROUP III
Irving Fisher's short-cut distributed lag (Palda, 1964a):

(*a*) $Y_{t+1} = f\left(\dfrac{2X_{t+1}+X_t}{2}\right)$

$\ \ Y_{t+1} = f\left(\dfrac{2X_{t+1}+X_t}{2},\ D_i\right)$

$\ \ Y_{t+2} = f\left(\dfrac{3X_{t+2}+2X_{t+1}+X_t}{6}\right)$

$\ \ Y_{t+2} = f\left(\dfrac{3X_{t+2}+2X_{t+1}+Xt}{6},\ Di\right).$

Subgroups (*b*) and (*c*) were also calculated, where Fisher's term was $3 \log X_{t+2}+2 \log X_{t+1}$ etc., but the denominator was not transformed.

GROUP IV
Koyck's distributed lag (Palda, 1964a):
(*a*) $Y_{t+1} = f(X_{t+1},\ Y_t)$
$\ \ Y_{t+1} = f(X_{t+1},\ Y_t,\ D_i)$
$\ \ Y_{t+2} = f(X_{t+2},\ Y_{t+1})$
$\ \ Y_{t+2} = f(X_{t+2},\ Y_{t+1},\ D_i).$

Subgroups (*b*) and (*c*) were also calculated.

GROUP V
$\Delta Y_{t+1} = f[\Delta(X_{t+1})],\quad$ where $\Delta Y_{t+1} = Y_{t+1}-Y_t$, etc.
$\Delta Y_{t+2} = f[\Delta(X_{t+2})]$
$\Delta Y_{t+2} = f[\Delta(X_{t+1})]$
$\Delta Y_{t+2} = f[\Delta(X_{t+2},\ X_{t+1})].$

All in all, seventy regressions were run.

The first three equations listed below show the three 'best' estimated regressions for the three time periods (i.e. for Y with subscripts t, $t+1$ and $t+2$, respectively). This statement includes not only, for instance, the form $Y_{t+2} = f(X_{t+2})$, but also $Y_{t+2} = f(X_{t+2}, X_{t+1}, X_t, D_i)$, etc. The criterion for inclusion into this group was the size of the standard deviation of regression residuals (also called standard error of estimate). This statistic is the one most closely associated with forecasting performance – the smaller it is, the smaller the forecast error is likely to be (Palda 1963):[11]

$Y_t = -1·176+0·741X_t$ *1*
             (0·087)

7·444   4·391

$N = 39$ $R^2 = 0·661.$

$Y_{t+1} = -0·722+0·667X_{t+1}$ *2*
             (0·078)

7·051   3·775

   $N = 30$ $R^2 = 0·723.$

$\log Y_{t+2} = -0·321+1·090 \log X_{t+2}$ *3*
               (0·099)

7·037*   3·427*

    $N = 39$ $R^2 = 0·765.$

*(Not expressed in logarithms.)

The following two regressions are also listed for further discussion:

$Y_{t+2} = -26·793+27·031 \log X_{t+2} +6·013 \log Y_{t+1}$ *4*
                 (4·354)   (2·834)

6·687   3·619

   $N = 30$ $R^2 = 0·727$

$\Delta Y_{t+1} = -1·470+0·896 \Delta X_{t+1}$ *5*
             (0·225)

6·289   5·118

   $N = 29$ $R^2 = 0·600.$

How should these results be interpreted? These three con-secutive surveys are in many ways typical of much commercial

11. Y is the market share and X awareness in periods indicated by the subscripts; N is sample size; R^2 is the coefficient of multiple determination; the figures in parentheses are standard errors of regression coefficients and the figures on the last line below each regression are, respectively, the standard deviation of the dependent variable and the standard deviation of regression residuals.

advertising research, in that quite a few data are generated without a rigorous attempt at getting unambiguous results. This was the reason why it was considered important to subject the data to as rigorous an analysis as possible.

Just as the preliminary chi-square analysis indicated, the regression results confirm the presence of a strong concurrent relationship between awareness and market share. One could have, however, more confidence in the existence of a causal relationship flowing from awareness to purchasing if two phenomena potentially obtainable from the data had been detected. First, the presence of higher levels of advertising activity should have strengthened the awareness-purchase relationship. But regression equations incorporating dummies, which represented varying levels of advertising activity, were of a lower quality than those which did not.

Second, lag correlations between awareness and market share would give a better indication of the direction of the causal flow between variables. But regressions using lagged awareness, the more refined Irving Fisher lag, or the sophisticated Koyck lag distribution simply did not fit as well as those of the concurrent form. (See, as evidence, the 'best' lag regression shown above, equation 4.) Even first differences performed poorly. (Equation 5 shows the best first-difference equation fitted.)

Thus, it cannot be said that the data from these surveys confirm the hypothesis that awareness tends to *precede* or even to *contribute* to rate of purchase. They only show that higher awareness *co-exists* with higher purchasing rates.

A few years ago a Canadian producer of a brand of a frequently purchased, very widely used, low cost consumer product started co-sponsoring a highly popular television program in a certain province. (The other sponsor was not new to the program.) While his sponsorship was new, his brand was well established in that province, holding a market share of almost 20 per cent. To assess the effectiveness of his advertising venture, the manufacturer's marketing research agency conducted three telephone surveys.

The purpose was, roughly, to get information on the awareness of the sponsor's identity, on the viewers' reaction to the sponsorship of such a program, on the extent of recall of the commercials, on the attitude toward the company and its products, and on buying.

The telephone interviews took place in the four principal cities of the province. The first one was staged just before the start of the telecasts, the second four weeks later, the third just after the TV series finished several months later. Five hundred different subjects were selected in each of the three surveys by a random procedure from the telephone directory. Two quotas were imposed: the subjects had to be users of the product (not the brand) and half of them had to be male. Thus, the universe was one of product users. The sex restriction (achieved by alternately asking to speak to the housewife or the husband) probably had little distorting effect, users and viewers not likely being – on *a priori* grounds – differentially distributed between the sexes. The time of the survey was after 5 p.m., and three callbacks were made.

Awareness of sponsorship

'Could you tell me what company, or companies, sponsor each of the following TV programs (six programs, rotating in order)?'

During the second interview, 23 per cent of all respondents correctly mentioned the sponsor's name. At the time of the third interview 48 per cent did. Among the users of the brand the percentage went from 33 to 57, among non-users it increased from 21 to 46. The results do not appear to need further statistical analysis.

Opinion of sponsorship

'As it happens, the telecasts are sponsored by Companies A and B (rotating company name from respondent to respondent). Are there any comments you would like to make about either or both companies and their sponsorship of the TV program?' The results are set forth in the following two tabulations, for brand users and those who are not purchasers of the brand:

Table 4 Brand Users

	Favorable opinion	Other opinion		Total
Second survey	(a) 44 persons	(b) 60	(n_1)	104
Third survey	(c) 46	(d) 71	(n_2)	117
Total	90	131		221

$z = -0.59$

Table 5 Users of Other Brands

	Favorable opinion	Other opinion	Total
Second survey	186 persons	210	396
Third survey	184	199	383
Total	370	409	779

$z = \cdot 23$

The analysis of the differences between proportions follows Wallis and Roberts (1956). The following statistic, z, is computed and reference is made to the normal distribution tables:

$$z = \left[bc - ad - \frac{n_1 + n_2}{2} \right] \sqrt{\frac{n_1 + n_2}{n_1 n_2 (a+c)(b+d)}}$$

It is apparent that analysis of the total sample (500) will not yield a higher value of z.

Recall of commercial content

'Let's discuss ... telecasts. Think back to the last few T V programs and describe the first/second commercial you can remember ..;'

Table 6 Results for all Respondents

	Second survey	Third survey
Sponsor's commercial		
Recalled first	11%	20
second	20	52

These figures do not need further statistical analysis.

Attitude toward company

'I am going to read a list of descriptions and for each one, would you please name the one of the four manufacturers that it best fits. If you think it describes more than one, name them.' (Rotate name of manufacturer; keep reminding respondents who the four manufacturers are.)

The z statistics appropriate to evaluate changes in attitudes toward the company are given for the averages:

First to second survey change:		Second to third survey change:	
Sponsor's brand users	1·76	Other brand users	2·38
Other brand users	2·36	All respondents	1·28

For the change recorded from the first to second survey, it is clear that since the two subgroups' z statistic exceeds 1·65, the z statistic for the whole group will also.

For the change recorded from the second to third survey, the change is clearly of little significance among brand users – 58–57 per cent. This small amount of change is enough to swamp the change among non-users.

However, the amount of change recorded between the first and the third surveys is considerable for all groups.

Table 7 Attitudes Toward Sponsor as Indicated by Respondents' Opinions About Four Companies, Including the Sponsor

	Per cent of respondents mentioning sponsor								
	Sponsor's brand users			Non-users			All respondents		
Attitude toward company	*1*	*2*	*3*	*1*	*2*	*3*	*1*	*2*	*3*
Most progressive	40	46	48	11	13	15	17	20	23
Best reputation	46	56	62	16	22	27	22	29	35
Most community minded	18	41	30	10	13	13	12	19	17
Most interested in his customers	54	72	64	29	39	39	34	46	45
Most popular	40	52	50	11	12	15	17	20	23
High quality products	63	78	78	30	34	45	36	43	53
Fastest growing	38	40	37	10	15	14	16	21	19
Most reliable company	57	72	71	27	38	46	33	45	52
Independent company	38	61	69	13	27	40	17	34	47
Average	44	58	57	17	24	28	23	31	35

Brand usage

'Now, speaking about ('the product') only, which brand of it do you use mainly?'

The proportion of all respondents claiming to use sponsor's brand mainly increased from 19 per cent on the first survey to 20·8 per cent on the second and 23·4 on the last survey. The first change being a small one, the change between the first and third surveys will be assessed.

Table 8

	Sponsor's brand users	Non-users	Total
First survey	95	405	500
Third survey	117	383	500
	212	788	1000

The z statistic used to evaluate this change yields the value of 1·62.

It should be pointed out that the dependent variable here is *not* sales, but rather the number of respondents who say they use the sponsor's brand *mainly*. This is far from a reliable revenue yardstick. Thus, it is *not* possible to say whether, as a result of the advertising, revenue increased or users bought at a higher rate than previously while some new customers were acquired, etc. It is only possible to say that among the total respondents, the number of users grew from 95 to 117 out of 500.

What overall conclusion can be reached from this study with regard to the hypothesis of hierarchical effects? It is clear that many of the communication objectives of the sponsor were reached: awareness of his sponsorship increased strongly from the time the T V series started; recall of commercial content was very good and increased considerably. Slightly more ambiguous results were obtained when opinions were sampled. Some, but only a small amount, of increase of favorable opinion towards the sponsorship of the T V series (really, toward this type of advertising) was registered. However, on the highest rung of the hierarchical ladder a considerable increase in favorable attitude toward the company was recorded, especially between the first and third surveys.

No such clear-cut results were obtained with regard to brand usage. Keeping in mind that brand usage is not a perfect substitute for sales, it cannot even be said, at least on non-Bayesian grounds, that it showed a significant amount of change. Thus, while 'significantly' large numbers of respondents moved 'up the hierarchical ladder' of awareness, liking of the advertising and of attitudes, performance on the last 'rung' is difficult to assess. Add to this the uncertainty of the causal direction (awareness $\rightarrow$ opinion $\rightarrow$ recall $\rightarrow$ attitude $\rightarrow$ usage) and we end with an unsatisfactory feeling. At that, this study appears to have been a rather good one, unwittingly perhaps, but nevertheless persistently testing the hierarchical hypothesis.

As a concluding remark, it is suggested that the only satisfactory and lasting answer to the doubts or unwarranted assertions concerning the hierarchical hypothesis would be a well-designed experiment. Only an experiment can approach the assessment of the direction in the causal flow unambiguously. Many problems can be foreseen, especially with pre-test effects in such experimentation, but it is not the task here to advise on its feasibility.

A table was constructed (Table 9), leaning on the Lavidge-Steiner representation, to point out in condensed form most of the substantive weaknesses of the hypothesis of hierarchical effects. Singled out for inclusion are also certain methodological weaknesses, most of them not mentioned above, which appear to be connected with each step in the hierarchy.[12] The considerable number of these methodological problems, quite apart from the substantive objections, brings up forcefully this question: Is it, on balance, really more difficult and expensive to investigate the direct link between advertising expenditure and sales than it is to undertake research into each step of the hierarchy – *even if the existence of a hierarchy of effects were actually established?*

12. Each methodological objection has been raised elsewhere. Indeed, Lucas and Britt (1963) provide a compendium of them, on which the fourth column of Table 9 is based.

Table 9 A Summary of Substantive and Methodological Weaknesses of the Hierarchy-of-Effects Hypothesis

Behavioral dimension	Examples of information sought	Typical related research	Some unresolved problems in such research	Substantive weakness
COGNITIVE	Brand awareness	Sample survey	Discrimination between awareness as consequence of advertising and awareness as consequence of word of mouth	In general, no logical necessity for awareness of brand to precede its purchase by any significant fraction of time, particularly in self-service store
	Recognition, recall	Starch, Gallup & Robinson	Incomplete elimination of factors other than the one advertisement or commercial	Purchasers of brand may be better 'rememberers'
			Little sensitivity	
	Portfolio tests			
AFFECTIVE	Liking of and preferences between ads	Order-of-merit and paired comparison of ads	Assumption that at least one ad is liked; halo effect	No logical connection between (esthetic) enjoyment of ad and disposition to buy brand
		Program analyser	Quality of sample, naturalness of setting	
		Semantic differential	Polarity of adjectives; no allowance for no opinions; comparison of profiles does not give indication of their possible profitability	
		Inquiry tests with offers	Coupon clippers bias results; if offer attractive, contamination by word of mouth	Can anything be said about preference among ads when relevant stimulus is a 'non-brand' offer?

		Interpretation	
Attitudes toward and preferences among brands	Attitude surveys	Unidimensionality of meaning, validity of indirect questions	'A causal relationship and a "meaning" relationship between attitude and behavior can be distinguished. When attitude is changed first, the aim is to cause change in behavior. On the other hand, if behavior changes first, a change in attitude is involved and serves to give a meaning to the already achieved behavior. Attitude may thus be viewed either as a mechanism directing behavior, or as a modality which confers on behavior its meanings (Moscovici, 1963).
	Schwerin	Quality of sample, naturalness of setting (e.g. attitude change through communication easier to achieve, according to Hovland, in laboratory than in real world)	
	Projective techniques		
CONATIVE Intention to buy	Sample surveys	Predictive power of intention-to-buy surveys with regard to classes of consumer durable goods has been massively documented by the Survey Research Center, University of Michigan. Predictive power of advertising-induced intentions with regard to branded non-durables has scarcely been investigated at all by any organization	The problem of 'impulse' purchases

References

ACHENBAUM, A. A. (1964), 'Is copy testing a predictive tool?',
Proc. 10th ann. Conference, Advertising Research Foundation, p. 66.

COFFIN, T. E. (1963), 'A pioneering experiment in assessing advertising
effectiveness', *J. Marketing*, vol. 27, no. 3, pp. 1–10.

COLLEY, R. H. (ed.) (1961), *Defining Advertising Goals for Measured
Advertising Results*, Association of National Advertisers, p. 55.

COPLAND, B. (1963), 'An evaluation of conceptual frameworks for
measuring advertising results', *Proc. 9th ann. Conference*, Advertising
Research Foundation.

DEUTSCH, M., and COLLINS, M. M. (1951), *Interracial Housing – A
Psychological Evaluation of a Social Experiment*, University of
Minneapolis Press.

DUBOIS, C. (1960), 'The story of brand XL: How consumer attitudes
affected the market position', *Proc. 15th ann. Conference Am. Assoc.
Public Opinion Res.*, reprinted (1960) in *Public Opinion Q.*, vol. 24,
no. 3, pp. 479–80.

FESTINGER, L. (1964), 'Behavioral support for opinion change', *Public
Opinion Q.*, vol. 28, no. 3, pp. 404–17.

HASKINS, J. B. (1964), 'Factual recall as a measure of advertising
effectiveness', *J. Advertising Res.*, vol. 4, no. 1, pp. 2–8.

HELLER, N. (1956), 'An application of psychological learning theory to
advertising', *J. Marketing*, vol. 20, no. 1, pp. 248–54.

JUSTER, F. T. (1964), *Anticipations and Purchases*, Princeton University
Press for the National Bureau of Economic Research.

KRUEGER, L., and RAMOND, C. (1964), *Sales Measures of Advertising:
An Annotated Bibliography*, Advertising Research Foundation.

LAVIDGE, R. C., and STEINER, G. A. (1961), 'A model for predictive
measurements of advertising effectiveness', *J. Marketing*, vol. 25,
no. 4, pp. 59–62.

LORIE, J. H., and ROBERTS, H. V. (1951), *Basic Methods of Marketing
Research*, McGraw-Hill, ch. 14.

LUCAS, D. B., and BRITT, S. H. (1963), *Measuring Advertising
Effectiveness*, McGraw-Hill.

MENDELSOHN, H. (1962), 'Measuring the process of communication
effect', *Public Opinion Q.*, vol. 26, no. 3, pp. 411–16.

MINDAK, W. A. (1956), 'A new technique for measuring advertising
effectiveness', *J. Marketing*, vol. 20, no. 2, pp. 367–78.

MOSCOVICI, S. (1963), 'Attitudes and opinions', *Ann Rev. Psychol.*,
vol. 14, pp. 249–50.

MURPHY, G., MURPHY, L. B., and NEWCOMB, T. M. (1937),
Experimental Social Psychology, Harper & Row, pp. 909–12.

NATIONAL BROADCASTING COMPANY (1950), *The Hofstra Study:
A Measure of Sales Effectiveness of TV Advertising*, NBC.

NATIONAL BROADCASTING COMPANY (1953), *Why Sales Comes in
Curves*, NBC.

NATIONAL BROADCASTING COMPANY (1955), *Strangers into Customers*, NBC.

NATIONAL INDUSTRIAL CONFERENCE BOARD (1962), *Measuring Advertising Results*, NICB.

PALDA, K. S. (1963), 'The evaluation of regression results', in S. A. Greyser (ed.) *Toward Scientific Marketing: Proc. Winter Conference*, American Marketing Association, pp. 279–90.

PALDA, K. S. (1964a), *The Measurement of Cumulative Advertising Effects*, Prentice-Hall, ch. 2.

PALDA, K. S. (1964b), 'Sales effects of advertising', J. *Advertising Res.*, vol. 4, no. 3, pp. 12–16.

PEAK, H. (1955), in M. R. Jones (ed.), *Nebraska Symposium on Motivation*, University of Nebraska Press, pp. 151–2.

ROENS, B. B. (1961), 'New findings from Scott's special advertising research study', *Proc. 7th Ann. Conference*, Advertising Research Foundation, pp. 65–70.

ROTZOLL, K. B. (1964), 'The Starch and Ted Bates correlative measures of advertising effectiveness', J. *Advertising Res.*, vol. 4, no. 1, pp. 22–4.

SANDAGE, C. H., and FRYBURGER, V. (1963), *Advertising Theory and Practice*, Irwin, p. 240.

SEMON, T. T. (1964), 'Assumptions in measuring advertising effectiveness', J. *Marketing*, vol. 28, no. 3, pp. 43–4.

STARCH, D. (1961), *Measuring Product Sales Made by Advertising*, Daniel Starch.

STRAITS, B. C. (1964), 'The pursuit of the dissonant consumer', J. *Marketing*, vol. 28, no. 3, pp. 62–6.

STEWART, J. B. (1964), *Repetitive Advertising in Newspapers*, Harvard Business School.

VROOM, V. A. (1964), 'Employee attitudes', in G. Fisk (ed.), *The Frontiers of Management Psychology*, Harper & Row, pp. 127–43.

WALLIS, A., and ROBERTS, H. V. (1956), *Statistics – A New Approach*, Free Press, p. 430.

WELLS, W. D., and DAMES, J. (1962), 'Hidden errors in survey data', J. *Marketing*, vol. 26, no. 4, pp. 50–53.

WOLFE, H. D., BROWN, J. K., and THOMPSON, G. C. (1962), *Measuring Advertising Results*, National Industrial Conference Board.

18 D. Lowe Watson

Advertising and the Buyer–Seller Relationship

D. Lowe Watson, 'Advertising and the buyer-seller relationship',
Journal of the Market Research Society, vol. 11, no. 2, 1969, pp. 125–46.

In a paper given at the 1967 Annual Conference of the Market Research Society, S. King drew attention to the need for a more satisfactory theory of how advertising works.

He underlined the need for such theory to provide the conceptual framework both for the creation and planning of advertising campaigns, and for the design and interpretation of the advertising research which we use to make decisions about which campaign to run, and to evaluate the effectiveness both of individual advertisements and of campaigns.

He pointed out that most of the generally accepted theories implied that advertising performed some kind of sequential process, converting people through a series of mental states from non-buyers to buyers. Some, like the DAGMAR model, implied that this is achieved through memory or conviction about claims. This type of model led to the use of measures of recall, interest, attention value and belief in claims, as indicators of successful advertising. Others, such as the Advertising Planning Index theory, implied a succession of mental states, relating to the brand rather than the advertising. This led to the use of measures of brand awareness, brand image and intention to buy.

He suggested that such theories tended to be based on *a priori* arguments rather than empirical evidence, and drew attention to an increasing weight of circumstantial evidence which seems to suggest that advertising does not work this way.

Other writers have drawn attention to the lack of empirical support for the sequential concept. Copland (1963) suggested that it was perhaps possible that a person might not always have to pass through the full range of mental states before reaching the final stage of becoming a buyer of the brand.

More recently, Palda (1966) reviewed the published empirical evidence and concluded that there was little support for the hypothesis that successive changes in a hierarchy of intermediate variables, such as awareness, knowledge, recall, recognition and attitude, increased the probability of purchase.

King also pointed out that recent analyses of consumer buying behaviour by A. S. C. Ehrenberg in a number of stable but heavily advertised markets, have produced results which are not consistent with the theory that advertising 'converts' users from one brand to another.

Ehrenberg has shown that in such markets people tend to have a very stable multiple brand pattern of purchasing. That is, they do not seem to veer from one brand to another but regularly buy a number of brands with different frequencies, and these purchasing patterns are systematic and predictable.

This evidence does not seem to support the theory that buyers are 'switched' from one brand to another by some kind of conversion process. It is more consistent with the hypothesis that each buyer has a pattern of brand preferences, reflected in the frequency with which he or she buys each brand, and that these preferences change relatively slowly over time.

Interesting support for this brand preference hypothesis is found in one of the markets studied by Ehrenberg: the petrol market. In this market are to be found a number of motorway sites at each of which the motorist is offered a limited selection of brands on approximately equal terms (there are minor variations at some sites due to the layout of the islands).

At such sites the distribution of sales between the brands represented tends to be proportionate to each brand's share of the national market. This is consistent with the theory that each motorist has a pattern of brand preferences, giving a certain probability of purchase for each brand.

It can be shown that an alternative model, more consistent with the 'conversion' theory, which presupposed that each motorist tended to be loyal to a single brand, would result in a different pattern of sales. For in this case any motorist who found himself at a motorway site at which his preferred brand was not available would presumably be indifferent to the choice offered. Such motorists would therefore distribute their purchases evenly between the islands.

The basic similarity found by Ehrenberg between the petrol market and the numerous other markets he has studied suggests that the same kind of model should apply to all.

A study by Bird and Ehrenberg (1966), based on over 100 brands, demonstrated a mathematical relationship between spontaneous brand awareness and brand usage. This, of course, is what most people would expect.

To examine the influence of other factors they studied the deviations from this awareness-usage relationship. They found a relationship between these deviations and past advertising expenditure over a long (five year) period such as we would expect from the theory described in this paper. Yet they did not find any consistent relationship with recent advertising. These results, therefore, do not support the DAGMAR-type (Defining Advertising Goals – Measuring Advertising Results) conversion theory that advertising is continuously influencing usage by a chain of events which includes awareness.

Alternatively we can hypothesize that users are most likely to be influenced by the advertising for the brand because they are predisposed to notice and accept it. The proposition that users of a brand are more aware of its advertising than non-users is well established. Table 1 shows a typical set of results.

The pattern shown will be familiar to any advertising researcher. It is of interest to note that users' attitude to the advertising for the brand is also more favourable than non-users. This observation is confirmed by the findings of the recent IPA survey of *Attitudes to television advertising* (BMRB, 1967).

An explanation for the higher awareness and more favourable attitude to a brand's advertising among users than non-users is offered in this paper. Some mention must also be made of the explanation frequently put forward in terms of the theory of dissonance associated with Festinger (1957). This hypothesis suggests that in order to eliminate the tensions of 'dissonance' which result from the making of choices, people are likely to seek rationalizations for having bought the brand, after the purchase has been made.

Such an explanation seems plausible in a case such as the

Table 1 Motorists' awareness of, and attitudes to, petrol
advertising (*a*) Recall of petrol advertising

Advertising recall of	All motorists	Usual brand		
		Brand A	Brand B	Brand C
Brand A	69	84	61	62
Brand B	64	59	72	60
Brand C	44	42	34	69
Base	593	148	135	42

(*b*) Advertising found especially interesting (all who recall
some advertising)

Interesting	All	Usual brand		
		Brand A	Brand B	Brand C
Brand A	27	41	26	11
Brand B	25	23	39	19
Brand C	16	15	13	36
Base	536	140	120	36

purchase of a motor car (the example quoted by Festinger). A
motor car is an important possession to most people, and the
role of ownership is one in which they may take some pride. So
it is not unreasonable to suppose that the purchaser might actively seek evidence and reassurance to justify so important a
choice.

But can we so readily assume that the housewife is equally
anxious to justify her choice of a brand in a hundred and one
relatively unimportant household products – particularly when
we know that she habitually buys not one, but a variety of
brands in regular proportions?

The IPA survey referred to above has provided further evidence inconsistent with the hypothesis that people look to advertising primarily as a source of information about products,

whether to guide their choice of brand or to give them post-purchase reassurance.

The survey showed that not only do people like commercials which make claims about the product, but they prefer commercials which make obviously exaggerated claims, over those without exaggerated claims. The latter finding is the reverse of what we would expect if people were looking for factual information as an aid to rational choice. So, too, is the finding that people prefer 'mood' to straight commercials.

These conclusions, however, are consistent with the theory put forward here.

If people looked on advertising simply as a source of information about competing products, they would not want to be repeatedly exposed to the same items of information. Yet the IPA survey shows that people like a commercial they have seen a number of times better than one they have only seen a few times, or have not seen before, and the more they like a commercial the more often they want to see it.

A further point of interest in this survey is the evidence of a 'halo' effect operating in the liking of commercials – a strong association between liking a commercial and liking particular aspects of it.

The operation of a 'halo' effect is a familiar experience among market researchers, not only in image and attitude studies, but also in the more 'factual' context of product-testing.

King (1967) points out that although in a blind product test Brand A may win comfortably over Brand B, when brand names are attached the results may be reversed. This suggests the existence of a total 'personality' for the brand, consisting of a closely-knit set of associations capable of being triggered off by the brand name, and sufficiently strong to overwhelm the present experience and perceptions of the product test.

The theory of advertising which is put forward in this paper is based on the concept of a set of relationships between the buyer, the 'personality' of the brand, and the 'personality' of the seller, or company. This theory, it is suggested, is more useful than the standard advertising theories of today because it can satisfactorily account for a number of discrepancies between existing theory and empirical observation such as those outlined above. It also embraces the role of the company image or personality – a notable omission from most current theories of advertising.

It has been suggested by Ehrenberg that theories should be based only on interpretation of empirical facts, never on speculation. Against this it can be argued that scientific methods involve observing discrepancies between existing theory and empirical observation, and formulating speculative theories to explain such discrepancies – as this theory attempts to do. If it is based largely on *a priori* assumptions, those assumptions are not repugnant to commonsense or common experience. They are in the main derived from established psychological theory, though in most cases the application of this theory to advertising has not been experimentally confirmed.

As a speculative theory, therefore, it remains to be tested by experimental research, and it is hoped that means of conducting such research may before long be found.

Man's relationship with his environment

Before we can consider how a persons' actions can be influenced by a persuasive communication, such as advertising, it is necessary to sketch in some basic concepts about human behaviour.

We start therefore with the assumption that man is an organism, capable of using a flow of information to adapt his behaviour to a changing environment.

To illustrate what is meant by adaptive behaviour we may borrow an example from F. E. Emery (1962) who contrasts a stone rolling down a hill with a man running down-hill for a bus. The path of the stone is determined from moment to moment by the reaction between its inherent qualities (such as size, shape, momentum) with the local contours of the hillside. The path of the man will be momentarily influenced by the shape of the local terrain but in general it will be governed by the relative position of the distant bus. If the bus is moving, he may direct his course to intercept it, using his powers of reasoning, and his judgement of their respective speeds, to determine his path.

D. Lowe Watson 327

We can extend Emery's analogy further. The man may be encouraged to attempt an apparently impossible task by the belief that the bus will stop at a particular point for a certain length of time. This expectation may result from information communicated by the bus company's timetable, confidence in this information being reinforced by past experience coupled with a favourable attitude to the company.

Perhaps social factors may enter the situation. The man may shout to attract the bus driver's attention, hoping to influence his actions through recognition of a common interest (the bus driver's desire to pick up a fare), or an appeal to a personal relationship (the bus driver's friendly feeling towards him). Finally, he may hope to enlist the sympathy of other passengers to influence the driver in his favour.

This example illustrates the complex range of factors which may simultaneously influence a person's behaviour. In this example they include the physical environment (the terrain), the evidence of his senses (his view of the bus), his ability to interpret this evidence in a predictive sense (the path to intercept the bus), belief in an informative communication (the bus timetable), reinforced by experience and by his image of the source of information (the bus company). Social factors include a possible common interest and personal relationship with the driver, and a group relationship with the other passengers.

All the time the man is receiving and interpreting a stream of information about this complex external situation and is adapting his behaviour so as best to achieve his object of catching the bus.

Let us now consider how a person handles the stream of information he receives from his senses about the world around him. Suppose he enters a room in which there is a table. A single glance will enable him to recognize it as a table, and if he is not interested the further information which he receives about the table is redundant and he will ignore it. But suppose, as he walks towards the table, fresh information reaches him which tells him the table is no longer an object of indifference but an obstruction to progress and a potential threat to safety. His relationship to the table has changed, and this has altered his attitude to the table. Action follows and he will stop or change direction. In more general terms, we say that a person interprets the information he receives about the objects around him as a set of relationships. Fresh information about his environment may change some of these relationships, and cause him to alter his course of action to achieve a certain end result.

A person may receive information about an object which he interprets in terms of the relationship 'not relevant to my needs'. As a result his attitude will be one of indifference and he is likely to ignore further information about this product as redundant. (Note the implication here of a carry-over effect in advertising.)

If, however, his attention is drawn to fresh information about this product, as a result of which the relationship changes to 'a possible means of satisfying my needs', his attitude will change to one of interest, and he may take action either to seek further information or to make trial of the product.

Studies of consumer behaviour in relation to major purchases (for example, a central heating installation) show that the period of 'search' may be quite prolonged. On the other hand, it seems possible that in the case of relatively unimportant and frequently purchased consumer items 'trial' may take place (either deliberately or fortuitously – as a result of limited availability of alternatives perhaps) without the relationship ever reaching the state of 'preferred brand'.

We can interpret Ehrenberg's description of multiple brand purchasing in terms of a series of relationships with the available brands, some frankly experimental, others reflecting varying degrees of acceptance in terms of the purchaser's needs. This would lead to the situation of varying pre-disposition or probabilities of purchase observed by Ehrenberg.

The buyer–seller relationship

We know that a person can have relationships with other persons as well as with objects. In the particular case of the type of persuasive communication which we call advertising, we suggest that the relationship with the advertiser, the source of the communication, is likely to be a critical factor.

An interesting example of this is the recent situation in which one of the 'pirate' radio stations has been broadcasting advertisements which have been publicly repudiated by the advertisers concerned. Clearly the resultant uncertainty about the source of the advertisement must have had some effect on its credibility.

It is clear that any meaningful communication between two people implies the existence of a relationship between them. Without such a relationship the communication could not be interpreted by the recipient and would remain ambiguous.

In fact, such a communication will of itself create a relationship, if none existed. Equally it may either change or reinforce any prior relationship.

In connection with 'information' theories of advertising, a point of some importance is that such communication need not necessarily convey 'information' in the narrow, factual sense.

Suppose, for instance, that I am walking down the street and I meet a lady of my acquaintance. I smile at her and say, 'Good morning, Mrs Jones.' The purpose of my remark is clearly not to convey information about the weather. Mrs Jones will interpret this remark simply as a desire on my part to convey a friendly feeling and thus reinforce our relationship. Had I, on the other hand, failed to give her the greeting she expected, she might well have interpreted it as a change in our relationship for the worse.

Suppose, instead of meeting me, Mrs Jones had seen a poster for a familiar brand of soup. Might she perhaps have interpreted its message in the following terms: 'Good morning, Mrs Jones, I know you walk down this street, and I value your custom, so I have taken the trouble to remind you that my tomato soup is deliciously warming on cold days!'

It is suggested that any effective communication implies a relationship between the speaker and the audience. For a persuasive communication, such as an advertising campaign, to be effective implies that some part at least of its function must be to establish and maintain a relationship between the buyer and the seller.

This of course is not a new idea. The importance of goodwill has been recognized by generations of advertising people. To quote Dorothy Sayers, for example:

330 Management of Communications

The advertiser's reputation is in the long run his livelihood. An anonymous purveyor may sand his sugar or put paper in the soles of the shoes he sells; but if the advertiser of branded goods does so, his victims will talk; his bad name will be bandied around.

And, she might have added, his subsequent advertising is likely to be ignored.

Today, of course, advertising for shoddy or inferior goods is unlikely to be accepted in the first place. The point remains however that an advertising campaign is likely to be interpreted by the consumer in the light of his or her previous experience of the company's advertising and its products.

It means that customers who have rejected a company's advertising as irrelevant to their needs may be less likely to pay attention to the campaign that follows; that customers who were disappointed in a product which did not deliver the promise of the advertising may be less ready to believe the next set of claims; but that customers who have been pleased and satisfied may develop a relationship with the company which makes them readily accept its subsequent advertising and eager to buy its products.

In general terms, it is suggested that our conceptualization of the advertising process is incomplete unless it includes not only the customer's view of the product and the claims made about it, but also his view of the advertiser who makes those claims.

Psychological theory and the buyer–seller relationship

In seeking to develop the 'relationship' theory of advertising, we have naturally looked to see what help could be got from established psychological theory. Much of the psychological theory and associated techniques commonly applied to advertising seem to have stemmed from psychiatry and the psychology of the individual and his personality.

Not a great deal of help, it would seem, can be found in the field of inter-personal relations, and still less in the particular area of persuasive communication or advertising. However, there is a body of theory, developed mainly in the field of public opinion, that would seem to be capable of application to the problem before us, and one in particular – the work of Emery

(1962) at the Tavistock Institute of Human Relations – that is directly concerned with the problem of advertising.

These theories are mainly derived from concepts of balance, symmetry, or congruity, similar to those which have recently become familiar to the advertising world in the particular context of Festinger's Theory of Cognitive Dissonance.

Heider (1946) put forward a theoretical formulation of the way in which an individual viewed his relations with another person concerning some object, idea, event or the like. He used the notation P to represent the subject individual, O the other person and X the impersonal entity, which in our case might be the product or an advertising message about it.

Heider postulated that the relations between these three as seen by P would be either 'balanced' or 'unbalanced'. For

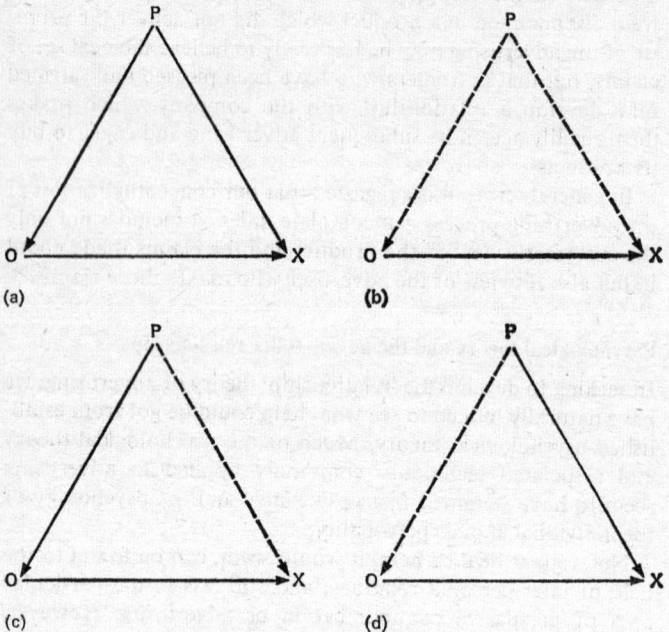

Figure 1 Examples of Heider's definition of balance applied to the buyer–seller relationship. Solid lines represent positive, broken lines negative, relations

example, if P liked both the person O and the object X, and O also liked X, the relationship would be 'balanced'. But if P liked X but disliked O and O liked X, the relationship would be 'unbalanced' (see Figure 1).

Heider postulated that an unbalanced state produces tension and generates forces to restore balance.

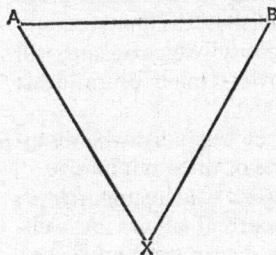

Figure 2 Newcomb's ABX notation

Subsequent experimental work confirmed that unbalanced states tended to produce feelings of unpleasantness compared with balanced states.

Newcomb (1953) put forward a rather similar theory of balance, but concerning social relationships and communications between people, rather than the situation existing in one person's mind. He also used a different notation, representing the two individuals by A and B. He postulated a 'strain towards symmetry' in the attitudes of A and B towards the object or idea X and suggested that this would influence communication between A and B so as to bring their attitudes to X into line (see Figure 2).

Experimental work amongst students showed that those who made friends with each other tended to agree on many matters and that similarities of opinion tended to increase over time.

Osgood and Tannenbaum (1955) put forward a 'Principle of Congruity'. This deals specifically with the situation in which an individual is presented with a statement by a person towards whom he has some attitude concerning some matter about which he also has certain feelings.

This is, in effect, a special case of Heider's theory of balance and says, for example, that congruity exists if a person the individual likes makes a statement with which he agrees, but if such a person makes a statement with which he disagrees the resultant incongruity may influence his attitude both towards the source and the object of the statement.

To give an example – suppose a Socialist hears that the Soviet Union, of which he approves, is beginning to favour the profit motive in industrial management, of which he disapproves.

The state of 'unbalance' or 'incongruity' which results will tend to lower his opinion of the Soviet Union or raise his opinion of the profit motive (or both).

The converse would be the case for the Capitalist who disapproves of the Soviet Union but approves of the profit motive.

This theory, and the experimental work which supported it, were concerned with statements on current affairs by well-known public figures. If, however, the theory were applied to advertising messages, it would suggest for example that an advertising claim by a well-regarded company for a brand which was considered unfavourably would produce a state of incongruity. The pressure to restore congruity would tend to result in a less favourable attitude to the company but a more favourable attitude to the brand. Conversely, an advertisement in favour of a well-liked brand by an unfavourably regarded company would tend to improve the attitude to the company but might adversely affect the attitude to the brand.

Whilst the idea of an unpopular company producing a popular brand may seem unlikely, the theoretical possibility of an advertising boomerang is somewhat alarming.

A less extreme example might be the case of a company committing some unpopular public act which would have unfavourable repercussions on the public attitude to its products.

A further derivation of this principle of congruity is that incongruity may not always produce attitude change, but may lead to incredulity or rejection of the evidence of the source of the statement.

This again would seem to have an advertising application, and suggests that belief in an advertising message may be influenced by the consumer's attitude to the advertiser as well as his attitude to the brand.

Other work on the subject of persuasion has shown the importance of the subject's relationship to the source of the communication. Hovland (1951) for example, has suggested that the ways in which a person deals with a communication that does not fit his established pattern of attitudes may include discrediting the communicator and distorting the message into a more acceptable form.

One theory which is directly concerned with the problem of persuasive selling was formulated by Emery (1962). He postulated a model of the marketing process which includes both the product and the persuasive communication. Using Newcomb's ABX notation, he uses X to denote the product whilst X^1 denotes the representation of the product made by B to A, in other words the advertisement (see Figure 3).

For our purposes we can call B the company or advertiser, A the advertisement audience, or customer, X the brand or product advertised, and X^1 the advertising communication.

B produces the advertisement X^1 and brings it to the notice of the customer A. If effective, X^1 modifies A's perception of X and this leads to the behaviour B wishes to produce, usually purchase or use of X.

It is clear that there is little difficulty, through the use of normal advertising skills and resources, in bringing the advertisement X^1 to A's attention. The critical problem, the problem of creative effectiveness, is whether the advertisement X^1

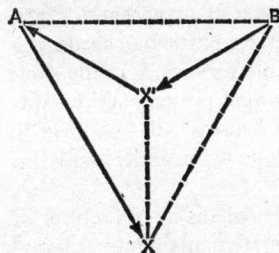

Figure 3 Emery's model of persuasion

D. Lowe Watson 335

can convey something about X which will induce the required change in AX.

The key point which Emery makes is that this effect depends not just on how A perceives the advertisement X^1 but on the whole system of relationships.

Take first the relationship AB. If A has an unfavourable image of the company B he will tend to discount both the product X and what is said about it by the company (i.e. the message X^1). On the other hand, if A's view of B is favourable he will be more ready to pay attention to the message X^1 and to believe what it says.

What is perhaps less obvious is that the AB relationship also involves the image which B the company holds of A his customer. If, for example, the company has an unfavourable or distorted view of its customers, this may be reflected in the tone and content of the advertising, in its behaviour to customers – such as the treatment of complaints, in the design of the product and its whole marketing strategy.

Apart from the danger that B may actually take wrong marketing decisions, there is a likelihood that A will sense B's attitude in a number of subtle ways and the AB relationship will be thereby affected.

Emery points out that the relationship between A and B is in effect a type of personal relationship even though, in the case of advertising persuasion there is no face-to-face contact. One important aspect of this relationship, which has a bearing on the effectiveness of B's attempts at persuasion, is that there must be an element of congruity in the way in which A and B respectively view X. Thus for A to be prepared to accept B's persuasion about the suitability of X for A's particular needs, it is necessary for A to accept that B is able to view X in the same way that A views it. So advertising which presents X in a way which A recognizes as relevant to his needs will also help to strengthen A's image of B as someone who understands his point of view.

At the same time if B is seen (in his role as manufacturer or seller) as being competent to make statements about relevant qualities of X which A cannot perceive for himself, this will further strengthen his power of persuasion.

For example, if B is a manufacturer of washing machines, he must first convince the customer that he knows all about her washday problems – the lack of space in her kitchen, her husband's dirty overalls, her fears of the children getting hurt by the machine, and so on. In this way he establishes a congruity of view about the washing machine. They must 'talk the same language'.

Secondly, he must establish his skill and experience in the design and manufacture of such machines, his ability to provide the technical solution to her needs. This, in effect, represents the relationship between B and X. Emery uses the phrase 'distinctive competence' to describe the extent to which B is seen as having the necessary 'know-how' for the type of product which X represents. Wilkinson's for example, have made use of their distinctive competence as sword manufacturers in producing fine cutting edges to advertise their razor blades.

Whilst A the customer is aware of B's interest in persuading him about X, he will also have expectations about B's own attitude to X which he would naturally expect to be enthusiastic. Thus A will accept and expect a degree of enthusiasm or exaggeration in the communication X^1 as consistent with B's expected relationship with his product X. Such exaggeration will doubtless be compensated for in A's perception of the message.

On the other hand, if B's communication about X is seen by A as being too cool or objective, this could create an inconsistency which might result in A revising his image of both B and X.

This point is well brought out in the I P A survey of television advertising, which shows clearly that customers tend to expect and like the advertiser to speak in enthusiastic and even obviously exaggerated terms about his product.

Then there is the question of the relationship of X^1 the advertisement to X the product. Is X^1 perceived as a statement that is likely to be truthful about X? Alternatively, is it a statement that is relevant to X as A perceives it?

This brings us to the question of A's relation to X. Clearly if A is to be persuaded to take action in respect of X, to buy or to use it, then X must be seen as having properties required by and

D. Lowe Watson 337

appropriate to his need. Thus the relation of A to X depends both upon the nature of A's need and the character of X as perceived by A. A Rolls-Royce may be a desirable object but we do not buy one to use for carting manure.

A further development of the model may occur if A recognizes that B has an interest in persuading him about X, so that his perception of the message X^1 is influenced by his image of B as truthful or reliable. To overcome this B may resort to testimonial or presenter advertising, and have his message put forward by an intermediary 'b' who has better standing with A, has no apparent self-interest in selling X, or who may be seen as capable of professional or expert judgement.

This introduces a new set of relationships. First b's relation to A; does A accept him as able to understand his needs? Then b's relationship to X; is he competent to make statements about the product?

Then there is b's relationship to X^1 – the message; did he really say the things attributed to him? and finally b's relationship to B; is b really being paid to say what B tells him to say?

Once again, a change in any one of these relationships must have repercussions throughout the system.

It is of some interest to note that a medium which carries the advertising may tend to fill a rather similar role to the presenter 'b', provided A believes that the medium accepts some responsibility for the advertising it carries.

It follows that if the medium is seen as a 'personality' this will

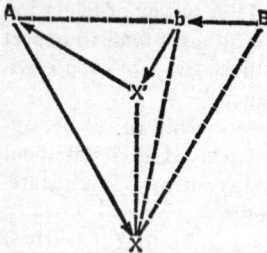

Figure 4 Emery's 'presenter' model

influence the interpretation of the message. In passing, it is of interest to compare this view of the role of the medium with Marshall McLuhan's detailed examination of the relationship between the characteristics of the medium and the nature of the message transmitted (1964).

This would seem to be an area which would reward further research and consideration

Implications of the theories

Two general conclusions seem to emerge from these theories, especially from Emery's work. In the first place they describe the nature of advertising in terms of a complex system of balancing relationships.

We have only described the system relating to one advertiser and his product. Such a system must be replicated for every

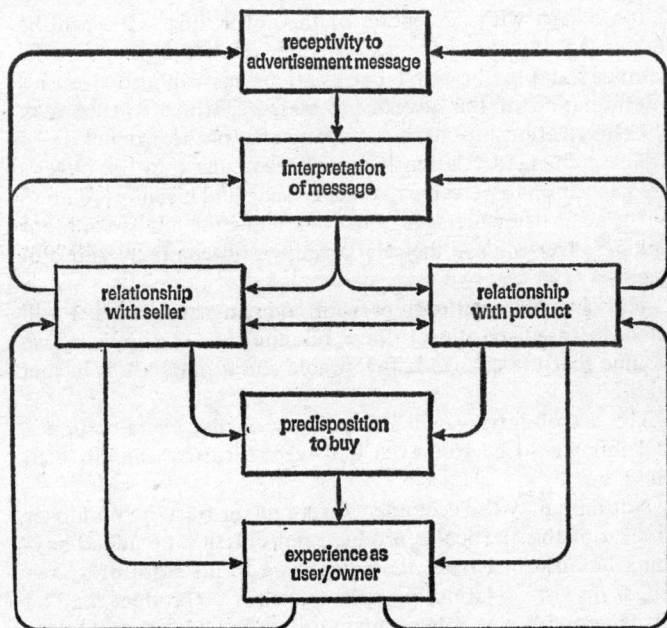

Figure 5

competitive product which some other advertiser is seeking to bring to A's attention.

In the second place, because of the assumption of 'balance' or 'congruity' a change in any one of these relationships will result in tensions tending to change the system as a whole.

This suggests we would expect to find a 'halo' effect embracing not only the 'personality' of the product, but the 'personality' of the advertiser, and the advertising as well. This indeed seems to be confirmed by the evidence cited above that users tend to have a more favourable attitude to the advertising of a brand than non-users.

The effect of this system of interlocking relationships will be to set up a series of 'chain reactions' or feed back loops.

The flow-chart in Figure 5 gives a simplified representation of the advertising–buying relationship from the point of view of the buyer.

If we start with perception of the advertising – this will be influenced by the person's existing relationships with the company and the brand. These relationships will also affect his interpretation of the advertising message, which in turn may alter his relationships to the company and/or the product.

These changed relationships will feed back into the buyer's predisposition to perceive that advertising and his interpretation of the advertising message, thus completing the first set of loops linking advertising to the relationships with company and product.

The changed relationships with company and product will affect his predisposition to buy. For the sake of simplicity we assume that the change is favourable and a purchase is in fact made.

The act of buying will immediately change the situation – and this would be true even if it were a casual, unmotivated purchase.

Not only may the customer, for a time at least, be no longer in need of this particular product; not only has he added anything he absorbed from the advertising to his store of knowledge; his own relationship with this class of product may be changed by his new role as buyer or owner – for example, of a new motor car of a certain make and model.

He now begins to accumulate experience of the product in use, and his perception and interpretation of this experience is conditioned both by his new role as owner and also by the expectations derived from his previous image of the company and the product.

His relationships both with the seller and with the product will be further changed by this experience. Incidentally his relationships with other competitive products and their sellers are also likely to be affected.

If the purchase is one of personal significance, such as clothes, cosmetics, or even a haircut, it may subtly influence his perception of how others see him. Or if the experience is shared by others – an expensive meal, a central heating system – it may influence his relationships with other people and he is likely to be sensitive to their reactions to it.

In this way the whole system of relationships will be altered. His perception of the product as owner or user will feed back into his relationships with the product and the seller. His new image of the company and of the product (in relation to his needs – which may also have changed) will be related to his recollection of previous advertising – its truthfulness and relevance for example – and this in turn will influence his predisposition to pay attention to future advertising from this source, and his interpretation of the message conveyed by such advertising.

It will also influence his receptivity to, and interpretation of competitive advertising, through his changed relationships with the companies and products concerned. Under these circumstances the question of what cause precedes what effect becomes, as King has put it, a matter of the chicken and the egg.

With the help of this model we can distinguish three key factors involved in effective advertising; the customer's image of the company, his image of the product, and his perception of the advertising. These three factors mutually support and reinforce each other like the three strands of a rope. If these relationships are strong and firmly interwoven then like a rope they will spiral upwards carrying the sales curve with them.

If one is weak, or is not properly interwoven with the other

D. Lowe Watson 341

two, then the whole rope is weakened and the campaign is likely to fail.

It is worth pointing out that our model has been deliberately limited to those aspects of the marketing process directly concerned with persuasion. The marketing rope has other strands of which product availability and price may be particularly important, but it is beyond the scope of this paper to extend the analogy in these directions.

There is one further word to be said about this 'relationship' theory of advertising.

The purpose of any descriptive theory of this type must be to provide a conceptual framework as a basis for prediction and for measurement. It might appear at first sight that the very complexity of the model suggested may inhibit its usefulness from this point of view. Against this it may be argued that a realistic model of a highly complex situation must necessarily include a certain degree of complexity.

From the point of view of measurement, it will not have escaped the notice of the technically-minded reader, that the concept of 'relationships' used in this model bears a certain similarity to the 'personal constructs' postulated by Kelly (1955). It seems likely therefore that the technique of repertory grid testing which Kelly has devised could be adapted and used as a tool to explore and quantify the relationships we have described.

Conclusion

This paper has drawn attention to the inadequacy of currently used theories of the advertising process to explain satisfactorily much of the empirical evidence about how advertising works.

A new approach is suggested, based on a completely different conceptualization in which the advertising process is seen as part of a network of relationships, linking the buyer, the seller and the product or service advertised. This new model is shown to account for many observed discrepancies between previous theories and observed facts.

It is further suggested that the new 'relationship' theory gives fresh insight into the nature of advertising. It shows how the company image is related to advertising effectiveness and emphasizes the quasi-personal nature of the relationships involved. This has several implications.

In the first place it underlines the importance of the concept of 'total communication'. This means coordination of policy in every part of the company's communications activity, advertising, sales promotion, packaging, product planning, public relations and corporate identification. All these forms of communication contribute to the company 'personality' as seen by its customers and can influence the effectiveness of its sales and advertising effort.

In the second place we have drawn attention to the role which the company image or personality is likely to play in the process of advertising persuasion. This role, it is suggested, may play an important part in the longer term effects of advertising. These longer term or 'carry over' effects are recognized by most advertising people, but are very imperfectly accounted for in the 'conversion' type of theory. We now suggest that the advertiser who can build up a strong and favourable relationship with his customers will establish a fund of goodwill from which he can derive future benefits. These benefits include not only a greater readiness on the part of the customer to pay attention to his advertising and a predisposition to put a favourable interpretation on the message received, but also a favourable attitude towards the product itself, an expectation of satisfactory product performance and a greater willingness to try a new product.

At this point some readers may observe that whilst certain advertisers make a point of featuring the company's name in all their advertisements, other advertisers, who appear equally successful, give little prominence to the company's name if indeed they mention it at all. Indeed it is very probable that many housewives are quite unaware whether their favourite washing powder is made by Unilever or by Procter and Gamble.

The question of whether to feature the company name in an advertising campaign is one which must be considered on its merits. For example, when Van den Bergs moved into the soft drinks market with their Tree Tops range of products they might have considered that their 'distinctive competence' as food manufacturers would create goodwill for the new soft drinks brand; alternatively they might have considered that the image of a margarine manufacturer was too far removed from the particular skills involved in fruit drinks processing.

The important point is that the customer must have some image of the source of the advertising message.

As we suggested earlier, any meaningful communication between two people implies the existence of a relationship between them, and such a communication will of itself create a relationship if none previously existed.

If the housewife does not know that Omo is made by Lever Brothers, she will think of them as 'the Omo people'. She will build up in her mind a personality for 'the Omo people' in a similar way to mental pictures she would construct of, let us say, a politician addressing an election meeting, a TV personality, or a newspaper columnist, and it is probably true to say that this personality would be based not only on what he had to say, but perhaps even more on the way in which he said it.

We suggest that any advertiser who doubts this assertion should carry out appropriate research – which we are confident will prove that his advertising has built up an image of his company in the minds of his customers, whether or not this has been a part of his deliberate policy.

In the third place it is suggested that advertising strategies other than 'product sell' can be devised for use in established product fields where there is little meaningful difference between brands, where further technical improvement is difficult, or where competitive technology is so efficient that product improvements are almost immediately matched by rival brands.

It seems likely that misguided attempts to apply factual 'product sell' in these inappropriate fields may be a prime cause of the accusation that much advertising is concerned with trying to create trivial or imaginary differences between brands.

In such cases it may well be that less emphasis on factual product differentiation and a more conscious attempt to create a favourable aura for both product and company might be more appropriate.

In this connection we have referred above to the Total Communication concept. A particular facet of this is the role of promotional activities such as games, special offers and so on. According to DAGMAR-type theory, such activities can only have an ephemeral effect unless they also convey information or argument in favour of the product. According to such theory, any sales effect which lasts after the promotion has ended must be a result of the sampling by non-users – notwithstanding Ehrenberg's observations that promotions are often more effective in increasing the rate of purchase of infrequent buyers.

We can now see that a successful promotion, by creating goodwill among the customers, can have a longer term effect by strengthening their relationship with the company. Conversely, of course, an unpopular promotion would have the reverse effect.

Finally, the relationship theory exposes the fallacy of the 'economist's view' of advertising as a kind of intelligence service to buyers in a market place where decisions between brands are made on a strictly rational basis. It is comparatively easy to show that most advertising is wasteful and inefficient by this yardstick. The information it imparts is selective, incomplete and frequently obviously exaggerated.

The implication of this paper is that advertising on the contrary has an important social role to perform, by helping to create and to strengthen the essential relationship between the seller and the buyer on which the smooth and mutually satisfying performance of millions of commercial transactions ultimately depends.

In today's world of large scale production and complex distribution methods, the majority of the things we buy are produced by a faceless manufacturer whom the customer never meets.

Just as the manufacturer, through his market research and sales analysis can build up a picture of the personality, behaviour and needs of his customers, so can the customer make use of the manufacturer's advertising to interpret for himself the sort of company whose products he buys or is contemplating buying, and the intentions of the manufacturer in the design and marketing of his products.

In this way, it is suggested, the buyer–seller relationship, established primarily through advertising, plays a positive role in reducing the level of confusion, distrust, dissatisfaction and disappointment which would otherwise exist.

A world without advertising, if we can imagine such a place, would be a world in which the customer would be not only fumbling blindly in confusion and ignorance of the products offered for sale, but would also be angry and frustrated by his lack of contact with the manufacturer and, by implication, the manufacturer's lack of interest in him.

Effective advertising, we suggest, must always convey to the customer the manufacturer's intense interest in him, and his urgent desire to meet his customers' needs in the best possible way.

To underline the importance of this 'public relations' function we conclude by quoting Marshall McLuhan's comment that Arthur Miller's *Death of a Salesman* was symbolic of the changing face of advertising . . . 'he could as appropriately have titled his play *The Birth of a P R man*'.

References

BIRD, M., and EHRENBERG, A. S. C. (1966), 'Non-awareness and non-usage', *J. Advertising Res.*, vol. 6, no. 4, pp. 4–8.

BRITISH MARKET RESEARCH BUREAU (1967), *Attitudes to Television Advertising*, Institute of Practitioners in Advertising.

COLLEY, R. (1961), *Defining Advertising Goals for Measured Advertising Results*, Association of National Advertisers of New York.

COPLAND, B. (1963), 'An evaluation of conceptual frameworks for measuring advertising results', *Proc. 9th ann. Conference*, Advertising Research Foundation.

CHATFIELD, C., EHRENBERG, A. S. C. and GOODHARDT, G. J. (1966), 'Progress on a simplified model of stationary purchasing behaviour', *J. Roy. stats. Soc.*, vol. 129, pp. 317–67.

EMERY, F. E. (1962), 'Heuristic models of the marketing process', *Hum. Rel.*, vol. 15, pp. 63–76.

EMERY, F. E. (1962), *In Search of Some Principles of Persuasion*, Tavistock Institute of Human Relations (unpublished).

FESTINGER, L. (1957), *A Theory of Cognitive Dissonance*, Row, Peterson.

HEIDER, F. (1946), 'Attitudes and cognitive organization', *J. Psychol.*, vol. 21, pp. 107–12.

HOVLAND, C. I. and WEISS, W. (1951), 'The influence of source credibility on communication effectiveness', *Pub. Opinion Q.*, vol. 15, pp. 635–50.

HOVLAND, C. I., JANIS, I. L. and KELLEY, H. H. (1953), *Communication and Persuasion: Psychological Studies of Opinion Change*, Yale University Press.

KELLY, G. A. (1955), *Psychology of Personal Constructs*, vols. 1–2, Norton.

KING, S. (1967), 'Can research evaluate the creative content of Advertising?', Market Research Society Annual Conference.

LOWE WATSON, D. (1963), 'The function of advertising', Conference of International Marketing Federation, Hamburg.

McLUHAN, M. (1964), *Understanding Media*, Routledge & Kegan Paul.

NEWCOMB. T. M. (1953), 'An approach to the study of communicative acts', *Psychol. Rev.*, vol. 60, pp. 393–404.

OSGOOD, C. E., and TANNENBAUM, P. H. (1955), 'The principle of congruity in the prediction of attitude change', *Psychol. Rev.*, vol. 62, pp. 42–55.

PALDA, K. S. (1966), 'The hypothesis of a hierarchy of effects: a partial evaluation', *J. Marketing Res.*, vol. 3, no. 1, pp. 13–24.

ZAJONC, R. B. (1960), 'The concepts of balance, congruity and dissonance', *Pub. Opinion Q.*, vol. 24, pp. 280–96.

19 S. Majaro

Advertising by Objectives

S. Majaro, 'Advertising by objectives', *Management Today*,
January 1970, pp. 71–3.

The famous statement that 'I know half the money I spend on
Advertising is wasted; but I can never find out which half' has
been attributed to at least two great sellers and advertisers; the
first Lord Leverhulme and John Wanamaker, the nineteenth-
century American merchant. Whoever first said it, the quotation is understandably popular among advertising men, who
must continually search for methods of measuring the
effectiveness of advertising. This long-standing problem has
been preoccupying an increasing number of marketing executives and company chairmen alike. Advertising is a major resource area in many companies, and it is inconceivable for no
heart-searching to follow the deployment of such substantial
sums. In Britain close to £500 million is spent on advertising –
1·4 per cent of the gross national product; in the United States
this expenditure exceeds £7000 million – 2·2 per cent GNP.
To spend these vast amounts without wanting to see results is
the sort of mindless extravagance which the modern manager
can hardly afford.

Not surprisingly, the subject has stimulated considerable
interest among academic researchers and businessmen. Management literature abounds with lengthy and interesting studies
on how advertising results can be measured and how the advertising effort can be made more effective. Panaceas grow and die
by the dozens; methodologies and techniques fill volumes; and,
like alchemists, a new breed of specialists has emerged ready to
turn advertising budgets to gold dust. Techniques for measuring
effectiveness have sprung from all directions. Some are simple
and naïve; others are sophisticated to the point of incom-
prehensibility, some are highly qualitative and conceptual;

others are quantitative and mechanical. The whole subject has become so riddled with methodologies that most marketing managers prefer to steer clear of this overwhelming battery of 'aids' developed to help them. They treat them as the bear-hug that should not be trusted.

A modern enterprise rarely fails to measure the effectiveness of its human resources. Similarly it is quite normal for a company to analyse carefully its raw material content and utilization. But how many companies measure systematically, if at all, the results of their advertising effort? How many companies are able to express in quantitative terms the impact that a specific campaign has achieved? This of course, leads one to ask the logical question: how many companies know precisely what they are trying to achieve through advertising? A recent survey among both UK and Continental companies, conducted by management consultants Urwick Orr & Partners, tried to answer these questions. The search was for a clearer picture of how companies on this side of the Atlantic treat their advertising effort in general and, specifically, how they measure the attainment of their advertising objectives.

Most of the companies approached, in a wide cross-section of industries, showed interest in the survey and felt challenged by the implications of what was for many the first opportunity to consider these questions in depth. A simple questionnaire was used which sought this information, in jargon-free language:

1. Historic data on the relationship, over a period of five years, between two ingredients of the marketing mix – advertising and sales management costs – and the resulting sales turnover.

2. Whether the company had actually formulated advertising objectives, and if so, the details of such objectives.

3. How the company measured its advertising effectiveness, and details of the methods used to do so.

4. How the company decided on its budgets.

Replies to this last question, although slightly away from the overall theme of the survey, helped to throw light on the companies' general attitude to advertising and its objectives. Such answers as 'we select an advertising budget in accordance with what we can afford in any given budget period', or 'percentage of budgeted sales', help to indicate a company's state of enlightenment towards advertising as an effective tool of the marketing process. These replies usually come from companies which slash their advertising appropriation the minute that turnover shows a tendency to decline. Thus, the questionnaire was simple but fairly comprehensive. It was designed to remove the obfuscating mystique that surrounds the subject in the minds of most managers.

The answers revealed that a surprisingly large proportion of British and Continental firms claim that they formulate advertising objectives. This claim was made by 70 per cent of the sample. Nearly all consumer goods firms select objectives for their advertising effort, or say they do. Most answers make it evident that the process rarely goes beyond a very basic and almost crude description of objectives. Many companies declared that they had advertising objectives but seemed to confuse them with overall marketing objectives.

The survey showed, however, that companies which formulate an Advertising by Objectives strategy fare better than those which do not. While most respondent companies reported increased sales during the period 1965–69 (whether or not they formulated advertising objectives), only 35 per cent of the total sample also reported *increased market share* during the same period. Of these high-fliers no less than 85 per cent believe in and actively pursue an Advertising by Objectives philosophy. This indicates that firms which clearly formulate their advertising objectives (and more than likely also have a total Management by Objectives approach to business) enjoy a marked competitive edge. However, although 70 per cent of the sampled companies formulate advertising objectives, only 55 per cent of the total sample actually reduce these objectives to a written form.

The majority of the companies which admit to having no advertising objectives at all market industrial goods. Most of them spend relatively small amounts on advertising. This, of course, is predictable – the less a manager spends on advertising, the less he is preoccupied by its effectiveness. Nevertheless, the replies suggested that even these companies have become aware of the need to evaluate the results of their advertising appropriation. Banks and hire purchase companies in the sample seemed to occupy a unique position. Their advertising budgets are on the increase; but none could point to clearly defined goals.

The question, what are the actual advertising objectives of companies, yielded the following list (in order of frequency of mention):

Increase or support sales;

create or increase product or brand awareness;

improve image of company's products;

improve company's image;

sales promotion;

influence attitudes;

inform or educate the consumer;

introduce new products.

The wording is extracted from the forms with minimum changes in order to reproduce accurately the general impressions gained from the survey.

On methods used for measuring effectiveness the survey aimed to unearth two aspects: what methods are being used by UK and Continental companies which actually purport to measure the effectiveness of their advertising effort, and are the methods disclosed by the companies used effectively? More specifically, are the individual measurement techniques used appropriate to the selected advertising goals?

The methods used, again in order of frequency of mention, can be summarized as follows:

'Sort and count' techniques, such as consumer mail or coupon response;

group interviews or panel discussions;

recall tests;

comparison of sales results (monthly, quarterly or annually);

psychological depth interviews;

folder tests;

salesmen's monthly reports;

annual survey by market research department;

reports from dealers;

mathematical models.

The number of companies using fairly sophisticated mathematical models was small, and even such companies were not entirely clear about what precisely they were trying to measure.

An analysis of the questionnaires indicated a common failure to dovetail the measurement methods with the specific objectives; for instance, the psychological depth interview method is used by one company to measure attitude changes, although the advertising objective it gave on the questionnaire is 'to inform the public of a product's availability' – which is like using a thermometer to measure the humidity. Many similar instances were observed; in other words, the impression is inescapable that even progressive companies which have formulated clear advertising objectives do not always use the most relevant measurement methods to evaluate results.

The rationale behind the inquiry about methods used to determine appropriations was an attempt to establish whether a strong Advertising by Objectives approach helped in the task of determining the size of the advertising budget. The survey revealed that most of the companies in the sample used slightly dated methods for determining advertising budgets. 'Percentage of past sales'; 'as much as we can afford'; 'matching competitors' expenditure', and so on are phrases that recurred frequently. Only 25 per cent of the companies claimed, in so many words, that their advertising budgets were regulated to correspond with pre-defined advertising objectives. They set objectives and only then determine the advertising resources required to carry out the task to be performed. Thus size, shape and function of the edifice are determined before allocating the bricks and mortar needed for building. That this is the sole logical course is, unfortunately, only understood by a small minority of enlightened companies.

Most businessmen would declare that the basic objective of advertising is to aid sales, and that the only criterion of effectiveness is the 'cause and effect' relationship between advertising and sales volume. This is a practical approach but it does not always correspond to the true state of affairs. An extreme example of an advertising objective which is not set in *action terms* (e.g. to increase sales), but in *communications terms* (e.g. to impart information, or to change attitudes) is that of eliminating 'cognitive dissonance'. That technical phrase means the post-purchase anxiety or doubt which the buyer, especially the buyer of an expensive product, sometimes develops *after* acquiring the product. This doubt may be a partial carry-over from the pre-purchase period, when the customer had trouble making a choice. If, for example, the product was a car, each possibility had attractive and unattractive qualities: the customer chose a specific product because, after careful consideration, he decided that the atttractive qualities outweighed the unattractive ones. Once the product is in his possession, however, the less attractive qualities start bothering him and doubts set in.

Dissonance is common among purchasers of homes, motor cars, major appliances; it is also common among investors in shares and unit trusts. The tension caused by dissonance leads the buyer to seek its reduction. He may wish to rid himself of the offending product through its return to the seller, or its disposal, or its concealment in the attic. He may, on the other hand, try to resolve the nagging doubt by seeking proof that he has made the right choice. The manufacturer's aim is to provide the doubting purchaser with reassurance and confirmation of the product's excellent properties. Unless the seller makes some positive effort to dispel the dissonance he may lose the purchaser as a future customer. If this effort is the main objective of the advertising, it should be clearly spelt out, and a method of measurement should be provided. The effectiveness of the campaign can then be monitored. The measuring of such results may admittedly require the use of complex techniques (such as the 'projective technique' or the 'thematic apperception test'), but measurement is nonetheless possible.

Most managers, however, see advertising's main objective as 'increasing sales' or 'increasing market share'. But these aims

S. Majaro 353

describe the *total* marketing objectives, not the objectives of one element of the marketing mix. It is hardly reasonable to expect advertising to shoulder the full burden of attaining basic marketing objectives, unless it is the single variable in the marketing mix used. So what is really the basic goal of advertising? The subject is full of controversial notions which have stimulated a voluminous and fascinating literature. There are two main opposing schools of thought, basically either that advertising should be stated in terms of sales objectives; or that advertising, together with other forms of promotion, aims to accomplish clearly defined communication objectives; thus advertising succeeds or fails depending on how well it communicates pre-determined information and attitudes to the right people at the right time and the right cost. This philosophy is often referred to as DAGMAR (*D*efining *A*dvertising *G*oals – *M*easuring *A*dvertising *R*esults).

What happens when these two concepts are applied to specific situations? Where advertising is used to alleviate 'cognitive dissonance', or post-decision doubt, especially in relation to expensive items, DAGMAR supporters carry the day. Again, advertisements aiming at the creation of *primary demand,* say, for wool or steel or aluminium in their generic form, are mounted by or on behalf of a large number of manufacturers acting collectively, in order to enhance the general awareness by readers or audience of the excellent properties of the product – irrespective of a specific manufacturer. The rationale is that once public awareness is generated, the wide demand for the product will facilitate the promotional efforts of individual manufacturers. The success of such a campaign cannot be measured in terms of sales; the time-lag between the campaign and the possible purchase of a specific brand ('selective demand') is too prolonged to be of measurable significance. DAGMAR wins the day again!

Another example is financial. Unit trusts advertise heavily nowadays; and each advertisement carries a coupon, clearly identified with a 'key' or code and ready to be used. The effectiveness of each advertisement or each campaign in each medium can be evaluated by reference to the number of coupons returned. The DAGMAR protagonists may have some difficulties here. Sales are the real target, and sales volume can be readily measured. In another case, two large detergents manufacturers advertise their respective brands; both extol the many virtues of their splendid products – they both wash 'whiter than white'; both claim to be God's gift to housewives. Each company would like to increase sales and raise its market share at the expense of the other. If the firms are of comparable efficacy it is difficult to see how advertising can help them to achieve this aim; yet if one manufacturer were drastically to reduce his advertising effort, the other would obtain some market benefits.

If both companies were to reduce their advertising expenditure simultaneously, if not by agreement, then by some telepathic intuition, it is likely that they would gradually both lose part of their market shares to smaller and hitherto less successful competitors and/or own-label brands. We are thus dealing here with a *defensive* type of promotion, designed to maintain brand loyalty at all levels of the marketing process. Measuring sales attainment after each campaign or even at the end of the year is not a valid yardstick of advertising effectiveness. The advertiser's objectives must be clearly defined if the results are to be meaningfully measured; and the objectives here would be expressed in DAGMAR communications terms rather than in action terms.

A bank advertises the many services it is able to offer the public. The advertisement is specially worded to appeal to young students – potential clientele for the bank; the bank considers that the student of today is the tycoon or the professional man of tomorrow. Here advertising fulfils a communication function in the sense that it attempts to create awareness of what the bank can offer; it can also improve the reader's attitude to banks, to bankers and to the advertiser. If the bank tried to judge the effectiveness of its advertising effort by counting how many students rushed to one of the bank's branches to open an account, it would be very disappointed; but in communication terms the advertisement may have attained significant results – another good example of a DAGMAR situation.

A large electronics firm advertises in order to make the

S. Majaro 355

market generally aware that the company is in the electronics business; it wishes to convince people that this is a company capable of bringing out new or improved electronic products. Ideally the company would wish to create a level of awareness among readers which would result in their associating anything which is good in electronics with its name. This is a perfectly legitimate ambition, and it can be couched in measurable terms such as: 'We wish to raise awareness of Proposition A from its present level of 20 per cent of our target group to an appreciably higher level . . .' DAGMAR once again.

A synthetic fibre manufacturer runs a very substantial campaign emphasizing the excellent qualities of the product incorporated in finished garments which the firm does not manufacture itself. It is inconceivable that readers will respond by dashing out to the nearest store and buying the garment made from this wonder fibre; so it is pointless to measure the effectiveness of such a campaign in action terms. Underlying the campaign may be this type of Advertising by Objectives reasoning:

(a) 'We recognize that our product is in no way superior to that of our major competitors.'

(b) 'Our major strength is the fact that our range of colours and textures is modern in appearance and conforms to the taste of a specific market segment' (the segment, or the target group, being clearly defined).

(c) 'We therefore wish to communicate this message to the market with the view of increasing the level of awareness (i) among customers – here we wish to increase the level of awareness of our brand and its attributes from its present level, which is known to us, by 20 per cent; (ii) among manufacturers of finished garments – here we wish to increase the level of awareness of our special range of colours from its present level by 40 per cent; (iii) among members of the channels of distribution – here we wish to increase the level of awareness of the fact that our brand is synonymous with fashionable colours from the present level by 25 per cent.'

These are clear, simple and measurable communication objectives which support the DAGMAR theory.

On the other hand, a mail order firm advertises a special offer. A coupon is provided at the bottom of the advertisement soliciting orders accompanied by a remittance. It would be impossible to find a simpler example of advertising effort that can be measured in action terms: the larger the number of responses, the more successful the campaign.

All these examples have been taken at random from current advertisements appearing in well-known media; they show clearly that while sometimes advertising can, and should, be measured in terms of sales achieved, there are other occasions when communication objectives are more relevant. The DAGMAR versus SALES controversy is futile: each situation should be taken on its merits. Whichever way one looks at it – in action terms or communication terms – clearly defined objectives are needed, and their attainment can be measured. Conceptual controversy as to what advertising is all about in no way detracts from the basic fact that an effective advertising effort needs pre-set goals.

An Advertising by Objectives approach can yield considerable benefits. The following are, briefly, some of the specific advantages:

1. *It helps to integrate the advertising effort with the other ingredients of the 'marketing mix', thus setting a consistent and logical marketing plan.* In the absence of advertising objectives there is every danger that the advertising appropriation will fail to maximize the contribution of advertising to the marketing effort. The mental exercise of preparing objectives and reducing them to a written form is in itself effective stimulus to the clear thinking and consistent reasoning which are so badly needed in any planning task.

2. *It facilitates the task of the advertising agency in (a) preparing and evaluating creative work and (b) recommending the most suitable media.* The chances of an advertising agency performing successfully in both creative work and media selection are greatly enhanced when a well-formulated set of objectives is presented. These objectives can, of course, be formulated with the agency's help, but it is neither wise nor fair to leave the setting of advertising objectives entirely to the agency. To do so

S. Majaro 357

resembles leaving the selection of your meal to the chef or the head waiter; it can be done, but there is no guarantee of satisfaction.

3. *It assists in determining advertising budgets.* It is easier to decide upon an appropriate budget with a specific task in view: without objectives the determination of budgets is a highly pragmatic affair.

4. *It enables marketing executives and top management to appraise the advertising plan realistically and approve or disapprove.* It facilitates the control of advertising expenditure: in the absence of such control criteria, top management tends to be suspicious of the validity of the advertising effort and often presses for drastic cuts, especially during cost-reduction drives.

5. *It permits meaningful measurement of advertising results.* This is probably one of the greatest benefits of the Advertising by Objectives approach. This aspect alone can justify the time and effort spent on formulating the objectives of a company's advertising effort in general and of a specific campaign in particular. The reward stemming from performance measurement cannot be over-emphasized.

Before any useful work on setting advertising objectives can begin, all relevant information on the product, the market and the consumer must be available. Of prime importance is a thorough assessment of consumer behaviour and motivation, with particular reference to the company's target group. A full appreciation of the overall marketing plan and its objectives is an essential part of the input information. The advertising planner can now consider which of the marketing objectives can best be achieved through advertising. 'Best' here implies a combination of effectiveness and minimum cost. Advertising objectives can then be formulated and should be consistent with the overall marketing objectives and with the objectives of the other ingredients of the marketing mix.

Whenever possible, they should be expressed in quantitative terms: for communication objectives, clearly-defined and accurate 'benchmark' bases should be incorporated in the plan. (If an increase in 'awareness' from 20 per cent to 50 per cent is sought, and the basic 20 per cent figure is suspect, the whole exercise could be futile). The help of the company's advertising agency in the important task of formulating objectives can be called for; whether this is done depends on the experience and degree of sophistication of the company.

A detailed plan can now be prepared to show how the objectives can be attained. It will incorporate details such as budgets (funds required to attain the set task), the message, media selection, and scheduling. The next step is to obtain management approval. This will be more readily provided if evidence can be produced to show that the hypotheses put forward in the plan are tenable. Successful pre-testing of an advertisement (both as to message and media) and a favourable response from a representative sample of the target group are useful proofs that the plan is soundly conceived and structured. With the campaign under way, with the budget being spent, with objectives clearly defined – whenever possible in quantitative terms – the company can measure results and evaluate the performance of the advertising plan. This is not always simple; there can be difficulties in finding a representative sample of the target audience; the cost of evaluation can turn out to be excessive. Yet *without* objectives, there cannot be so much as an attempt to measure results.

An example of the Advertising by Objectives approach at work comes from the Common Market. A Continental domestic appliance manufacturer recently added a novel type of hair-drier to his range. The marketing department collected a wealth of information about the market and the potential customers. The marketing plan envisaged a market share of 7 per cent within three years, with the upper-middle class segment as a target group. Successful launching of this new product depended, according to the marketing plan, on the following conditions: firstly, that 30 per cent of the target group should become aware of the existence of this hair-drier and of its novel properties; secondly, that a strong association should be found in the mind of those becoming 'aware' that this hair-drier was the product of this acknowledged leading manufacturer of top-class appliances; thirdly, that there should be effective communication with the target segment of the outlets where the drier can be seen and purchased; fourthly, that encouragement should be provided to the stores selected as distributors to stock the new product and display it conspicuously.

The advertising manager realized that the main brunt of realizing the above aims would fall on his shoulders; he studied the information available and translated it into a plan which set out the following objectives:

1. To create among our 'well-defined target group' an awareness (currently *nil* awareness) of the following: (a) Availability of new hair-drier – 30 per cent awareness at the end of the campaign; (b) the brand – 30 per cent awareness; (c) special features of the product – 20 per cent awareness; (d) stores where available – 20 per cent awareness.

2. To generate enough interest among the target audience to produce further inquiries about the new product, either direct or through appointed distributors. The objective is to stimulate 5,000 direct inquiries and 10,000 inquiries through distributors. The plan is that attractive brochures will be available to those showing interest.

3. To instil in the mind of the target audience a strong link between the new brand and the company's corporate image – 60 per cent 'made aware'.

The advertising manager could now work out his plan and the budget required to reach his basic objectives. To eliminate residual doubts he was in a position to pre-test his plan, trying out both message quality and media effectiveness. Following the campaign he was in a strong position to evaluate the results of his department's work in relation to the campaign. He knew what the advertising objectives were and thus could measure the extent to which they were achieved. He could further measure the contribution of his work and effort to achieving the marketing objectives and hence the firm's overall objectives.

In this way the Advertising by Objectives approach can be a valuable tool in the effort to cut the waste out of advertising. It can help companies to obtain better results from their advertising effort, often at lower costs. It can go a long way towards making the effectiveness of advertising measurable – and that in itself is an aid to, as well as a consequence of, better management.

20 R. J. Lawrence

How to Test Advertising

R. J. Lawrence, 'How to test advertising', *Management Today*,
May 1968, pp. 86–90.

It is sometimes said that advertising is not subject to scientific measurement, that it operates in a field of intangibles and imponderables, where the lightning-flash of creativity is the only illumination. This argument is a smoke-screen through which the businessman often peers in vain in an attempt to see what he is getting for his money. Advertising is partly an art, but it is also a science with appropriate measurement techniques. Unfortunately it is not a generalized science which yields universal principles, like the Law of Gravity. Each market, each product, is a study of its own. Consequently every marketing man needs to put in hand the investigations which show how his market thinks, reacts, desires and buys.

The need for an experimental approach to the planning of advertising campaigns is becoming increasingly recognized. The object is to improve the allocation of the advertising budget and so to obtain a better return on the advertising investment. Today advertising is the biggest single item in the marketing bill for many products. Yet more thought, planning and calculation are likely to go into the decision to spend £500 on a new machine than into a project for spending £50,000 on an advertising campaign.

Responsibility rests squarely on the individual company. There are no experts who can be called in to give immediate correct solutions to problems. The expert may have a wide knowledge of the general field, but there is no certainty that this knowledge will apply satisfactorily to a particular case with unique features of its own. The marketing man has to become his own expert. To do so, he has to learn. Learning means the accurate assessment of cause and effect relationships. The emphasis is on 'accurate'. Because a lot of money was spent on advertising and sales went up, it does not necessarily mean that one caused the other. Sales might have increased, anyway, thanks to the product itself, or to better distribution, or to many other factors.

Learning does not mean turning to textbooks. It means planning action with the object of finding things out. The problem is intensely practical, it involves doing as well as thinking. It is like the problem facing a mouse put down in a maze. It cannot merely think its way out; it must try different alleys until practical experience shows the one which works. The marketing man is worse off than the mouse. Not only is he in his own private maze, but the escape route keeps changing. The way out last year, which produced a good profit, may be a long detour this year, or even a dead-end. Learning is a ceaseless process. In a changing world it is never complete.

This is not an argument of despair. It does mean that the rate of learning is vital. The way to learn accurately is to experiment. Experimentation means no more than a plan to do different things in different areas, and to measure the results. Other factors may affect the outcome, but often their influence can be allowed for in the final assessment. Unless a conscious effort is made to experiment, learning is certain to be relatively slow. And, like the Red Queen, we have to run pretty fast these days to stay where we are.

The first fact that has to be faced is that, in most consumer goods markets, the established brands are relatively 'fixed'. The majority of consumers have tried them. For good or ill the brand image of the product is implanted in the public mind. All the evidence shows that it costs relatively large sums of money to win an increase in market share, and that any increase tends to be temporary. To use a term from economics, such products are 'inelastic' to advertising expenditure.

Suppose that sales of a brand are 1000 tons per year and that it is supported by an advertising budget of £50,000. If the brand has been on the market for many years, it is possible that a cut in the advertising budget to £25,000 would not reduce sales below 850 tons. If the advertising budget is doubled to £100,000, the most that can be hoped for is a sales level of 1200 tons, and even that may not be held in subsequent years. Brands such as this, for which a reasonable expectation is that halving or doubling the advertising budget will only produce a 20 per cent movement in sales at the most, are 'inelastic'. Assuming a gross profit of £100 per ton, the product would show the following results at the three levels of sales and advertising discussed:

Sales, tons	850	1000	1200
Gross profit	£85,000	£100,000	£120,000
Advertising	£25,000	£50,000	£100,000
Sum*	£60,000	£50,000	£20,000

* Gross profit after advertising, before indirects.

Other brands, especially new brands, may be very elastic, or responsive to advertising expenditure. A brand will be relatively elastic if

1. many consumers have not yet tried it;

2. many consumers are not yet aware of the brand and the advantages which it offers them;

3. existing users are not using the brand for all the purposes which it is suitable for;

4. attitudes are not firmly set in favour of competitive brands which are just as good or better in terms of price, flavour, efficiency, packaging, etc.;

5. the product has, or will have at the time for which plans are being prepared, a genuine advantage discernible to the consumer over other products in terms of price, flavour, efficiency, packaging, etc.;

6. competitors are underspending on advertising in relation to the business they are doing.

Each brand can be evaluated on these criteria and assigned to the relatively elastic or inelastic group on a 'best judgement' basis, aided by research evidence. The logical next step is that inelastic products should experiment with total advertising budgets by *reducing* them, and elastic products should experiment with total advertising budgets by *increasing* them. The logic of this recommendation in terms of profits is inescapable. The inelastic produce can *only* take advantage of its position by reducing advertising, since sales will fall off less than proportionately. Any attempt to increase market share will be unduly expensive and certainly reduce profits. At first sight it seems unthinkable to budget for lower sales next year than this (although sales do have a habit of going down in successive years, despite estimates of an increase). The argument is that sales once lost are gone forever and must be maintained whatever the effect on profits.

The counter-arguments are, first, that the wonderful year when it will be possible to sit back and enjoy profits on sales kept up at great expense somehow never comes. Competitors seldom give up entirely and reduce the pressure. Many companies hang on grimly to tonnage from year to year in the hope that better days will come. There are often better ways in which the money to keep going could be spent. Second, products have a life cycle. They grow, mature, age and die. When a product is past its peak, the aim should be deliberately to budget for the declining sales which are going to occur anyway. In this way old age can be very profitable. The waste occurs when old products pay for an advertising face-lift costing thousands of pounds in an effort to look young again. Rejuvenation seldom seems to work as well as expected. Third, advertising alone will not stem the tide. A basic rethinking of marketing policy or a substantial improvement in the product and its fundamental appeal is likely to be needed.

A genuine substantial improvement rarely comes. Until it does, a loss of tonnage may have to be faced. If the above arguments are accepted, the experimental approach is required to find out whether a product is in fact as elastic or inelastic as analysis indicates. As a guide, the gross profit per ton (£200 in the example below) can be used to set out a table of results at different levels of sales and advertising:

R. J. Lawrence 365

Sales (tons)	Ad appropriations in thousands of pounds				
	Nil	20	40	60	80
900	180*	160	140	120	100
950	190	170	150	130	110
1000	200	180	160	140	120
1050	210	190	170	150	130
1100	220	200	180	160	140

* Gross profit after advertising before indirects in thousands of pounds.

Likely sales figures are entered in the left-hand column and possible advertising appropriations along the top. Multiplying the sales tonnage by the gross profit per ton, then deducting the advertising figure at the top of the column, enables the total gross profit after advertising, before indirects, to be entered up. The table is completely factual. It contains no guesswork and no estimates except the gross profit per ton. The end result in terms of profit is thrown into relief. It is better to fix a target in terms of profit and then find out how to get there. The method often used, of fixing the *sales* estimate first and arranging the other figures to fit, can be misleading.

In the example, a profit of £160,000 may be selected as the required yield for the brand. This result will be achieved in three ways, within the limitations of the table, by selling 900 tons with an advertising appropriation of £20,000; by selling 1000 tons and spending £40,000; or by selling 1100 tons at £60,000. Each combination is equally satisfactory from a profit point of view. But which will work out in practice? Or if none of them work, which will come closest to achieving the profit objective? If sales of the brand are currently around 1000 tons per year with a budget of £40,000 or £50,000, the elasticity concept should be used to decide the direction in which to experiment. Inelastic brands should experiment with a £20,000 appropriation. Elastic brands should try the £60,000 appropriation. In both cases a £40,000 budget should be used in at least one sales area as a control. The figures in this example have been kept in round numbers for the sake of simplicity, but intermediate budget levels such as £30,000 and £50,000 may also justify separate experiments. The appropriate sales figures to give the same £160,000 profit are a straightforward arith‹metical calculation.

Having fixed the advertising appropriation on a basis of profitability, the best use must be made of the available money. A first consideration is the split between *theme* and *schemes*. Certain basic jobs automatically call for an allocation of funds, and these basic jobs must be done.

Schemes: competition and trade practice will establish that a certain level of discount offers and other incentives, which may include deal packs, is necessary to induce *the trade* to buy stock in sufficient quantity, to retain display positions and encourage 'specialling', and to prevent competitors obtaining advantages through their offers.

Theme: if many people are unaware that a brand exists, or do not know what advantages the brand offers and the uses to which it can be put, or have misconceptions about the brand, then there is a *basic* theme job to be done. Note that this job is *measurable*, thanks to the efficiency of research. We can find out how many people are aware of each brand, etc. If the figure is 40 per cent, then a target can be set for achievement over a given period of time – say, 60 per cent by the end of the year. The relative success of the theme expenditure can then be assessed. It is strongly suggested that all basic jobs for theme advertising should be defined numerically, in the form of current scores and objectives.

In many cases there will be a large amount of the advertising budget left over when enough money has been allocated to the basic jobs. In the case of some long-established brands, no theme expenditure may be required for the communications job outlined above, because it has already been done. This balance of money is the striking force, mobile and uncommitted. Should it be spent on deal or theme? The answer will vary from brand to brand, and there is very little definite evidence to go on. Only one thing is certain. Most of the money will be wasted.

The waste is inevitable on either front. In the case of deals, most of the packs will be bought by existing users, who get a free present. The deal may help the marginal user to stay loyal a little longer, but the deal cannot last forever and a housewife who is thinking of trying something else may do so sooner or later. The deal is also wasted on those who have tried the brand or product category and do not like it. It can only affect the 'floating' housewife, who uses several brands in rotation and is attracted to bargains, and some 'never-users'. Even to attract the bargain-hunters, presumably the offer has to be the best going, because otherwise the housewife will buy the better bargain on another brand.

So far as theme is concerned, advertising which has no new thought to communicate is doing a reminder job. We do not know how many reminders are necessary, or how many sales are made because of reminder advertising which would not have been made without it – the only criterion of success. Even if reminder advertising does create a higher level of conscious recall of the brand, there is little evidence that recall correlates with sales. In view of these factors, there are obvious advantages in an experimental approach to the allocation of money between theme and deal, to find out whether one is less wasteful than the other for a particular brand.

There are three main types of media experiment: 1, varying the total media expenditure in different places so that housewives in comparable areas get different levels of advertising per head; 2. varying the allocation of money between media, again in comparable areas; and 3. varying the scheduling pattern within each medium, for example, comparing short, very high-frequency bursts with lower frequency advertising over a longer period.

The natural question is: if this is done, how are results to be measured? Ideally, all other factors should be equal and the only difference between two experimental areas should be the media schedule for the brand in question. In practice this does not often happen, because competitors will not cooperate. The situation is not entirely hopeless, however. Statistical techniques can allow for differences between areas, provided that the right research design is adopted and the differences are measured accurately. In multi-product companies there is often a brand selling in a relatively stable market where local competitive retaliation is unlikely. New products may have the field to themselves at least for a time.

It remains true that media experiments are comparatively delicate. The problem can be overcome in two ways. First, by making the media experiment sufficiently drastic. It is no good thinking of a 10 per cent difference either way. Some or all media may have to be dropped altogether, or raised to three times the current rate. Reducing expenditure can be done in a large area if results are closely watched, so that the tap can be turned on again if necessary. Increased expenditure can either be financed from savings elsewhere, or the experiment can be limited in scale. Second, by making the experiment run over a long period of time, deals and other temporary factors are averaged out.

Media experiments can be measured in two ways. The ultimate pay-off is in sales and market share, measured through consumer or retail panel audits and cross-checked with sales figures. An intermediate measurement is from Recall of Advertising Content. Content recall shows which elements of the campaign are registering. Sales may not follow directly, but the media campaign is basically doing a communications job, and content recall indicates how well it is being done. Content recall measurements should be read in close conjunction with weight of advertising figures for the product category. Recall for one brand may go down because less money was spent on theme advertising, *not* because the message is losing interest. Expenditure on competing brands must also be taken into account. If one brand's spending goes down, there may actually be an increase in the brand's share of all advertising for the product category, because competitive spending has been reduced even more.

Since on-pack deals also inevitably involve considerable waste, there is scope for experimentation to minimize the loss. The main variants come into the categories:

Number of deals – how many per year?

Value of deals – big or small saving? Small or large packs?

Type of deal – money-off, on-pack premium, trade discount (various types), write-in offer, multiple or single packs?

Apart from deals associated with the pack, there are many other types of promotion, including sampling, contests, 'write in for a free packet', 'money back on proof of purchase', and so on.

R. J. Lawrence 369

The complication with large-scale deal experiments is that special packs should be delivered only to designated areas. Distribution problems arise, shops with multiple branches have no interest in cooperating, and retailers complain that another district is getting better treatment. One answer is to concentrate on small-scale experiments, taking pairs of shops which have been matched for location, turnover value, etc., and assigning a deal to one shop of a pair at random. It is easier to get individual retailer cooperation, but such experiments need careful supervision, both to measure results accurately and to avoid differences arising through accidental displacement of stock or supplies running short in one of the two outlets. It should be remembered that not dealing at all is the simplest experiment to carry out and also the cheapest. A non-deal area is a valuable yard-stick against which to measure what deals elsewhere really do achieve.

Finally there is the creative experiment, which means keeping media coverage, promotions and other factors constant in two areas, but varying the creative message which the advertising carries. The points made about the media mix also apply to creative experiments. The measurements are the same; sales, market share and content recall. Again it is no use trying to test a minor variation of creative treatment, such as one shot in a television commercial against another. The difference must be drastic if it is to have a measurable effect. The two campaigns must either have two basically different appeals, or a similar appeal with very different treatments, perhaps humour against mood against straight sell. Another variation, which is half-way between creative and media experiments, is the use of different length television commercials. One area might have a ten second off-peak campaign, another sixty second commercials in evening time. The basis of comparison can be either 'equal money' or 'equal impacts'.

Many types of experiment have been suggested. It would be impossible to operate all of them simultaneously for any one brand. But amongst the list must be at least one experiment which could have a major bearing on the sales or profitability of every product. Experimentation has many difficulties. Some of them are technical, such as the problem of finding truly comparable areas, or of measuring the factors which might affect sales other than the experimental influence. Perhaps the biggest difficulty is getting started at all. Experiments involve a great deal of planning, organizing and measurement. Frankly, they are a bother and many managements do not want to be bothered; they find enough to keep themselves busy coping with the routine of telephone calls and in-tray. It requires a board-level decision to make an investment in learning about advertising and promotional effectiveness, and to insist that evaluation of results through experimentation is a required part of the executive's job.

There are two questions to put to the advertising man. One is 'are you certain that the way you are spending the company's money is the best one?' No one can in honesty answer 'yes', because human behaviour and the effects on it of advertising influence are too complex. The follow-up question is 'what steps are you taking to find out how to get better value for your expenditure?' A variety of answers can be expected, but many of them will boil down to this: best judgement, expert advice, years of experience or careful analysis (unspecified) show how improvements can be made. Being interpreted, such answers mean that the company's money is riding on somebody's guess. It is better to insist that the advertising department enters more than one horse in the race so that measured performance in the market place confirms which of several alternatives produces the most promising results.

21 R. Le Kashman and J. F. Stolle

The Total Cost Approach to Distribution

R. Le Kashman and J. F. Stolle, 'The total cost approach to distribution', *Business Horizons*, vol. 8, no. 4, 1965, pp. 33–46.

The more management focuses the company's efforts on cutting distribution costs, the less successful it is likely to be in reducing the real costs of distribution. This apparent paradox is no abstract or armchair play on phrases. It explains why so many companies have diligently pruned distribution costs – in the warehouse and in inventory, in order processing and in transportation – only to find that these hard-earned savings are

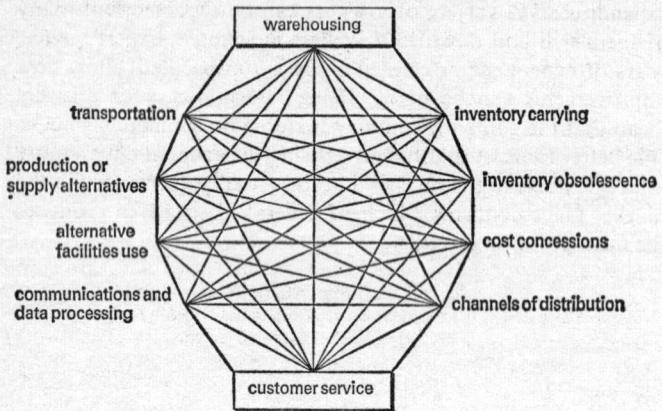

Figure 1 The real cost of distribution[1]

1. The real cost of distribution includes much more than what most companies consider when they attempt to deal with distribution costs. In a sense, any major distribution decision can affect every cost in the business and each cost is related to all the others. Our experience indicates that the following ten cost elements and interrelationships are the ones that are most likely to prove critical in evaluating the impact of alternative distribution approaches on total costs and total profits.

somehow not translated into improved profit margins. They have been watered down or actually washed out by increases in other costs scattered throughout the company.

It is these 'other costs', motley and miscellaneous as they first seem, that turn out on closer analysis to be the *real* cost of distribution. (See Figure 1.) They never appear as distribution costs on any financial or operating report, but show up un-identified and unexplained at different times and in assorted places – in purchasing, in production, in paper-work processing – anywhere and everywhere in the business. When the gremlin-like costs are traced to their roots, however, one finds that they are, in fact, all intimately interrelated, linked together by one common bond. They all result from the way the company dis-tributes its products.

It is this aggregation of distribution-related costs – rather than what managements usually mean when they complain

---

Warehousing To provide service through the company's chosen channels of distribution, some warehousing is required, involving from one in-plant warehouse to a multiple-unit network dispersed across the country. Service usually becomes better as the number of warehouses is increased, at least up to a point. However, as the number of warehouses increases, their average size decreases; this will begin to reduce the efficiency of service to customers. Also, costs increase. Thus, any change in the three variables – number, type, or location of warehouses – will affect both service and costs.

Inventory carrying The ownership of inventory gives rise to costs for money, insurance, occupancy, pilferage losses and custodial services, and sometimes inventory taxes. Depending on the business involved, this group of costs may range from 10 per cent to 30 per cent of average annual inventory value. Customer service will be improved by keeping inventory at many storage points in the field near to customers, but this will increase total inventory and the cost for carrying that inventory. Thus, inventory carrying cost is closely linked to warehousing cost and customer service.

Inventory obsolescence If (at a given level of sales) total inventory is in-creased to provide better customer service, then inventory turnover is decreased. Also, the greater the 'pipeline fill' in the distribution system, the slower the inventory turnover. This automatically exposes the owner to greater risks of obsolescence and inventory write-down. This is a partic-ularly important cost for companies having frequent model changeovers, style changes or product perishability.

Production or supply alternatives Production costs vary among plants and vary with the volume produced at each individual plant. Plants have different fixed costs and different unit variable costs as volume is increased. The decision of which plant should serve which customers must give about the cost of distribution – that represents the important and increasing drain of distribution on earnings. These are the costs – rather than those usually defined and dealt with as distribution costs – that have eluded even the most earnest cost-cutting drives. Because of its size and its elusiveness, this cost complex remains for many companies a promising profit-improvement potential.

---

weight not only to transportation and warehousing costs, but also to production and supply costs; these will vary significantly with the volume allocated to each plant.

Cost concessions A special aspect of production or supply alternatives arises from the fact that distribution decisions can affect costs otherwise incurred by suppliers or customers. For example, when a retailer creates his own warehouses, this may free suppliers from packing and shipping small quantities or from maintaining small local warehouses in the field. A retailer who establishes his own warehouse network may be able to recoup some of these costs by negotiation with the supplier.

Channels of distribution The choice of distribution channels profoundly affects the nature and costs of a company's sales organization, its selling price and gross margin structure, its commitment to physical distribution facilities. These in turn will affect production and supply costs.

Transportation Changing the number or location of warehouses changes transportation costs, sometimes in unanticipated and complex ways. For example, an increase in the number of warehouses may initially reduce total transportation costs; but past some determinable point, the cost trend may reverse because of the decreasing ratio of carload to less-than-carload tonnage.

Communications and data processing These costs vary with the complexity of the distribution system and with the level of service provided, including costs for order processing, inventory control, payables, receivables and shipping documents. These costs rise as more distribution points are added to the system. Additionally, as the cycle time or response time of the communications and data processing system is shortened, costs of this service are increased.

Alternative facilities use Changes in inventory requirements or in other aspects of the distribution operation will change space requirements and utilization in a plant-warehouse facility or a retail store. Space used for distribution may be convertible to selling space which yields incremental sales and profits. In the case of retail business, this is actually a variation of the customer service factor since it increases the availability of goods with which to fill customer requirements.

Customer service Stock-outs, excess delivery time, or excess variability of delivery time all result in lost sales. Any change in the distribution system will influence these elements of customer service, and therefore must either gain or lose sales for the company. These effects, while difficult to measure, must be considered part of the real cost of distribution.

374 Management of Communications

The total cost approach
When to use it

For earnings-minded management, the dimensions of this profit potential and a practical technique for tapping it, have now been tested and proved. A handful of companies have faced up to the across-the-board impact of distribution on costs and profits. They have accomplished this by applying an approach – we call it the 'total cost approach' – that is designed to convert these intangible and intricate cost interrelationships into tangible dollars-and-cents improvements in profit margins. A major food manufacturer, after applying effectively an assortment of rigid cost-cutting techniques, has found that this new approach is enabling the company to add 1·7 per cent to its margin on sales. A major merchandiser, already enjoying the benefits of advanced distribution techniques, found that this same new approach could cut from its corporate costs an additional $7·5 million – 3 per cent of the sales value of its products – while at the same time significantly improving service to customers. At Du Pont, a company well known for its general management excellence, this same new approach underlies the announcement that programs recently instituted are expected to cut $30 million from its total cost, a 10 per cent reduction of the costs attributed to distribution. These success stories shed some light on how distribution drains profits – and on what can be done about it:

The real impact of distribution on profits is much greater than most managements think. In companies in which distribution-connected costs have been studied, they turned out to be significantly greater than management estimated – as much as from a third to a half of the selling price of the product.

This untapped profit-improvement potential exists because these costs lie in a managerial no-man's-land, where they can increase because they are outside the scope of responsibility or control of any operating executive. These distribution-related costs are not strictly the responsibility of the man in charge of distribution, because they are costs of purchasing, manufacturing, or some other function of the business. But they cannot be dealt with effectively by the executive in charge of

R. Le Kashman and J. F. Stolle 375

these other functions because they are actually caused by distribution decisions, for which only the man in charge of distribution has any responsibility. They are the result of complex interrelationships involving all of the functions of the business Distribution lies at the crossroad of these complex interactions, and that is what is so different about distribution. In no other function of the business can decisions made at the operating level look so right and be so wrong.

These costs will not respond to the usual cost-cutting approaches. Management has achieved near miracles in cutting costs in one function of the business after another, including costs within the distribution function, notably in warehousing, transportation and order-filling. But conventional cost-cutting approaches are limited to costs that fall within any one operation of the business; for cutting these costs, management can hold some executive responsible. Distribution-related costs are organizational orphans, beyond the reach of even the most diligent, skillful cost-minded executives.

These costs will respond only to a high level across-the-board re-examination of how distribution affects the total costs and total profits of the business, and of what management action is necessary to tap this profit opportunity.

Thus the problem and the opportunity are deposited squarely on the desk of the chief executive. The pursuit of these added profits has to get its start, its support and its sanctions at the top management level. With this high-level effort, even companies that have tightened and tidied their distribution operations can greatly increase earnings by a frontal attack on the basic framework of their distribution decisions and practices.

This broad, basic approach has a continuing payoff, for once the most profitable pattern of distribution has been defined for the present operations of the business, management has in its hands a yardstick for measuring the impact on total profits of any proposed management move. This makes it possible to define the impact on total profits of a new plant or a new product, or a cluster of new customers, and so makes it possible to determine what changes in distribution – if any – will ensure peak profits from these new ventures.

What is this total cost approach? What is new about it? Why have we not heard more about it?

The approach simply stated

This approach sounds simple. First, analyse the distribution impact on each cost of the business, and select for more detailed study those activities the cost of which is significantly affected by distribution policies and practices. Second, develop the data necessary to measure the profit impact that alternative distribution decisions would have on each of these activities. Finally, determine which distribution decision will maximize profits.

Obviously, if it were as simple as it sounds, more companies would long ago have beaten a path to this better mousetrap. Three sets of facts explain why this has not been so:

1. The impact of distribution costs is more difficult to unravel than is the effect of other business decisions. All functions of a business are somewhat interrelated, but distribution is more complexity intertwined with each. And it is these interrelationships – rather than the costs of the distribution functions *per se* – that are the cause of high distribution costs and the key to understanding and reducing these costs.

2. Because corporate accounting has historically been oriented to finance and production, rather than to marketing or distribution, the operating reports that guide managerial action do not tot up in any one place the full impact of distribution on costs. The real cost of distribution never stares management in the face.

3. Even where managements have become aware of these costs and their impacts on profits, there was until recently very little that anyone could do about the pervasive effects of distribution. Even a relatively simple problem in distribution system design can involve hundreds of bits of information that interact in thousands of ways. So there was no way of dealing with the distribution cost complex until techniques were developed to manipulate this mass of material as a single integrated entity.

This last is, in fact, the major reason why these distribution-related costs have continued to rise and to depress profits margins throughout our economy. And for that same reason the total cost concept remained until recently a topic for textbook discussion, theoretically provocative but of little practical use. But techniques have been developed to deal with information in these quantities and with interrelationship of such complexity. They have converted this sound but previously unworkable concept into a practical management approach.

The examples that follow are composites of a number of companies. The relevant facts and figures have thus been disguised without in any way changing the practical significance of the results. The first example traces the step-by-step process involved in the analysis of the factors that enter into the application of the total cost approach in a business engaged primarily in the retail distribution of a wide range of consumer products; the second shows how this complex array of information is analysed and manipulated to provide management with profitable answers to some familiar distribution problems.

What makes distribution different

Consider the problem facing the management of a large company whose business consists of a widely dispersed chain of retail stores and a few factories that produce some of the merchandise sold in these stores. This company has shipped directly from its suppliers and its factories to its stores, but wants to determine whether there would be any profit advantage in shifting to a national system of field warehouses. When the company looked at the combined cost of warehousing and of transportation that would result from introducing various combinations of field warehouses, it appeared, as shown in Figure 2, that the lowest cost system was one with six warehouses. But this would *increase* its distribution costs by $12·9 million. Thus, on the basis of apparent distribution costs alone, there was no profit advantage in any field warehouse system.

However, when this study investigated how alternative distribution networks would affect other costs in the company, the answer was quite different. As shown in Figure 3, the most efficient warehouse system turned out to be one with five, rather than six, field warehouses. And this five-warehouse system would cut the total costs of the company by $7·7 million; an increase of 1·4 per cent on sales.

Looking at distribution from a standpoint of total costs, this company discovered an opportunity to increase its profits that it could not have identified or taken advantage of in any other way. What explains the difference? What legerdemain turned up this handsome profit potential that represented a 22·4 per cent return on the investment required to design and install this field warehouse system? The answer, in this case as in other similar corporate experiences, involves following through the various steps of the total cost approach – that is, to determine the total cost of the present operation and then compare it with the total costs that would follow from alternative distribution systems.

At its very inception, the total cost approach is different in a number of ways from the traditional functional approach to

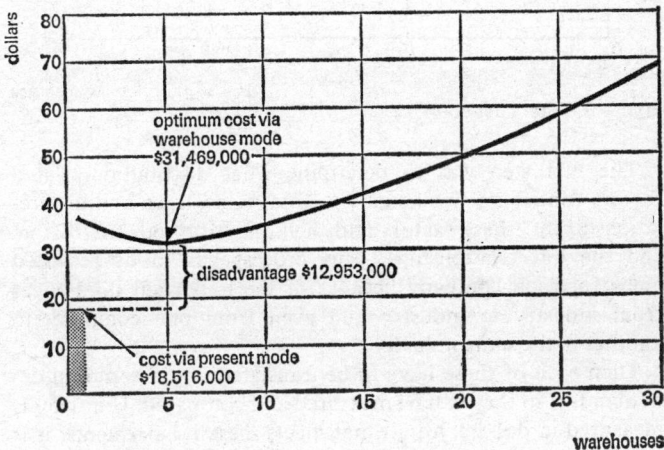

Figure 2 Distribution cost solution

distribution management. In the first place, it deals with the impact of distribution decisions on business costs wherever these costs appear. Secondly, many important cost factors and many critical relationships between distribution and other parts

R. Le Kashman and J. F. Stolle 379

of the business are not usually translatable to quantitive terms. Customer service is a classic example.

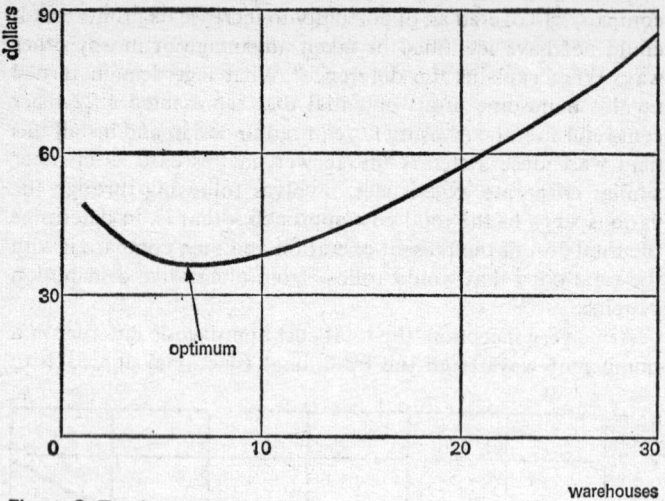

Figure 3 Total cost solution

The first step was to determine what distribution-related factors contribute significantly to total costs, trace and interrelationships of these factors and then quantify both the factors and the interrelationships. This process has to be repeated anew for each company because of the important differences from industry to industry and even from one company to another in the same industry.

Then each of these have to be translated into a common denominator, so they can be measured and compared. If impact is measured in dollars, a unit that meets these requirements, it is possible to reduce all of the cost and profit considerations and all of these intricate interrelationships to one final total dollar cost for each alternative course of action.

The significance of this for management is seen in Figure 4; graphs show, for each major activity affected, the impact of different field warehouse systems (indicated by the numbers along the base of each graph) on the total cost of this operation.

380 Management of Communications

These graphs clearly show that for each factor of costs, a certain number of warehouses would yield the lowest costs and the maximum profit. Because each of these factors has its own built-in logic, each curve takes on its own configuration. The sum of all of these curves – each with its own optimum – is one final curve that defines the total cost. That in turn defines the optimum number of warehouses for this operation, when all considerations are taken into account. Except by chance coincidence, this point will differ from the optimum of each of the component curves. Obviously, a piecemeal approach to cost reduction will not yield the maximum profit impact achieved by this total cost approach.

These graphs show that even though one or several elements of distribution cost are cut to their lowest practical level, total costs may actually increase, and dealing with these costs one at a time will not produce the best result. They show the pitfalls of considering these various factors as single and static, instead of as interrelated and dynamic. The first and second graphs in the series make apparent the process whereby the consideration of distribution costs alone – the cost of warehouse plus the cost of transportation – led to the conclusion that no change in distribution could add to the profitability of the business. Only the final graph, summing up all of the interacting factors involved, demonstrates unmistakably that a shift to the five-warehouse system would be a very profitable move for this management.

Actually, in this case as in so many others, a reduction in warehouse and transportation could in fact lead to increases in other distribution-related costs, with the result that total costs would be increased and this significant profit opportunity missed. Only by increasing these distribution costs could total expenses be cut and total earnings increased in this company. By this kind of trade-off the total cost approach brings a company closer to achieving its maximum potential profit. The actual figures from this company's calculations for the five-warehouse system are shown in Table 1.

It is difficult to conceive of a distribution problem in a company of any substantial size that could not show near-term benefits from this kind of analytical approach; the approach does much more than offer a one-time solution to what is

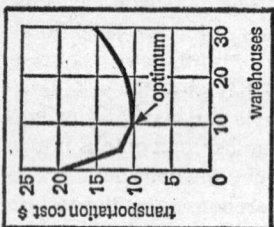
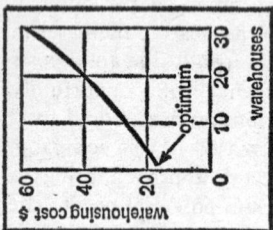
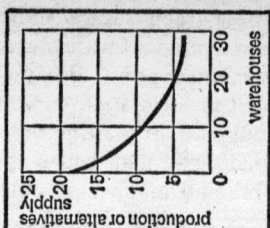

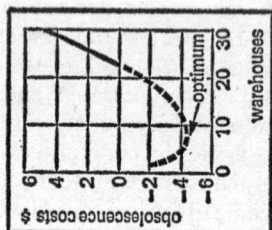

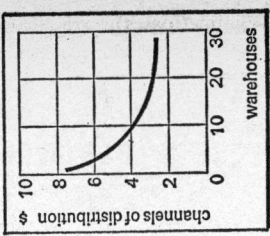

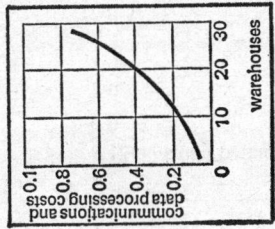

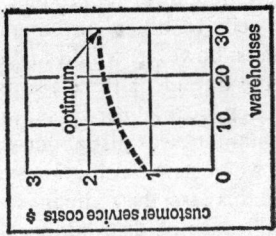

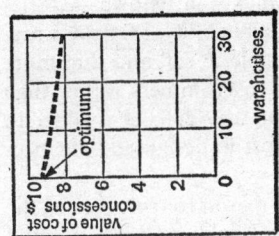

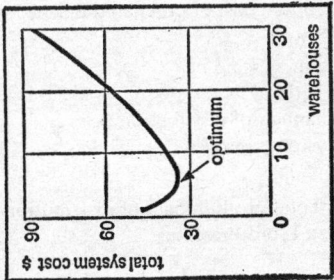

Figure 4 Total cost approach

Table 1 Profit impact of distribution – gains (losses)
(in millions of dollars)

Warehousing	(14·4)
Transportation	0·5
Total distribution costs	(13·9)
Inventory	
Carrying costs	1·4
Obsolescence costs	4·3
Value of alternative use of facilities	7·8
Total	13·5
Production and purchasing	
Production and raw materials costs	0·2
Reduced cost of purchased finished goods	6·7
Total	6·9
Data processing	(0·2)
Marketing	
Channels of distribution	0·2
Customer service	0·4
Total	0·6
Total profit impact of distribution-related items	21·8
Pretax Profit Increase	7·9

actually a perennial problem. Because this company distributes mostly through its own retail outlets, the channels of distribution are not currently an important variable. They involve only the small amount of its product that it makes in its own factories but sells to other customers. The availability of field warehouses, however, would make it possible to sell and ship more of the output of these plants direct to customers rather than through local jobbers. As it turned out, the $200,000 it added to profitability was just about what it cost to design and engineer this whole new distribution system.

In this case, the company had good reason for considering the significance of distribution channels. Looking ahead, it could see the possibility of integrating backwards, then becoming more heavily involved in manufacturing. In that case, alternative channels of distribution might become more important. The point is that in this kind of analytical exercise it is essential to consider all possible directions for company growth. Otherwise, a new distribution system, however profitable it may be under present conditions, might freeze the company into a set of cost factors that would preclude an otherwise profitable growth opportunity. The total cost approach offers management this built-in flexibility in assessing alternatives.

Every time management makes a decision of any magnitude, it ought to be in a position to get an answer to the question, 'how will it affect distribution costs throughout the company?' The total cost approach puts the company in a position to make continuing gains by applying a rigid yardstick to any proposed corporate venture. Whenever manufacturing management designs a new plant, develops a new production process, or turns to a new source of raw materials, the pattern of distribution-related costs will be changed throughout the business. Similar far-flung changes will take place whenever marketing management adds a new product or a promising new group of customers. The total cost approach enables management to define how these changes will interact with distribution to affect the company's total cost and its total profits. It tells management what distribution decisions need to be made to avoid the loss of potential profits, or to add to them. So both short-term and long-term benefits result from management's recognition of these complex cost and profit relationships.

From data to decision

How these complex inter-relationships and the mass of related data enable management to put a dollar value on alternative courses of action can be seen quite readily in the following case. The total cost approach was used by a division of a large manufacturing company. This division does an annual business of about $45 million, with over 3,000 customers located in every state. It has manufacturers and warehouses at five points across the country, shipping to customers via both rail and truck.

The profit problems this management posed have a familiar ring; some are long-range problems.

Without any major investment, can we increase our profits by changing our distribution system?
Can total costs be reduced by shifting some of our available equipment from one factory to another?

Can we further reduce costs and increase profits by changing our marketing approach?

Is there any profit in changing the capacity of one or more of our present plants, or perhaps building a new facility at another location?

Could we further improve profitability by changing our warehouse capacities or locations?

An analysis of this company's business showed quite readily what factors and what interactions determined the total profit of the product delivered to the customer.

Finding relevant facts

Every distribution study has to start with a definition of where the customers are located and what requirements they impose on their suppliers. In this case, some customers requested that products be shipped to them by rail, and others stipulated that they be served by truck. Some buy f.o.b., others at a delivered price. Options, consolidation requirements, or other ingredients of the customer service package are often relevant.

Different companies will have differing requirements for details. In this case, it was important that the data be broken down by sales districts. Therefore, it was determined for 160 sales districts what percentages of sales came into each district by rail and by truck, and percentages were found in each sales district for f.o.b. and delivered prices.

The company then knew where the products were going and how they were going to get there. Next, information was needed that would help determine from which of the five plants and warehouses each sales district should be supplied. This involved an in-depth analysis of the cost of production and warehousing per unit in each of the plants and warehouses for various volume levels.

Figure 5 shows the total plant and warehouse cost for the Indiana installation of this division, for amounts from 0 to 2,100,000 hundredweight. The total plant cost is built up by analysing the cost for varying production volume of materials, inbound freight, direct labor and plant overhead. Each of these cost elements will, of course, differ at each plant, even within the same company. Total warehouse costs over this same

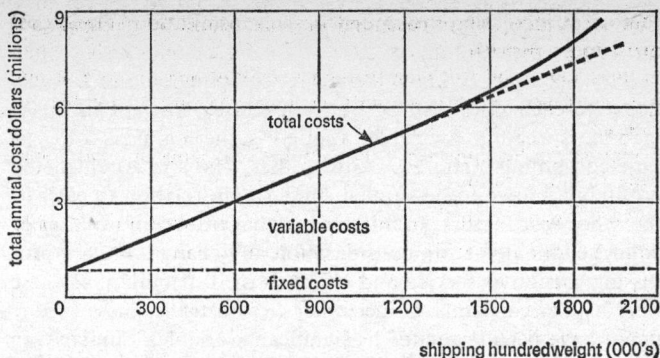

Figure 5 Total plant and warehousing cost, Indiana plant

volume range were similarly analysed. The same calculations were made for each of the company's five facilities.

Figure 6 shows these total cost curves for all of the plants and

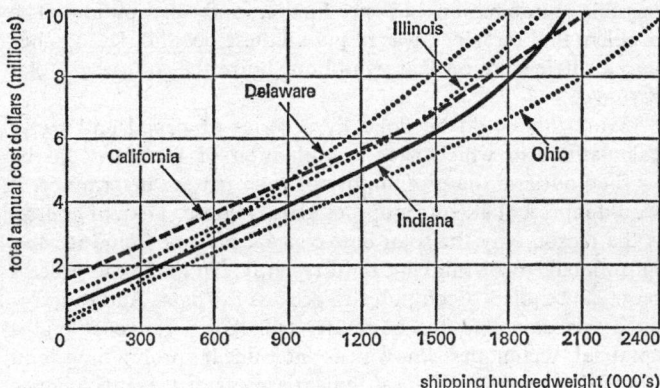

Figure 6 Total plant and warehousing cost, five plants

warehouses. These costs are, of course, different for each facility at each point on the curve. Not only does each curve start at a different point, reflecting different overhead costs, but the rate of increase is also different, reflecting different variable cost

R. Le Kashman and J. F. Stolle 387

factors at increasing volumes for each installation. These cost differences play an important role in the calculations. It then became necessary to know the cost of shipping from each warehouse to each sales district, by train and by truck. This information is readily available, though gathering it is often a time-consuming chore. Any other factors influencing profitability have to be studied similarly, in relation to each of the other cost factors. In this case, management, as a matter of policy, eliminated from consideration any changes in data processing, customer service and channels of distribution, so these were held as constants. Under other circumstances these factors might have been evaluated as significant variables. Similarly, in other company situations, other cost factors might have required analysis so that their impact could be introduced into the final decision.

Manipulating the data

At this point, available information showed for each unit of product and for each customer the profit contribution under all possible combinations of production and distribution. The problem that remained was to put all these possibilities together into a single solution that would maximize the company's total earnings.

While this could be done by a series of pencil and paper calculations in which each combination of factors could be worked out and the profitability of each pattern determined, it would represent an enormous and costly chore. That, of course, is the reason why the total cost concept has not found its way into management thinking until recently. To make the process practical requires a computer to process the data. And to introduce this data into the computer calls for a range of mathematical techniques known as non-linear programing and simulation modeling. The technical aspects of these techniques are not important for their managerial implications. What is significant is that they do exist, that they do work, and that once the computer program has been written, this kind of distribution problem can be solved in a matter of minutes.

Concerning the questions confronting the management of

this company, the total cost approach was able to provide a very precise answer to each of them:

1. By rearranging the company's distribution pattern and making appropriate shifts in production and warehousing loads, it was possible without any change in facilities to increase this company's profits by $492,000 a year. The largest ingredient in this change would come from reduced materials cost at $126,000, with warehouse savings contributing $138,000, direct labor saving in the plants adding $57,000, and plant overhead $27,000. Transportation, so often overstressed in distribution decisions, contributed only $54,000 to this total profit improvement package.

2. Additional savings of $180,000 could be effected by shifting equipment from one plant to another at minor cost. To determine this, it was necessary to develop new production cost curves for alternative arrangements of equipment and run these through the computer, comparing them with the most profitable way of using the equipment as presently located.

3. Further savings of $447,000 a year would result if about half of the customers could be persuaded to shift from truck to rail delivery. These reduced costs could be added to earnings or passed on to the customer, thus giving the company a competitively significant price advantage.

4. It was determined that there was no plant addition that would provide an acceptable return on investment. Although building a new plant in Michigan would result in lower production and warehousing costs amounting to $225,000, the return on the investments would be only 2 per cent, and the 'other costs' discussed above more than offset any possible gains, so that this investment would not be a wise one.

5. On the other hand, an addition to the capacity of the warehouse at the Delaware plant would add $75,000 a year to profits and represent a sound investment. This was determined by setting up new warehousing cost schedules and running them through the computer alongside the costs under existing conditions. The comparison showed that the investment in the added Delaware warehouse capacity would return almost 25 per cent a year.

R. Le Kashman and J. F. Stolle 389

The total addition to profits adds up to almost $750,000 a year, from changes in distribution and facilities, that were well within the company's capabilities. These would add 1·7 per cent to this company's margin on sales. The important point is this: these profits could not have been generated by decisions based on the insight or the experience of the most competent line executive. Only the total cost approach could have established, for example, that the earnings of this business could be increased by supplying its customers in the Dakotas from a plant in Ohio rather than from a much nearer facility in Illinois. Yet when total profits were calculated, this turned out to be an element in the most profitable use of the existing facilities of this company.

Similarly, only a total cost calculation could provide the background for estimating the return on investment that could be expected from building a new facility in Michigan. Actually, that new plant would have reduced production and warehousing costs by an appreciable figure. However, other costs would be incurred in serving customers from this facility rather than from the present plant in Illinois; these other costs substantially reduced the potential savings and made the investment an unsound one. This ability to put precise price and profit tags on each pattern of alternatives makes the total cost approach a particularly effective management tool.

Making the total cost approach work

The successful applications of the total cost approach illustrated by these examples leave no doubt that this approach can, for many companies, uncover profit opportunities previously obscured by established ways of looking at distribution costs and by existing methods of managing distribution functions. But the experience of the successful companies also serves as a warning to those who are tempted to use the term 'total cost' lightly. Understanding of many factors is required in order to undertake the kind of analysis required to define what all these costs are and what they really amount to, to develop a way to recover the profits they represent, and then to translate that solution into actual practice.

Though experience shows that the approach works out

differently in every practical application, the sequence of steps that management has to take is always the same and it always involves the same inexorable logic:

To succeed, the total cost approach must have the active endorsement of top management. The total cost concept can be initiated at any place in the company, but unless it receives strong support from the top, it will not progress successfully, for the simple reason that only top management can insist that the real cost and profit impact of distribution be defined and measured, and at regular intervals. Only top management can see to it that there is a senior executive actively concerned with doing something about this impact of distribution on costs and on profitability. And only top management can assign to this executive the authority necessary to tackle this problem across organizational lines, in order to identify and take advantage of this profit opportunity.

Only a carefully conceived feasibility study can determine whether or not a restructuring of the distribution system is likely to be profitable. This thorough kind of study requires a wide range of technical and managerial skills. The team that can do such a study has to include transportation, production, and materials handling specialists, warehousing and logistics experts, as well as analysts with backgrounds in economics, mathematical decision making and operations research.

Some companies have found it appropriate to assemble these skills within the company, while others have preferred to bring the necessary talent in from outside; this is a decision that management must make. But one fact cannot be avoided: this kind of study involves a much wider range of talents than is usually brought to bear on distribution problems, as well as a broad experience in the application of these capabilities to these total cost problems.

A more substantial and more time-consuming study is then required to determine in detail what changes are indicated, what profits can validly be expected from alternative ways of effecting these changes and what improvement in profits can be anticipated from the most practical solution.

To succeed in this effort the firm must develop quantitative information on the variables that affect each cost factor and the inter-relationships among the various factors. Much of this information may be available in company records and some of what is not available can usually be derived from existing reports. In most cases, it will be necessary to generate additional data.

Then, all of the significant inter-relationships must be traced through the operation, the significant correlations defined and quantified, and all of this data subjected to mathematical analysis.

Next, the appropriate mathematical models must be constructed and then tested against past experience to validate their effectiveness. Then, alternative solutions to present and foreseeable problems have to be developed, and these studied by putting them through the model. This puts dollar values against each alternative and defines the optimum solution – the one that is most practical and most profitable.

Finally, the business implications of this solution need to be checked against organizational requirements, implications for competitive strategy, and ultimately for practicality in terms of timing and return on investment.

The final stage in the application of the total cost approach is the actual implementation of the solution. Initially, this involves putting into place the distribution system that matches the company's existing needs and its requirements for the short-term future. Since the business itself and its external environment are both changing inevitably with the passage of time, with changes in product and in marketing policies and practices, as well as in response to changes in competitive forces and strategies, it is likely to prove profitable to re-run the problem at regular intervals. This process will redefine optimum distribution decisions and adjust plant loads and shipping schedules.

The companies that have been successful in using this approach have found that along with this restructuring of their distribution system, certain additional steps are likely to be critical. The assignment of responsibility for distribution has to be clarified. An information system has to be developed that will provide data on distribution costs and performance to whomever is responsible for controlling these activities. The company's data-gathering and data-processing system must be adapted so that it will pick up routinely the necessary informational input. Procedures must also be established to feed into the information system intelligence concerning conditions in the marketplace and notably a continuing reassessment of prevailing customer service levels.

Thus the accumulated experience not only confirms the practicality and profitability of the total cost approach, but it also defines some clear-cut guidelines for managements who propose to put this approach to work. Experience in applying this approach suggests, too, that a number of additional considerations need to be clarified.

The fact that this substantial profit opportunity exists in a company is no implicit criticism of its operating management. No traffic manager or transportation specialist can be expected to deal with a problem the roots of which extend far beyond his sphere into manufacturing and marketing. Nor can the best warehouse manager be expected to come up with solutions to problems the causes and conditions of which extend from purchasing and supplier relationships at one extreme, to customer service considerations at the other. Even those companies that have centralized distribution responsibility in the hands of a single high-level executive rarely can provide this executive with the wide range of supporting capabilities and in-depth experience necessary to deal with this profit potential.

Nor does the fact that the necessary action requires top management support mean that the chief executive has to become an expert in the complexities of the mathematical tools involved, any more than he has to become knowledgeable in computer technology or the relative merits of the hardware and software. No one intends to suggest that management has to do or know anything specific or technical about distribution. What is required is management's insistence that something be done, by someone with the appropriate capabilities and experience.

In this sense, the challenge of the total cost approach has another interesting management meaning. The relentless and increasing impact of distribution on profits is one of a growing category of management problems that are not going to be solved satisfactorily within the framework of traditional organizational and decision-making approaches. The most effective solution to any company's distribution problem requires looking at the company as a whole and dealing with the profitability of the entity. More and more, management is being faced with problems requiring this kind of across-the-board attention.

At the same time new concepts, new techniques and new technology are becoming available that are peculiarly able to cope with this very kind of problem. The more we learn about the computer and about such techniques as simulation, the more apparent it is that they are used to fullest advantage when they are used to deal with problems like these for which no other problem-solving technique is truly appropriate.

There is every reason to believe that with the increasing complexity of modern businesses and the mounting competitive pressures in their environment, the ability of companies to forge ahead and to grow profitably may have a direct relationship to the ability of management to put these new tools and their vast new capabilities to work. In the days ahead, competition between companies may in large measure reflect the skill with which competing managements take advantage of these new management tools.

Further Reading

Books

W. Alderson, *Marketing Behavior and Executive Action*, Irwin, 1957.

J. Arndt (ed.), *Insights into Consumer Behavior*, Allyn & Bacon, 1968.

F. M. Bass, C. W. King and E. A. Pessemier (eds.), *Applications of the Sciences in Marketing Management*, Wiley, 1968.

M. L. Bell, *Marketing: Concepts and Strategy*, Houghton Mifflin, 1966.

P. Bliss (ed.), *Marketing and the Behavioral Sciences*, Allyn & Bacon, 1963.

S. Broadbent, *Spending Advertising Money*, Business Books, 1970.

M. Fishbein (ed.), *Readings in Attitude Theory and Measurement*, Wiley, 1967.

G. Fisk, *Marketing Systems*, Harper & Row, 1967.

R. E. Frank, A. A. Kuehn and W. F. Massey (eds.), *Quantitative Techniques in Marketing Analysis*, Irwin, 1962.

C. I. Hovland, I. L. Janis and H. H. Kelley, *Communication and Persuasion*, Yale University Press, 1953.

J. A. Howard, *Marketing Theory*, Allyn & Bacon, 1965.

J. A. Howard, and J. N. Sheth, *The Theory of Buyer Behavior*, Wiley, 1969.

W. T. Kelley, *Marketing Intelligence: The Management of Marketing Information*, Staples Press, 1968.

R. P. Kelvin, *Advertising and Human Memory*, Business Publications, 1962.

P. Kotler, *Marketing Management, Analysis, Planning and Control*, Prentice-Hall, 1967.

J. U. McNeal, *Dimensions of Consumer Behavior*, Appleton-Century-Crofts, 1969, 2nd edn.

N. E. Marks and R. M. Taylor, *Marketing Logistics*, Wiley, 1967.

D. B. Montgomery and G. L. Urban, *Applications of Management Science in Marketing*, Prentice-Hall, 1970.

F. M. Nicosia, *Consumer Decision Processes*, Prentice-Hall, 1966.

A. R. Oxenfeldt, *Executive Action in Marketing*, Wadsworth, 1966.

A. R. Oxenfeldt and C. Swan, *Management of the Advertising Function*, Wadsworth, 1964.

E. A. Pessemier, *New Product Decisions*, McGraw-Hill, 1966.

E. M. Rogers, *Diffusion of Innovations*, Free Press, 1962.

C. H. Sevin, *Marketing Productivity Analysis*, McGraw-Hill, 1965.

S. V. Smith, R. H. Brien and J. E. Stafford, *Readings in Marketing Information Systems*, Houghton Mifflin, 1968.

M. E. Stern, *Marketing Planning: A Systems Approach*, McGraw-Hill, 1966.

J. B. Stewart, *Repetitive Advertising in Newspapers*, Harvard Business School, 1968.

M. J. Thomas, *International Marketing Management*, Houghton Mifflin, 1969.

A. Wilson (ed.), *The Marketing of Industrial Products*, Hutchinson, 1965.

Papers

J. B. Haskins, 'Factual recall as a measure of advertising effectiveness', *Journal of Advertising Research*, vol. 4, no. 1, 1964, pp. 2–80.

J. A. Lunn, 'Perspectives in attitude research: methods and applications', *Journal of the Market Research Society*, vol. 11, no. 3, 1969, pp. 201–13.

R. E. Quandt, 'Estimating advertising effectiveness: some pitfalls in econometric methods', *Journal of Marketing Research*, vol. 1, no. 2, 1964, pp. 51–60.

J. N. Sheth, 'A review of buyer behavior', *Management Science*, vol. 13, no. 12, 1967, pp. 718–56.

A. Shuchman, 'The market audit: its nature, purposes and problems', *American Management Association*, Report no. 32, 1959.

Acknowledgements

Permission to reproduce the Readings in this volume is acknowledged to the following sources:

1 R. D. Irwin Inc. (publishers of *Marketing Behavior and Executive Action*) and W. Alderson
2 Prentice-Hall Inc. (publishers of *Economic Theory and Operation Analysis*) and W. J. Baumol
3 University of California at Berkeley
4 *Harvard Business Review*
5 American Marketing Association
6 *Management Today* (Management Publications Ltd)
7 *Management Science*
8 McGraw-Hill Inc. (publishers of *Marketing Productivity Analysis*) and C. H. Sevin
9 *Management Today* (Management Publications Ltd)
10 *Harvard Business Review*
11 *Management Today* (Management Publications Ltd)
12 *Business Horizons* (Indiana University)
13 *Management Decision*
14 American Management Association
15 American Marketing Association (*Journal of Marketing*)
16 Association of National Advertisers Inc.
17 American Marketing Association (*Journal of Marketing Research*)
18 *Journal of the Market Research Society* and D. L. Watson
19 *Management Today* (Management Publications Ltd)
20 *Management Today* (Management Publications Ltd)
21 *Business Horizons* (Indiana University)

Author Index

Subject Index

Abrasive products marketing, 77–80
Absorption costing, 229, 233
Acquisitions, 35–7, 78
Action (purchase), 286–7, 294
Adler, M., 122
Advertising
  and sales promotion, distinguished, 283
  as a defensive measure, 355
  as a sequential process of persuasion, 286–92, 293–5, 316–19, 322–3
  as mass, paid communication, 284
  budget setting, 49–51, 245–6, 284
    company methods, 349–50, 352
    experimental approach to, 365–7
  by testimonials, 338
  communications task approach, 285–92
  cost allocation, 151–2, 157
  effectiveness criteria: sales or communications effects, 294–320, 354–7, 369
  effectiveness measurement: Mead Johnson's example, 84–5
  effectiveness measurement problems, 91–2, 348–9
  effectiveness measurements used by companies, 351–2
  effects of company image, 329–31
  effects of repetition, 271, 326
  elasticity of response to, 363–5
  exaggeration in, 326, 337
  for dissonance reduction, 353–4
  objectives set by companies, 350–54

  policy statement: Salada Foods example, 245
  product manager's role in, 243–7, 256–7
  relationship theory of, 342–6
  waste in, 348, 367–9
Affect, 293–4, 300
Aske Research, 118
Attention, 294
Attwoods, 117
Audits of Great Britain, 117, 123
Audley, B., 123
Awareness (of product or company), 286–7, 294, 296
  higher among brand users, 324–5

Backward costing, 228
Balance theory, 332–5
Banks
  advertising objectives, 355
Behavioural models
  Freud (psychoanalytic), 271–4
  Hobbes (organizational factors), 278–9
  Lavidge-Steiner (sequential motivational states), 293–4
  Marshall (economic), 267–9
  Pavlov (learning), 269–71
  Veblen (social-psychological), 274–8
Behavioural theory of the firm, 56
Black box
  analogue of buyer's psyche, 265
Borg-Warner Corporation, 87
Brainstorming, 203
Brand
  buying, 323
  links with company image, 326–7, 334–46
  manager, 239–59
  personality, 326

limitations of, 8–9
Marketing intelligence
 as a company policy input,
  100–101
 system, 11, 107–9, 128
 system in use: Mead Johnson's
  example, 81, 84–6
Marketing profitability analysis
 basis of cost allocation, 146–9
 cost allocation to customers,
  153–8
 cost allocation to products,
  149–53
 cost allocation to territories,
  158–9
 functional classification of
  costs, 144–6
 methods, 132–4
Market research
 agency briefing, 119–20, 123
 choice of agencies, 121
 in new product development,
  202–3
 personnel, 125–6
 precision required, 121–2
 uses and misuses, 115–19
Markets
 decline stage, 177
 growth stage, 175
 heterogeneity in, 58
 maturity stage, 177
Market stretching, 185–97
Matching, 59
Maximization
 of earning power of prime
  resources, 169–71
 of profits, 40, 42–56, 224–7
 of rate of return on capital, 226
 of rate of return on total sales,
  226–7
 of sales revenue, 41, 47–56, 64,
  132, 163
Medium, 338–9

Mergers, 32, 177
Metrecal, 195–6
Milk, 276
Misinformation systems, 127–40
Models, 80, 86, 88, 90–4, 100,
  107, 130, 137–8, 309–11, 352
 see also Behavioural models
Monopolies Commission, 227,
  233
Motivation, 116, 122
 see also Behavioural models
Motivation research, 124, 202,
  272–4
Moulson, T., 118, 123
Mousetraps
 paths not beaten to doors of
  makers of better, 178

National Biscuit Company, 247
National Economic Development
  Council, 235
New product development
 see Innovation
Nielsen, 117
Nylon
 progressive development of new
  uses, 186–90

Objectives of the firm
 see Firm; Maximization
Obsolescence
 in hosiery, 187–8
Omo, 344
Order assembly and handling
  expense, 150, 152, 155, 157
Organizational overhaul, 78–9
Orwell, S., 117, 125
Output quantity decisions, 43–9,
  51–4, 166–71

Packing and shipping expense
  allocation, 150, 155
Parker Pens, 238

Penguin Modern Management

Readings

Business Strategy
Edited by H. Igor Ansoff

Consumer Behaviour
Edited by A. S. C. Ehrenberg and F. G. Pyatt

Design of Jobs
Edited by Louis E. Davis and James C. Taylor

Management and Motivation
Edited by Victor H. Vroom and Edward L. Deci

Management Decision Making
Edited by Lawrence A. Welsch and Richard M. Cyert

Management Information Systems
Edited by T. W. McRae

Management of Change and Conflict
Edited by John M. Thomas and Warren G. Bennis

Management of Production
Edited by M. K. Starr

Marketing Research
Edited by Joseph Seibert and Gordon Wills

Modern Financial Management
Edited by B. V. Carsberg and H. C. Edey

Modern Marketing Management
Edited by R. J. Lawrence and M. J. Thomas

Systems Analysis
Edited by Stanford L. Optner

Systems Thinking
Edited by F. E. Emery

Texts

Management and the Social Sciences
Tom Lupton

Simulation and Business Decisions
G. T. Jones

Writers on Organizations
D. S. Pugh, O. J. Hickson and C. R. Hinings